Taxonomy of instructional design functions

Design Functions	Components	Description
Identifying instructional problems	Needs assessment	Normative, comparative, felt, expressed, future, critical incident needs
	Goal analysis	Aim, goals, refinement, rank, refinement, final rank
	Performance assessment	Knowledge or skills, motivation or incentive, environmental, management, interpersonal

Design Functions	Components	Description
Learner analysis	General characteristics	Age, grade level
	Specific entry competencies	Ability to understand abstract information
Contextual analysis	Orienting context	Learner's perspective
	Instructional context	Lighting, noise, seating
	Transfer context	On-the-job support

Design Functions	Components	Description
Task analysis	Topic analysis	Knowledge, concepts, principles
	Procedural analysis	Steps
	Critical incident method	Interpersonal communication

Design Functions	Components	Description
Objectives	Behavioral	Verb, criterion, condition
	Cognitive	General instructional objective, samples of performance
Expanded performance-content matrix	Content	Fact, concept, principle or rules, procedure, interpersonal, attitude
	Performance	Recall, application

Design Functions	Components	Description
Sequencing	Learning related	Identifiable prerequisites, familiarity, difficulty, interest, and development
	World related	Spatial, temporal, physical
	Concept related	Class, propositional, sophistication, logical prerequisites
	Content expertise	Conceptual sequence, theoretical sequence
	Task expertise	Simplifying conditions

Design Functions	Components	Description
Strategies	Recall	Rehearsal, mnemonics
	Integration	Paraphrasing, generating questions
	Organizational	Outlining, categorization
	Elaboration	Mental images, diagrams, sentence elaborations

Design Functions	Components	Description
Preinstructional strategies	Pretest	Alerts learner
	Objectives	Precisely inform learner
	Overview	Prepares learner
	Advance organizer	Clarifies content
Message design	Signals	Explicit, typographical
	Pictures	Decoration, representation, organization, interpretation, transformation

Design Functions	Components	Description
Development	Concrete	Pictures/images
	Step size	Terminology, references
	Pacing	Examples and elaborations
	Consistency	Terminology used
	Cues	Highlighting points

Design Functions	Components	Description
Evaluation	Formative	Questionnaires, interviews, observations, records
	Summative	Questionnaires, interviews, observations, records
	Confirmative	Questionnaires, interviews, observations, records
Assessment	Standards of achievement	Relative and absolute standards
Student self-evaluation	Pretesting	Testing for prerequisites, improved performance

Design Functions	Components	Description
Testing for knowledge items	Objective tests	Multiple choice, true/false, matching, constructed response items
Testing for skills and behavior	Direct, analysis of naturally occurring results	
	Ratings of performance	
	Rubrics	
	Anecdotal records	
	Indirect checklist	
	Portfolio assessment	
	Exhibitions	
Testing for attitudes	Observation/anecdotal records	Rating scale
	Assessment of behavior	Observation, questionnaire/survey, interview

Design Functions	Components	Description
Proposal preparation	Purpose	Each proposal should include this information. If no format is provided by the funding group, these tools can also serve as the headings
	Plan of work	
	Milestones and deliverables	
	Budget	
	Schedule	
	Staffing	
Project planning	Scope of work	Prepared prior to beginning the work
	Scheduling	
	Budgeting	
Management	Managing resources	Used to monitor, report, and revise the project planning materials
	Tracking	
	Reporting	

Design Functions	Components	Description
Implementation plan	CLER model	Configurations, linkages, environment, resources
Implementation decisions	Instructional delivery	Classroom facilities, media equipment, other equipment, transportation, housing, and food
	Materials	Packaging, duplicating, warehousing, and shipping
	Instructors	Scheduling, training

Design Functions	Components	Description
Formative evaluation	Planning	Purpose, audience, issues, resources, evidence, data-gathering techniques, analysis, reporting
	Techniques	Connoisseur-based, decision-oriented, objectives-based, public relations–inspired studies
Summative evaluation	Planning	Specify objectives
		Determine evaluation design for each objective
		Develop data collection instruments
		Carry out evaluation
		Analyze results
		Interpret results
	Disseminate results and conclusions	
Confirmative evaluation	Educational programs	
	Training programs	Appropriateness of training, competencies, benefits

Design Functions	Components	Description
Project team	Instructional design	Designs the instruction
	Media production	Graphic artist, scriptwriter, video production staff, still photographers, programmers, network administrator
	Evaluator	Develops evaluation plan
	Performance consultant	Helps with nontraining interventions
	Subject-matter expert	Provides content information

Designing
Effective
Instruction

Fourth Edition

Gary R. Morrison
Wayne State University

Steven M. Ross
University of Memphis

Jerrold E. Kemp
Professor Emeritus
San Jose State University

WILEY

John Wiley & Sons, Inc.

Acquisitions Editor   *Brad Hanson*
Marketing Manager   *Kevin Molloy*
Senior Production Editor   *Valerie A. Vargas*
Senior Designer   *Madelyn Lesure*
Cover Image   *Roy Wieman*

This book was set in 10/12 New Baskerville by Argosy and printed and bound by Malloy Lithograph. The cover was printed by Phoenix Color.

This book is printed on acid-free paper.

ISBN 0-471-21651-8
ISBN 0-471-45154-1 (WIE)

Printed in the United States of America

10 9 8 7 6 5 4 3 2

We would like to dedicate this book to our mentors.

I would like to thank Denny Pett, my advisor and chairman at Indiana University, for providing the opportunities and challenges that made graduate school an important part of my career.

—Gary Morrison

I thank Frank Di Vesta, who was my advisor and chairman at Pennsylvania State University, for the training and mentoring that so well prepared me for writing, research, and teaching.

—Steven Ross

I would like to express my appreciation in the memory of Dick Lewis, who was director of audiovisual services at San Jose State University, as my career started in instructional technology.

—Jerry Kemp

PREFACE

Although this edition is the fourth edition of *Designing Effective Instruction*, it has evolved from one of Jerry's early textbooks. In 1971, *Instructional Design: A Plan for Unit and Course Development* was published by Fearon Publishers. In the preface Jerry wrote, "Planning for student learning should be a challenging, exciting, and gratifying activity." Over 30 years later, experienced instructional designers would agree with Jerry's statement. We believe that this edition of our textbook will help instructional designers to accept the challenge of designing effective and efficient instruction, to find the process is stimulating, and to believe that there is a great deal of satisfaction to gain from completing an instructional design project.

CONCEPTUAL FRAMEWORK

The model presented in this book is eclectic in that it borrows ideas from many different disciplines and approaches to instructional design. We believe that there is never one perfect approach to solving an instructional design problem. As a result, we have incorporated both behavioral and cognitive approaches into the model so that we can reap the benefits of each.

An effective instructional design model is both flexible and adaptable. No two designers will approach a problem in the same manner, and no two problems are exactly alike. The model in this book is circular rather than a more traditional linear flow chart. Our experience has shown that projects start and end at different places in the design process. Often, designers are not able to complete each and every step because of external constraints. Other times, it is not efficient nor necessary to complete each step. The design model must be flexible to accommodate the demands of the job, yet maintain the logic to produce an effective product.

A design model must grow with the instructional designer. We have approached instructional design as the application of heuristics that one can apply to a variety of instructional problems. These heuristics are modified and embellished based on each instructional designer's experiences, observations, and interpretations of the literature. This approach to instructional design allows designers to both modify and add to our list of heuristics.

We continue to provide a strong emphasis on designing instruction in a business setting. Our approach in this text is one that is applicable to designers in business, military, medical, and government settings as well as to higher education and P–12 classrooms. Designers in each of the environments will take different approaches because of the opportunities created and the constraints imposed by each situation. However, instructional designers will have the common goal of using the instructional design model to guide them in the development of effective instruction.

INTRODUCTION TO THE FOURTH EDITION

With each of our editions, several of our colleagues strongly encouraged us to maintain the integrity of our model. With each edition, there is always the consideration of how and where to expand the book. We have carefully considered various options and suggestions. Our focus in this book is on the basics of instructional design that will help a student develop a solid foundation in the design process. Students and designers can then use and adapt these basic skills in a variety of settings such as multimedia, classroom, and distance education instruction.

The organization of this book allows the instructor to adapt the sequence to the class as well as to the instructor's own perspective. An instructor can also vary the emphasis in each chapter. For example, an introductory course might place the most emphasis on Chapters 2 through 12 (the basic design process). An advanced course might place more emphasis on Chapters 13 to 15 (project management, role of the designer, and implementation). Another approach is to start with the chapters on evaluation and assessment (10–12) or project management (14), and then teach the basic design process (2–9).

We have made minor fine tunings of the model in our updates of all the chapters. As part of this revision process, we have updated each chapter by adding new examples and references to relevant literature. The chapter organization in this edition is very similar to that in the third edition.

Features

We have created a design for the book that includes five features in each chapter. The quality management and sample design plan features appear only in Chapters 2 through 9, whereas the other features are found in each chapter. The following paragraphs describe these features of the book.

Getting Started.   Each chapter begins with the "Getting Started" section that provides a real-world scenario of an aspect of the chapter. Instructors can use these scenarios as stimulus for discussion during class time or as part of a dicussion conducted via a mailing list or online forum discussion.

Expert's Edge.   What happens when an instructional designer tries this in the real world? The "Expert's Edge" pieces were contributed by practicing instructional designers who share their knowledge, successes, and failures from the real world. In this edition, we have added several new Expert's Edge pieces that now reflect an international perspective as well as different contexts in which instructional design is conducted.

Quality Management.   In Chapters 2 through 9, we have added a section that will help the designer conduct a quick quality check of the design project. Key questions and issues are presented to help the designer keep the project aligned with solving the instructional problem. If you require your students to develop a project as part of this course, they can use this feature to do a quality check during the design and development process.

The ID Process.   Instructional design texts, as most scholarly texts, tend to take a sterile approach to writing. The "ID Process" sections allow us to present a "here's how it is really done" discussion of each element of the model.

Applications and Answers.   At the end of each chapter, we present one or two exercises for the readers to test their skills and knowledge. Many of the chapters present the reader with realistic problems where they can apply and expand their knowledge.

Sample Design Plan.   At the end of the primary design chapters, we have included a sample plan developed by Deborah Armstrong. This unit on time management provides another example of instructional design application.

ACKNOWLEDGMENTS

We would like to thank Gary Anglin, Barbara Bichelmeyer, Rob Foshay, Howard Kalman, and J. Michael Spector for providing us with feedback and suggestions as we prepared this edition. We would also like to give a special thanks to James Hartley, Deborah Jones, Richard F. Kenny, Dewey Kribs, Fred Pass, Robert Reiser, and Roderick C. Sims who contributed the new Expert's Edge pieces to this edition.

Like any instructional design project, this book has gone through a lengthy formative evaluation process. We would like to thank Amy Ackerman, M. K. Hamza, Paulina Kuforiji, Dan Surry, and Michael Spector. Last, we would like to thank the numerous colleagues and students who shared their expertise, experiences, and examples for all four editions of the book.

ABOUT THE AUTHORS

Gary R. Morrison received his doctorate in instructional systems technology from Indiana University in 1977. Since then, he has worked as instructional designer at the University of Mid-America, Solar Turbines International, General Electric Company's Corporate Consulting Group, and Tenneco Oil Company; and as a professor at the University of Memphis. He is currently a professor at Wayne State University, where he teaches courses in instructional design. His credits include print projects, multimedia projects, and over 30 hours of instructional video programs, including a five-part series that was aired nationally on PBS-affiliated stations. He has worked on projects involving pest management for farmers, small business management, gas turbine troubleshooting, systems engineering for electrical engineers, beam-pumping performance analysis, vessel design, microcomputer sales, and microcomputer repair.

Gary has written more than 100 papers on topics related to instructional design and computer-based instruction, as well as contributing to several book chapters and instructional software packages. He is senior author of *Integrating Computer Technology into the Classroom*. He is the associate editor of the research section of *Educational Technology Research and Development* and a past president of Association for Educational Communication and Technology's (AECT) Research and Theory Division and Design and Development Division.

Steven M. Ross received his doctorate in educational psychology from the Pennsylvania State University in 1974. He joined the faculty at the University of Memphis in 1974, and he is currently a professor in educational psychology and research there. He is the author of three textbooks and more than 125 journal articles in the areas of educational technology, computer-based instruction, program evaluation, and at-risk learners. He is the editor of the research section of *Educational Technology Research and Development*. In 1993, he was the first recipient of the University of Memphis Board of Visitors award for distinguished accomplishments in teaching, research, and service. In 1999, he testified on school reform for the House of Representatives Education Committee and also served on an invited panel chaired by Secretary of Education Richard Riley.

Jerrold E. Kemp received his doctorate in audiovisual education from Indiana University in 1956. For 30 years, he served as professor of instructional technology and coordinator of instructional development services at San Jose State University, California. Jerry first wrote *Instructional Design: A Plan for Unit and Course Development* in 1971 (Fearon), from which the present book, as the fourth version, emerged. In addition, he has authored or coauthored three other books dealing with training and technology. Jerry has been an instructional design consultant and conducts training workshops for many computer and electronics companies in Silicon Valley, California, and elsewhere.

BRIEF CONTENTS

CONTENTS

CHAPTER SIX
Designing the Instruction: Sequencing   134

CHAPTER THIRTEEN
The Role of the Instructional Designer   342

CHAPTER FOURTEEN
Planning and Project Management   360

CHAPTER FIFTEEN
Planning for Instructional Implementation   382

Introduction to the Instructional Design Process

GETTING STARTED

At last, you have finished your degree and are now ready to start practicing instructional design at your new job with a corporation in the top Fortune 25. Your first day on the job, however, holds a few surprises. Of most concern is that the manager you thought you were going to work for has transferred to a different division. Your new manager does not have a background in instructional design, but rather has worked as a chemical engineer and project manager for this corporation for the past 15 years. Needless to say, you are a little apprehensive about your predicament, considering that you are the *first* instructional designer hired by this corporation.

Shortly after the morning coffee break, your manager invites her staff in for an introductory meeting. The staff includes three trainers who have more than 35 years' combined experience in teaching courses for the corporation, an administrative assistant who schedules and makes arrangements for courses, two engineers (who have worked in the department for four years each) who write new curricula, and you. The meeting starts with each individual describing his or her background and role in the department. The other staff members can easily impress the new manager with their mastery of company lingo and number of hours of training they produce each quarter.

QUESTIONS TO CONSIDER

"Why examine the teaching/learning process?"

"How does curriculum planning differ from instructional design?"

"What are the components of a comprehensive instructional design plan?"

"What premises underlie the instructional design process?"

"What benefits can result from applying the instructional design process?"

"What is the value of instructional design to teachers?"

"What is the relationship between instructional design and human performance technology?"

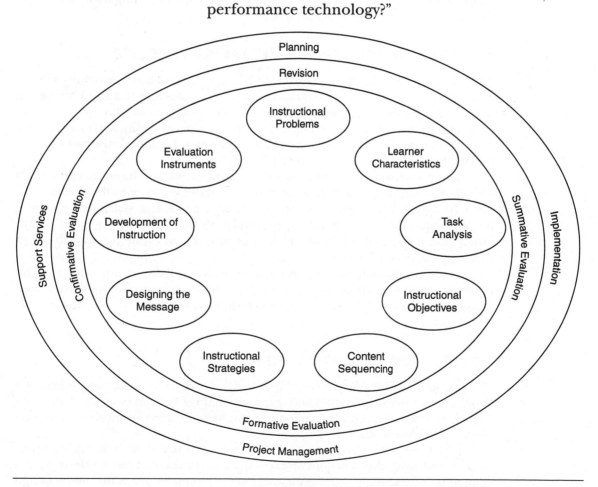

Turning slowly, the manager sizes you up and asks you to describe your background and your role in *her* new department. The manager and other staff members are not impressed by your degree in instructional design or the fact that you received it from a leading program in the area—probably because they have never heard of instructional design, although one of the engineers was familiar with your university's basketball coach. After a brief pause and a few frowns, one of the senior trainers asks you to explain exactly what it is that you do—seems they all thought you said "interior designer" and that you were there to spruce up their offices and classrooms.

The next few minutes are critical. You can either win over this manager and staff to a new way of viewing training, or you can overwhelm them with your knowledge so they decide you are one of those intellectual types. What will you say to this group that will help ensure your longevity with the company?

The Questions to Consider listed on the previous page represent the important concepts treated in this introductory chapter. Understanding them is the basis for systematic instructional planning.

WHY EXAMINE THE TEACHING/LEARNING PROCESS?

The United States is moving toward a global, information-based economy with an increasingly diverse workforce. One result of these changes is a need for better-trained, competent managers, professionals, and technicians who are capable of using complex technologies to improve services, increase quality, and raise productivity. Also, more jobs require individuals to reason in high-level, abstract terms to make inferences and solve intricate problems.

The conventional structure and delivery of education, however, are at odds with these societal changes. Learning must be more effective and efficient. This need has given rise to the instructional design process, a systematic planning method that results in successful learning and performance. Learning is haphazard; instruction is planned. Thus, our goal as designers is to create sound instruction that will lead to appropriate learning.

Before examining the elements of the instructional design process, it is useful to have a basic understanding of curriculum and its relationship to instructional design. Developing curriculum is often considered the starting point for instructional planning.

A DEFINITION OF CURRICULUM

The purpose of education or training is to provide a series of structured learning experiences for the learner. These experiences may be classes in an elementary school, courses in a secondary school or a higher education institution, or a training program in a business setting.

The term *curriculum* refers to the subject content and skills that make up an educational program. A school or curriculum includes the course offerings; at a company, the training programs may represent the curriculum. Curriculum design is a process of formulating a specific educational platform that defines the beliefs of what should be in the curriculum (Henderson & Hawthorne, 1995).

The emphasis of a curriculum depends on philosophical, social, and cultural forces that affect the school in terms of the broad society and the specific community it serves. For a business concern, a training curriculum reflects the organization's management policies, strategic plans, identified needs, and market trends. One caution we offer is to avoid building a curriculum in business that serves no other purpose than to offer a series of courses. All courses should serve to improve employee performance, thus supporting the mission and goals of the organization. The following questions help determine a curriculum:

1. What is the purpose or mission of the institution or department or the strategic plan of the organization?
2. What goals for education or training are necessary to serve the mission or plan?
3. How can instruction be categorized and organized to accomplish the goals?

Answering these questions can help in selecting subject areas, courses, instructional themes, or content categories (Table 1-1).

FROM THEORIES TO PLANS

The major goal for this book is to illustrate how to plan, develop, evaluate, and manage the instructional design process effectively so that it will ensure competent

TABLE 1-1
Organizing subject contents for curriculum

Education		
Subject Areas	**Courses**	**Themes across Courses**
Physical science	Physics	Patterns of change
Earth science	Chemistry	Scale and structure
Life science	Geology	Stability
	Biology	Systems and interactions

Training	
Training Areas	**Content Categories**
Management development	Managing change
Employee development	Effective presentations
Product development	Project management
Marketing development	Negotiating skills
Field training	Product troubleshooting
	Economic analysis

performance by learners. In the following pages of this chapter, the roles for instructional designers are explained and an overall instructional design plan (or "model") is introduced. At this beginning stage of your reading, it is important to understand that skilled instructional designers do not apply design strategies mechanically or arbitrarily. What is most effective in a given situation not only depends upon the particular context (e.g., high school versus corporate training) or target audience (e.g., preschool students versus senior financial managers), but also on judgments made logically and scientifically in accord with theories of learning and instruction. Such theories help designers to decide what type of instructional orientation is most likely to produce the desired results with the given group of learners. To help you differentiate among (1) a learning theory, (2) an instructional theory, and (3) a design plan, we briefly examine each in the following sections. An additional benefit should be increased understanding of the interrelationships between your instructional design course and courses that you might take in areas such as educational psychology, curriculum, and teaching methods.

LEARNING THEORY

A learning theory tends to be *descriptive*. It explains how learning takes place to achieve certain types of outcomes. A behavioral learning theory, as one might associate with B. F. Skinner's work (Skinner, 1954, 1965), emphasizes the effects of external conditions such as rewards and punishments in determining future behavior. In contrast, cognitive theory, as represented by the work of Jean Piaget (Inhelder and Piaget, 1958) and Jerome Bruner (Bruner, 1963, 1973), focuses on how individuals perceive, process, store, and retrieve information that they receive from the environment. A social-cognitive theory, such as that of Vygotsky (1962), might stress how students learn from others in cooperative settings. Most contemporary instructional designers draw from multiple theoretical paradigms, favoring whatever ones apply best to the design task at hand. Despite their importance as explanatory frameworks, learning theories don't tell the designer what to do specifically to achieve the goals of the particular task. For example, a designer hired to develop an advanced training unit on corporate tax law may consider, on the basis of learning theory, using small steps and frequent overt feedback (behavioral theory), including numerous examples and nonexamples to strengthen conceptual learning (cognitive theory), and practicing in small teams of students (social learning theory). These are sensible general thoughts, but will they fit the specific instructional goals and conditions of the learning context? Instructional theory can be invoked to shape these theoretical ideas into actual strategies of teaching.

Instructional Theory

While learning theories are descriptive and generic, instructional theories should be *prescriptive* and situation-specific (see Reigeluth, 1983). The instructional theory, in essence, applies the principles and assumptions of learning theory to the instructional design goal of interest. The focus, as is explained in detail in Chapter 5, is the learning objectives of instructional material being designed. To return to the tax law example, suppose that one key objective from the training unit is that students could "accurately apply two approved state formulae for calculating exemptions from gross profits." Drawing from instructional theory, the designer would analyze the types of content and performance involved (e.g., facts, concepts, principles, rote, or application) to determine (prescribe) the specific teaching strategy components to be used. Such may involve, for example, rehearsing the definitions of important terminology, paraphrasing, and engaging in guided practice on actual problems. Some instructional objectives for the lesson, as in this example, might rely predominantly on cognitive learning theory, whereas others (e.g., "work cooperatively with an accounting team on the audit to form a consensual recommendation") might be more sociocognitive or behavioral in nature.

Instructional Design Model

At the risk of sending some readers into jargon overdose, again consider the different frameworks of knowledge that guide instructional design. *Instructional theory*, as informed by *learning theory*, defines the core teaching strategies to be incorporated in the lesson or training unit. However, developing, refining, and producing a completed product in real life requires the integration of many more elements that must operate interdependently. As you will learn later, these elements together compose the *instructional design plan*, or model. By following such a plan, the instructional designer can ensure that the design process is both comprehensive and systematic, thus leading to a quality product and, most critically, successful learner performance. So, in summary, the three frameworks provide the following hierarchical functions:

Learning theory:	How you learn
Instructional theory:	How you ensure that the desired learning occurs
Instructional design plan:	How you apply instructional theory to create an effective lesson or unit

THE ROLE FOR INSTRUCTIONAL DESIGN

The systematic method of implementing the instructional design process is termed *instructional design* (often abbreviated as ID). It is based on what we know about learning theories, information technology, systematic analysis, and management methods. Dewey (1900) saw a need in the early part of the twentieth century for a science that could translate what was learned through research into practical applications for instruction. This science would make decisions about instructional practices that are based on sound research rather than intuition. Snellbecker (1974) and others have proposed that instructional design is the linking science described by Dewey. We agree with Snellbecker and see instructional design as the process for designing instruction based on sound practices.

The ID approach considers instruction from the perspective of the learner rather than from the perspective of the content, the traditional education and training approach. The traditional approach simply asked, "What information should I include in this course?" In some courses, the chapters in the textbook determined the content.

In contrast, the ID approach focuses on many factors that influence learning outcomes, including the following:

- What level of readiness do individual students need for accomplishing the objectives?
- What instructional strategies are most appropriate in terms of objectives and learner characteristics?
- What media or other resources are most suitable?
- What support is needed for successful learning?
- How is achievement of the objectives determined?
- What revisions are necessary if a tryout of the program does not match expectations?

Other issues, inherent in the instructional design process, also influence student learning. This process is applicable for designing instruction in public education, higher education, and skills training. The information, concepts, and procedures presented here can aid teachers and instructors, instructional designers, and planning teams—anyone who wants to develop effective, appealing instruction.

How would you answer this question: "If you were about to start planning a new unit in a course or training program, what matter would first receive your attention?" Various individuals might answer as follows:

Primary grade teacher: "I think first about the state and district benchmarks and how this content aligns with those benchmarks. Then, I would ask how well prepared are my students to study it (physically, emotionally, intellectually)?"

High school teacher: "First, I would start by identifying the relevant state standards, then I'd start writing down what I want to accomplish in teaching the unit to meet these standards. These statements become the goals around which I'll plan the instruction."

College professor: "My approach is to list the content that needs to be covered relative to the selected topic. This list would include the terms, definitions, concepts, and principles that I feel need to be communicated to my students."

Instructional designer in industry: "I would start by determining whether the problem the training is to address is an instructional problem. If instruction will help solve the problem, then it's important to start by listing the competencies the trainees are to develop as a result of this instruction. These would be the outcomes or objectives to be accomplished."

The foregoing replies represent a sampling of approaches that might be taken as different individuals initiate their instructional planning. There could be other replies to the question. For example, one community college instructor always starts by writing the final examination for a new unit. He believes that passing the final exam is the students' greatest concern. Therefore, he writes questions that indicate what should receive emphasis in his teaching. His reasoning seems plausible.

As you read the replies to the question and formulated your own answer, two conclusions should have become apparent. First, a number of different considerations appeal to educators and instructional designers as each starts planning. Second, each of us selects an order or sequence of our own to treat these elements.

KEY ELEMENTS OF THE INSTRUCTIONAL DESIGN PROCESS

Of the planning elements identified by the four individuals in the previous section, four are fundamental in instructional design. You will find them addressed in almost every ID model. They can be represented by answers to these questions:

1. For whom is the program developed? (characteristics of learners or trainees)
2. What do you want the learners or trainees to learn or demonstrate? (objectives)
3. How is the subject content or skill best learned? (instructional strategies)
4. How do you determine the extent to which learning is achieved? (evaluation procedures)

These four fundamental components—learners, objectives, methods, and evaluation—form the framework for systematic instructional planning (Figure 1-1).

These components are interrelated and could conceivably make up an entire instructional design plan. In actuality, there are additional components that should require attention (i.e., the context in which the learner learns and works) and that, when integrated with the basic four, form a complete instructional design model. The following section introduces nine elements of the instructional design process necessary for a comprehensive design plan.

THE COMPLETE INSTRUCTIONAL DESIGN PLAN

The nine elements in a comprehensive instructional design plan are as follows:

1. Identify instructional problems and specify goals for designing an instructional program.
2. Examine learner characteristics that will influence your instructional decisions.
3. Identify subject content, and analyze task components related to stated goals and purposes.
4. Specify the instructional objectives.
5. Sequence content within each instructional unit for logical learning.

6. Design instructional strategies so that each learner can master the objectives.
7. Plan the instructional message and develop the instruction.
8. Develop evaluation instruments to assess objectives.
9. Select resources to support instruction and learning activities.

The nine elements of this instructional design plan are illustrated in Figure 1-2.

The starting place for instructional planning is deciding whether instructional design is appropriate for a potential project. The diagram shows this first element, instructional problems, at the twelve o'clock position.

Although the list of nine elements forms a logical, clockwise sequence as illustrated, the order in which you address the individual elements is not predetermined. For this reason, the oval pattern is used. An oval does not have a specific starting point. Recall the answers to the question asked of various persons earlier in this chapter. Individuals may proceed through the instructional design process in their own preferred way, starting with one element or another and following whatever order they consider logical or suitable.

In Figure 1-2, the elements are not connected with lines or arrows. Connections could indicate a sequential, linear order. The intent is to convey flexibility yet some order in the way the nine elements may be used. Also, some instances may not require treating all nine elements. For example, in some programs evaluation instruments may not be necessary. Similarly, someone working on an instructor-led course might only analyze the content, specify the objectives, and then sequence the content because of time or resource constraints. The instructional strategies, message design, unit development, and evaluation instruments might be developed by one or more instructors who deliver the course. Although we do not see this approach as ideal, the reality of the situation often limits how much instructional design we do.

Another reason for using the oval form is that a flexible interdependence exists among the nine elements. Decisions relating to one affect other decisions. For

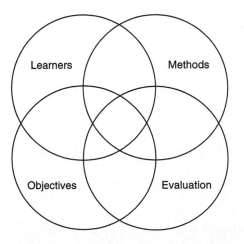

FIGURE 1-1
The fundamental components of instructional design

FIGURE 1-2
Components of the instructional design plan

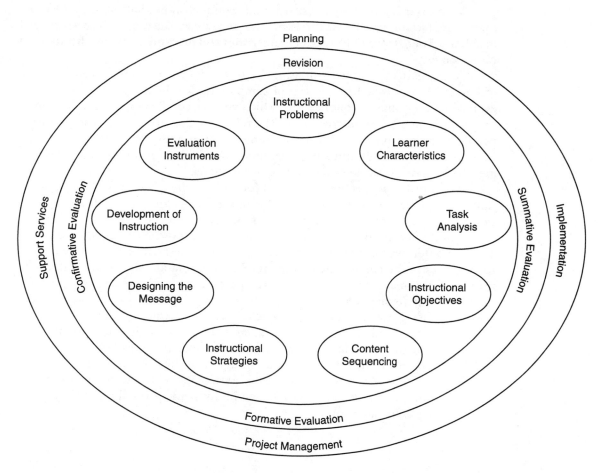

example, determining that your learners are not available for travel to a central training location for a weeklong course impacts how you deliver the instruction. As instructional objectives are stated, items of subject content may be added or reordered. Or, while the instruction is developed, the intent of an instructional objective may become clearer than as initially stated and may require revision. Consequently, the procedure permits and encourages flexibility in the selection of elements, the order of their treatment, and back-and-forth activity among the elements. This procedure allows for additions and changes as the instructional design plan takes shape.

Many instructional design models identify and use features similar to those described in this book. Such models are often represented by a diagram with boxes and arrows as a series of steps in a set order, as shown in Figure 1-3. The intent of such a model is to establish a 1-2-3 sequential order. In actual use, the process often is not linear. The open, circular pattern seems more appropriate and useful.

When starting to design instruction, if you feel somewhat insecure with the open, flexible format, follow the logical arrangement, starting with instructional problems. Then, move to learner characteristics and proceed clockwise through the nine elements.

As you gain experience with using this instructional design plan, you no doubt will establish your own arrangement of components for the design of a course. But even when following a sequence with which you are comfortable, you will need to make adjustments. Romiszowski (1981) refers to this approach as a heuristic, problem-solving approach. With each project, you modify your strategy based on how things work in each situation. Over time, you will develop a repertoire of strategies that you can adapt to new and unique situations.

The word *element* is used as a label for each of the nine parts of our instructional design plan. This term is preferable to the terms *step, stage, level,* or *sequential item,* which are expressions in keeping with the linear concept.

Another part of our diagram is the indication of revision around the elements. The two outer ovals illustrate the feedback and management features, which allow for changes in the content or treatment of elements at any time during development as well as managing the design, development, and implementation. The treatment of elements may require revisions when, for example, data about learning are collected during instructional tryouts (called *formative evaluation*) or at the end of a course offering (called *summative evaluation*). If you want learners to succeed, accomplishing instructional objectives at a satisfactory level of proficiency, then you will want to improve any weak parts of the program as they are discovered.

Various expressions are used to label systematic instructional planning. In addition to the term *instructional design* used in this book, you will find reference to the following in the literature:

FIGURE 1-3
A typical instructional design model

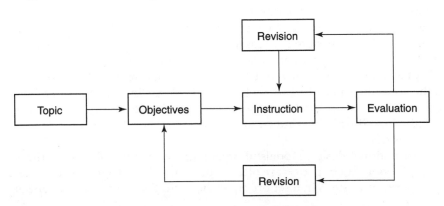

- Instructional systems
- Instructional systems design
- Instructional systems development
- Learning systems design
- Competency-based instruction
- Criterion-referenced instruction
- Performance technology

Another expression, *instructional development*, is interpreted in different ways. One approach is to define instructional development as the production process, that is, the translation of the instructional design plan into the instructional materials such as print, video, multimedia, or web-based materials. Another definition describes instructional development as the management function in systematic instructional planning. This term includes assigning and supervising personnel, handling allocated budgets, arranging for necessary support services, and checking time schedules for compliance.

The chapters that follow focus mainly on the instructional design elements shown in Figure 1-2. But Chapter 14, "Planning and Project Management," focuses on the instructional development procedure for managing a project.

PREMISES UNDERLYING THE INSTRUCTIONAL DESIGN PROCESS

We have identified seven basic premises to help you understand the ID process and apply it successfully. These premises can influence both your thinking and your treatment of the instructional design plan.

Premise 1: The instructional design process requires attention to both a systematic procedure and specificity for treating details within the plan.

The term *systematic* refers to an orderly, logical method of identifying, developing, and evaluating a set of strategies aimed at attaining a particular instructional goal. This task is accomplished using the nine interrelated elements of the instructional design plan.

Treating each element requires exacting mental effort. Each element of the plan (if it is relevant to your project) must be applied with attention to precise details. This means being specific. For example, an instructional objective is a statement that includes a particular verb that guides the development of an instructional strategy and indicates how achievement will be evaluated. The details of the instructional strategy used to present the instruction supporting an objective are another indication of the specific treatment required when implementing the instructional design process.

Attention to detail is critical for the success of any instructional design work. By applying systematic procedures and being attentive to specific details, you can design effective instruction.

Premise 2: The instructional design process usually starts at the course development level.

Decisions about curricula and broad goals for a school or training program precede the design of specific courses. Although instructional designers can help administrators, managers, and committees make decisions about the purposes, directions, and emphasis of a program, instructional design work usually starts with identification of the instruction or training needs to be served. Units or topics composing a course are then selected. This selection is followed by the development of instructional components related to the various planning elements. In recent years, designers have taken a more active role in curriculum development in business, using such skills as needs assessment, learner analysis, and sequencing.

Premise 3: An instructional design plan is developed primarily for use by the instructional designer and planning team.

Some people believe that all details developed during planning (instructional needs analysis, instructional objectives, content sequencing, etc.) are to be given to learners, often in the form of a study guide. This assumption is not true. The learners will use many of the items written as elements in the plan, but not always in the form or order in which they are being developed and stated. We distinguish between the planning documents (instructional needs, instructional strategies, etc.) and the instructional materials the learners will actually see and use. The design team uses planning documents to design and develop the instructional units. Once the instructional materials are in final form, the planning documents lose their value and usually are filed.

Also, the order in which elements are treated during planning may differ substantially from the order in which they are eventually presented to learners. For example, a pretest might be developed after the final examination is devised even though students will complete it prior to the start of instruction.

Premise 4: While planning, every effort should be made to provide for a level of satisfactory achievement for all learners.

A study by Bloom (1976) concluded that up to 95 percent of all public school students can accomplish what is required of them if each individual has suitable academic background, appropriate instruction, and sufficient time for learning. Other research has shown that if a student is prepared to learn and puts forth the effort to study but is unsuccessful in learning, a more careful design of the instructional plan can help overcome this shortcoming. This conclusion applies to training as well as to education. It justifies the need to test a plan before its implementation, as indicated by the revision oval in Figure 1-2.

Premise 5: The success of the instructional product is dependent on the accuracy of the information flowing into the instructional design process.

To solve a performance problem, the designer must identify what the exact training needs are through the use of needs assessment, goal analysis, and/or performance analysis. Creating instruction for a task that is not a performance problem is not likely to lead to an improvement in learner performance. Similarly, the designer must accurately identify the target audience to design materials that are appropriate for the audience's reading and skill levels. The information obtained from the subject-matter expert must be accurate and complete. Selecting an appropriate instructional strategy for the content and objectives is essential for both efficient and effective instruction. And last, accurate information is needed from the formative evaluation of the materials to make appropriate modifications. Failure to obtain accurate information and to make the correct decisions can result in ineffective instruction.

Premise 6: The instructional design process focuses on the individual rather than the content.

Instructional design focuses on the individual and how to improve individual performance rather than on what content to cover. During learner analysis, the process focuses on audience characteristics. As we design the instruction, we consider these characteristics in the selection of the instructional strategies and delivery methods that are adapted to the individual members of the target audience. Throughout the design process, the designer focuses on the individual learner and what the learner must achieve to alleviate a problem rather than focusing on what content to cover.

Premise 7: There is no single best way to design instruction.

Applying the instructional design process can reduce reliance on intuition or trial and error in planning. Yet the instructional design process has not reached a level of scientific exactness. Many paths can reach the same goals and objectives. Instructors and designers are unique individuals, just as learners are unique. Each designer formulates activities and applies elements of the instructional design plan in individual ways. The proof of an instructional plan's success is whether a satisfactory level of learning is achieved in an acceptable period of time.

BENEFITS OF USING THE INSTRUCTIONAL DESIGN PROCESS

For any enterprise to be successful, those involved in the endeavor must derive some benefit. In a business operation, the owner makes a profit, the customer is satisfied with the price and quality of the product or service, and the worker or craftsperson receives sufficient pay while feeling a sense of pride in workmanship. Those of us associated with instructional design must have equal benefits as well.

- The program manager or administrator wants evidence of effective, efficient learning within an acceptable cost base. The time is past when we could say, "It looks like a good program" or "It's acceptable because the students certainly enjoyed the course." We need hard evidence of success.
- The instructional designer wants evidence that a satisfactory program has been designed. The best indication is the accomplishment of program objectives by learners within an appropriate time period.

- The instructor wants to see learners achieve the required competencies and also personally wants to develop a positive relationship with learners.
- Learners want to succeed in their learning and also to find the learning experience to be pleasant and satisfying.

When the design of an instructional program follows the procedures outlined in this book or those of another suitable model, such benefits as these are realized. In other words, employing the instructional design process increases the probability of goal attainment.

In addition to enhancing learning of knowledge and skills, instructional design can foster a positive attitude toward the subject and better study habits. In our evaluation of a variety of instructional materials, we have found that well-designed instruction fosters a positive attitude and motivation. In many cases, the students inquire whether more instruction will be available in the same format. We have also noticed similar responses when evaluating prototypes that present only a sample of the content.

FROM LEARNING THEORY TO INSTRUCTIONAL THEORY

If you have studied education, psychology, or instructional design, then you will probably have had or will take a course on learning theories. As you read the instructional design literature, you see references to different learning theories such as behavioral and cognitive theories. A reasonable question is, "How do these learning theories relate to instructional theories?" Let's examine these two terms and see how they influence the process of instructional design.

Learning theories are *descriptive*. They describe the process of learning. For example, Thorndike's law of effect states that responses that are followed by satisfaction are repeated, while those followed by displeasure are not. We can use this law to describe a rat's or a student's reaction to positive and negative reinforcements. In contrast to the learning theories are instructional theories that Bruner (1966) describes as *prescriptive*. That is, instructional theories describe the most effective way of designing the instruction to achieve an objective. Instructional theories focus on how we can best design instruction rather than on describing the learning. An instructional theory would use Thorndike's law of effect and other ideas to develop a set of prescriptions to design an optimal set of instruction. The instructional theory might describe a type of reinforcement (e.g., food) and the timing of the reinforcement (e.g., frequently at first, then remove it a little at a time). But how are learning theories and instructional theories related?

Instructional theories are based on the learning theory that describes learning. For example, the research supporting the behavioral learning theory has been very rich and has provided instructional theories based on this theory with a firm foundation. More recently, we have seen the development of cognitive learning theories that have lead to the similar development of cognitive-based instructional theories. Our instructional design models are based on and are influenced by the instructional theories and learning theories. You can find a more detailed discussion of learning theories, instructional theories, and instructional design models in Reigeluth (1983, 1999).

APPLYING THE PROCESS TO BOTH ACADEMIC EDUCATION AND TRAINING PROGRAMS

Specific job training has precise, immediate requirements with identifiable and often measurable outcomes. The program must stress the teaching of knowledge and skills for the performance of assigned tasks. Academic education, on the other hand, often has broad purposes and more generalized objectives. Application of the knowledge and skills to be taught may not become important until sometime in the future.

Whether one is studying history or carpentry, the identical principles of learning apply to structuring experiences for individuals. While the emphasis, certain details, and terminology differ, both situations treat similar elements of the instructional design plan. Thus, the procedures presented in this book can be effective for either an academic or a training situation. Where particulars differ, special explanations and examples are included in either the academic instruction or the planning for training.

Benefits of Instructional Design in Business

The benefits of the application of instructional design in business can take many forms. Results can vary from simply reducing the amount of time it takes to complete a course to solving a performance problem by designing effective instruction that increases worker productivity. In the late 1980s, Motorola University conducted three limited studies of the benefits of training. Researchers found that for every dollar invested in training, they realized a return on investment of $30 (Brandenberg, 1987; *The Value of Training*, 1995). Although we do not have the specifics of how the return on investment was calculated, it is interesting to note that many corporations consider a return of 13 percent acceptable for most projects. The role of instructional design and training varies from company to company, as do the benefits. For example, Speedy Muffler King, which experienced high revenues and profits for 1994, made extensive use of training. During 1994, it provided more than 100,000 hours of employee training to improve customer satisfaction and loyalty (Canada NewsWire, 1995). Appropriate training can produce a return on investment for both tangible (e.g., increased output) and intangible (e.g., worker loyalty) measures.

Benefits of Instructional Design in P–12 Education

Do P–12 teachers have to be instructional designers in addition to their traditional roles of classroom managers, presenter–lecturers, and mentors? Our definitive answers are "to some degree" and "it all depends." By saying "to some degree," we mean that textbooks, workbooks, basal readers, and other standard instructional resources rarely, if ever, are sufficient to satisfy formal curriculum objectives while keeping students engaged and interested. There are numerous occasions (many teachers might say "every day") in which the need for teacher-developed materials—drill-and-practice exercises, remedial lessons, problem-based lessons, or even full-fledged instructional units—arises. Knowing the basic principles of instructional design (see the preceding seven) can help to ensure that what is produced serves a necessary purpose, meets the needs of students, is attractive and well organized, is delivered in an appropriate mode, and is continually evaluated and improved. Unlike professional instructional designers, however, the typical teacher is not likely to need formal expertise in the various instructional design processes. However, basic familiarity with major principles and procedures (e.g., how to present text, write and deliver a lecture, or prepare a test) can be extremely helpful, both for the teacher's own work and for evaluating commercial educational products.

How much teachers use instructional design also depends a great deal on situational factors. Teachers working in today's restructuring schools may find themselves increasingly involved in design activities. Specifically, in recent years, national initiatives for educational reform (Sarason, 1995; Bradford, 1999) have generated support for activity-oriented, student-centered methods of teaching that stress meaningful learning applied to real-world problems. Following the classic ideas of Dewey and Piaget, modern constructivist theories view knowledge as primarily created (constructed) by the learner rather than transmitted by teachers (Prewat, 1995).

To promote active learning both schoolwide and district-wide, comprehensive restructuring models, such as those developed by New American Schools (Kearns & Anderson, 1997), are being disseminated nationally. Nearly all of these models emphasize extensive use of project-based activities in which learners integrate concepts and skills across multiple subjects to develop products, perform experiments, and solve problems. One example is the Expeditionary Learning–Outward Bound model (Campbell et al., 1997). By participating in learning expeditions around the school and community (e.g., interviewing local police and citizens about neighborhood crime and presenting the findings in a group report and exhibition), the students acquire opportunities to connect learning and curriculum objectives to real-world events. Another approach is to provide teachers with a model specific to designing classroom instruction. Morrison and Lowther (2002) provide a constructivist instructional design model for teachers to use in integrating computer technology into the classroom.

Implementing these approaches obviously requires well-designed expeditions and projects. Where do they come from? For the most part, that responsibility falls on the individual teachers. Not surprisingly, however, many teachers find themselves unprepared for the task, and the implementations of the new strategies suffer as a result (Bodilly, 1998). By learning more about instructional design, teachers should become better equipped to either create high-quality student-centered lessons or adapt commercial materials to fit their course needs.

Expert's Edge

Instructional Design: You've Come a Long Way, Baby!

It Seems Like Only Yesterday.   It was 1968 and I wanted to get a Ph.D. and study more about the psychology of learning and creating instructional materials and programs, mostly using programmed instruction techniques. I didn't know what this was called but soon found myself talking to people in an Instructional Technology program.

Question: Does this mean I have to figure out how to thread a film projector?
Answer: No. *(Thank goodness! I thought.)*
Question: Where are the jobs?
Answer: Well, with a Ph.D., the women usually work in curriculum jobs in school districts and the men work in universities. *(I'm out of here!)*

However, I did enter the program. My discrimination-programming experience and past study of learning theory, human development, and the systems approach (with Leonard Silvern) prepared me well for instructional design. There was one other female student, a middle school principal who is now retired from the public schools and is a teacher education professor. I did much of the data analysis on my dissertation research on a Frieden calculator and then punched the data into cards so I could complete the task on a mainframe computer. The graduate school just began to allow photocopies of typed dissertations rather than carbon copies. Then in 1971, I was a card-carrying Ph.D. with a research position at Wayne State University, actually leading a design team. I had flirted briefly (and not too seriously) with the thought of getting a job in business, but this seemed a remote possibility.

Look What's Going on Now!   The differences in the instructional design field today are astounding. Foremost, people are not only working in the field, but are doing well. The promise of teachers working full-time as school-based designers is long forgotten, however, and the profession has largely become part of the world of employee training and education. To a great extent, this phenomenon, coupled with the development of computer technology, has shaped the field from both theoretical and practical points of view.

Theoretically, the field emerged from a merger of behavioral learning theory and general systems theory. Learning and instruction were both performance oriented. Even though cognitive orientations were dominant by the 1980s, the field still incorporated vestiges of behaviorism. Today, the theoretical bases of design are far more diverse—cognitive, constructivist, and still, behaviorist. Systems theory remains current as evidenced by the importance of "systems thinking" and "systemic change."

However, the more important evidence of systems thinking today is demonstrated by performance improvement or performance technology language. The object of instructional design efforts is no longer simply a product, nor is it learning. Instead, the object is improvement in on-the-job performance and ultimately in solving organizational problems. The foundational design theories now include the nature of organizations, human motivation, management, and change.

The practice of instructional design has changed throughout the years, again because of changes in the business work environment. Most design projects are team efforts that increasingly rely on new technologies for instructional delivery, as well as on tools to automate the design process. Designers, like other professionals, are under pressure to produce high-quality products in less time. Moreover, they are required to provide concrete evidence that their efforts substantially impact organizational profits.

As with other aspects of life, technology has changed the character of instructional design over the past 30 years. Not only are technologies such as the Internet increasingly used to deliver instruction, but also technology is used to automate design processes and make them more efficient. Today, designers find it far more difficult to avoid demonstrating technology competence than in the early years.

Finally, instructional design expertise no longer resides only in the United States. Designers are trained worldwide and many practice worldwide, necessitating that instructional products be adapted to the idiosyncrasies of many cultures and many nations.

Clearly, designers have more job options today than previously, but expectations are that designers will be highly skilled professionals. They must master not only traditional design processes, but also advanced technology skills, project management capabilities, and business acumen. I believe that today's novice designers are typically more competent than yesterday's "experts." Correspondingly, they have the potential to earn higher incomes. However, they work under more pressure and with more demands than did designers of the past.

Rita C. Richey is professor and program coordinator of instructional technology at Wayne State University. She has over 30 years of experience in instructional design and is widely published in the areas of instructional design research and theory.

WHO'S WHO IN THE INSTRUCTIONAL DESIGN PROCESS

As you prepare to study the instructional design process, you will want to view it from your own perspective. What role or roles will you assume in planning? What specific responsibilities might you have? What relationship do you have with other persons in your organization who are involved in aspects of teaching or training? These are all matters to keep in mind as you study the elements of instructional design.

In Chapter 13 we examine in detail the roles and responsibilities of those persons engaging in instructional planning, development, implementation, and evaluation. At this point, however, you should recognize that four essential roles must be performed during instructional planning. You may be expected to fill one or more of these positions:

- **Instructional designer:** A person responsible for carrying out and coordinating the planning work; competent in managing all aspects of the instructional design process. The instructional designer has the primary responsibility for designing the instruction.
- **Instructor:** A person (or member of a team) for and with whom the instruction is being planned; well informed about the learners to be taught, the teaching procedures, and the requirements of the instructional program; with guidance from the designer, capable of carrying out details of many planning elements; responsible for trying out and then implementing the instructional plan that is developed.
- **Subject-matter expert (SME):** A person qualified to provide information about content and resources relating to all aspects of the topics for which instruction is to be designed; responsible for checking accuracy of content treatment in activities, materials, and examinations. The teacher or instructor may also serve as SME.
- **Evaluator:** A person qualified to assist the staff in developing instruments for pretesting and for evaluating student learning (posttesting); responsible for gathering and interpreting data during program tryouts and for determining effectiveness and efficiency of the program when fully implemented.

INSTRUCTIONAL DESIGN AND PERFORMANCE TECHNOLOGY

An interesting area to the instructional designer is the applied field of performance technology or performance improvement. This field focuses on "maximizing the valued achievements of people within work settings" (Stolovitch & Keeps, 1999, p. 4). Performance technology places a very strong emphasis on front-end analysis to identify the performance problem and the cause. Similarly, a performance technologist takes a broader perspective on performance problems than a trainer by considering nontraining interventions as a solution to a problem. To a trainer, every problem "looks" like a training problem much like everything looks like a nail to a child with a hammer.

Performance technology includes instructional design as an important tool for solving *some* instructional problems. In addition, the performance technologist might involve an organizational development specialist, a compensation specialist, an information technologist, an ergonomics specialist, or an industrial engineer to provide a nontraining intervention. These interventions might include restructuring the job compensation, redesigning the workstation, or designing a simple job aid. This text focuses on instructional design and provides the instructional designer or performance technologist with essential skills for developing training interventions as well as some nontraining interventions such as job aids and electronic performance support systems (EPSS).

ANSWERING THE CRITICS

"Isn't the instructional design process actually a mechanistic rather than a human-istic method of instructional planning? Doesn't this procedure discourage creativity in teaching? Isn't teaching more of an art than a science?" These and similar ques-tions are frequently raised and must be answered realistically. After studying this book, you should make up your own mind about how to answer them. Following are our responses to such questions:

> **Question: Isn't the instructional design process actually a mechanistic rather than a humanistic method of instructional planning?**

As explained earlier, some ID models exhibit a rigidity when only a single, linear path for planning, as created with boxes and arrows, is followed without exception. Figure 1-3 illustrates this approach. The sequences should be flexible, with elements developed in different orders or arrangements as necessary. An instructional designer's style of working, the nature of a subject, or the learners' needs can all influence how the components are handled in planning. The ID process would only be mechanistic if elements were treated in a fragmented manner rather than in an integrated approach.

A humanistic approach to instruction recognizes the individual learner (stu-dent or trainee) in terms of his or her own capabilities, individual differences, pres-ent ability levels, and personal development. It should be apparent that these matters do receive attention in the instructional design process. Elements of the process include examination of learner characteristics and identification of readi-ness levels for learning. Furthermore, the application of systematic planning for designing various forms of individualized or self-paced learning also can allow for various individualized styles of learning.

Philosophically, as the planning starts, the instructional designer or instructor might have the following perspective: "I am designing a program of learning expe-riences for learners so that together we will be successful in accomplishing the stated goals and objectives. While it is important for each person to learn, it is equally important to me that the learner becomes proficient."

Therefore, a successful instructional program is one in which as many stu-dents as possible have succeeded, reaching a mastery level for accomplishing the specified outcomes. Grading on a bell-shaped normal curve and assigning letter grades would have no place in such instruction.

> **Question: Doesn't the ID procedure discourage creativity in teaching?**

When a fine work of art is created, the artist has used a number of widely accepted design elements (unity, emphasis, balance, space, shape, color, etc.) cre-atively. This same principle applies to instructional planning. The effective instruc-tional designer considers all the elements of the process to design a creative instructional approach.

Certain accepted learning principles, characteristics of individual compo-nents, and necessary relationships among elements require consideration in planning. These nine design elements, discussed earlier, can be developed and manipulated in imaginative and creative ways. Although the nine elements are the basis for good instruction, innovative and creative approaches result from how you the instructional designer apply the process.

Two persons teaching the same subject or topic and targeting the same outcome goals might very well design different plans. Both can result in equally satisfactory student learning. The process demands dynamic interactions between students and instructor and between student and content, and different activities may be developed to satisfy those demands. This process encourages creativity, even to the extent of providing for open-ended or unanticipated learning experiences.

Expert's Edge

Does He Know that I Know that He Knows that I Know?

Why Should I Care about Philosophy?   Our philosophies shape what we think and do. Few of us, however, take the time (or *have* the time these days) to examine our beliefs or to contemplate life. I barely have enough time to figure out what to wear each day, let alone the meaning of life. Yet, understanding our beliefs can go a long way toward removing the roadblocks we face each day—in life—and in instructional design.

Whether it's life in general or an applied field of study, some things are black or white whereas others are in gray. Yet, when we take the time to understand the beliefs that guide and direct us, we become better prepared to solve problems or manage difficult situations. Our philosophies are the beliefs, values, and attitudes that filter how we interpret situations and make decisions.

In addition, those of us who work in the field of instructional technology will most likely encounter those core values that underlie our profession, including these:

1. The systems approach is the field's foundation.
2. Learning is a change in knowledge or behavior.
3. Achievement is the desired outcomes of the instructional design process.

Our philosophies influence how we make sense out of these core values. Sometimes we become so wrapped up in living our lives that we forget to consider our values and beliefs. Our philosophy sheds light on what we do, how we do it, and why we do it because philosophy is all about *thinking*. Long ago when Socrates claimed that "the unexamined life is not worth living," philosophy was a way of life intended for ordinary people. It provided practical advice for living. So, let's take a look now at how all of this might apply to instructional design.

Is It a Line or an Oval?   The systems approach means different things to different people. Some interpret the systems approach to mean systematic, a concept best illustrated by the vast array of procedural models that describe instructional design as a linear, step-by-step process. Others believe that the systems approach is a systemic orientation that is more recursive and organic than linear. Of course, gray areas between these two extremes integrate bits and pieces of both explanations. What do you think? Is the systems approach a line, an oval, or something else? Does it ever make sense to follow a rigid plan or should you always plan to follow a flexible process?

Is Learning Internal or External?   Speaking of gray areas, the field has yet to discover a single theoretical perspective that completely explains the complex phenomenon of learning. Generally, the black-and-white opinions on this subject describe learning as either something that occurs in the mind or as a behavior that must be observed. Added to this issue are various beliefs about how learning occurs. Some believe knowledge is what the learner acquires through instruction. Others suggest that learning is an active process of constructing rather than acquiring knowledge. Clarifying *your* views about the nature of learning helps you make sense out of the perspectives and expectations that stakeholders hold about instructional design. As an instructional designer, you will be constantly challenged to understand multiple viewpoints and interpret theories of learning into appropriate strategies.

Stuff, Experiences, or Environments?

Student: Is the focus of instructional design on instruction or learning?
Professor: Yes!

The instructional design process yields achievement that aligns with various orientations to the field. A *product* orientation often focuses on development of instructional materials. A *process* orientation reflects a focus on structuring meaningful learning experiences, whereas a focus on the *environment* is oriented toward creating an atmosphere that fosters learning. But there are no absolutes, and, more times than not, instructional design integrates all these views. From a philosophical perspective, however, these various orientations often lead to learning outcomes that include anything from knowledge to skills to attitudes. If you're clear about whether your focus is stuff, experiences, or environments, you'll be more likely to deliver the results you desire.

Is Unexamined Instruction Worth Designing?   When was the last time you came face to face with your philosophies about learning and instruction? Philosophy can help instructional designers find solutions that are compatible with those beliefs surrounding the instructional design process. Some believe that instructional design needs to address more than practical issues—it should provide for the human spirit as well. The ultimate benefit of this approach is insight into the impact of our actions on the learner . . . and it may help a few people figure out what to wear tomorrow!

David L. Solomon has more than 13 years' experience designing, developing, and implementing training and performance improvement solutions for multinational and privately held businesses. David teaches part-time at the secondary and postsecondary level, and his research interests include explicating the role of philosophical inquiry in our field.

Question: Isn't the main attention in ID given to low-level, immediate-learning outcomes rather than to higher-order, long-term outcomes?

Examine the test questions in a typical unit or end-of-course examination. Frequently, they are multiple-choice or true/false items that involve defining, labeling, naming, recognizing, and other memory or recall of subject content. The ID process, in keeping with the goal to be accomplished, logically emphasizes more advanced intellectual thought processes that build on basic factual information. This emphasis may include learning related to comprehension, application, analysis, synthesis, and evaluation.

In many academic subject areas, learners achieve major learning outcomes only after they have completed a class and then enroll in an advanced course or begin working on the job. Instructional design includes procedures for directly and indirectly evaluating postcourse behavior and content application outcomes.

These answers to the critics may seem unconventional. Many teachers and trainers, based on their beliefs and experiences, might not accept them. Often people must become dissatisfied with present practices or results before they recognize the need for change and improvement (e.g., getting beyond passive learning and rote memorization to attaining higher-level objectives and providing more meaningful educational experiences). At that point, they are probably ready to explore a fresh approach to instructional planning. Providing explanations and offering opportunities, as described in this introductory chapter, can help counter criticism of the instructional design process.

QUESTIONS . . . QUESTIONS . . . QUESTIONS

As you read and study the following chapters, you will frequently see questions being raised or referred to in relation to the topic under consideration. Such questions may appear at the beginning of a chapter to indicate the important matters that follow. Then, as the discussion proceeds, other questions help direct thinking toward decisions that must be made.

An instructional designer continually probes for clarification, explanations, and details. You must help the persons with whom you carry out instructional planning to communicate effectively with you. This can best be done by using questions. Therefore, pay particular attention to the questions raised throughout the book. Then, let questioning become a common part of your behavior as you explore and eventually practice the instructional designer role.

SUMMARY

1. Curriculum includes subject matter, skills, and courses that constitute an educational program.
2. The key elements of ID are learner characteristics, objectives, instructional strategies, and evaluation of learning.

3. A complete ID plan consists of nine elements arranged in a flexible configuration and formative and summative evaluations for potential revisions and judgments of success.

4. A number of expressions may substitute for the term *instructional design* in the literature and in practice. The expression *instructional development* applies to the management of ID projects.

5. The ID process has the following qualities: it follows a systematic procedure with specific details, it usually starts at the course development level, it can enhance learning at a satisfactory level, and it may result in different planning results by different designers.

6. The ID process can benefit program managers, administrators, instructional designers, instructors, and learners.

7. The ID process applies to both business (i.e., nonschool settings) and academic education.

8. Roles in the ID process include instructional designer, instructor, subject-matter expert, and evaluator.

9. Criticism of the ID process that needs answers includes the opinions that it is a mechanistic rather than humanistic planning method; it discourages teacher creativity; and its main attention is given to low-level, immediate outcomes. The approach to ID emphasized in this textbook is counter to these criticisms.

10. Asking questions during all phases of the ID process can help direct thinking toward decisions.

THE ID PROCESS

As you read through this book, you will use the instructional design process to create a unit of instruction similar to the one in the Appendix. In this section, we provide guidance for applying the concepts, skills, and processes described in the chapter. This section also provides you with additional heuristics on the design process.

To start, we recommend that you reflect on your own definitions and philosophies. First, what is your definition of instructional design? Second, which learning theory or theories do you subscribe to for designing instruction? Third, what is your view of the learner?

APPLICATION

In the "Getting Started" section at the beginning of this chapter, we described an unfortunate scenario of an instructional designer's first day on the job. How would you respond to the group's questions?

Write a job description for your ideal job. Next, refer to the nine elements in Figure 1-2 and see how many of them are described in your job description. Which elements did you include in your description?

ANSWERS

How would you respond to the getting started scenario? It seems the key issue is not to overwhelm your new colleagues with instructional design terminology. A more friendly approach might be to discuss what you can do in concrete terms that they can understand. One of our professors always cautioned new graduate students not to overwhelm their new boss with all they know in the first month, as they would have nothing left for the rest of the year! This job is going to take some gradual selling and building of both rapport and support with the manager and staff. We suggest proceeding cautiously, but doing everything you can to be helpful.

Which design elements would you include in your job description? Asking us to pick one or two is like asking parents to select their favorite child! Each of us enjoys doing certain tasks more than others, but we recognize that all the different elements are essential and important in the design, development, and implementation of an effective and efficient product. We hope that you have a real interest in two or three of the elements but that you also develop your skills in all aspects of the design process.

REFERENCES

Bloom, B. (1976). *Human characteristics and school learning.* New York: McGraw-Hill.

Bodilly, S. (1998). *Lessons learned from New American Schools scale-up phase.* Santa Monica, CA: RAND Corporation.

Bradford, D. J. (1999). Exemplary urban middle schoolteachers' use of five standards of effective teaching. *Teaching and Change, 7*(1), 53–78.

Brandenberg, D. C. (1987). Communicating evaluation results: The external evaluator perspective. In L. S. May, C. A. Moore, & S. J. Zammit (Eds.), *Evaluating business and industry training.* Boston: Kluwer Academic Publishers.

Bruner, J. S. (1963). *The process of education.* New York: Vintage Books.

Bruner, J. S. (1966). *Towards a theory of instruction.* New York: W. W. Norton.

Bruner, J. S. (1973). *The relevance of education.* New York: W. W. Norton.

Campbell, M., Farrell, G., Kamii, M., Lam, D., Rugen, L., & Udall, D. (1997). The Expeditionary Learning–Outward Bound Design. In S. C. Stringfield, S. M. Ross, & L. J. Smith (Eds.), *Bold new plans for school restructuring: The New American Schools Development Corporation designs.* Mahwah, NJ: Erlbaum.

Canada NewsWire (1995). Speedy Muffler King announces second quarter results. [On-line]. Available: www.newswire.ca/releases/August1995/03/c2085.html.

Dewey, J. (1900). Psychology and social practice. *Psychological Review, 7,* 105–124.

Henderson, J. G., & Hawthorne, R. D. (1995). *Transformative curriculum leadership.* Englewood Cliffs, NJ: Merrill.

Inhelder, B., & Piaget, J. (1958). *Growth of logical thinking from childhood to adolescence.* New York: Basic Books.

Kearns, D. T., & Anderson, J. L. (1997). Sharing the vision: Creating New American Schools. In S. C. Stringfield, S. M. Ross, & L. J. Smith, (Eds.), *Bold new plans for school restructuring: The New American Schools Development Corporation designs.* Mahwah, NJ: Erlbaum.

Morrison, G. R., & Lowther, D. L. (2002). *Integrating computer technology into the classroom* (2nd ed.). Columbus, OH: Merrill.

Prewat, R. (1995). Misreading Dewey: Reform, projects, and the language game. *Educational Researcher, 24,* 13–22.

Reigeluth, C. M. (Ed.). (1983). *Instructional-design theories and models: An overview of their current status.* Hillsdale, NJ: Erlbaum.

Reigeluth, C. M. (Ed.). (1999). *Instructional-design theories and models: A new paradigm of instructional theory, Volume II.* Hillsdale, NJ: Erlbaum.

Romiszowski, A. J. (1981). *Designing instructional systems.* New York: Nichols.

Sarason, S. B. (1995). Some reflections on what we have learned. *Phi Delta Kappan, 77,* 4–85.

Skinner, B. F. (1954). The science of learning and the art of teaching. *Harvard Educational Review, 24,* 86–97.

Skinner, B. F. (1965). Reflections on a decade of teaching machines. In R. Glaser (Ed.), *Teaching machines and programmed instruction II.* Washington, DC: National Education Association.

Snellbecker, G. (1974). *Learning theory, instructional theory, and psychoeducational design.* New York: McGraw-Hill.

Stolovitch, H. D., & Keeps, E. J. (1999). What is human performance technology? In H. D. Stolovitch & E. J. Keeps (Eds.), *Handbook of performance technology: Improving individual and organizational performance worldwide* (pp. 3–23). San Francisco: Jossey-Bass/Pfeiffer.

Tyler, R. (1949). *Basic principles of curriculum and instruction.* Chicago: University of Chicago Press.

The value of training. (1995). [On-line]. Available at: http://tidbit.fhda.edu/BII/News-Notes.html.

Vygotsky, L. S. (1962). *Thought and language.* (E. Hanfmann & G. Vakar, Trans.). Cambridge, MA: MIT Press.

Identifying the Need for Instruction

GETTING STARTED

You have just transferred to the U.S. division of Deep Well Chemical Company. This company supplies chemicals for oil well work in the United States for land and off-shore oil rigs. When you arrive, your manager is very agitated because he has a problem. They have had two deaths due to trucking accidents in the first eight months of this year, plus they are averaging 5.3 more accidents per 100,000 miles driven than the national average for trucking companies. The chief executive officer has told the division manager that he wants a perfect driving record in three months.

Your manager is convinced that the accidents are caused by drivers not obeying the speed limit, and he wants to initiate a program that will impose a company fine for every speeding ticket a driver receives. However, he is not sure how effective this approach will be since he does not always receive information on speeding tickets. He knows that the drivers are not performing at their best. Thus, he is giving you this problem to solve.

There are eight areas in the division (two in Texas, one in Louisiana, one in Oklahoma, one in Colorado, two in California, and one in Alaska). He quickly explains that each area has a dispatcher who assigns jobs to the drivers, two to five supervisors who each manage 12 to 15 drivers, and a safety manager. All training is done at the west Texas training facility. You have permission to travel to each area, where a manager will provide you with access to all personnel. Your manager would like to discuss your plan of action for addressing this problem tomorrow morning. What is your plan?

QUESTIONS TO CONSIDER

"What is the problem we are asked to solve?"

"Will instruction solve the problem?"

"What is the purpose of the planned instruction?"

"Is an instructional intervention the best solution?"

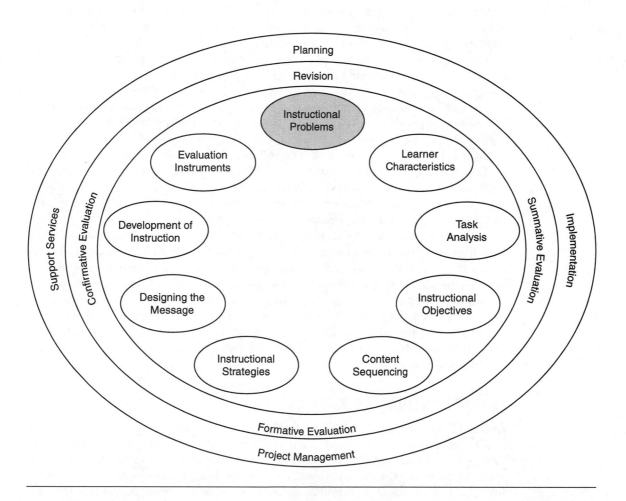

29

Before starting an instructional design project, we should ask, "Why do we need instruction? Under what conditions is it advisable to undertake a task that is both costly and time-consuming?" Let's examine some situations that might require an instructional intervention.

First, suppose performance is not meeting expectations. For example, emergency personnel who answer 911 phone calls are not providing accurate, complete information to the police and fire departments responding to emergency situations; or the mean score for a fifth-grade class on the fractions section of the state's achievement test is below the state and district means. In these two situations the operators and students are not performing to expectations.

Second, the work environment can change as a result of modifications in procedure or the installation of new equipment. When one corporation purchases another corporation, there will likely be procedural changes for minor operations such as requesting travel or completing travel expense forms. More complex procedures can also change—for example, preparing packages for exportation. In an elementary school the principal may decide to adopt a problem-based learning approach, requiring staff development and changes in teaching methods. Or a school might receive money to purchase five computers for every classroom. Teachers would then need training not only on how to operate the computers, but how to integrate this technology into their curricula.

Third, a company or industry can expand so rapidly that qualified personnel are in short supply. In the 1970s, the petroleum industry grew faster than the industry could prepare engineers for higher-level positions and faster than universities could provide qualified graduates. The solid-state electronics industry experienced similar growth in the late 1970s and early 1980s, which created problems. A similarly rapid industry growth occurred for information technology specialists in the 1990s. Inexperienced professionals were often hired, promoted to higher-level positions, and advised to learn through experience on the job.

In situations like the three types just described, training interventions *might* help improve productivity or achievement. More specifically, instructional design would provide a means for developing appropriate training or increase the cost-effectiveness of existing training. For example, a corporation might hire an outside consulting group to teach a course on time management. Could a similar course be designed in-house to reduce costs and more directly reflect the corporation's work environment? Similarly, an existing course might require an employee to attend for five full days. Perhaps a mixture of self-paced instruction and classroom instruction would reduce time away from the job.

IS INSTRUCTION THE ANSWER?

At first glance, it seems that the 911 operators mentioned earlier need training in how to record correct information and the fifth-grade students need to study one or more units on fractions. But do we know that more instruction will solve these problems? Considering the 911 operators, could something in the environment account for their inaccuracies? A careful analysis of the situation might reveal that the earpieces on the phones may not fit the operators properly or that transmissions have an unacceptable level of static. Training for the operators would not solve any of these problems. The fifth-graders' low test scores might be the result of the students' taking the year-end achievement test before they have completed the planned unit on fractions.

The purpose for identifying the problem is to determine *whether* instruction should be part of the solution. A team who developed new training for the 911 operators or required them to repeat existing training would squander company resources. Similarly, simply rescheduling the teaching of fractions or the achievement test might easily solve the fifth-graders' performance problem. Consider our Deep Well Chemical Company problem. What are the potential solutions for this problem? One option might be training or improved training. Another option to consider is the scheduling of the jobs. Further analysis might indicate that the time frame for each job is scheduled with little flexibility, resulting in the need for drivers to drive above the speed limit and take risks. A problem of this nature would require a change in policy and procedure as well as the work environment. Last, an analysis of the driving conditions might indicate that roads are hazardous, requiring additional training for drivers.

The instructional design process begins with the identification of a problem or need. Why is performance below expectations? Once we know the root cause of the problem, we can determine whether an instructional intervention will solve the problem. Instructional designers can use three different approaches to identify instructional problems: needs assessment, goal analysis, and performance assessment. Once the problem is identified, the instructional designer must determine the most appropriate intervention. Problems that on the surface seem to require an instructional intervention can often be solved with a change in policy, coaching, or the environment. Our focus in this book is designing instructional interventions *when instruction is an appropriate solution to the problem.*

When does an instructional designer conduct an analysis to determine whether there is a problem to address? Rossett (1999) identifies four opportunities for identifying performance problems. First is the introduction or rollout of a new product. When an automobile company introduces a new vehicle such as an electric or hybrid car, this change represents an opportunity to provide some type of support—either training or other—to improve the mechanics' ability to troubleshoot the vehicle. Second is responding to an existing performance problem. If a computer mail-order company notices an increase in power supplies that are incorrectly installed, then an analysis is probably warranted to determine the cause of the problem. Third, a company recognizes a need to develop its people so they can continue to contribute to the growth of the company. For example, in the early 1980s many appliance-manufacturing companies found that the knowledge of their design engineers was suddenly out of date due to the introduction of microprocessors into home appliances. Companies were faced with either replacing their current staff with new college graduates or developing their existing staff. An analysis was used to identify an appropriate solution—retraining the existing staff. Fourth is strategy development, where an analysis provides useful information for making decisions for strategic planning.

Individual and organization needs are ever changing. The needs or performance problems you identify today are likely to change in a month or six months. Similarly, training or change in the workplace implemented to address the problem affects existing needs and may change priorities. Needs assessments, goal analyses, and performance assessments often have a limited life span and require continual updating to identify critical performance problems.

NEEDS ASSESSMENT

Kaufman and English (1979) and Kaufman, Rojas, and Mayer (1993) describe needs assessment as a tool for identifying the problem and then selecting an appropriate intervention. If the designer fails to identify the problem properly, then the intervention may address only the symptoms, with no resultant change in the target audience's performance. The needs assessment process serves four functions:

1. It identifies the needs relevant to a particular job or task, that is, what problems are affecting performance.
2. It identifies critical needs. Critical needs include those that have a significant financial impact, affect safety, or disrupt the work or educational environment.
3. It sets priorities for selecting an intervention.
4. It provides baseline data to assess the effectiveness of the instruction.

Gathering baseline data is not always possible or cost-effective. For example, a designer may determine that one cause of meter damage is water-meter inspectors using the wrong technique for turning off meters. Is it feasible or cost-effective to observe a number of individuals in order to document the incorrect procedure, since no records exist that indicate the cause of the damage? Or could the designer simply record the total number of meters replaced before and after the training is implemented?

We define *needs* as a gap between what is expected and the existing conditions. Instructional designers are primarily interested in gaps when actual performance does not equal or exceed expected performance. Others view the term *need* as a noun and as a verb (Witkin & Althschuld, 1995). Our definition of a need as a gap in performance uses the word as a noun, whereas defining it as the solutions needed to fill the discrepancy uses the word as a verb. The next section describes how to plan and conduct a needs assessment.

Types of Needs and Data Sources

Six identifiable categories of needs are used for planning and conducting a needs assessment (Burton & Merrill, 1991). These six categories provide a framework for designers to determine the type of information to gather and a means to classify needs.

Normative Needs.   A normative need is identified by comparing the target audience against a national standard. Normative needs in education include national achievement test norms such as performance on the California Achievement Test (CAT), the Scholastic Aptitude Test (SAT), or the Graduate Record Exam (GRE). Normative data for identifying training needs in industry often do not exist because of the lack of record keeping at the national level. Some normative data exist for safety records (e.g., plant safety and transportation), service (e.g., an airline's on-time rating), and sales (e.g., projected sales of a product or service for a metropolitan area). A normative need exists when the target population's performance is less than the established norm. Thus, a fifth-grade class that scores 15 points below the norm on the math section of the CAT has a defined normative need. A trucking company that averages six more accidents than the industry norm per million miles driven has an identified normative need.

The first step in defining a normative need is to obtain the normative data. The test administrator's handbook or test publisher typically provides test norms. Norms related to specific industries (e.g., insurance, transportation) may be available from professional societies, trade groups, and government agencies (e.g., the Department of Transportation). Once the norm is defined, the instructional designer must collect data from the target audience for comparison with the norm. Again, summarized test data are often available in schools. Sales, manufacturing, and safety data are often included in company reports, databases, internal newsletters, and annual reports.

Comparative Needs.   Comparative needs are similar to normative needs in that both are defined by comparing the status of the target audience to an external measure or status. A comparative need, however, is identified by comparing the target group to a peer that is another company or school as opposed to a norm. In education, a comparative need is identified by comparing one class to another equivalent class (e.g., two sixth-grade classes) or comparing two equivalent schools to identify differences such as available equipment or test scores. However, federal and school district regulations involving privacy protection, as well as human subject review committees in the case of university-based studies, have made such data collection more difficult in recent years. Still, the data gathering may be even more challenging in a business environment. For example, public schools in many states administer an achievement test developed by the state each spring. School districts can prepare profiles for all of their schools for the different subtests. Administrators, teachers, and parents can then compare their school to comparable schools to identify comparative needs. Many universities and colleges maintain a list of institutions they use for comparisons of faculty salaries, class size, and budgets. Businesses often study competitors to define training needs, facilities, compensation, and incentives. A comparative need exists when there is a gap between the groups. This difference, however, may not reflect a *true* need that can be addressed through training, but rather an attitude of "keeping up with the Joneses."

To identify comparative needs, the designer must first determine areas for comparison (e.g., math scores, facilities, management development). Data are then collected on the target audience to determine the current status. Next, data are collected from the comparative audience. In education, this process may be as simple as calling the other school and requesting the information. Data gathering is usually not as simple in the business environment because of the proprietary nature of information and government antitrust regulations, which often prohibit such discussions between different companies. A designer may need to revert to interviewing employees who have a knowledge of other organizations and to reading journals (e.g., *Performance and Instruction, Training and Development*) to obtain the comparative data. When identifying comparative needs, the designer *must make sure* that the need is a viable training need as opposed to a status need.

Felt Needs.   A *felt need* is a desire or want that an individual has to improve either his or her performance or that of the target audience. Felt needs express a gap between current performance or skill level and desired performance or skill level. When searching for felt needs, designers must identify needs related to improving performance and individual wants that are motivated by a desire other than performance improvement. For example, one company offered a training course that involved travel to several locations in the United States and the Bahamas to study and observe various geological formations. The training manager had to determine who had a need for the course to improve job performance and who had a need to travel to interesting places. Another example is a college professor who decided to revise a course. She "felt" the need to add the new information to the course to make the course current, which would result in an improvement for the learners.

Felt needs are best identified through interviews and questionnaires. Face-to-face interviews are often more effective, since the designer can alleviate anxieties and probe for additional details. Questionnaires are only effective when individuals are willing to express their needs on paper. Typical questions to elicit felt needs are, "What could be done to improve your work performance?" or "What could be done to improve the performance of (target audience)?" Such questions may open a Pandora's box of problems; the designer would need to separate needs into those that are addressable by training (e.g., "a better understanding of the accounting system") and those that require other interventions (e.g., "reduce the amount of paperwork, add more lights to the work area").

Expressed Needs.   Bradshaw (1972) defines an *expressed need* as a felt need turned into action. People are often willing to pay to satisfy expressed needs (Burton & Merrill, 1991). An individual who chooses one of two or more options—for example, enrolling in a specific course or workshop—is also demonstrating an expressed need. Again, instructional designers are primarily interested in expressed needs that improve the performance of the target audience or person. An example of an expressed need is the list of students who are placed on a waiting list for a training course. The students have expressed a desire to enroll in the course and wait for an opening. The expressed need is the waiting list, which indicates a need for another section, a larger room, or a change in course formats to allow more students to take the course. In industry, professionals are often encouraged to attend one or more training courses a year as part of their professional development. Expressing an interest in attending such a course or having a manager recommend that an employee attend a specific course are means of identifying expressed needs. Recently, a number of principals and teachers have requested workshops and in-service training on how to integrate the use of microcomputers into the curriculum. This request is an expressed need.

Data on expressed needs come from a variety of sources. A need for more sections of a course is expressed in the enrollment data. Individual personnel files and performance reviews often include goals in the form of either expressed or felt needs. Although the right to privacy may restrict an individual designer from reviewing files, a designer could ask the appropriate supervisor or manager to review the files and report any needs. Finally, expressed needs are often identified in suggestion boxes and in-house publications with a question-and-answer or suggestion column.

Anticipated or Future Needs.   The instructional design process often focuses on identifying needs related to existing performance problems. *Anticipated needs* are a means of identifying changes that will occur in the future. Identifying such needs should be part of any planned change so training can be designed prior to implementation of the change. For example, a school principal and supervisors might decide to implement a new instructional technique (e.g., cooperative learning) next year. An anticipated need is the knowledge teachers need to use the cooperative learning method effectively in a classroom. By anticipating the need, a designer can prepare appropriate training before the teachers start the year and difficulties develop with the method. Similarly, the introduction of new software in a customer service center at a major corporation would likely require training for customer service representatives. Anticipating this need as the software is developed will allow the designers an opportunity to design the training so that it is ready prior to the transition to the new software. The customer service representatives are then knowledgeable of the new software and better able to do their job when they start using it.

Anticipated needs are often identified through interviews and questionnaires similar to those used with felt needs, but with additional questions about what future changes the employee anticipates that will affect the way the job is done. A second approach to identifying anticipated needs is to identify potential problem areas. For example, assume that a manually controlled drill press will be converted to a computer-controlled machine next year. An analysis of this change might find that the maintenance staff will need training on repairing and replacing the digital controllers on the drill presses.

Critical Incident Needs.   Mager (1984b) identifies *critical incident needs* as failures that are rare but have significant consequences—for instance, chemical spills, nuclear accidents, medical treatment errors, and natural disasters such as earthquakes, hurricanes, and tornadoes. A typical reaction to a critical incident need was the planning and education that occurred in Memphis, Tennessee, in 1990 in the wake of the 1989 San Francisco earthquake. An earthquake was predicted to occur in Memphis in December 1990. In anticipation of the disaster, several government agencies, schools, and corporations developed earthquake awareness programs by analyzing the events associated with the 1989 San Francisco earthquake.

Critical incident needs are identified by analyzing potential problems. For example, chemical plants, manufacturing facilities, and petroleum refineries often develop employee training programs for handling emergencies such as fires, explosions, or spills. Other critical incident needs are identified by asking "what if" questions; for example, what would happen if the main computer or phone system failed?

CONDUCTING A NEEDS ASSESSMENT

Four phases constitute a needs assessment: planning, collecting data, analyzing data, and preparing the final report. Figure 2-1 identifies the individual steps under each of these four phases.

FIGURE 2-1
Needs assessment process

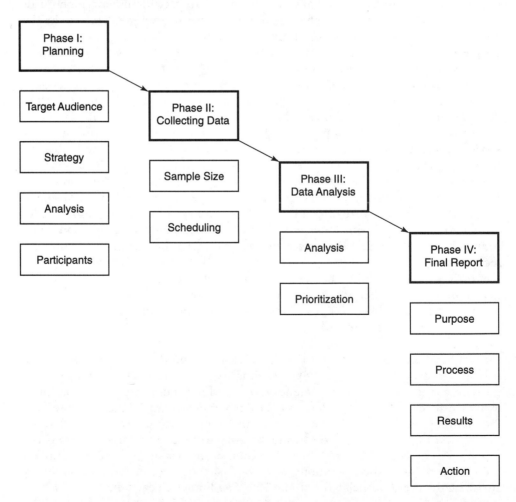

Phase I: Planning.   An effective needs assessment focuses on one job classification or target audience. Once the audience is defined, a strategy is developed for collecting the needs data. The designer first determines whether data are required for each type of need. For example, normative needs might not be essential when identifying anticipated needs due to a change in telephone systems.

The next step of the planning phase is to determine who will participate in the study. In industry, the participants (i.e., individuals to interview) might include a sampling of the target audience, supervisors and managers of the target audience, and experienced individuals who once were members of the target audience but have received promotions to higher levels. Figure 2-2 illustrates a sample organizational chart for a telephone company and identifies target participants (installers). Members of this target audience and the managers are asked to share their perceptions of the current needs. The line workers and repair people are also interviewed because they once worked as installers (the target audience) and can provide a different perspective. Experienced individuals provide another perspective based on their experiences and their interactions with the target audience.

Similar decisions are also required for school-based needs assessments. Major participants in those assessments are parents, students, and outside consultants. For example, we conducted a technology assessment for a school to identify teacher training needs and hardware and software needs. Our focus was primarily on felt and anticipated needs. We collected data by interviewing teachers and asking teachers, parents, and students to complete surveys.

The last step of the planning phase is to determine how to collect the data. Common data collection techniques include questionnaires, rating scales, interviews, small-group meetings, and reviews of paper trails. Consider the population who will participate in your assessment and determine the best means for collecting the data. For example, sending a questionnaire via e-mail to an audience that is not

FIGURE 2-2

Needs assessment participants (boldface box indicates individuals participating in needs assessment)

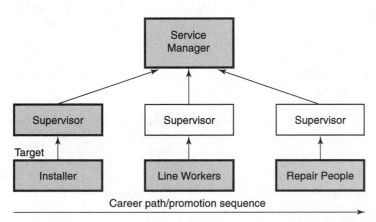

composed of frequent e-mail users could result in a low return rate. Similarly, paper questionnaires mailed to a group of executives may also yield a small return rate. Find one or two data collection methods that will produce the best results. Needs assessment results are often reported as frequencies (e.g., 60 percent of the employees indicated they did not know how to complete an expense advance request). Identification of the analysis methodology early in the process aids in designing the instruments and ensures that appropriate data are collected. The planning step is complete when you have designed the data collection instruments.

Phase II: Collecting the Data.   Careful consideration of the sample size and distribution is required when collecting data. It may not be logistically or economically feasible to interview every participant at each company site, plant, or division. Thus, the sample must include individuals from representative sites and regions. For example, manufacturing companies produce a variety of products at a number of different locations. Interviewing employees in only one area could provide a false picture of the training needs for a company-wide target audience. Data collection also includes scheduling appointments, making travel arrangements, and distributing and collecting questionnaires. Individual experience will determine the optimum number of interviews to plan per day and the return rate for questionnaires. Note that a 100 percent return rate often is unrealistic. Although a 75 to 85 percent return rate is desirable, the acceptable level depends on the context. Also, unlike experimental or basic research, large samples may be less important than samples that are representative relative to the target population of employees or students.

Phase III: Analyzing the Data.   Once the data are collected, you are ready to analyze the data. The output of the analysis is a prioritization of needs. Needs can be prioritized on the basis of economic value (e.g., cost value to the company), impact (number of people affected), a ranking scale, frequency of identification, or timeliness. One method for prioritizing the needs, the Delphi method, is an iterative process: we might mail a list of goals to a group of managers and ask them to rank the goals. In a second mailing, we might send the same group the top 40 goals and ask them to rank them again, and then the top 20 in a third mailing. This process is repeated until it establishes a focus. The advantage to the Delphi approach is its systematic and thorough data-gathering process; its disadvantage is its relatively high effort and time demands. Another method for prioritizing is to use the identified needs as an input to a goal analysis (see "Goal Analysis" later in this chapter), which is then used to set the goals for training intervention.

Phase IV: Compiling a Final Report.   The last phase of needs assessment is to prepare a final report. A needs assessment report should include four sections:

1. Summary of the study's purpose
2. Summary of the process (how it was done and who was involved)
3. Summary of the results with one or more tables and a brief narrative
4. Necessary recommendations based on the data

The recommendation should be appropriate to the problem. If the needed intervention focuses on restructuring wages or an organizational development intervention, then either a new team or additional team members may be needed to implement the solution. If instruction is an appropriate intervention, the designer can proceed with the design and development process.

Example Needs Assessment Plan

The Electronic Phone Company (EPC) offers business customers discounted day-time phone rates for domestic and overseas calls. EPC has customer service and operator information centers in New York, Atlanta, St. Louis, and San Francisco. The caller information department consists of information operators (entry level), operator supervisors, and chief operators. Information operators are promoted to operator supervisors. Operator supervisors monitor operator activity, provide coaching to entry-level operators, and handle problem situations for 10 to 15 operators. Chief operators monitor the activities of 5 to 10 operator supervisors and have the final authority and responsibility for all actions. EPC has decided that training is needed to improve the skills of the operator supervisors.

Phase I.   A decision was made to collect data on five types of needs: comparative, felt, expressed, anticipated, and critical incident. The decision was made in part because of an international conflict that began at the beginning of the needs assessment. Operator supervisors are the target audience (approximately 74 in the four locations). Face-to-face interviewing was selected as the primary method for data collection. Two operators at each of three levels were interviewed individually. A structured interview form was developed to guide the interviews.

Phase II.   A decision was made to interview employees at all four locations, since the New York and San Francisco locations had a greater percentage of overseas calls, and the St. Louis and Atlanta locations primarily handled domestic calls. The designers scheduled two days in each location to conduct six interviews (two operators at each of three levels) for a total of 24 at the four locations. Table 2-1 includes the interview questions that were used.

Phase III.   A frequency count was made for each need identified in the interviews. The needs were categorized as either customer oriented or employee oriented. Customer-oriented needs were ranked by estimated loss of income (e.g., inability to find a phone number, misdirection of customer complaints). A group of operator supervisors and chief operators participated in a ranking process using the Delphi method to rank the employee-oriented needs.

Phase IV.   The final report identified three training problems. First, operator supervisors needed training in the use of advanced searching techniques to identify phone numbers. Second, they needed training in handling difficult customers. Third, they needed training in coaching entry-level operators in communication techniques.

TABLE 2-1
Interview questions

How long have you served as an operator?
What resources do you use to help to answer caller questions?
How well do the resources work for you?
Does anything get in your way while doing your job?
What changes do you want to see?
Are there any things/issues that impact employee efficiency and effectiveness?
If you could change one thing about your job, what would it be?
How do you learn about new products that affect your job?
What changes might affect your job?

Needs assessment is a useful tool for identifying training needs. It is particularly effective when very little is known about an organization. Interviewing a number of individuals provides a broad perspective for correctly identifying the problem or needs.

GOAL ANALYSIS

Sometimes, conducting a needs assessment is neither practical nor feasible. An alternative approach is to use a goal analysis to define the problem. Mager (1984b) describes goal analysis as a method for "defining the undefinable." Some designers consider goal analysis as an integral part of the needs assessment process. Unlike needs assessment that seeks to identify problems, a goal analysis begins with input suggesting a problem. For example, a manager might determine that supervising operators are having a problem coaching the information operators. Goal analysis is then applied to this "need" to develop the goals for the training intervention. Applying goal analysis to a need suggested by one individual *assumes* that the need exists and that a training intervention is required to address the need. For example, a principal might ask you to conduct an in-service workshop on web page development for the teachers in her school. Since you are unfamiliar with the teachers, you might attend a faculty meeting and conduct a goal analysis to determine what the teachers feel they would like to accomplish in the workshop.

A goal analysis could also use the data from a needs assessment to set priorities. Take, for example, a needs assessment that identifies the need to train managers in how to conduct hiring interviews. A goal analysis would use this need, interview training, to determine goals for the instruction.

Six Steps of Goal Analysis

Klein et al. (1971) and Mager (1984b) have suggested similar steps for conducting a goal analysis. Our six steps for a goal analysis are a synthesis of theirs.

(**Expert's Edge**)

"Getting Blood out of a Turnip": An Instructional Design Approach

In an ideal world, focus groups would consist of 8 to 10 participants—experts in the field—who take turns addressing issues, allow the facilitator to control the conversation, and have unlimited time to participate. What happens, however, when you have 15 to 20 participants who are experts at their jobs, many of whom refuse to share information because supervisors are present, and have only one hour to spend? Clearly, such a situation calls for some changes to the traditionally run focus group. Here's what our training team did.

Prior to the focus group, we circulated a list of 10 questions we would ask and requested that participants review them. At the beginning of the session, we handed out the list again, this time with room for the participants to write down potential answers. They were told that we would collect these notes at the end of the session, and we requested that they not write their names on the notes unless they wanted to be contacted directly for their answers.

The facilitator read each question, clarifying, if necessary, and allowed a couple of minutes for the participants to make the notes. Discussion followed with note takers recording answers. (We were not allowed to tape these sessions.)

As with any focus group this large, there were a few who did not participate. With 10 minutes to go, we stopped the process and gave each person an opportunity to make one last statement about anything he or she felt strongly would affect training. These ideas were also captured.

In the debriefing session that followed, we reviewed the participants' notes and were surprised to find that many mentioned topics that we didn't have time to discuss. We also received some strong comments that may not have been politically correct to express in a focus group setting. Finally, we had substantial reinforcement for all the comments that were made, making it easier for us to determine consensus of opinion. In one hour we had collected more data than we normally gained in much longer sessions.

Bailey F. Hanes, Ed.D., is an independent consultant and educational psychologist specializing in performance management and employee training. He has over 30 years' experience in working with major corporations all over the United States.

Carol Diroff is an instructional technologist at Ford Motor Company's Powertrain Core Competency, where she has done extensive work in technical training. She is currently working on training for complex problem solving.

Identify an Aim. Using a group of experts familiar with the "problem," determine one or more aims related to the need. An *aim* is a general intent that gives direction. Example: Conduct an effective interview for a real estate sales position.

Set Goals. Have the group of experts generate a number of goals for each aim. These goals should identify behaviors that describe learner performance. Examples:

> Prepare an agenda for the interview.
> Prepare a series of questions to ask during the interview.
> Prepare a structured interview form.
> Identify people to take the interviewee to lunch.
> Identify individuals to provide transportation for the interviewee.
> Identify a real estate agent to work with the interviewee.
> Obtain benefits information.
> Identify the steps for conducting an interview.
> Determine the type of questions to ask.

Refine Goals. Sort through the goals and delete duplicates, combine similar goals, and refine those that are vague. This step is primarily a refinement stage to clarify the goal statements. Examples:

> Prepare a series of questions to ask during the interview.
> Prepare an agenda and transportation for the interview.
> Identify a real estate agent for the interviewee.
> Obtain benefits information.
> Identify the steps for conducting an interview.
> Determine the type of questions to ask.

Rank Goals. Rank and select the most salient goals. Ranking can be by order of importance, items most likely to cause problems if ignored, or other relevant criteria. Some goals may be eliminated and others identified as critical to job performance. Examples:

1. Prepare an agenda for and transportation to and from the interview.
2. Obtain benefits information.
3. Prepare a series of questions to ask during the interview.
4. Determine the type of questions to ask.
5. Identify the steps for conducting an interview.
6. Identify a real estate agent for the interviewee.

Refine Goals Again. Identify discrepancies between the goals and existing performance. This step verifies that the need exists and that the goals are related to the job task(s) by identifying differences between existing performance and the goals. Examples:

> Goal 2 was dropped because the personnel office handles benefits information.
> Goal 6 was dropped because it was not considered part of the interview process.
> The remaining goals represented existing performance problems.

Make a Final Ranking. Develop a final ranking of the goals. Determine how critical or important the goal is to performing the tasks. Second, consider the overall effect of the goal. Relevant factors may be the cost of not doing the training, the probability the need will disappear if ignored (e.g., an impending change in the system), or the number of people affected by the training intervention. The final ranking is then used to design the training. Examples:

1. Determine the type of questions to ask.
2. Prepare a series of questions to ask during the interview.
3. Identify the steps for conducting an interview.
4. Prepare an agenda for and transportation to and from the interview.

Comparing Goal Analysis and Needs Assessment

Goal analysis takes less time than a needs assessment and its focus is typically much narrower. The goal analysis starts with a problem someone has identified, and then it focuses on a solution (i.e., expressed in the goal analysis). A goal analysis is typically conducted with a few individuals who are knowledgeable of the problem and target audience. The designer is relying on this small group of individuals to provide accurate input rather than gathering a variety of data from a number of sources as with a needs assessment. Deciding which method to select depends on a number of factors, including cost, time, scope of the project, and validity of the information the designer obtains from the participants. Typically, a needs assessment is reserved for projects that can justify the time and cost involved. A goal analysis is used when a problem is identified and the designer has confidence that the problem is valid. For example, a university implements a new online record system so that faculty and advisors can access student and class information. Since this system is new, training of some sort is probably needed. A goal analysis with appropriate individuals could be used to further define the training.

PERFORMANCE ASSESSMENT

Instructional designers often receive requests to design a training program to address a perceived problem. A manager, chairperson, principal, or vice president may offer additional funding or rewards as an incentive to complete the project. Although it is often tempting to "take the money and run" with the project, the first step prior to initiating design is to determine whether training intervention will actually solve the problem. Some problems, for example, may result from a failure to follow procedures rather than from the improper execution of a task. An overnight shipping company saved thousands of dollars on training by recognizing such a problem. One facility had a consistently large number of package-sorting errors. Initial reaction might have been to design a training program to improve the sorters' skills. After careful observation of the process, however, the manager found that the crew loading the packages on the conveyor was starting the sort earlier than scheduled and before the full complement of sorters arrived. The few sorters who arrived early were overwhelmed by the packages and made errors trying to keep up with the packages loaded by the crew. Simply enforcing the procedure that the sort would not start until the designated time solved the sorting problem. The appropriate solution to this problem was one of following procedures rather than one of providing retraining for the employees.

Similarly, a request was made to develop a course to help petroleum engineers plan an acid treatment on an oil well to increase oil production. An analysis of the problem indicated that treatments were adequately planned, but they were done on wells that were already producing as much oil as possible given the pipe diameter and well pressure. Any increase in oil production would not be physically possible or economically feasible compared with the cost of the treatment. The training emphasis shifted from planning the treatment to determining when a treatment was needed. The performance assessment, in this case, identified a *different* problem that was addressed with training.

For training to be effective, it must address the appropriate problem and not a symptom. Mager (1984a) describes a performance analysis as an aid to identifying performance problems. Rossett (1999) describes this process as finding the source of the problem. *If* we know the source of the problem, *then* we can determine the appropriate solution! Developing training for the sorting problem just described would be a waste of company resources and would fail to solve the problem. Often, there is a simpler solution (such as reaffirming the starting time) than developing and implementing a training program. Rossett (1999) and Kalman (1987) suggest a number of causes of performance problems. We have combined these two approaches in Table 2-2. If you discover a problem during a needs assessment or goal analysis, or someone "identifies" a performance problem, you can use Table 2-2 to help guide your assessment of the problem. By identifying the real cause of the problem, you can determine the appropriate intervention strategy. Your analysis may require additional interviews, observations, surveys, and focus groups (Rossett, 1999).

Another technique, job analysis, is a listing of all the tasks an individual performs in a job. Such an approach is useful for developing a curriculum for training rather than identifying performance gaps or problem areas. While this method is very time-consuming, it does yield a complete task listing for a job. The use of job analysis to define a program assumes that training is needed on the tasks. Such an approach is appropriate for certain environments, such as a trade school course or military training that involves entry-level learners who have little knowledge or skill in the area. The outcome is typically a series of courses based on a body of knowledge the learner must master.

SUMMARY

1. Like a good problem-solving model, instructional design begins with identification of the training problem. Needs assessment, goal analysis, or performance assessment can help identify the problem. In practice, problem identification often involves a combination of these techniques rather than just one.
2. Needs assessment is an effective tool for identifying a range of problems in an organization, particularly if the designer is unfamiliar with the organization.

TABLE 2-2

Causes of performance problems

Cause	Example	Intervention
Lack of knowledge or skills	Production personnel do not know how to set the computer controller for the drill press.	Training.
	New-hire insurance sales personnel do not know the difference between whole life and term life insurance.	
Lack of motivation or incentive	Employees are not returning unused parts to the correct bins.	Improve motivation and/or offer incentives for performance.
	Students are not completing homework assignments due on Mondays	
Environmental factors	Professional staff are experiencing an increase in carpal tunnel syndrome after receiving PCs.	Modify environment or change workstation to facilitate task.
	Lighting in the shop is not adequate to perform tasks.	
Management factors	Manager fails to provide adequate direction for staff concerning scope and time frame for jobs.	Change management practices or train/ coach manager.
	Manager's style is confrontational.	
Interpersonal relations	Dispersed workgroup flounders on collaborative projects.	Change work environment; provide coaching, conflict resolution; change management practices or policy.
	Rivalry between staff members disrupts job/task.	

3. A needs assessment can identify six types of needs: normative, comparative, felt, expressed, anticipated, and critical incident.

4. A goal analysis can use either a needs assessment or a request for instruction as a starting point to establish priorities. The goal analysis process first identifies aims, then establishes, refines, and prioritizes the goals.

5. Performance assessment helps determine whether the goals of the training program actually address a training problem or whether another intervention is more appropriate.

6. The problem identification process may require multiple techniques to refine the problem (see Figure 2-3). For example, you might start with a needs assessment or performance assessment, and then you use a goal analysis to refine the problem.

FIGURE 2-3
Identifying instructional problems

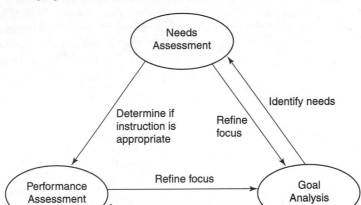

THE ID PROCESS

This element of the ID process provides the first contribution to instructional design documentation. During this phase, you meet with your manager to identify your client and maybe the target audience. In most cases, one of your clients will have an idea or focus area for the performance problem. That is, someone will have identified a gap where performance is not meeting expectations. Or, in some instances, you might be asked to identify where a performance problem might develop because of changes in the job or work environment. There are also times when you might identify a performance problem during your analysis of an unrelated problem.

Now is the time to delve into your toolbox and determine the best tool or tools to use to define the problem. You must find an approach that is both effective and efficient. If instructional design is a new concept in your company, you may need to sell your management on the concept of defining the correct performance problem.

The output of this phase is a definition of a performance problem. If it is a problem that you can solve with training, then you further refine the problem statement with a goal analysis that will guide the next phase–task analysis. If the performance problem is easily solved with a job aid, then you can begin the process of developing the job aid. If the problem is one that is not best addressed by an instructional intervention, then you must determine who can more appropriately provide a solution. Depending on your own skills, you might provide the solution, or you could find another resource in the company to provide the appropriate solution.

APPLICATIONS

Consider the next two problems you might face as an instructional designer. What actions would you take?

It is your first day on the job at Global Plastics and you are meeting with your manager in her office. Looking around, you notice that it is professionally decorated and has various symbols indicating her success in the company (and probably access to the corporate interior designer). Obviously, she is someone who is viewed favorably by upper management and has the necessary political connections. As you talk with her, she is fumbling with a malfunctioning mechanical pencil. From her actions, you might infer that she lacks any mechanical ability and wonder what effect it might have on her ability to understand technical training problems. Noticing that you are not paying full attention to what she is saying, she places the pencil in her desk drawer and closes it with extra effort for emphasis. She explains that she wants videotape instruction developed on how to change the oil in all the diesel engines in the 10 manufacturing plants. She is unsure how many engines there are, but there are four in this plant. Furthermore, she explains that the in-plant technical training program must start with the basics. As you walk out the door, she mentions that her neck is on the line for the $2.5 million video studio she installed last year. She needs to show management that video instruction can affect the company's bottom line. She urges you to collect data to support this point. "Now," she charges, "determine where you want to begin shooting, and I will make the arrangements for you to begin tomorrow afternoon."

After your two-day meeting with the regional field service managers, you have a list of 56 "training" courses they generated. A quick analysis of the topics suggests that they are potential performance problems caused by either a lack of knowledge or skill, or they are tasks that are not performed frequently. These managers are quite adamant that their field service staff definitely needs this type of training if they are to continue offering a quality product to clients.

After some investigation, you grow weary of the list. It seems some of your sources question the need for certain topics and some topics are deemed too simple to need training. Your task is to improve the performance of the field service engineers, who have acquired the reputation of replacing parts until the equipment is fixed rather than troubleshooting the problem.

What is your plan of action? One of your clients is the group of managers who fully believe they have identified the training needed to solve the problem. On the other hand, these training topics do not appear to support troubleshooting, but rather to support removing and replacing parts. Considering you are new to the company, what will you do?

A N S W E R S

What is the real problem with changing the oil in the diesel engines? There are two issues. First, your manager needs to justify the expensive purchase of the video equipment that you will *use* for producing video-based training. Second, there may be a need for in-house technical training. You are new on the job and you do not have a lot of credibility or support yet. This situation may be an instance in which it is best to "bite the bullet" and spend an afternoon producing a simple tape on how to change the oil. You will gain the support of your manager, who can then show upper management the nice product you have produced. Then, she might more readily listen to your plan for addressing the larger issue. Presenting her with reasons why the company does not need the videotape might fall on deaf ears.

In every situation, there are typically two or more clients. Your manager is one of your clients. The field service managers are also clients. And the field service engineers are clients—probably the most important because you are trying to improve their productivity. Although it might be politically expedient to develop the 56 courses identified by the managers, the burden of not solving the performance problem would probably ultimately fall on you. Given the results of your initial research, it appears that the problem is not defined. We would recommend that you sell your manager and the field service managers on trying to identify the "real" problem—lack of troubleshooting skills.

To accomplish this task, you might do a needs assessment and an analysis of the type of work completed during the past two years on the job. Obvious trends might emerge, such as the fact that the engineers replace the heat transfer element whenever a problem occurs. A check with your engineering department might indicate that the number of failures reported by this service department far exceeds those expected or performed by other service groups. The combination of the needs assessment data and repair data might convince the managers to take a different approach to solving the problem. This problem illustrates that there is a political side (not only in business, but also in education) of instruction. The successful designer must often balance the political and instructional needs of the organization and individuals. Designers must consider the political issues to ensure that all stakeholders buy in and that they understand and support the plan. Similarly, the designer must report the needs to the stakeholders and help them make the most appropriate decision for addressing the problem.

QUALITY MANAGEMENT

There are two questions to ask at this stage of the instructional design process. First, is the problem correctly identified? A needs assessment should provide adequate data to support your problem identification. However, there is often a lack of such data if you used *only* a goal analysis or peformance assessment. Before proceeding, you should verify that you have correctly identified the problem by either reviewing your data or posing some additional follow-up questions to those familiar with the target audience and/or problem. Second, is this problem one that is best addressed by an instructional intervention? If instruction is the answer, then you should proceed with the instructional design process. If you have determined that another intervention is more appropriate, such as by using the peformance assessment process, you must determine the most appropriate action. You might add new members to your team or suggest another specialist form a team to address the problem.

SAMPLE DESIGN PLAN

PROBLEM IDENTIFICATION

The Student Services department has documented a growing number of graduate students requesting help with time management principles. The director has decided that a unit of instruction on time management principles should be developed and made available to any student requesting it. Because of limited support staff, the instruction must be paper-based and self-paced.

Graduate students often juggle a wide variety of roles with all the attendant demands on their time: one can have family obligations, extracurricular interests, career goals, and work responsibilities. Add to that one to four graduate-level courses per semester, and time management becomes a critical skill. Time-constrained graduate students often need help mastering the principles of time management. Electronic calendars and personal digital assistants (PDAs) are found in many a graduate student's briefcase, but these are only electronic devices without a guarantee of efficient and effective use. The student services director has requested an instructional unit that will guide graduate students through the basic principles of time management: how to set goals and establish priorities, how to construct realistic time lines for projects, and how to stick to those time lines. Only after mastering this process will electronic calendars and PDAs become useful tools for managing the multiple demands on the graduate student's time.

The graduate students have expressed their need for better time management skills, but I want specific information on the nature of their need. To make this instruction effective I want to know two things: (1) how they manage their time now and (2) where their time management skills are lacking. Fortunately, the Student Services director keeps careful contact notes and has a database that will give me a picture of the scope of the problem, but I'll also conduct a needs assessment to get more specific data. I will also do a goal analysis once the needs assessment is done.

Needs Assessment

Expressed Needs.   The database was used to identify expressed needs from students. The database data suggests that those who most often ask for time management guidance are first-year graduate students. One problem came up several times: important projects are left to the last minute and then done hurriedly at the expense of quality. It seems the students need help prioritizing tasks.

Felt Needs.   What data should I collect to get more specific information on the level of the graduate students' existing time management skills and where their time management skills are most lacking? I know these are busy students, so interviews and focus groups are probably out. I might get better results if I design a short survey and mail it. Whatever I send must be brief. A survey should work; it will be easy for them to complete, easy data for me to analyze, and it won't take too much time to create and mail. I also need to decide to whom to send the survey. The instrument will be sent to a sample taken from the population of students who have used the Student Services facility in the last academic year. I'll target all first-year graduate students in this population. Then, I'll take a random sample from the rest of the population—undergraduates. I'll include the undergraduate students in the survey because I suspect they will have something to say about their time management skills. The database has home addresses plus e-mail addresses for every student who uses the student center, so sending out the instrument should not be very difficult. The director will fund a mailing to 350 students. I will request that the surveys be returned within two weeks of the mail date.

The response rate for the survey was 53 percent, 185 surveys returned! The data analysis revealed two major problems: procrastination and difficulty prioritizing the many tasks that make up a project. In the open-ended section of the survey, students indicated they do not like using a daily planner to its fullest potential.

Now, I can do a goal analysis based on the needs I have identified. I'll work with a couple of my subject-matter experts for this step.

Goal Analysis

Step 1: Identify General Aims.

- Learners will use time management principles to construct an assignment plan.

Step 2: Set Goals.

- Prioritize tasks.
- Write goals.
- Break down tasks into subtasks.
- Break down goals into tasks.
- Organize workspace.
- Use a daily planner.
- Overcome procrastination.
- Write a project plan.
- Turn a list into a plan.
- Construct a time line.
- Identify one time management principle to adopt.
- List everything that must be done to achieve a goal.
- Create a master goal list.
- Create a monthly task list.
- Create a weekly task list.
- Create a daily task list.

Step 3: Refine Goals.

- Prioritize tasks.
- Write goals.
- Break down goals into tasks.
- Break down tasks into subtasks.
- Use a daily planner.
- Overcome procrastination.
- Write a project plan.
- Create a master goal list.
- Create a monthly task list.
- Create a weekly task list.
- Create a daily task list.
- Organize workspace.

Step 4: Rank Goals.

1. Prioritize tasks.
2. Write goals.
3. Break down goals into tasks.
4. Write a project plan.
5. Overcome procrastination.
6. Use a daily planner.
7. Create a master list.
8. Create a monthly task list.
9. Create a weekly task list.
10. Create a daily task list.
11. Organize workspace.

Step 5: Refine Goals Again.

- Goal 11 was dropped because it was not identified as a performance problem.
- Goals 2 and 3 were dropped because they are subgoals to goal 4.
- Goals 7, 8, 9, and 10 were dropped because they are subgoals to goal 6.

Step 6: Make a Final Ranking.

1. Prioritize tasks.
2. Write a project plan.
3. Overcome procrastination.
4. Use a daily planner.

Recommendations

Based on the goal analysis, this instruction will consist of four units: (1) prioritizing tasks, (2) creating a project plan, (3) overcoming procrastination, and (4) using a daily planner. Because prioritizing tasks is a foundational skill for the other units, the project will begin with it. The Student Services director will be given the opportunity to review this first unit before design on the other three units begins.

REFERENCES

Bradshaw, J. (1972). The concept of social need. *New Society, 19*(4), 640–643.

Burton, J. K., & Merrill, P. F. (1991). Needs assessment: Goals, needs, and priorities. In L. J. Briggs, K. L. Gustafson, & M. H. Tillman (Eds.), *Instructional design: Principles and applications* (2nd ed., pp. 17–43). Englewood Cliffs, NJ: Educational Technology Publications.

Kalman, H. K. (1987, March). *Is it a training problem?* Paper presented at the National Society of Performance and Instruction, Washington, DC.

Kaufman, R., & English, F. W. (1979). *Needs assessment: Concept and application.* Englewood Cliffs, NJ: Educational Technology Publications.

Kaufman, R., Rojas, A. M., & Mayer, H. (1993). *Needs assessment: A user's guide.* Englewood Cliffs, NJ: Educational Technology Publications.

Klein, S. P., Hoepfner, R., Bradley, P. A., Wooley, D., Dyer, J. S., & Strickland, G. P. (1971). *Procedures for needs-assessment evaluation: A symposium.* (Report No. 67). Los Angeles: University of California, Center for the Study of Evaluation.

Mager, R. F. (1984a). *Analyzing performance problems* (2nd ed.). Atlanta: Center for Effective Performance.

Mager, R. F. (1984b). *Goal analysis* (2nd ed.). Belmont, CA: Lake.

Rossett, A. (1999). Analysis for human performance technology. In H. D. Stolovitch & E. J. Keeps (Eds.), *Handbook of performance technology: Improving individual and organizational performance worldwide* (pp. 139–162). San Francisco: Jossey-Bass/Pfeiffer.

Witkin, B. R., & Altschuld, J. W. (1995). *Planning and conducting needs assessments: A practical guide.* Thousand Oaks, CA: Sage Publications.

CHAPTER 3

Learner and Contextual Analysis

GETTING STARTED

Your manager has asked you to design a training program to improve the collaborative skills of cell phone designers who are using a new online collaborative design tool. Each of the designers or groups must bargain with the other designers or groups. For example, the group working on the battery power might ask all the teams for a few more ounces of weight in exchange for a longer talk time. It is November and the documented training design is due in late January. Time is therefore short, and, as you soon discover, the target employees are very busy and not highly accessible for providing information. First, what do you need to know about your target audience that might influence the design of the materials? Second, how will you collect the information?

Suppose that you had never heard about the instructional design process. You start giving a lecture at the first class meeting of your course. You have put a lot of work into developing this new introductory unit so as to impress students with the value of the subject. The lecture contains detailed statistical content from recent research and complex explanations. As you proceed, you sense reactions: a few students are listening intently and rapidly taking notes; others look puzzled; some appear completely indifferent. This is a one-time opportunity for all of them to get this important information! What is wrong? Perhaps, in your preparation, you have given little consideration to the nature of the student group, the students' preparation levels, degree of motivation, or other traits that contribute to their interest and success in learning. One of the key elements of the instructional design process mentioned in Chapter 1 is the need to consider the learners for whom a program is being developed. Obviously, the measure of success of an instructional plan will depend principally on the learning level accomplished by the learners involved. Learner populations, from elementary levels through high school and college and in training areas (whether industrial, business, health, government, or military), are composed

"Why is it important to give attention to learner characteristics when planning instruction?"

"Which characteristics are most useful, and how is information about them obtained?"

"What limitations might these characteristics place on your design?"

"What factors in the environment will affect the instruction?"

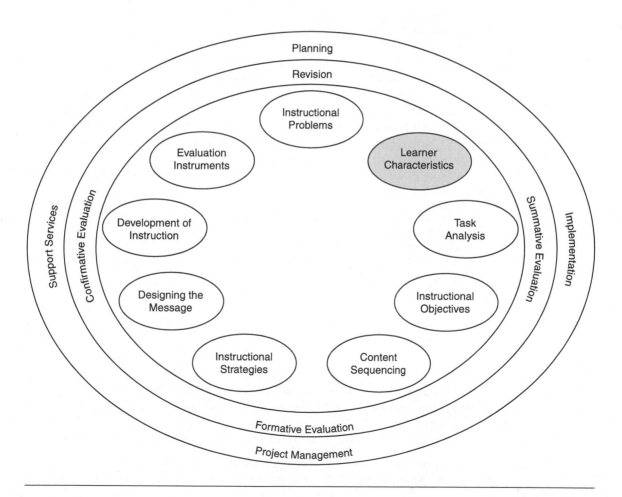

of varied types of people. As designers, we need to understand the relevant characteristics of our learners and how those characteristics provide either oportunities or constraints on our designs.

Just as people differ in many respects, so do ways in which they learn. Some of these differences are evident in the kinds of experiences each person requires to learn and, if competence in a skill is to be acquired, in the amount of time and practice each person needs to acquire it. It is essential, therefore, early in the planning process, to give attention to the characteristics, abilities, and experiences of the learners—both as a group and as individuals. To serve either a training group or an academic classroom, the instructional designer must obtain information about the capabilities, needs, and interests of the learners. This information should affect certain elements in planning, such as the entry point, selection of topics (and the level at which topics are introduced), the choice and sequencing of objectives, the depth of topic treatment, and the variety of learning activities. Related to learner analysis is environmental analysis; that is, what variables in the learning environment can or will affect the design and delivery of the instruction.

When designing an instructional plan, decide early in the initial design stages which characteristics of your learners or trainees are most useful to identify. Then, decide how to acquire the necessary information. As you complete the design process, you may find that you need additional information about your learners or the learning environment.

Often in learning, it is easier to understand a process by seeing an example of a final product. Here is one to consider from a learner analysis that two of the authors (Ross and Morrison) conducted for a project involving the design of computer-based support tools. What follows is the summary section (using fictitious labels in places) of our final report:

- The employees to be trained are generally motivated to improve their skills and efficiency.
- New employees often start the job without adequate training.
- More employees with experience work in section GM than in section EO.
- Most employees are very knowledgeable about their jobs.
- Employees are generally positive about their jobs, but feel that they are inhibited by limitations of the existing computer system.
- Other employee frustrations stem from a perceived lack of understanding by other groups as to what their group needs. This frustration is particularly strong among section EO employees, who feel that section A's staff needs to better understand section EO's needs for orders and other tasks.
- Most users characterize themselves primarily as problemsolvers.
- Employees are generally well educated and have good reading and cognitive skills.
- Employees feel great time pressure to complete their job requirements.

Based on the preceding characterizations and more detailed, job-specific information, we were able to make much more informed decisions about different aspects of the instructional design plan. For example, we determined that computer support tools requiring any substantive off-task time (e.g., receiving a computer-based instruction [CBI] tutorial lesson on a particular job procedure) would rarely be used by the target audience. To derive this information, however, we needed to orient our learner analysis around characteristics most likely to impact the learning task. Let's now examine strategies and schemes for identifying these key learner differences.

TYPES OF LEARNER CHARACTERISTICS

Countless traits differentiate learners. In initiating a learner analysis, the important task for the designer is to identify those characteristics most critical to the achievement of the specific training objectives. Also, in most applied contexts, the accessibility of learner information is a major factor in deciding which characteristics to consider. For example, where general intellectual ability is considered an important variable relating to success in the training program, administering individual IQ tests at several hundred dollars per student may be viewed as extravagant, or certainly impractical, relative to using some existing ability or aptitude score. On the other hand, a variable such as gender or prior jobs may be highly accessible but have little relevance to the particular instructional design decisions.

Heinich, Molenda, Russell, and Smaldino (1999) suggest that designers initially consider three categories of learner characteristics: general characteristics, specific entry characteristics, and learning styles. Let's briefly examine each category, while remembering that on an actual design project (for example, training accountants to use a new tax preparation application) the importance of specific traits within each category depends on both task relevance and accessibility of the learner information.

General Characteristics

General characteristics are broad identifying variables such as gender, age, work experience, education, and ethnicity. We examine several of these variables in more detail later, but for now consider the example of training employees to use a new tax preparation application. Recognizing that you have not yet conducted a needs analysis (Chapter 2) or task analysis (Chapter 4), try to form preliminary impressions of some training approaches you might use. Would you rely primarily on a workshop or lecture? A printed manual? On-the-job coaching? Job aids or guide sheets? Some combination? At this point, it's probably pure speculation, but would your "best-guess," first idea change if you were told that the employees were all novice workers in their early twenties? What if all were disadvantaged teenagers hired for the summer on a school-to-work program? What if they were senior accountants with extensive experience in numerous accounting applications? And, finally, the designer's frequent challenge—what if the employees comprise a mixture of experts, novices, and paraprofessionals with diverse job and software experiences? Given these variables, the importance of a prior needs (or goal) analysis and present understanding of how general learner characteristics may impact addressing those needs in the training design should be evident.

Specific Entry Competencies

Specific entry competencies are prerequisite skills and attitudes that learners must possess to benefit from the training. Based on our experiences, we have found the analysis of such competencies is important at two stages in the design process. One stage precedes the design of the instruction and determines the *entry* characteristics of typical target students or trainees. In the example of the accounting project, it would certainly help to know that the majority of employees to be trained have had limited experiences in using computers in their work; or that most are highly educated with strong reading skills; or that most are extremely negative about using the new application and are likely to resist the training. Knowing the learners' skills, attitudes, or aptitudes is obviously important in determining the appropriate difficulty level of instruction. We recommend making the difficulty level slightly higher than that considered optimum for the average learner. Consequently, the instruction will be challenging, but not overly demanding for most learners; and it is usually easier to provide supplementary support for learners experiencing difficulty than it is to make too-easy content interesting and challenging for the majority.

The preceding sentence suggests the second stage of design during which the assessment of specific entry competencies comes directly into play. Once the instruction is designed, it is highly useful and often essential to include entry tests that determine the learners' readiness. For example, if one of the accounting trainees was completely unfamiliar with the computer used in the training (e.g., switching from a Macintosh to a PC), a prerequisite training session to provide the needed background could prevent a situation in which that individual becomes lost and frustrated during the actual instruction. At the opposite extreme, an entry assessment might identify several trainees who have already mastered the instructional objectives and, therefore, do not need the training. Heinich et al. (1999) suggest clearly stating prerequisite competencies as part of the instructional program: "The accounting trainee must be able to start up the computer and format a floppy disk for saving files." We might expect to revise our specific entry competencies after completing the task analysis or after completing the strategy design.

Learning Styles

Learning styles are traits that refer to how individuals approach learning tasks and process information. Simply put, some learners find certain methods of learning more appealing and effective than others. For a long time it has been known that, rather than attending lectures and reading textual material, some individuals learn better from a visual approach to studying and others learn from physical activities and the manipulation of objects. Attempting to identify a person's unique learning style preference might aid planning for small-group or individualized instruction.

Despite the extensive literature on learning styles, questions remain regarding the degree to which such styles can be matched to teaching methods with any benefits for learning (Knight, Halpin, & Halpin, 1992; Snow, 1992). This concern has been raised in general with the research that attempts to systematically adapt instructional methodologies to individual learner characteristics (see the review by Jonassen & Grabowski, 1993). For the designer, then, the potential value of knowing students' learning styles must be weighed against the effort required to obtain that information (e.g., administer and score a learning styles inventory) and the likelihood that useful and practical adaptations of instructional strategies can be achieved. In our view, the primary context in which you may want to consider learning styles is one-to-one instruction for which materials and strategies can be easily adapted to accommodate individual needs.

The Kolb Learning Style Inventory (Kolb, 1984, 1985) and the Myers-Briggs Type Indicator (Myers & McCaulley, 1985) are examples of self-scoring inventories that can help both individual students and instructors identify cognitive learning styles. Students who study individually and have choices can adapt activities and resources to their own styles. Instructors can use the information to address the various cognitive learning styles.

Again, you, as the instructional designer, must weigh, on the basis of practical considerations and instructional needs, the degree to which assessing learning styles is useful to the design project. Academic information, our next focus, is more often a key variable for instructional planning and delivery.

ACADEMIC INFORMATION

Probably the most easily obtainable and the most often used category of information about individual learners is an academic record. This record would include the following:

- School grade or training level completed and major subject areas studied
- Grade point average or letter grades for academic studies
- Scores on standardized achievement tests of intelligence and in such basic skills as reading, writing, and mathematics
- Special or advanced courses completed relating to the academic major or area of training

Much of this information is available from student records on file in a school's administrative office. Some of it is available from employment applications, in personnel files, or in the individual's training history. Confidentiality and ethical considerations must be kept in mind when referring to student or personnel records. If a specific kind of information about learners is not available, specialized tests can be obtained and administered through a testing or personnel office.

Closely associated with the academic information about learners are the knowledge and skills that learners may already possess directly relating to the subject content or skills to be learned. Obtaining knowledge and skills information is one of the purposes for the pretesting element of the instructional design process (see Chapter 10). Thus, there is a close relationship between the information gathered about learner characteristics and the data to be acquired from pretests.

PERSONAL AND SOCIAL CHARACTERISTICS

You should also consider personal and social characteristics of the learners for whom the program is intended when those characteristics might impact the design and delivery of the course. Typically, information about the following types of variables is helpful to the designer:

- Age and maturity level
- Motivation and attitude toward the subject
- Expectations and vocational aspirations (if appropriate)
- Previous or current employment and work experience (if any)
- Special talents
- Mechanical dexterity
- Ability to work under various environmental conditions, such as noise, inclement weather (for those working outdoors), or high elevations

Looking at this list and thinking of your recent experiences, which variables do you feel are most important for instruction or training? Much depends on the nature and conditions of the learning activities. For many instructors, learner motivation is actually considered to be the most important determinant of success (Driscoll, 2000; Keller & Litchfield, 2002; Pintrich, Roeser, & De Groot, 1994). Learners who "just don't care" or, worse, are actively resistant to the instruction are not likely to respond in the same way to the learning activities as would highly motivated students. Design strategies that create interest and keep attention would be appropriate for the former group.

Learner attitude is somewhat different from motivation. For example, a learner may be interested in taking a basic electronics course, but he may feel doubtful that he can pass it based on his poor abilities. This type of self-fulfilling prophecy breeds failure by anticipating failure (Slavin, 1994). If the designer finds such negative attitudes are common for the target learner groups, she might employ strategies specifically intended to build confidence in the learner's abilities as the lesson proceeds (Jonassen & Grabowski, 1993). One possibility is to start the instruction with very easy content and gradually increase difficulty over time. (B. F. Skinner, in fact, employed a similar orientation, called "successive approximations," or "shaping," in designing programmed instruction.)

The manual dexterity and other special motor skills of the learner may be of major importance in certain training programs. As discussed in Chapter 5, the classification of motor skills has had less acceptance and less practical impact than has that of the cognitive and affective domains. Yet, several potential useful taxonomies exist, such as those by Heinich et al. (1999) and Kibler (1981).

Learner analysis may also reveal physical characteristics of potential students, such as health, physical fitness, weight, or disabilities, that are relevant to training decisions. For example, one training program recently offered by a school district included, as a team-building exercise for administrators and teachers, an outdoor expedition requiring hiking and climbing. For several participants, these activities proved highly strenuous and produced negative feelings about the training (not to mention soreness and muscle aches the next day as a continuing reminder!).

Useful data about personal and social characteristics may be obtained by observation, interviews, and informational questionnaires, as well as from attitudinal surveys completed by learners. (See Chapter 11 for further discussion about these information-gathering methods.) If special groups constitute a significant percentage of the student population, social characteristics peculiar to each group should be given due consideration.

CHARACTERISTICS OF NONCONVENTIONAL LEARNERS

While it is important during planning to gather and use the usual kinds of information—academic, personal, and social—about all learners, attention also should be given to the special characteristics of those individuals described as nonconventional learners, whose preparation, behavior, and expectations may not be typical. These groups include individuals who are culturally diverse, learners with disabilities, and adult learners.

Culturally Diverse Learners

Learner groups may include members of ethnic cultures with backgrounds and behaviors that differ markedly from those of the majority of learners or trainees. Also, both the instructional designer and instructors who deliver the instruction may differ in ethnic background from members of the student group. For these reasons, characteristics of culturally diverse learners need special attention during planning.

One obvious problem may be deficiency in the English language. If this is true, remedial training in English (or the language in which the instruction will be conducted) must be provided as needed (Ovando, 1989). Cultural and social differences should be recognized because they can affect such things as the ability to take responsibility for individualized work or to engage in creative activities. In some cultures, an accepted strong authority figure, such as, for example, the father in a family, influences the freedom and decision-making abilities of children. If background experiences are limited, a resulting naïveté and lack of sophistication may affect a learner's readiness for and participation in a program. In planning instruction for culturally diverse learners, take care in selecting bias-free materials and providing alternative resources and activities to support instructional objectives.

Five "standards" for effectively teaching minority students and culturally diverse learners have been proposed by researchers (see Bradford, 1999; Tharp, 1998). The standards include the following:

- Joint productive activity, where teacher (expert) and students (novices) work closely together to accomplish joint projects
- Developing language and literacy across the curriculum, where language development is continually emphasized and assisted through modeling, eliciting, probing, restating, clarifying, questioning, and praising
- Making meaning, where learning is highly situated within and connected to the real-world contexts of students' lives
- Teaching complex thinking, where students are involved in complex tasks and instruction shifts from basic skills to complex manipulation of problem solving in content domains
- Teaching through conversation, where students are engaged in learning through the use of language and dialogue, especially in relation to real-world tasks

Information about the abilities of learners in ethnic groups can be obtained through the usual testing, interview, and questionnaire procedures, as well as from the literature (e.g., Garcia, 1991). In addition, another source of information is counselors in an organization or the community who have had direct experience working with such individuals. However, at the same time, it is extremely important for designers to avoid stereotyping different ethnic or cultural groups to create adaptations that aren't needed or, worse, unequal opportunities to learn (Pollock, 2001). We advise carefully checking the appropriateness of such design variations using formative evaluation and expert review (see Chapter 12).

Learners with Disabilities

The category of learners who are disabled includes individuals with physical disabilities and others with learning disabilities such as hearing and vision loss, speech impairment, and mild mental retardation. Each type of disabled learner has unique limitations and requires special consideration. While some persons with physical disabilities can participate in regular classes, others cannot. A careful analysis of individual abilities should include observation, interviews, and testing.

Many learners with disabilities require special training and individual attention. Therefore, an instructional program may require extensive modification to serve such learners appropriately. Specialists who are capable of working with individuals with disabilities should be a part of any instructional-planning team.

Adult Learners

An important factor reducing the homogeneity of learner populations is the increasing number of adults who have become learners in these settings: those returning to colleges and universities; engaging in community adult education programs; and participating in job training or retraining for new skills in business, industry, health fields, government service, and the military.

The field of adult education, known as andragogy, has been studied at length. Those who work in this field recognize a number of generalizations regarding adults and their accommodations in the educational process:

- Adults enter an education or training program with a high level of motivation to learn. They appreciate a program that is structured systematically with requirements (objectives) clearly specified.
- Adults want to know how the course's content will benefit them. They expect the material to be relevant, and they quickly grasp the practical use of the content.
- To adults, time is an important consideration. They expect the class to start and finish on schedule, and they do not like to waste time.
- Adults respect an instructor who is fully knowledgeable about the subject and who presents it effectively. Students quickly detect an unprepared instructor.
- Adults bring to class extensive experience from their personal and working lives. These experiences should be used as major resources for helping students relate to the subject being studied.
- Most mature adults are self-directed and independent. While some adults lack confidence and need reassurance, they would prefer that the instructor serve as facilitator to guide and assist rather than as an authoritarian leader.
- Adults want to participate in decision making. They want to cooperate with the instructor in mutual assessment of needs and goals, the choice of activities, and decisions on how to evaluate learning.
- Adults may be less flexible than younger students. Their habits and methods of operation have become routine. They do not like to be placed in embarrassing situations. Before they accept a different way of doing something, they want to understand the advantages of doing so.
- Adults like to cooperate in groups and socialize together. Small-group activities and an atmosphere for interaction during breaks are important.

For adults, as well as for other learners, the same principles of human learning and behavior must form the basis of an instructional program. (These principles receive attention in Chapter 7.) The degree and specificity for applying the principles among certain groups differ during planning, when media are designed, and when instructional activities are carried out. By being sensitive and alert to the characteristics of special groups of learners, a designer can plan programs especially effective for them.

CONTEXTUAL ANALYSIS

Cognitive science research has found that embedding the instruction in a familiar context enhances both student achievement and student attitudes (Bransford,

Expert's Edge

Old Technology Is Still Good Technology . . . for Some

A major industrial corporation had its top executive-level suites completely remodeled during the last part of 1998. The work was to be completed after the New Year's holiday break and included remodeling all the executive conference rooms. In addition to a more comfortable and plush headquarters, the design team for the remodeling also wanted to include the latest technology wherever possible. In their zeal to impress the executives, they equipped every conference room with new electronic whiteboards—boards that could download scribed information directly to a computer for saving. "They'll love this!" was the general thinking.

Within the first week of activity after the holidays, I began receiving the usual requests to scan, digitize, and transcribe the executives' flip-chart musings from the old paper easels. After a week or two of business as usual, I asked one of the vice presidents why they weren't using the nifty computerized whiteboards. It seems the executives, while technically aware, were not very technically knowledgeable. In addition, the use of paper easel flip charts with colored felt-tipped pens was ingrained in the corporate culture for use at any meeting or brainstorming session involving scribing. They would scribble and write like crazy on these pages, then tear them off and hang them around the room so they could refer to them during the meeting. None of them had a clue as to what the whiteboard with the computer even did, much less how to use it.

Nobody took the time to analyze how the executives used conference rooms. The executives generally were 40-plus years old and well paid to make major decisions and conduct strategic planning. Each executive had one or two assistants who dealt with any technology such as faxing, preparing presentations, using voice mail, and using various computer applications. A few interested assistants eventually found the time to study the instruction manual and experiment with the boards to discover, on their own, what they could do. I later learned that some of them tried to encourage their bosses to be innovative and use the boards; only two were successful after a year. They reported results of slowed meetings, too much focus and wasted time on learning what they were doing, and nearly instantaneous grumbling to "get those easels back in here!" The effort failed. Currently, the boards mostly just sit there, unused. A small monument to wasted effort and cost, and a reminder to take the time to understand the learners and the environment!

Paul Burry works in customer service, providing projection room and conference support for the executive staff of a Fortune 500 company. For the past five years, he has been responsible for digital still reproduction, multimedia applications, video conferencing, and projection systems management.

Sherwood, Hasselbring, Kinzer, & Williams, 1990; Dorsey-Davis, Ross, & Morrison, 1991; Ku & Sullivan, 2000; Morrison, Ross, & Baldwin, 1992). Context, for example, plays a key role in the design and development of problem-based learning (Barrows

& Kelson; 1996; Morrison & Lowther, 2002) and anchored instruction (Bransford et al., 1990). For example, consider a course for legal professionals on searching electronic databases. A very simple approach to teaching how to use a database such as WestLaw would be to display the search screen and point to where to enter data and which button to click to search. This same presentation could be enhanced by embedding the teaching of the search strategy within a context. For example, the instruction could create a scenario in which the student is searching for information on disputed property lines to keep Big Al's Super Food Market from encroaching on a client's backyard. Providing a context for teaching the search strategy makes the content concrete and realistic and helps the student understand not only the search strategy, but also how it can be applied on the job.

Analysis of the instructional context provides rich data for designing real-world examples and scenarios (Tessmer & Richey, 1997). Why should a designer be concerned with this larger environment? First, instruction and learning do not take place in a vacuum. The context influences every aspect of the learning experience. Second, context is a collection of factors that can inhibit or facilitate instruction and learning. For example, a classroom across the hall from the break room will likely have noise and other distractions from other students that can disrupt the instruction. Similarly, a classroom that is well equipped with a video projector and computers for each student can facilitate instruction in creating database queries. Third, a single class can require multiple contexts. For example, a fifth-grade classroom using a problem-based learning approach might survey historical buildings in the neighborhood, do research at the assessor's office, use a computer lab, and conduct small group meetings in the hallway. Learners in a popular geology course offered by an oil company visited various geological sites in Texas and the Grand Canyon and ended with a snorkeling trip in the Caribbean, all to observe different geological structures. Each of these contexts provided a unique learning environment for the course. A thorough context analysis ensures the planned instruction fits the instructional environment (Tessmer & Harris, 1992).

Types of Context

There are three types of context an instructional designer should analyze when designing instruction (Tessmer & Richey, 1997). First is the orienting context that focuses primarily on the learner. Second is the instructional context, which provides information about the physical environment and scheduling of training. Third is the transfer context that considers the opportunities for transferring the knowledge and skills to new situations. The following is a description of each of these context types.

Orienting Context.   The first part of this chapter focuses on learner characteristics; that is, the knowledge, skills, and attitudes the learner brings to the instruction. A designer might want to consider three other variables. First, what goals does the learner have for taking or attending this course or instruction? Some individuals in business approach a course simply as another week of paid vacation! As a new student, what were your goals for your first course? Were you simply concerned with getting an A, or were you more concerned with learning new knowledge and skills? With a knowledge of the learner's goal or lack thereof, you can consider how to design the preinstructional strategy (see Chapter 8) as well as the instruction.

Second, what is the learner's perceived utility of the instruction? Do the learners see the course as providing them with useful information? For example, a university installed new Touch-Tone phones in each faculty member's office many years after they had Touch-Tone phones at home. The communications department prepared a four-hour training program on the new phones. Faculty and staff perceived little utility in the training since the only features the phones had were receiving incoming calls and making calls. Voice mail, call forwarding, and conferencing would not be available for a year or more. As a result of the low perception of utility, only a few people attended the training.

The third factor to consider is the learner's perception of accountability. Is the learner accountable for mastering the content presented in the course? For example, many faculty members have discovered that students will not participate in an online discussion or create a personal web page if it does not count toward their grades. Similarly, adults attending a course that does not lead to certification or some other form of accountability (e.g., pay increase or promotion) may have a low perception of accountability and may demonstrate less transfer of the knowledge or investment in the course. A designer who understands the learners' goals, utility, and accountability can use this information in the design of the instruction.

Instructional Context.   Simple strategies such as planning to use a cutaway of a sewing machine on Thursday to explain how it works can turn to disaster when you discover the sales force has taken the cutaway to a trade show and you lent your 35mm slides to an instructor teaching a similar course in Paris!

Some of the common instructional environment factors to consider are described in Table 3-1. Many corporations employ meeting coordinators who help instructors address some of these issues. Each of these factors requires careful consideration. For example, you might plan a course on using Excel to calculate the return on investment (ROI) of a project or improvement. Such a course assumes that students have access to computers; thus, you need a computer lab. If you are planning to offer the course at a hotel, is it feasible to set up a computer lab? Your only option might be to create a self-paced course using printed materials, a CD-ROM, or the Web so that learners can complete the training at their computer workstations. Careful consideration of the instructional environment early in the design process is essential.

Another instructional environmental factor to consider is the scheduling of the course. For example, what are the problems with offering a course in January in Minneapolis or another city in the snowbelt versus Houston or Atlanta? Similarly, offering a two-week course the second week of December may not generate a large enrollment because of the holidays. If you are planning a workshop for teachers, what are the days and time limitations during the schoolyear? Another factor to consider is the length of a course and its meeting times. It is not unusual to find one-week or even six-week courses offered in business. But how do you accommodate a course you planned as a weeklong course (e.g., 5 days for 8 hours a day) when management dictates that the course must be offered one or two days a week for only two hours and that it must start one hour *before* the regular workday begins? What modifications will you need to make? Some companies also require courses be offered on weekends. For example, one Fortune 500 company's introductory management course is always held on Saturdays. Management's philosophy is that only those employees who are really interested in moving into the management track will be willing to give up a few Saturdays to make the transition.

Transfer Context.   A goal of any instruction should be the continual application of the knowledge and skills learned. This last type of context analysis focuses on creating an environment that promotes the application of the newly learned knowledge and skills to a diverse range of situations. Learners are more likely to transfer the knowledge if they perceive that it can help them do their jobs. Similarly, a learner needs access to the tools and resources required to apply the skills. For example, work assignments that require the use of spreadsheets to perform calculations will need access to a computer with Excel installed if students are to use the information learned in the course. Thus, sending an engineer to a course on using an Excel template to calculate ROI requires that the engineer has access to a computer in the work environment if the engineer is to transfer the new knowledge to the job.

TABLE 3-1
Analysis of the instructional environment

Factor	Considerations
Lighting	Can you control the lights for presentations by turning off the lights above the screen and dimming the other lights? Are the controls easily accessible and usable? Are there shades or blinds on the windows?
Noise	Are there sources of noise such as mechanical devices (e.g., elevators, motors), office areas, hallways, or break rooms that will distract the learners? Is there any way to control these noises?
Temperature	Can you or someone else easily adjust the temperature in the room?
Seating	Are the tables the correct size and shape for activities? Can you move the chairs for small-group exercises? Does everyone have a clear view of the screen and presenters?
Accommodations	Are there hotel or housing accommodations in close proximity? Can learners eat lunch on site to avoid disruptions? Are facilities or entertainment available after course hours?
Equipment	Is equipment such as projectors, computer labs, tools, shops, and other equipment available or available for renting?
Transportation	Do students and instructors have easy access to the meeting area and accommodations? Do you need to arrange for transportation?

Two other factors that can inhibit the transfer of knowledge and skills are opportunities and support. If learners do not have frequent opportunities or need to calculate expected ROI, then they are unlikely to transfer the skill to new situations. If learners' managers do not support the use of Excel or even punish learners for using it, then they are less likely to transfer the knowledge to new situations.

Conducting a Contextual Analysis

The common tools for conducting a contextual analysis include surveys, observations, and interviews. Start by identifying factors that might affect your instructional design plan by providing either opportunities or constraints. Then, determine how to collect the necessary data. You may need to refine your contextual analysis after you start designing the instruction (see Chapter 7) and when you refine your delivery strategy and instructional strategies.

Collecting Data.   Rich data are needed to provide the designer with an accurate picture of the instructional environment. Surveys using both forced-choice (e.g., rating scales and multiple-choice items) and open-ended questions can provide a quick picture of the environment. For example, a designer might send a survey to several sites to gather information about the training room facilities or type of computers and software available in the labs. Surveys can also be used to assess learner perceptions and the organizational support for the instruction. A designer might send such an instrument to both the target audience and the supervisors and/or managers of the audience.

Consider an instructional designer planning a multimedia unit on how to operate cash registers in a national chain of grocery stores. The designer might start first with a survey to determine the availability and the type of computer(s) each store has for training. Second, the designer might want to know what type of cash registers each store is using. By collecting these two pieces of data, the designer can determine the lowest common denominator for the computers used to deliver the instruction. If over 35 percent of the stores have computers that are three years old, the designer can make some initial assumptions about the speed of the machines and take this limitation into consideration when designing animations. If the results of the survey indicate that more than one type of cash register is used, the instruction will need to include instructions for each type. To make the instruction more efficient, the software will need to have a means of selecting or preselecting the appropriate cash register for the training.

Observations provide the instructional designer with a firsthand picture of the environment. Designers can observe the layout of facilities to determine their applicability for various instructional strategies. A room with fixed seating might not be appropriate for a course that relies heavily on small-group work or role plays. We once presented in a room that was touted as a well-equipped state-of-the-art presentation room. Yes, it had a large screen and video projector. Unfortunately, there was no way we could connect our laptop to the video projector, the windows faced east and let the morning sunlight shine on the screen and in the presenter's face, and the two entrances to the room were on either side of the screen and behind the presenter. While we could use the facility's desktop computer and deal with those arriving late, we could not control the air-conditioning vents placed directly behind the projection screen, which caused it to wave continuously! While a survey might suggest the rooms are appropriate, a direct observation can reveal any problems or enhancements.

Interviews can provide a picture of potential learners in their work environments. Interviewing members of the target audience and their supervisors can provide a rich source of contextual information. Tessmer and Richey (1997) suggest using open-ended questions that allow for a wide range of potential answers. Interviews conducted in the workplace can also provide insights into the factors that can support or inhibit the transfer of learning.

Analyzing Data.   The collected data are analyzed to identify environmental factors that will influence the design and delivery of instruction. The analysis should identify factors that place limitations on the design and delivery of the instruction, that facilitate the design and delivery, and that are missing from the analysis.

SUMMARY

1. By considering the results of task or goal analysis and the likely conditions of training (practical constraints, setting, duration), the designer must to identify the learner characteristics most likely to have an impact on instructional outcomes.
2. Three categories of learner traits are general characteristics (gender, age, ethnicity), specific entry characteristics (prerequisite skills for the instruction), and learning styles (preferred ways of learning).
3. Knowing about students' learning styles provides a potentially valuable basis for adapting instruction, but valid learner classifications and beneficial instructional adaptations may be difficult to achieve in practice.
4. Academic records reveal the extent and quality of schooling or training that learners have already received.
5. Through observation, interviews, and questionnaires, indications of learners' personal and social characteristics can be obtained.
6. Nonconventional learners include culturally diverse learners, adult learners, and learners with disabilities. Special characteristics of such individuals should be recognized and considered during planning.
7. Contextual analysis provides information about environmental factors that will affect the design and delivery of the instruction.

THE ID PROCESS

Learner analysis and contextual analysis are easily viewed as identifying constraints to the design or delivery of the instruction. Learners who do not have the prerequisites expected, who cannot be away from work for extended periods to attend a course, or who have a short attention span may require the designer to make necessary changes in the design plan. On the other hand, a learner analysis might reveal a highly motivated group of learners, and the contextual analysis might reveal not only a supportive environment from management, but a state-of-the-art training facility! If you approach learner and contextual analysis as a means of identifying both limitations and opportunities, then you are likely to generate a more positive attitude and product.

When initiating a learner analysis, consider the performance problem you have identified. Then, reflect on practical considerations involving your time schedule and the accessibility of information about the prospective trainees. General characteristics of interest might include age, work experience, work level, education, and ethnicity as relevant, easily obtainable information. A good source of specific characteristics is the subject-matter expert who helps you with the task analysis. This individual can help you identify specific characteristics related to the task or content that are needed to solve the problem. Your initial contextual analysis may be very broad at this stage of the design process. You can refine it and the learner analysis as the design plan gathers more information in the task analysis and strategy design steps.

Based on your data collection and analysis of findings, you will begin the next phase of the design process—task analysis (see Chapter 4)—with an initial conceptualization of the target audience and the instructional environment. This information facilitates your decisions throughout the remainder of the design process.

APPLICATION

Your design consulting group has just accepted a contract to revise a conflict resolution course for managers for one of the largest accounting companies in the country. This course met for three full days and had a one-day, follow-up meeting six weeks after the course. According to the training manager, the majority of the managers have already completed the course. The focus now is on managers who need to take it again and on the 10 to 20 new managers promoted or hired each month. Currently, the course is taught by six different instructors who use a combination of excellent videotapes, lecturettes, and role plays. The training manager wants the course revised so that it can be offered at a variety of company locations rather than at the corporate training center. He also wants the course to be offered in two- to four-hour blocks over a period of four weeks.

What type of information would you want to collect in a contextual analysis before beginning your design?

ANSWER

The following is our initial list of data we would want to collect to determine the factors to consider when revising this course:

1. The best times and days to offer the training
2. The type of video equipment that is available

3. The expected number of new managers in each location each quarter
4. The layout of the training rooms
5. The closeness of the training room to the place of work (i.e., how much travel time is needed between work and the class)
6. The amount of time learners might have for studying outside of class
7. Any distractions the place of work might present during the training
8. Perceived benefits of training

QUALITY MANAGEMENT

Updating and verifying your learner analysis is an ongoing process as you design the instruction. Initially, you need to confirm that you have identified the correct target audience—these are the individuals who will receive the instruction. Next, you need to consider how the audience characteristics and environmental characteristics can provide opportunities or limitations to the design of the course. For example, discovering that your course cannot run for five continuous days but can only be offered for two hours a day creates opportunities to build in self-reflection time after each class meeting. If you find that many of the students taking a computer course have physical limitations, you can collect additional information on their fine motor skills and then determine if adaptive technologies (i.e., large keypads, large buttons, or voice-activated software) can be used to enhance the functionality of the computers.

SAMPLE DESIGN PLAN

LEARNER ANALYSIS

Okay, what do I want to know about these students? The Student Services database gave me some good demographic information on the students, but I'd like to know how well prepared they are to go beyond just knowing time management principles to really managing events situated in a time frame. What metacognitive skills are needed here and which of those skills do they possess? I think I'll interview the director and perhaps some of the learning consultants who have recently interacted with my target population. I also want to know about

- their existing time management practices;
- their time constraints;
- their typical work/course load;
- their motivation;
- their attitude toward successfully mastering time management principles;
- their physical constraints or disabilities;
- whether they use English as their primary language;
- their prior knowledge;
- learner preferences (Is this necessary given my short time frame? Probably not!).

I interviewed the director and three learning consultants. I took those findings and combined them with demographic data from the database to create a learner analysis.

General Characteristics

- The group is 37 percent male, 63 percent female.
- They possess graduate-level education (although some students are just out of their undergraduate program).
- Their Flesch-Kincaid grade-level reading score is 11–12.
- They are Adult learners (average age is 31).
- They are culturally diverse.
- The majority hold full-time jobs.
- They are carrying 4 to 6 graduate credit hours.

Specific Characteristics

The learners must have the following specific characteristics:

- Be computer literate (Mac or Windows)
- Have access to the Internet
- Know how to locate a website
- Have access to a computer that can read a .pdf file
- Have access to a printer
- Know how to print files
- Be motivated to develop habits of time management
- Have an appreciation for time management skills
- Know how to deconstruct a whole into constituent parts (i.e., a project into goals, subgoals, and tasks)
- Possess a PDA (to work with goals and tasks)
- Have working knowledge of how to use the PDA

CONTEXTUAL ANALYSIS

It's kind of tough to do a contextual analysis since this instruction will be self-paced—the instructional context is pretty hard to determine. I can't possibly analyze the numerous and diverse physical environments in which the instruction will be administered (and so I have no control over that). I know that the instruction will be uploaded to the Student Services website as a .pdf file. Thus, some learners will access the tutorial in the Student Services computer lab. Other students will likely use a high-speed Internet connection from their dorm rooms. I will consider the Student Services computer lab to be the instructional environment and will design accordingly. As for transfer context, that will be embedded in the worksheets that will require the learners to work with a familiar project and perhaps select their own course project.

I can obtain more data from the orienting context. I know from the learner analysis that students who ask for time management support are motivated to learn the skills and want to work efficiently and complete projects on time. I expect that these students will see a high degree of utility in this instruction. Because there is no external accountability, I suppose these learners will print out the instruction, including the worksheets, and just use the tools that make sense to them.

REFERENCES

Barrows, H. S., & Kelson, A. M. (1996). *Problem-based learning: A total approach to education.* (Unpublished monograph). Springfield: Southern Illinois School of Medicine.

Bradford, D. J. (1999). Exemplary urban middle schoolteachers' use of five standards of effective teaching. *Teaching and Change, 7,* 53–78.

Bransford, J., Sherwood, R., Hasselbring, T., Kinzer, C., & Williams, S. (1990). Anchored instruction: Why we need it and how technology can help. In D. Nix & R. Spiro (Eds.), *Cognition, education, and multimedia: Exploring ideas in high technology* (pp. 115–141). Hillsdale, NJ: Erlbaum.

Dorsey-Davis, J. D., Ross, S. M., & Morrison, G. R. (1991). The role of rewording and context personalization in the solving of mathematical word problems. *Journal of Educational Psychology, 83,* 61–68.

Driscoll, M. P. (2000). *Psychology of learning from instruction* (2nd ed.). Needham Heights, MA: Allyn & Bacon.

Garcia, R. L. (1991). *Teaching in a pluralistic society: Concepts, models, and strategies.* New York: HarperCollins.

Heinich, R., Molenda, M., Russell, J., & Smaldino, S. (1999). *Instructional media and technologies for learning* (6th ed.). Englewood Cliffs, NJ: Prentice Hall.

Jonassen, D. H., & Grabowski, B. L. (1993). *Handbook of individual differences, learning, and instruction.* Hillsdale, NJ: Erlbaum.

Keller, J. M., & Litchfield, B. C. (2002). Motivation and performance. In R. A. Reiser & J. V. Dempsey (Eds.), *Trends and issues in instructional design and technology* (pp. 83–98). Columbus: Merrill Prentice Hall.

Kibler, R. J. (1981). *Objectives for instruction and evaluation.* Boston: Allyn & Bacon.

Knight, C. B., Halpin, G., & Halpin, G. (1992, April). *The effects of learning environment accommodations on the achievement of second graders.* Paper presented at the annual meeting of the American Educational Research Association, San Francisco, CA.

Kolb, D. (1984). *Experiential learning: Experience as the source of learning and development.* Englewood Cliffs, NJ: Prentice Hall.

Kolb, D. (1985). *Self-scoring inventory and interpretive booklet.* Boston: McBer.

Ku, H.-Y., & Sullivan, H. (2000). Learner control over full and lean computer-based instruction under personalization of mathematics word problems in Taiwan. *Educational Technology Research and Development, 48*(3), 49–60.

Morrison, G. R., & Lowther, D. L. (2002). *Integrating computer technology into the classroom* (2nd ed.). Columbus: Merrill Prentice Hall.

Morrison, G. R., Ross, S. M., & Baldwin, W. (1992). Learner control of context and instructional support in learning elementary school mathematics. *Educational Technology, Research, & Development, 40,* 5–13.

Myers, I. B., & McCaulley, M. H. (1985). *Manual: A guide to the development and use of the Myers-Briggs Type Indicator.* Palo Alto, CA: Consulting Psychologists.

Ovando, C. J. (1989). Language diversity and education. In J. Banks & C. McGee Banks (Eds.), *Multicultural education: Issues and perspectives* (pp. 208–228). Boston: Allyn & Bacon.

Pintrich, P. R., Roeser, R. W., & De Groot, E. A. M. (1994). Classroom and individual differences in early adolescents' motivation and self-regulated learning. *Journal of Early Adolescence, 14,* 139–161.

Pollock, M. (2001). How the question we ask most about race in education is the very question we most suppress. *Educational Researcher, 30*(9), 2–12.

Ross, S. M., Morrison, G. R., & O'Dell, J. K. (1989). Uses and effects of learner control of context and instructional support in computer-based instruction. *Educational Technology, Research, and Development, 37,* 29–39.

Slavin, R. E. (1994). *Educational psychology* (4th ed.). Needham Heights, MA: Allyn & Bacon.

Snow, R. E. (1992). Aptitude theory: Yesterday, today, and tomorrow. *Educational Psychologist, 27,* 5–32.

Tharp, R. (1998). *Theory into practice.* Santa Cruz, CA: National Center for Research on Cultural Diversity and Second Language Learning.

Tessmer, M., & Harris, D. (1992). *Analysing the instructional setting.* London: Kogan Page Limited.

Tessmer, M., & Richey, R. C. (1997). The role of context in learning and instructional design. *Educational Technology, Research, and Development, 45,* 85–111.

Task Analysis

GETTING STARTED

At last, you have the opportunity to work on a really neat project. The project focuses on teaching new hires how to design the interior of an automobile. This project will really test your skills as an instructional designer because it goes beyond the "simple" assembly tasks you designed in the past. In fact, your two subject-matter experts are legends within the company. Ms. Makeena is credited with the recent designs for women drivers that pushed your company's sales to new highs. Dr. Royce is the chief interior designer and has worked on over 30 different designs. If you can capture their knowledge and talent, you can develop a training program that will assure your status in the training department as well as the company.

Your initial meeting is going quite well. Ms. Makeena and Dr. Royce both explain the process and the many factors they consider. You have had a tour of their design lab and the usability-testing studio. Now that lunch is over, it is time to get to business and start defining the content to address the problem. Your first few questions are answered in detail, and it looks like this will be an easy task analysis. Then, Dr. Royce pauses and stares into the distance, much as you might expect him to do as he ponders the placement of the off–on switch for the cruise control. He states that he has two concerns. First, you are not an automobile designer so how can you expect to "write" a course on this topic. Second, this process of designing the interior of a car is an art and not something like teaching someone how to assemble a radiator. How could you possibly expect to teach someone this art?

It is apparent that Ms. Makeena supports Dr. Royce's concerns. How will you reply to obtain their confidence?

"What skills and information are necessary to address the identified needs?"

"What knowledge does the expert have that is essential for the task?"

"What related subject content should be taught?"

"How can the subject content items be organized?"

"How is a task analyzed to identify its components and then to sequence the actions required?"

"To what other elements of the instructional design process is task analysis most closely related?"

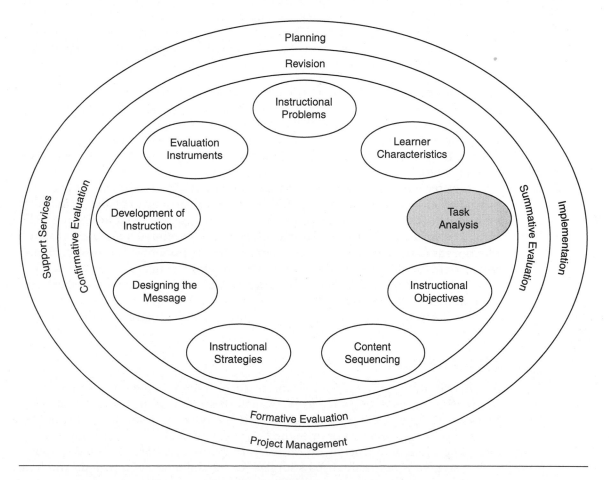

Task analysis is probably the most critical step in the instructional design process. If a designer has not defined the content to include in the instructional package, there is little value in or need for designing an instructional strategy, producing appropriate media, or conducting an evaluation. A survey of designers by Loughner and Moller (1998) found that over 78 percent of the designers agreed that it was not possible to design good instruction without first conducting a task analysis. Unfortunately, only 38 percent of the designers felt their clients understood the purpose of a task analysis. The instructional design process depends on the concise definition of the content that is the object of the instructional materials. Jonassen, Hannum, and Tessmer (1999) consider task analysis the most critical part of the instructional design process. The analysis solves three problems for the designer:

1. It defines the content required to solve the performance problem or alleviate a performance need. This step is crucial since most designers are working with unfamiliar content.
2. Because the process forces the subject-matter expert to work through each individual step, subtle steps are more easily identified.
3. During this process, the designer has the opportunity to view the content from the learner's perspective. Using this perspective, the designer can often gain insight into appropriate teaching strategies.

Jonassen and his colleagues (Jonassen, Hannum, & Tessmer, 1989) have identified 27 different task-analysis procedures that instructional designers can use to define the content for an instructional package. Selecting the best or most appropriate technique depends on a number of factors, including the purpose for conducting the task analysis, the nature of the task or content, and the environment in which the task is performed.

The terminology associated with topic and task analysis is often confusing. The instructional design literature frequently refers to the process of analyzing content as *task analysis*. Specific analysis procedures also go by a host of names. Some individuals refer to task analysis as a specific procedure for defining psychomotor skills, which leads to further confusion. The term *content analysis* is also confusing. Some researchers use this term to describe a methodology for analyzing text materials. Instructional designers use *content* or *subject-matter analysis* to define knowledge or content related to the instructional problem. In this book, we refer to *task analysis* as the collection of procedures for defining the content of an instructional unit.

TASK ANALYSIS

An analysis of the content required for instruction does not begin in a vacuum. It begins with the needs or goals derived from the definition of the instructional problem (see Chapter 2). These needs or goals provide an initial definition of the breadth of the project and provide the designer a focus. For example, if you were designing a unit of instruction on cardiac care for medical doctors, would you start with emergency-room care, bypass surgery, or rehabilitation of a patient who had suffered a heart attack? If you have properly defined the instructional problem, the problem statement and needs or goals will provide the initial direction and breadth of your analysis. Thus, a unit on cardiac care might focus only on rehabilitation as a result of the problem identification. A second input is from the learner analysis (see Chapter 3). An understanding of the learner's knowledge and background related to the topic helps the designer determine the beginning point for the analysis as well as the depth and breadth of analysis. The output of the analysis is the documentation of the content to include in the instructional materials. This output then serves as an input for developing instructional objectives (see Chapter 5).

Preparing to Conduct a Task Analysis

A task analysis can take many different forms. The methods and individuals involved vary depending on the circumstances. Designers most often work with a subject-matter expert (SME), an individual who is an expert in the content area. The SME is our link to the content; we rely on this individual (or individuals) to provide accurate, detailed information for use in developing the instructional unit. Our task as designers is to help the SME elaborate on the content and tasks in a meaningful, sequential manner. The designer is responsible for obtaining a complete analysis, whereas the SME is responsible for providing accurate information and suggesting where gaps may exist in the original goals.

In educational settings, the instructor often serves as both the SME and instructional designer, an often difficult but necessary combination of responsibilities. The teacher/SME/designer is responsible for providing a global view ("Are all the steps and information defined?") as well as a microscopic view ("What result or condition is required before doing the next step?").

In this chapter, we describe three specific techniques for analyzing content and tasks. First, we discuss how to conduct a topic analysis that is well suited for defining cognitive knowledge. Second, we explain how to conduct a procedural analysis for use with psychomotor tasks, job tasks, or cognitive sequences involving a series of steps. Third, we describe the critical incident method, which is useful for analyzing interpersonal skills.

TOPIC ANALYSIS

Assume you are a student attending a lecture. As the instructor delivers the lecture, what are you doing? Probably taking notes so you can capture the essence of the content. You may take notes in detailed sentences or in an outline form, such as the following:

Topic: The Circulatory System
  I. Types of vessels in closed circulatory system
      A. Arteries—carry blood away from heart
      B. Veins—carry blood toward heart
      C. Capillaries—final division of arteries that unite to form first small veins

II. Circulation
    A. Systemic—supplies most of body (aorta)
    B. Pulmonary—supplies lungs
    C. Coronary—within heart

We are all familiar with this procedure of outlining information as it is presented in a lecture. Now, reverse the procedure. You are the person who will deliver the lecture. What is your preparation? You might either write out the lecture in a narrative form you can read as written, or, with experience, you might prepare an outline consisting of the main headings, supporting details, and examples. This outline becomes the framework for reference as a guide to your presentation.

Change the situation yet again, and imagine you are a designer working for a hardware store who must prepare a manual for customers on how to select an appropriate wood fastener. Your manager has assigned an SME to work with you on the project. You would follow a similar process to define the content so the outline becomes a reference for designing the instruction.

The topic analysis or concept analysis is used to define the facts, concepts, principles, and rules that will make up the final instruction. Such an analysis is typically done in layers much like what an archaeologist finds when excavating a site. First, the top layer of soil is scraped away. Then layers of earth are removed, and each artifact's identity and location are recorded. Similarly, a designer working with the SME carefully reveals the first layer of information while looking for indicators of content structure (facts, concept, principles, and rules). Once the structure is revealed, additional detail is gathered for each structure, and new information appears as he or she digs deeper into the content.

A topic analysis thus provides two types of information. First, it identifies the content that is the subject of the intended instruction. Second, it identifies the structure of the components. Let's first examine these content, or knowledge, structures and then describe the process for conducting a topic analysis.

Content Structure

Most instructional design models provide a scheme for classifying information into discrete categories (Reigeluth, 1983). These classifications are then used to identify the appropriate instructional strategy (see Chapter 7). Six structures are often associated with a task analysis: facts, concepts, principles and rules, procedures, interpersonal skills, and attitudes.

Facts.   A *fact* is an arbitrary association between two things. For example, "The chemical symbol for potassium is K" is a fact that describes a relationship between potassium and K. Learning a fact requires only the memorization and recall of the fact. Examples of facts are listed here:

Names, symbols, labels, places, dates
Definitions
Descriptions of objects or events

Most topics include many facts, since they are the building blocks or tools of any subject—the "vocabulary" the learner must master for understanding. Verbal information or facts are preparation for more complex ways of organizing the content. Unless the facts are arranged in structured patterns, they will be of limited use to a learner and are often quickly forgotten. Facts are easy to identify but often confused with the second category, concepts. Consider our example, symbol for potassium is K: there was one potassium and one symbol—K. The fact refers to this *one* element.

Concepts.   *Concepts* are categories used for grouping similar or related ideas, events, or objects. For example, we might use the concept "soft drinks" to categorize the aisle in the grocery store that contains colas, orange drink, root beer, and so forth. The concept of fruit would include apples, oranges, bananas, and dates, but not potatoes. We use concepts to simplify information by grouping similar ideas or objects together and assigning the grouping a name (e.g., fruit). Some concepts such as fruit are considered concrete concepts because we can easily show an example. Concepts such as safety, liberty, peace, and justice are abstract concepts since they are difficult to represent or illustrate. As instructional designers, we have to be careful and not confuse facts with concepts. There is a concept related to our fact about potassium. Potassium is an example of the concept "elements." There are many members of this category including carbon, magnesium, and vanadium. Chemistry books are filled with facts about each of these elements.

Principles and Rules.   *Principles* and *rules* describe a relationship between two concepts. In microeconomics, we can derive several principles from a supply and demand curve. For example, "as price increases, the supply increases" is a principle that describes a direct relationship between the concepts (price and supply) that increase and decrease together. "As price decreases, the demand increases" describes a different relationship between price and demand that causes one to increase as the other decreases. "Stop at a red light" and "release the pressure before opening a pressure cooker" are also examples of principles.

Procedures.   A *procedure* is an ordered sequence of steps a learner must execute to complete a task. For example, the back of many bank statements lists a series of steps for balancing a checkbook. This series of steps is a procedure. Similarly, a recipe for making a cake or casserole is a procedure. A procedure could be a series of psychomotor steps needed to plant a rosebush, or it could be a complex series of cognitive processes required to debug a computer program.

Interpersonal Skills.   Verbal and nonverbal (e.g., body language) *skills* for interacting with other people are grouped in this category. This broad category includes behaviors and objectives related to interpersonal communication. An objective for a manager-training program requiring the development of interviewing skills is an example of this category. Content related to solving group conflict, leading a group, and demonstrating how to sit when interviewed are also examples of behaviors in this category.

Attitudes.   *Attitudes* are predispositions to behavior. Although often overlooked, attitudes are a part of many instructional programs. For example, a training program might emphasize the *safety* precautions for replacing a seal on a gas valve. Corporate employees who have access to confidential financial information must complete a course that explains the misuse of this information (e.g., insider training). Such programs contain information on the laws governing the use of this information (e.g., concepts and rules) as well as a component to develop appropriate attitudes toward corporate responsibility and proper behavior.

Analyzing a Topic

Let's examine a topic analysis on wood fasteners and define each of the content structures with an example. To begin, we first asked our SME to describe the different types of wood fasteners. Our question produced the following outline:

   I.   Nails
   II. Screws
   III. Bolts

Our SME considered these three major categories adequate to describe the various types of fasteners.

Next, we asked the SME to further define each of these categories. He expanded our outline as follows:

   I.   Nails
        A. Generally made from wire
        B. Range in size from 2-penny to 60-penny
           1. Length of nails 10-penny or less is determined by
              a. Dividing size by 4 and adding 0.5 inch
              b. Example: 7-penny nail is 2.25 inches long
        C. Typically driven into one or more pieces of wood with a hammer
   II. Screws
        A. Made from steel
        B. Size determined by the gauge (thickness) and length
           1. Length varies from 0.25 to 6 inches
        C. Usually twisted into a hole with screwdriver
        D. Screws provide a more secure joint than nails
   III. Bolts
        A. Made from steel
        B. Measured by length and diameter
           1. Available in fine or coarse threads
        C. Bolt is placed through a hole and then a nut is tightened from opposite side

Let's examine the content structure identified in the outline. Some of the facts identified in the outline are as follows:

Generally made from wire
Made of steel
Measured by length and diameter
Available in fine or coarse threads

The concepts identified in the topic analysis are these:

Nail
Screw
Bolt

One procedure was identified in the task analysis:

Length of nails 10-penny or less is determined by dividing size by 4 and adding 0.5 inch.

Our SME helped us identify one principle in the content:

Screws provide a more secure joint than nails.

Next, our SME decided to provide detailed information on each fastener category, starting with nails. Once we finished the analysis, we organized the content. This organization process included the following steps:

1. Review the analysis, and identify the different content structures (facts, concepts, principles, interpersonal skills, and attitudes).
2. Group related facts, concepts, principles, interpersonal skills, and attitudes. For example, in our full outline of wood fasteners, we would group all the information about nails, then the information about screws, and so forth.
3. Arrange the various components into a logical, sequential order.
4. Prepare the final outline to represent your task analysis.

The completed topic analysis on nails was as follows:

I.   Nails
    A. Generally made from wire
    B. Range in size from 2-penny to 60-penny
        1. Length of nails 10-penny or less is determined by
            a. Dividing size by 4 and adding 0.5 inch
            b. Example: 7-penny nail is 2.25 inches long
        2. Size is written as 2d for "2 penny"
    C. Typically driven into one or more pieces of wood with a hammer
    D. Types of nails
        1. Common nails
            a. Most commonly used nail
            b. Available in sizes from 2d to 60d
                (1) 8d size is most common
            c. Identified by flat head
            d. Used for general purposes

2. Box nails
   a. Smaller in diameter than common nails
   b. Available in sizes ranging from 2d to 40d
   c. Also identified by its flat head
   d. Used in lumber that may split easily
   e. Often used for nailing siding
3. Finishing nails
   a. Have a very small head that will not show
      (1) Head can be sunk into wood and hole filled
   b. Available in sizes 2d to 20d
   c. Used primarily for finishing work and cabinetry
4. Common brads
   a. Similar to finishing nails but much smaller
   b. Available in various lengths
      (1) Length expressed in inches or parts of an inch
   c. Used for finishing work
5. Roofing nails
   a. Similar to common nails but with a larger head
   b. Available in lengths from 0.75 inch to 2 inches
      (1) Available in various diameters
   c. Used for roofing[1]

How detailed should a topic analysis be? A designer needs to break down the content to a level appropriate for the learner. There are two sources for determining the needed level of detail. First, the learner analysis describes the learner's knowledge of the content area; it is used as a general guide for the amount of information needed. A course on home repair for apprentice carpenters, for example, will require a different amount of detail than a course for homeowners. Second, the SME is often a source of information concerning the learners' entry-level knowledge. A combination of these two sources provides a basis for determining the level of detail needed in this initial analysis. During the development and formative evaluation stages, you might find a need for additional information.

PROCEDURAL ANALYSIS

Procedural analysis is used to analyze tasks by identifying the steps required to complete them. The process breaks tasks into the size of steps needed for learning. Some designers distinguish between procedural analysis and information-processing analysis (Jonassen et al., 1989). The major distinction is that procedural analysis focuses on observable tasks (e.g., changing a tire), whereas information-processing analysis focuses on cognitive or unobservable tasks, such as deciding which stock to add to a

---

[1] Information from this task analysis is based on a chapter by Phipps (1977).

portfolio for diversification. In recent years, the distinction between the two methods has decreased because cognitive psychology has shown the importance of cognitive steps in observable processes. We use *procedural analysis* to refer to the analysis of both observable and unobservable behaviors.

Conducting a procedural analysis is a matter of walking through the steps with an SME, preferably in the environment in which the task is performed. For example, if you are conducting a procedural analysis for sharpening an ax blade, the SME should have an ax and the necessary tools. Similarly, if you are analyzing how to calculate your home's electric bill, you will need an electric meter (or at least a picture of the dial) and the electric rates. Sometimes it may not be possible to use the actual equipment for your task analysis. For example, you might analyze how to change the fuel filter on a gas turbine generator. Given the size, cost, and availability of the equipment, it may not be possible to actually conduct the analysis on the engine. However, you may be able to obtain a smaller valve unit that you can use for your task analysis. Each step of analysis includes three questions:

1. What does the learner do?
   - Identify the action in each step that the learner must perform.
   - These actions are either physical (e.g., loosening a bolt) or mental (e.g., adding two numbers).
2. What does the learner need to know to do this step?
   - What knowledge (e.g., temperature, pressure, orientation) is necessary?
   - What does the learner need to know about the location or orientation of the components that are a part of this step (e.g., how to position a wrench to remove a hidden nut)?
3. What cues (tactile, smell, visual, etc.) inform the learner that there is a problem, the step is done, or a different step is needed (e.g., a blinking light indicates you can release the starter switch)?

In the following procedural analysis, we visited a cabinetmaker and asked him how to prepare a piece of woodwork for the final finish. During the analysis, we asked him variations of the three questions described in the previous paragraphs to identify the steps, knowledge, and cues. As part of our analysis, he informed us that someone who finishes furniture would already know the basics of sanding and using a paint sprayer. Our analysis produced the following steps:

1. Inspect all surfaces for defects.
   Tactile cue: Feel for dents, scratches, and other surface defects.
   Visual cue: Splits or cracks are normally visible.
2. Repair defects in surface.
   a. Sand, glue, or fill minor defects.
   b. Reject pieces that you cannot repair for rework.
3. Spray two coats of lacquer sanding sealer on all surfaces.
   Visual cue: Dry, misty appearance indicates too-light application.
   Visual cue: Runs or sags indicate too-heavy application.

4. Prepare for final finish.
   a. Allow a 20-minute minimum drying time for sealer coat.
   b. After drying, rub out all parts with #400 grit silicon carbide abrasive paper.
   c. Remove dust from all surfaces with air gun, then wipe with clean, lint-free cloth.
5. Complete the final finish.
   a. Spray two coats of finishing lacquer on all parts.
      Visual cue: Dry, misty finish indicates too-light application.
      Visual cue: Runs or sags indicate too-heavy application.
   b. Allow a minimum of four hours for second coat to dry.
6. Inspect final finish.
   Tactile cue: Feel for grit or runs that may not be visible.
7. Rub out all surfaces with #000 steel wool.
8. Remove dust from all finished surfaces with air gun and lintfree cloth.
   a. Apply a thin coat of wax to all finished surfaces.
   b. Buff all surfaces to high gloss.
      Visual cue: Wax becomes dull prior to buffing.

In addition to an outline, designers often use flowcharts (see Figure 4-1) and tables (Table 4-1). The table format provides a visual prompt for the designer to ask questions to obtain information about the cues associated with each step. A flowchart is useful for identifying a specific sequence of steps the learner must follow as well as the key decision steps. Flowcharts are also useful for helping SMEs identify missing components and for identifying alternative procedures that may have been missed in the initial analysis. A rectangle indicates an action or knowledge in the flowchart. Diamonds indicate a question or decision point with branches off each tip to another question or action. The arrows indicate the path through the flowchart.

After you have collected the data for a procedural analysis, you need to organize the information in a logical fashion. Since most procedures are sequential, they are often organized in a linear manner by the order of the steps.

We could also use a procedural analysis for a task involving primarily cognitive operations, such as alphabetizing a collection of bibliographic cards for a research paper's reference section. Again, we need to identify the steps, the knowledge associated with each step, and any cues associated with each step:

1. Divide the alphabet into four groups (i.e., a–f, g–l, and so on).
2. Sort the cards according to the first letter of the last name of the first author and place in the appropriate stack.
3. When all the cards are sorted into one of the stacks, select a stack and sort the cards in the stack alphabetically according to the last name of the first author.
4. Search through the stack for cards with duplicates of the first author name.
5. If the duplicate card has the same authors, sort the cards by date, with the earliest date first.

FIGURE 4-1
Flowchart of a procedure

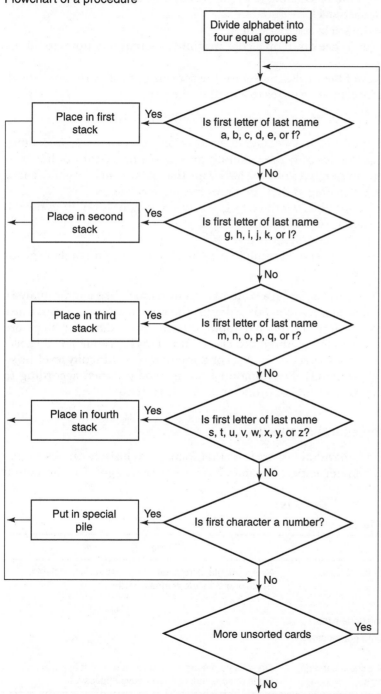

6. If the cards have different authors after the first, sort alphabetically by the second, then the succeeding authors. Sort identical authors by date.
7. Repeat for each stack.
8. Sequence the stacks starting with A.
9. Place the cards face down on a copy machine, overlapping notes to fill the copy area.
10. Make a copy of the cards, and repeat the process until all cards are copied.
11. Attach these reference pages to a draft of the paper.

Following is a checklist for conducting a procedural analysis:

- Are the relevant cues and feedback identified for each step of the procedure?
- Does the analysis identify the generally acceptable procedure rather than the personal preferences of the SME? Tips that make a step easier are usually acceptable so long as they do not violate a safety rule.
- Are the decision steps identified (e.g., "If the blue light is on, then turn to the right; if not, turn to the left.")?
- Are all steps accurately described?
- Are critical steps that could result in personal injury, equipment damage, or other loss identified?

Procedural analyses also reveal a content structure much like a topic analysis. For the cognitive information, you need to identify the related facts, concepts, rules, and principles to complete the related topic analysis. Procedures or steps are grouped in several ways. One method is to classify the steps by frequency of execution (frequently, occasionally, seldom). A second method is by difficulty level (easy, moderately difficult, difficult). Psychomotor tasks may be grouped according to gross- or fine-motor skills or level of proficiency (see Chapter 5).

Going beyond Procedural Analysis

The limitations of a behavioral task analysis that focuses exclusively on observable tasks of the subject-matter expert became clear a few years ago. This limitation

TABLE 4-1
Procedural analysis table

Step	Cue
1. Inspect all surfaces for defects.	Feel for dents, scratches, and other surface defects. Splits or cracks are normally visible.
2. Repair defects.	
(a) Sand, glue, or fill minor defects.	
(b) Reject pieces that are not repairable for rework.	
3. Spray two coats of lacquer sanding sealer on all surfaces.	Dry, misty appearance indicates too-light application. Runs or sags indicate too-heavy application.

became obvious while analyzing the tasks an air traffic controller performs (Chipman, Schraagen, & Shalin, 2000). This approach focused on the observable psychomotor skills of using the equipment, but failed to consider the various cognitive operations the controller performed. A new approach to task analysis, cognitive task analysis, was developed to analyze tasks that involved a cognitive component. Cognitive task analysis is typically used with a more traditional task analysis and provides additional information that is not obvious when the expert performs the task. The goal of cognitive task analysis is to identify those covert cognitive operations associated with the overt behaviors we can easily observe.

There are many approaches to conducting a cognitive task analysis. For example, GOMS (Card, Moran, & Newell, 1983) focuses on the *goals* the expert has when doing the task, the *operations* or small tasks the expert performs, *methods* that are the approaches or means used to achieve the goals, and *selection* of the most appropriate method. GOMS has been used extensively to design human–computer interfaces (Williams, 2000). Militello and Hutton (1998) describe the applied cognitive task analysis (ACTA) process that is very flexible and applicable to a wide variety of tasks. This method involves four steps. First, the [designer asks] subject-matter expert identifies three to six broad steps that are performed as part of this task. The purpose of this step is to identify broad steps rather than a sequence like a procedural analysis. The second step is a knowledge audit that is used to generate examples of the task. Questions [designer asks] used for the knowledge audit can include probes asking what is important about the big picture, describing a situation in which the expert immediately knew the problem after studying it for just a few minutes, or asking whether the expert has ever noticed things others did not. The knowledge audit is conducted for each of the broad steps identified in the first step. The third step is to conduct a simulation interview in which the expert describes how he or she would solve a realistic problem. As part of this interview, the expert is asked to first identify the major events. Next, the expert is asked a series of questions for each event including what actions to take, what is going on, and what errors a novice might make. The last step of the process is to create a cognitive demands table that synthesizes the information from the first three steps. A designer should focus on those steps that require complex cognitive processing when performing a cognitive task analysis. The cognitive demands table is used along with the traditional task analysis to design the training.

Teaching the process of cognitive task analysis is beyond the scope of this book. A CD-ROM training program on ACTA is available from www.decisionmaking.com/approach/ACTA_CD.html. The Militello and Hutton (1998) article also provides an excellent description of the ACTA process. There are, however, some ideas we can borrow from cognitive task analysis to enhance a procedural analysis.

First, we can use a talk-aloud protocol when conducting a procedural analysis. When working with a subject-matter expert, you can ask him or her to verbally describe each action and step as it is performed. You may need to use continual prompting of the subject-matter expert to talk aloud (e.g., "Could you tell me what you are [doing, seeing, thinking, hearing, smelling, feeling]?"). Second, you can use the talk-aloud protocol to identify important cues. These cues are used by the experts to complete the task and make decisions. It is important to collect with the cues information identifying errors a novice might make. Table 4-2 provides examples of different types of cues an instructional designer might identify in a task analysis and the types of errors a novice might make.

TABLE 4-2
Cues for enhancing a procedural analysis

Input	Example	Questions to Extract Cues from SME	Errors a Novice Might Make
Decisions	Determining when a board is sanded smooth	What do I do next? Is the procedure finished?	Might not know alternative steps to take when a problem arises
	Determining when a wood joint is a good fit	Do the two pieces fit properly?	Might misinterpret a snug fit for a secure fit
Visual	The closed lock at the bottom of browser window indicating a secure website	How do we know the website is secure?	Sending a credit card number to a nonsecure website
	A good recording is distortion-free	What is the correct recording level on the meter?	Setting the recording level too high, which results in unintelligible recording
	Swelling in the lower leg	What are the symptoms of a blood clot?	Diagnosing a blood clot as a sprained ankle
	Patterns in a data set or display	What does the initial inspection of the data set indicate?	Might miss an incorrect piece of data that is out of range, creates problems with the analysis
Tactile	A physical exam	How do you identify a lump in the breast?	Failing to identify a lump could result in cancer
	Stiffness of dough as it is kneaded	How long do you knead the dough?	Not kneading the dough enough will result in bread not rising
	The resistance of nut as it is tightened or loosened	How do you know when a bolt is tightened enough?	Overtightening the nut can result in weakening or breaking the bolt
Aural	The pitch of the sound produced by a turbine engine or generator	What do variations in the pitch or sound indicate?	A change in pitch can indicate a different speed or part failure
	Sounds of a fire crackling or metal stressing	What sounds does a burning building make?	Failing to recognize the crackling of a fire or sound of metal stressing could cause injury or death due to building collapse
	Car engine making a knocking sound	What types of unusual noises might one hear from an engine?	Failure to identify engine knock can result in costly damage to internal engine parts

TABLE 4-2 (*continued*)
Cues for enhancing a procedural analysis

Input	Example	Questions to Extract Cues from SME	Errors a Novice Might Make
Smell	The smell of gasoline at a fire	What can you tell about a fire from the odor of the smoke?	Smell of gasoline changes as it heats up and might be missed
	The aromas of a wine	What can you detect from the aroma of a wine?	May miss subtle fruit aromas
Taste	The "message" sent by a food	What taste sensations are aroused by the food?	Failing to discriminate between sour and bitter
	Patient complaints of frequent metallic taste	What can a metallic taste indicate?	A patient taking certain oral medicines could experience a metallic taste, which might be mistaken for a symptom of kidney disease

THE CRITICAL INCIDENT METHOD

The two methods we have described—topic and procedural analyses—work well with concrete content and highly structured tasks that are easily analyzed. Analyzing a process, such as how to conduct an interview, resolve an interpersonal conflict, or close a sales opportunity, is more difficult because processes vary from instance to instance. Although the instances share certain elements, typically the breadth of skills and techniques account for one's success. Procedural analysis works quite well for analyzing how to apply the final finish to a wooden table, for example, because the basic process is repeated time after time, with variations due to size and type of wood. Closing a sale, however, depends on several conditions (e.g., personality of the buyer, financial status of the buyer) that change with each sale. To define the content for this type of training adequately, we need a method that provides different points of view. For example, we might interview a salesperson who uses a very calm approach as opposed to another individual who uses high-pressure tactics.

A critical incident analysis, then, can identify the commonalities of various approaches. Interviewing several individuals for the critical incident analysis provides a rich context for analyzing interpersonal skills. In some situations, you may need to combine the results with a procedural analysis to define content for designing the instruction.

The critical incident method was developed by Flanagan (1954) during World War II to determine why Army Air Force pilots were not learning to fly correctly. Pilots were interviewed to determine which conditions led to a successful mission and which conditions led to an unsuccessful one. A critical incident interview is based on three types of information:

1. What were the conditions before, during, and after the incident?
   - Where did the incident occur?
   - When did it occur?
   - Who was involved?
   - What equipment was used and what was its condition?
2. What did you do?
   - What did you do physically (e.g., grabbed the rudder)?
   - What did you say and to whom?
   - What were you thinking?
3. How did this incident help you reach or prevent you from reaching your goal?

Primhoff (1973) suggests two questions to ask as part of a critical incident analysis. First, ask the SME to identify three instances when he or she was successful in doing the task. Second, ask the SME to identify three instances when he or she was not successful in doing the task. An analysis of the interviews will identify knowledge and techniques the SME used to accomplish the task. Once this information is identified, performing a topic and/or procedural analysis can further define the content.

The critical incident method is well suited for analyzing interpersonal skills and attitudes. If you were designing a course on classroom management for prospective teachers, you might use a critical incident analysis to determine how teachers handle disruptive students. Similarly, you might use this method to determine the content and skills needed to teach a workshop on conducting job interviews or employee performance reviews. It is also useful for initially defining complex tasks that an SME might consider an "art." For example, a designer might use this method for initial analysis when determining where to drill an oil well, predicting successful stocks or mutual funds to purchase, or determining which type of psychotherapy to use on a patient.

CONDUCTING A TASK ANALYSIS

Your SME and the environment will influence how you conduct a topic, procedural, or critical incident analysis. If you are a classroom teacher or a part-time instructor, such as a nursing supervisor responsible for training your staff, you will most likely be your own SME. If you are an instructional designer working in a hospital, university, government agency, or business, a knowledgeable SME will most likely be assigned to work with you on the project. The environment may vary from your office to a retail store, an operating room, or an offshore oil-drilling rig. Each environment offers advantages and disadvantages.

Expert's Edge

Hitting an Invisible but Moving Target

Our experience with task analysis over the years has led to tailoring the procedures to meet characteristics of the organization and tasks themselves. No one situation should be expected to be the same as others.

For example, in large organizations with many job incumbents who are geographically and organizationally disbursed, there may be variations in how tasks are performed and under what conditions. Even trying to sample these differences through a few SMEs is often not satisfactory. To ensure that differences and commonalities of task performance are identified, a stepwise approach is used. First, we define a task list with representative SMEs and then administer a task questionnaire to a large sample of the jobholders. The questionnaire asks for criticality, difficulty, and frequency judgments under various conditions of the task. The results are then analyzed to determine priorities for training as well as any differences among organizational elements.

Another organizational factor is the maturity of the job. In some cases, the job does not yet exist or is evolving. For example, a job might evolve because a new concept of operations is anticipated due to a major equipment change. In such situations it is necessary to both lean on existing SME experience and to analyze details of the differences as the changes emerge. It is often the case for emerging jobs that the task analysis and resulting training will lead to the actual job development and standards for the job.

Primary among the task factors is the type of learning, including the category of knowledge. There is an increasing awareness among analysts that higher-level cognitive tasks need more attention than straightforward procedural or skill tasks. For example, many cognitive tasks require looking at the task structure conditions. A task can be ill or well structured. An ill-structured task is one that may have more than one solution, more than one path to a solution, or unknown task constraints and one for which not all of the information needed is available. These tasks require deeper interviews with SMEs, and not all SMEs can verbalize the task well. This process may require some SMEs to develop examples to help other SMEs explain what they do under such situations and various conditions. The analysis then becomes a cognitive task analysis. There are many types of content domains this applies to such as medical diagnosis, troubleshooting complex equipment, any decision making under uncertainty, and engineering design problems.

Higher levels of cognitive tasks, such as designing, planning, strategic, and tactical decision making and problem solving, often require a deeper interview even when the task is well structured. An overlooked aspect of task analysis is the executive processing or metacognitive-type task elements involved. Many job incumbents have developed, through experience, cognitive techniques for processing the knowledge of the task. This is what makes them expert. It is part of the information needed if future experts are to be trained. Contrasting interviews with experts and novices sometimes help identify the differences.

   The job of the task analyst is to structure the analysis including interviews, questionnaires, and other instruments to account for these aspects of the organization and the task characteristics. Each situation should be approached with a view that there may be something different needed from the last analysis.

Dewey Kribs, president of Instructional Science and Development, has over 30 years of experience in the development of interactive training systems and computer-based courseware.

Being Your Own SME

Being your own SME has two major advantages. First is the ease of access to and scheduling of meetings—you need only motivate yourself! Second, you are already familiar with the learners and the problems they have with the task. The major disadvantage is your familiarity with the content, which may cause you to skip steps and fail to identify important cues. Four techniques can counter this disadvantage. First, find another SME and assume the role of the designer. In the latter role, you need to "forget" everything you know about the task and approach it from a naïve point of view. Second, if you are conducting a procedural analysis, once you have the initial version done, ask someone else to perform the task. As the other person does the task, ask him or her to verbally describe the task. You can then check this description with your own. Third, have another expert review or actually work through your analysis to identify any missing steps, cues, or topics. Fourth, talk both a novice and an expert through the task using your task analysis. Their feedback can help you revise your analysis.

Techniques for Gathering Data

Each designer develops a repertoire of techniques for analyzing content. The first rule is to be prepared when working with SMEs. Typically, they are on loan for an hour or a few days from their regular jobs. These individuals are usually experts who perform a valuable service for the organization. Adequate preparation on your part is not only courteous but shows that you respect their expertise and time. Adequate preparation includes your materials as well as adequate knowledge of the goals and problems you are trying to reach and solve. This information was defined when you identified the instructional problem (see Chapter 2). Review those materials and, if necessary, contact some of the individuals who helped you define the problem to obtain additional clarification and understanding. The following paragraphs describe three techniques for conducting content and procedural analyses. You might use only one or a combination of all three.

Literature Research.   Reading technical manuals and other materials is the least preferred method for conducting an analysis. It is an inefficient way to master the content in a relatively short time. However, if the materials can give you an expert's understanding, they may be adequate for use as training materials. Reading materials to prepare for a meeting with an SME may be beneficial, but reading the materials to become an expert is often counterproductive.

Interviewing an SME.   This technique is the most preferred method of defining information for all three analyses. Loughner and Moller (1998) found the individual interview was the task analysis methodology designers reported using most often. Meeting in the SME's office for an analysis that involves primarily a cognitive task has the benefit of providing easy access to the SME's resources. These resources include books as well as data to use for examples and case studies in your instruction. For example, one of the authors was developing a course on how to prepare engineering proposals. During the analysis, the SME was able to retrieve several good and bad examples from the office files. Analyzing these proposals helped in developing a procedure and checklist for proposal development as well as examples for instruction.

When conducting a procedural analysis that depends primarily on psychomotor skills, it is beneficial to schedule the SME meeting in a location where the SME can demonstrate the skills. These meeting locations can range from an operating room to a manufacturing plant. Sometimes a location is not available or travel or access is prohibited. For instance, one of the authors needed to analyze the tasks involved in setting the vanes on gas turbine engines that the client company manufactured but was unable to visit a site. After several phone calls, the SME found that each new turbine engine was run through a series of operational tests in a test cell at the plant. The SME was able to obtain the use of one of the engines for an afternoon while the analysis was conducted. For other analyses, a part was often obtained from the parts warehouse, and then a meeting was scheduled with the SME in a shop to analyze the repair and maintenance of that specific part. A network of key individuals, built and maintained by the designer, is a necessary resource.

Developer Modeling.   This method is typically used after the initial analysis with the SME to confirm the accuracy of your analysis. You can model the analysis by explaining the content in the topic analysis or demonstrating the steps in the procecural analysis. If an instructional designer is conducting a topic analysis, the information is explained to the SME. This technique helps the designer check his or her understanding and interpretation of the content. Explaining the information to the SME also identifies topics that were not adequately explained and prompts the SME to provide additional details and examples. In a procedural analysis, the task should be demonstrated or simulated. Walking through the steps and doing the motions helps identify cues and steps that were missed in the initial analysis. For some tasks (e.g., those that are hazardous or require a great deal of skill), the designer may need to resort to simulated actions only.

Recording Methods

Another aspect of task analysis is recording the information for use in developing the instruction. Notepads and index cards are helpful for recording the topics and steps. If the task analysis is outdoors, a notepad is often preferable because it will not scatter if dropped. Index cards provide flexibility in adding new topics or steps; it is very easy to label an index card as 10A and place it in the stack between cards 10 and 11. Another tool for recording information is a laptop computer, but the user should make sure it has adequate battery life or an extension cord and power source. A laptop computer with an outliner provides a very flexible method for conducting an analysis. Simply clicking at the appropriate point allows you to easily insert a new step or rearrange other steps and information. Tape recorders are also useful for taping the analysis; however, they are difficult to reference later unless transcribed.

A 35mm or digital camera is very helpful when conducting a procedural analysis. Taking pictures of the equipment, tools, and various steps is useful for refreshing the designer's memory. Some of the photographs can be printed in the manuals to illustrate a procedure. Designers should check first, however, to make sure they are allowed to take photographs—some locations have security regulations or may prohibit the use of flash lighting. A portable video camera is also useful for documenting a procedural analysis. The SME describes each step as it is performed. One author's project involved the development of a training program for maintaining a portable computer. The procedural analysis involved the only prototype available, and it was in a different location than the author's office. When the notes were inadequate, the videotape was cued and played to review the specific steps. Still, the SME was called several times to ask for clarification (e.g., "Do you need to rock it as you remove the board or pull it straight up?").

SUMMARY

1. One of the key steps of the design process is defining the content needed to address the instructional need or problem. This content is then used to identify the objectives, design the instructional strategies, develop test items, and create the instruction.

2. Topic, procedural, and critical incidence analyses are three methods for defining the content. A topic analysis is used to identify the facts, concepts, principles, and rules needed for the instruction. Procedural analysis is applied to a task to identify the individual steps, cues, and sequence for performing steps. Finally, critical incidence analysis is used to identify the content related to interpersonal interactions and attitudes.

3. Our experience has shown that almost every project uses at least two of these methods. The designer may switch between a topic and procedural analysis several times during an interview with the SME. When conducting a task analysis, the designer must keep accurate records of the transactions. Notepads and index cards can be supplemented with photographs or videotapes.

THE ID PROCESS

You are now ready to analyze the content and tasks needed for the instruction. The first step is to identify an SME who can provide you with the needed information. We always start by contacting individuals with whom we have worked in the past and getting their recommendations. Once you have identified the expert or experts, contact them and discuss the problem. They can help you determine whether you need to meet in an office or at a location that has the appropriate equipment or conditions. Also, during this initial contact, inquire about whether any special equipment or training is needed. For example, you might need to complete a course in first aid, winter survival, or hydrogen sulfide training, or you might need special equipment such as a hard hat and safety shoes. Arriving unprepared can result in a lack of access.

Next, you need to set a time and place for your meeting. You might also mention to your SME what type of examples (e.g., written reports, diagrams, pictures) you might need for the final unit. Finally, you need to prepare for the analysis. We always like to take one or two notepads, note cards, and a camera. If the conditions are favorable, we like to take a portable computer for notetaking.

Remember to respect the expert's time during your meeting. Simply preparing a brief summary of the problem or goals and the target audience can set the stage for the analysis. While you are conducting the analysis, ask plenty of questions and seek clarification rather than waiting until you return to your office. Once you finish the analysis, you will develop the objectives for the instruction.

APPLICATION

What are the steps for creating a peanut butter and jelly sandwich? Assume that the learner is given a knife, two pieces of bread, peanut butter, jelly, and a paper plate. Now, perform a task analysis.

ANSWER

The following is our task analysis for making a peanut butter and jelly sandwich. (Rather than using "dominant" and "nondominant hand," we have used "right" and "left hand.")

I. Place paper plate with top side facing up directly in front of you.
II. Place two pieces of bread side by side on plate with top edge of each facing same direction.
   Visual cue: Top edge of bread is usually round.
III. Remove lid from jelly jar.
IV. Grasp jelly jar with left hand and hold between thumb and fingers.
   A. Move jar 3 inches above and over slice of bread on right side of plate.
   B. Position so mouth of jar is one-third of way between top and bottom of bread and approximately 6 inches above bread.
   C. Tilt mouth of jelly jar approximately 45 degrees toward center of bread.

V. Grasp knife handle in right hand so that top (dull, smooth, flat side) of blade is facing up.
   A. Place index finger on top edge of knife blade for control.
       Visual cue: One edge of knife may be rounded as opposed to straight. This edge is pointing down.
   B. Insert knife approximately 1 inch into jelly with index finger on edge of blade closest to ceiling.
       1. Gently pull knife through jelly to accumulate approximately 1 tablespoon of jelly on tip.
       2. Slowly twist knife clockwise so that flat part of blade with jelly is facing ceiling.
       3. Gently remove knife from jar while keeping jelly on blade.
       4. Set jar down out of the way with mouth up.
       5. Place bread in palm of left hand.
   C. Carefully maneuver knife to center of bread on right side without dropping jelly.
       1. Turn knife blade over and gently brush jelly onto bread.
       2. Working from center out, use knife blade to spread jelly over the bread, leaving an eighth-inch border at each edge.
           a. Hold knife blade barely off of bread and at a 25 degree angle to bread to spread jelly.
       3. Spread jelly evenly over piece of bread.
           a. Add additional jelly as needed to meet personal preferences.
       4. Place bread back on plate in original position with jelly up.
VI. Move knife to second piece of bread.
   A. Hold blade flat against piece of bread and gently wipe both sides of blade clean.
   B. Set knife down on clean surface.
VII. Replace lid on jelly jar and tighten.
   A. Place jelly jar out of immediate workspace.
VIII. Remove lid from peanut butter jar.
   A. Grasp peanut butter jar in left hand between thumb and fingers.
   B. Position mouth of peanut butter jar approximately one-third of distance from top to bottom of second piece of bread, approximately 6 inches above bread.
   C. Tilt mouth of peanut butter jar approximately 45 degrees toward center of bread.
IX. Grasp knife handle in right hand so that top, dull, or smooth side of blade is facing up.
   A. Place index finger on top edge of knife blade.
       Visual cue: One edge of knife may be rounded as opposed to straight. This edge is pointing down.
   B. Insert knife approximately 1 inch into peanut butter with index finger on edge toward ceiling.

    1. Gently pull knife through peanut butter to accumulate approximately 1 tablespoon of peanut butter on tip.
    2. Slowly twist knife clockwise so that flat part of blade is facing ceiling.
    3. Gently remove knife from jar while keeping peanut butter on blade.
    4. Set jar down with mouth up and out of way.
    5. Place "clean" bread in palm of left hand.
  C. Carefully maneuver knife to center of bread without dropping peanut butter.
    1. Turn knife blade over and gently brush peanut butter onto bread.
    2. Working from center out, use knife blade to spread peanut butter gently on bread, leaving an eighth-inch border at each edge.
      a. Hold knife blade off of bread and at a 25 degree angle to bread to spread peanut butter.
    3. Spread peanut butter evenly over piece of bread.
      a. Add additional peanut butter as needed to meet personal preferences.
      b. Gently scrape each side of knife blade on edge of bread to remove excess peanut butter from knife blade.
      c. Place bread on plate in original position.
    4. Place knife in a clean spot.
  D. Gently grasp crust at top edge of bread of peanut-buttered piece with fingers of left hand and crust of bottom edge of same piece with right hand.
    1. Grasp only edge to avoid getting peanut butter on fingers.
  E. Lift bread approximately 1.5 times width of bread above plate.
  F. Move piece of bread directly over piece of bread with jelly.
  G. Carefully rotate piece of bread with peanut butter so that peanut-buttered side is facing down.
    Visual cue: Clean side of bread is facing up.
  H. Align two pieces of bread so that tops and right edges are aligned.
  I. Slowly lower bread with peanut butter toward piece that's jellied so that all four corners align.
  J. When two pieces of bread are barely touching, make any final adjustment in alignment.
  K. Release hold on bread.
  L. Gently pat top piece of bread to ensure adhesion of peanut butter and jelly.
 X. Place lid on peanut butter jar and tighten.
  A. Move jelly and peanut butter jars out of way.
XI. Determine how sandwich should be cut.
  A. To cut at angle from edge to edge
    1. Turn left corner of edge toward you at a 45 degree angle.
    2. Hold bread in position with gentle pressure from left hand on left corner.

      3. Grasp knife with right hand as before.
      4. Cut bread from top right corner to bottom left corner to create two right-angle triangles.
    B. To cut sandwich in half creating two equal rectangles
      1. Turn bread so that the longest side is parallel to your body.
      2. Gently hold bread into position with left hand by grasping top or bottom edge.
      3. Grasp knife in right hand as before.
      4. Select position halfway on longest edge on farthest side.
      5. Cut bread by drawing knife toward you.
    C. Arrange two pieces into pleasing presentation.
    D. Place knife in sink or dishwasher.

There several potential ways of doing this task analysis. For example, one designer might start with a trip to the grocery to gather the materials. Another might start with the gathering of all the materials in the kitchen. Similarly, another SME might suggest putting the top of the bread closest to the learner, whereas another might start with applying the peanut butter. The task analysis simply defines the content, it does not specify the sequence. As the process progresses, you may need and want to make changes in the task analysis.

QUALITY MANAGEMENT

There are two tasks to help ensure quality. First, you need to verify that your task analysis is thorough and accurate. For procedures, you can have another SME or naïve person walk through the steps as you read them. An SME can help you identify inaccurate information and missing steps, whereas the naïve person can help you identify missing steps and missing cues. For a topic analysis, you can conduct a review with one or more SMEs. We recommend giving them your verbal explanation rather than having them review your topic analysis because they may not know how to accurately read the topic analysis. The second task is to determine whether your task analysis is in alignment with your needs assessment and goal analysis. That is, will the content and skills you have identified alleviate the instructional problem? If not, you can take two actions. First, you can revise your task analysis to correct the error. Second, you can revise your goals to more accurately reflect the task analysis. This second solution may be the result of new or additional information that has resulted in a refinement of the problem. Such a decision should not be made haphazardly, but should include information from multiple sources.

SAMPLE DESIGN PLAN

TASK ANALYSIS

Okay . . . for this module I'm just going to concentrate on skills needed to prioritize tasks. The nature of this instruction is mostly cognitive . . . though if I have them use their PDAs to prioritize tasks, there will be some procedural skills involved. I'll do both a topic analysis and a procedural analysis and then combine them into my final task analysis.

My SME is one of the learning consultants who is familiar with time management literature and practices. Her input, in combination with my own reading and training in time management principles, will give me a good start on the content. I need my SME to help determine what specific content I will need to meet the goals and resolve the problem of setting priorities.

Task Analysis

Define important terms
Goal
    Definition: Broad objectives or aims toward which to work
        Includes a verb that illustrates an action such as
            Attend
            Purchase
            Complete
        Includes content that gives meaning to the goal
            Attend a conference
            Purchase a new car while there is an offer of 0 percent interest
            Complete my dissertation next year
        Goals are very explicit
    Example: Write a 25- to 30-page comparative essay on three taxonomies of
        educational outcomes
Task
    Definition: Constituent component of a goal; the actions that will help
        achieve the goal
        Includes an action verb and an object of the verb
    Example: Select a hotel; call the hotel
    Example: Outline the chapter; write the introduction
Priority structure
    Definition: A scheme for ranking the importance of the tasks
        Need to determine what tasks must be completed first
            Can base priority on
                Importance
                Criticality (problems if not completed)
                Time criticality
    Example: Locate primary resources first, then work on secondary sources
Criticality
    Definition: A state of being of the highest importance
        Tasks can be classified according to criticality
    Example: Locating primary resources has a high degree of criticality when
        writing about Bloom's taxonomy
Time frame
    Definition: A schedule that assigns deadlines for completing goals and tasks

Example: Locate primary resources before February 1; locate secondary
    sources by February 14

Prioritize tasks

    Identify project goal

      Example: Attend educational technology conference in Boston

    List all tasks that must be accomplished in order to meet the goal

      List tasks in no particular order

      Examples: Select a hotel

        Make hotel reservation

        Determine optimal departure and arrival times

        Contact travel agent for flight reservations

        Pick up airline tickets

        Find out if hotel has airport shuttle service

        Arrange for shuttle to and from airport

        Locate appropriate form to complete for travel authorization

        Obtain division director's signature for expenses

        Do laundry

        Lay out clothes

        Pack

        Fill out conference registration form

        Fax conference registration form

        Decide what work projects to take (budget reports for review, etc.)

    Create a priority structure, allocating priority levels and sequencing to tasks

      Use the priority/time-frame matrix (see Figure 4-2)

        The matrix has three rows

        Each row represents the priority allocation

        Essential tasks = priority rank 1

          Must be done without delay or face serious consequences

FIGURE 4-2

Priority/time-frame matrix

Time Frame ⇒ Priority ⇓	Today	Tomorrow	In one week	Later (Specific date)
Essential **(1)**				
Important **(2)**				
Not Critical **(3)**				

Important tasks = priority rank 2
  Something you should do, but the consequences of not doing this
    task are less acute
Not critical tasks = priority rank 3
  The consequences of neglecting this task are insignificant
The matrix has four columns
Each column represents the time allocation
  Today
  Tomorrow
  In one week
  Later (specify date)
Write each task in its appropriate cell
  Select a hotel
  Make hotel reservation
  Determine optimal departure and arrival times
  Contact travel agent for flight reservations
  Pick up airline tickets
  Find out if hotel has airport shuttle service
  Arrange for shuttle to and from airport
  Locate appropriate form to complete for travel authorization
  Obtain division director's signature for expenses
  Do laundry
  Lay out clothes
  Pack
  Fill out conference registration form
  Fax conference registration form
  Decide what work projects to take (budget reports for review, etc.)
 Record prioritized tasks in a PDA
  Turn on the PDA
  Use the stylus to click the *To Do List* icon
  Create a new category for the project
    Click on category in upper-right corner of screen
    Click on *Edit Categories*
    Click on *New*
    Enter the project goal beneath the words *Enter a new category name*
    Click *OK*
      Be certain that the category you created is highlighted
        If the new category you created is not highlighted, click on it to
          highlight it
      Click *OK* again to begin putting tasks into that category
Set *To Do Preferences*
  Click on *Show*
  Be certain that *Sort by* says *Priority, Due Date*
  Be certain that the following preferences are selected

> Show Completed Items
> Show Due Dates
> Show Priorities
> Show Categories
>
> To select a preference, click in the box to the left of that preference
>
> A check mark appears in the box when the preference is selected
>
> To deselect a preference, click on the box again and the check mark will disappear
>
> Click *OK* when preferences are selected

Enter a new task

> Click on *New* to enter a task
>
> Enter the task description
>
> Add a note to the task description
>
> > Click *Details*
> >
> > Click *Add Note*
> >
> > Enter text
> >
> > Click *Done*
> >
> > > Each new task is prioritized as a 1; you will reorder these priorities later
>
> Click on New and continue entering tasks

Assign priorities to tasks after all tasks have been entered

> Determine which tasks should remain at the number 1 priority level
>
> > Changes should not be made to these tasks, they are already prioritized as number 1
>
> Change priorities for non–number 1 tasks
>
> > Determine which tasks should be prioritized at the number 2 level
> >
> > Locate the first task you want to rank as number 2 priority
> >
> > Click on the number 1 to the left of this task and select 2 from the drop-down menu
> >
> > Do the same for priority levels 3, 4, and 5
> >
> > > Notice how the list order redistributes itself so that number 1 priority tasks remain at the top of the list, number 2 tasks come after number 1 tasks, and so on

Assign due dates to tasks

> Return to the first priority level 1 task
>
> Click on that task to select it
>
> Click on the dash mark (–) to the far right of that task
>
> Assign the appropriate due date from the drop-down menu
>
> > Today
> >
> > Tomorrow
> >
> > One week later
> >
> > No date
> >
> > Choose date
>
> Assign a specific date to a task

Click on *Choose date*
   A calendar will appear
   Locate the appropriate date on the calendar
   Click on that date to select it
   Notice that the date is automatically associated with the task
Change a date
   Click on the task
   Click on the date
   Select *Choose date*
   Select new date
   Notice that the date automatically changes on the *To Do* list
The list order now reflects the chronology you have established as well as the priority rankings

SMEs referred to the following texts for part of this analysis:

Covey, S. R. (1990). *The seven habits of highly effective people: Powerful lessons in personal change.* New York: Simon & Schuster.

Tracy, B. (2001). *Eat that frog! 21 great ways to stop procrastinating and get more done in less time.* San Francisco: Berrett-Koehler.

REFERENCES

Card, S. T., Moran, T. P., & Newell, A. (1983). *The psychology of human-computer interaction.* Hillsdale, NJ: Erlbaum.

Chipman, S. F., Schraagen, J. M., & Shalin, V. L. (2000). An introduction to cognitive task analysis. In J. M. Schraagen, S. F. Chipman, & V. L. Shalin (Eds.), *Cognitive task analysis* (pp. 3–23). Mahwah, NJ: Erlbaum.

Flanagan, J. C. (1954). The critical incident method. *Psychological Bulletin, 51,* 327–358.

Jonassen, D., Hannum, W., & Tessmer, M. (1989). *Handbook of task analysis procedures.* New York: Praeger.

Jonassen, D., Hannum, W., & Tessmer, M. (1999). *Task analysis methods for instructional design.* Mahwah, NJ: Erlbaum.

Loughner, P., & Moller, L. (1998). The use of task analysis procedures by instructional designers. *Performance Improvement Quarterly, 11,* 79–101.

Militello, L. G., & Hutton, R. J. B. (1998). Applied cognitive task analysis: A practitioner's toolkit for understanding cognitive task demands. *Ergonomics, 41,* 1618–1641.

Phipps, C. J. (1977). *Mechanics in agriculture.* Danville, IL: Interstate.

Primhoff, E. (1973). *How to prepare and conduct job element examinations.* Washington, DC: U.S. Civil Service Commission.

Reigeluth, C. M. (1983). Current trends in task analysis: The integration of task analysis and instructional design. *Journal of Instructional Development, 6,* 24–30, 35.

Williams, K. E. (2000). An automated aid for modeling human-computer interaction. In J. M. Schraagen, S. F. Chipman, & V. L. Shalin (Eds.), *Cognitive task analysis* (pp. 165–180). Mahwah, NJ: Erlbaum.

CHAPTER 5

Instructional Objectives

GETTING STARTED

For the past six years, you have worked for a petroleum company and are responsible for the training of civil, electrical, and chemical engineers at the various company refineries. When you visited one of the refineries recently while working on an instructional program for new engineers, you met an engineer, Ms. Calle, who had developed a program to determine the maximum output for the refinery based on the type of crude oil being refined. Ms. Calle demonstrated the program and pointed out that many engineers were requesting what she thought was unnecessary maintenance work. She had determined that the refinery was working at its maximum for the quality of crude oil input and the output it was producing. The problem, she said, was that the engineers were spending money for maintenance and repairs that simply were not needed. As a follow-up, you did your own analysis and verified the problem. Seeing the opportunity for fame and immediate recognition, you rushed to complete the task analysis and develop the objectives for a training program to teach engineers how to use the software to solve problems.

After returning to your office, you showed your plan to the chief engineer who thought it was a good idea—except, that is, for your objectives. He stated that his engineers knew how to solve problems and that there was no need for any problem-solving objectives. The unit should focus on how to enter the data and run the software. You pled your case with your data that clearly showed money was wasted on needless maintenance. Again, the chief engineer directed you to remove the problem-solving emphasis from the proposed training.

What would you do in this situation?

QUESTIONS TO CONSIDER

"What is the purpose of this instruction?"

"What can learners do to demonstrate they understand the material?"

"How can you assess whether the learners have mastered the content?"

"If you have good test items, do you really need objectives?"

"Don't instructors know what needs to be taught in a course?"

"What type of content and performance are specified in the objectives?"

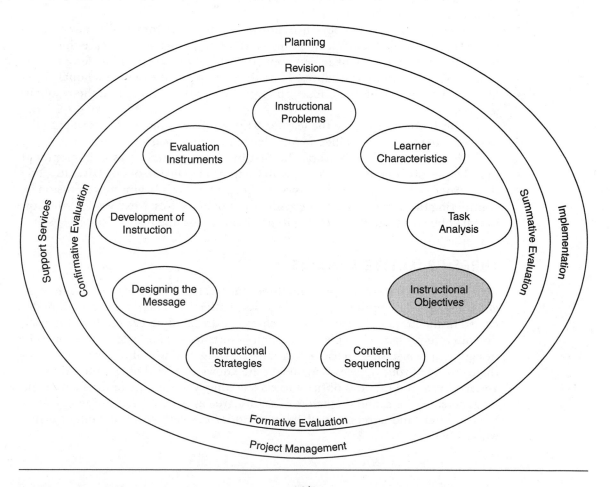

Why do instructional designers need instructional objectives? Unless the requirements are specifically defined, the instructional designer will not know what to include in the instruction. Also, without such a definition, the designer will have difficulty measuring the specific learning achieved. The benefits of the instruction are indicated in terms of what the learner is to accomplish—hence the expression *instructional objectives*. Clearly defined objectives are also essential for selecting the optimum instructional strategies to facilitate the learner's achievement of the objectives.

FUNCTION OF OBJECTIVES

Objectives perform three important functions for instructional designers, instructors, and teachers. First, they offer a means for the instructional designer and teacher to design appropriate instruction, specifically to select and organize instructional activities and resources that facilitate effective learning. The result is a very focused unit of instruction.

Second, instructional objectives provide a framework for devising ways to evaluate student learning. Since written tests and performance activities are the major means of measuring student achievement, objectives should guide the design of relevant testing items and procedures. Thus, the writing and use of instructional objectives can have a worthwhile impact on improving both teaching and the resultant learning.

Third, objectives guide the learner. The rationale is that students will use the objectives to identify the skills and knowledge they must master.

In this chapter, we focus on the first function, objectives as a development tool. The second function is addressed in Chapter 11. The use of objectives to guide the learner is the subject of discussion in Chapter 8. Let's begin our discussion by considering the three domains or classifications of objectives. Next, we describe how to write objectives and then how to classify them for making instructional decisions.

THREE OBJECTIVE DOMAINS

Objectives are typically grouped into three major categories (or *domains*, as they are generally called): cognitive, psychomotor, and affective. These areas are often discussed in the literature related to objectives. Understanding the levels within each domain is important when planning a unit of instruction. For example, if you were designing a course that focuses on problem solving, you would not expect to have the majority of your objectives written at the knowledge level of cognitive domain. You may also find that it is difficult to classify some verbs at one level of a domain. Designers, teachers, and evaluators often disagree as to the classification of a verb. We can often find agreement when we consider the verb and the content or the whole objective.

Cognitive Domain

The domain receiving the most attention in instructional programs is the cognitive domain, which includes objectives related to information or knowledge, naming, solving, predicting, and other intellectual aspects of learning. Bloom, Englehart, Furst, Hill, and Krathwohl (1956) developed a widely used taxonomy for the cognitive domain. (A *taxonomy* is a method of sequential classification on different levels.) The taxonomy is organized within two major groups: (1) simple recall of information and (2) intellectual activities. Bloom labels the lowest level *knowledge,* and the higher mental abilities are classified into five increasingly more intellectual levels of comprehension, application, analysis, synthesis, and evaluation. Table 5-1 illustrates several examples of instructional objectives in each of the six levels in the cognitive domain.

TABLE 5-1
Taxonomy of cognitive objectives

Level of Bloom's Taxonomy	Course: Chemistry Topic: Gas Laws	Course: Fundamentals of Electricity Topic: Connecting a Three-Way Switch
Knowledge: Recall of specific information	Define pressure.	List the tools required to wire a three-way switch.
Comprehension: Lowest level of understanding	Describe the relationship between pressure and volume.	Explain the purpose for each of the three wires used in connecting a switch.
Application: Application of a rule or principle	If you have a fully inflated basketball and you add more air, what is the effect on pressure inside the ball?	Sketch a diagram for connecting a three-way switch to an existing circuit.
Analysis: Breaking an idea into component parts and describing the relationships	Explain why an automobile's tire will not appear under-inflated after being driven several miles at a high speed.	Determine the gauge and length of wiring needed to connect a three-way switch to a junction box.
Synthesis: Putting the parts together to form a new whole	If you double the absolute temperature of a gas and double the pressure of the gas, what is the effect on volume?	Develop a plan for converting a dining room chandelier on a single switch to a three-way switch.
Evaluation: Making judgments about materials and methods	Before you is a container of water vapor with a temperature of 150°C and a container of oxygen at 150°C. Which gas is more likely to behave in accordance with the gas laws?	Given a diagram of an existing two-way switch for a dining room light, determine whether it can be converted to a three-way switch.

Too often, major attention is given in a course to memorizing or recalling information—the lowest cognitive level. One of the challenges in an instructional design plan is to devise instructional objectives and then design related activities that can direct students to accomplishments on the five higher intellectual levels. Although Bloom's taxonomy is used to design learning strategies, others such as Merrill (1983) have developed specific strategies for classifying objectives and then prescribing appropriate instructional strategies. We describe these methods in Chapter 7.

Psychomotor Domain

The second category for grouping instructional objectives is the psychomotor domain, which encompasses the skills requiring the use and coordination of skeletal muscles, as in the physical activities of performing, manipulating, and constructing. Although no taxonomy is universally accepted for this domain, Heinich, Molenda, and Russell (1993) present a taxonomy based on the degree of coordination that is applicable to many design projects (Table 5-2). Most muscular movements required for performing a task, whether it's doing a somersault or using a screwdriver, can be derived from this taxonomy.

Another grouping of psychomotor skills, proposed by Kibler (1981; see Table 5-3), is not a sequential taxonomy (in other words, the different levels are not sequentially organized). The value of Kibler's grouping is the recognition of separate gross- and fine-movement skills in the first two psychomotor behavior categories. Because each one requires the use of different sets of muscles, teaching such skills can be better organized by giving attention first to gross movements and then to fine movements.

TABLE 5-2

Domain of psychomotor objectives

Level	Description	Example
Imitation	Demonstrates an observed action	After watching the videotape on drilling countersink holes, you will drill a countersink hole for a wood screw.
Manipulation	Performs an action	After practicing on scrap wood, you will drill a hole for connecting two pieces of wood, scoring 8 of 10 points on the performance checklist.
Precision	Performs an action with accuracy	You will catch 75 percent of the ground balls hit to your position.
Articulation	Performs a coordinated activity in an efficient and coordinated manner	During a tennis game, you will properly execute a backhand swing as required by the volley.

TABLE 5-3
Kibler's psychomotor skill grouping

Level	Examples
Gross bodily movements of arms, shoulders, feet, and legs	Throwing a ball for a distance, picking up a heavy object so as not to strain the body, performing a backward dive
Finely coordinated movements of hands and fingers, of hand and eye, of hand and ear, and of hand, eye, and foot	Knitting a scarf, guiding wood through a table saw, using a typewriter, driving a car, sight-reading music while playing an instrument
Nonverbal communication through facial expression, gestures, bodily movements	Showing emotions through facial expressions, employing gestures to communicate directions, pantomiming a message
Speech behavior in producing and projecting sound, coordinating sound and gestures	Giving instructions in a foreign language or presenting a literary reading with gestures for emphasis

Affective Domain

The third category of instructional objectives is the affective domain, which involves objectives concerning attitudes, appreciations, values, and emotions such as enjoying, conserving, and respecting. This area is typically believed to be very important in education and training, but it is the one area in which we have been able to do the least, particularly in writing useful instructional objectives.

Krathwohl, Bloom, and Masia (1964) organize the affective domain into five levels (Table 5-4). The levels of the affective domain, like those of the cognitive domain, form a continuum for attitudinal behavior, from simple awareness and acceptance to internalization, as attitudes become part of an individual's practicing value system.

Interrelation of Domains

As you plan your instruction, keep in mind all three domains and attempt to treat the higher levels as they affect your topics and general purposes. Remember, too, that even though we are examining the three domains separately, they are closely related in two ways. First, a single major objective can involve learning in two or even all three domains. For example, when a technician learns to mix chemicals, he or she must first acquire knowledge about the different chemicals and their relationships as well as the psychomotor skills of performing the mixing operation. To this knowledge we might add the affective behavior of neatness and the practice of safety during the mixing procedure.

Second, attitudinal development may even precede successful learning in the other domains. Learners often need to be motivated to learn subject matter before instruction is successful. This step may be particularly true in a self-paced learning or distance education program, since these students must take responsibility for

TABLE 5-4
Affective domain

Level	Description	Example
Receiving	Willing to give attention to an event or activity.	Listen to, aware of, perceive, alert to, sensitive to, show tolerance of
Responding	Willing to react to an event through some form of participation.	Reply, answer, follow along, approve, obey, find pleasure in
Valuing	Willing to accept or reject an event through the expression of a positive or negative attitude.	Accept, attain, assume, support, participate, continue, grow in, be devoted to
Organizing	When encountering situations to which more than one value applies, willing to organize the values, determine relationships among values, and accept some values as dominant over others (by the importance to the individual learner).	Organize, select, judge, decide, identify with, develop a plan for, weigh alternatives
Characterizing by a value complex	Learner consistently acts in accordance with accepted values and incorporates this behavior as a part of his or her personality.	Believe, practice, continue to, carry out, become part of his or her code of behavior

their own learning, and both receptiveness and cooperation can, in some measure, determine their level of achievement. Once motivation is established, a well-organized program in which the learners participate successfully usually encourages them to have a positive attitude toward the subject and instructor.

DEVELOPING INSTRUCTIONAL OBJECTIVES

Some instructional designers insist that instructional objectives be defined immediately after formulating the goal or statement of general purposes for a topic. Sequentially, this approach may sound correct, but in actual practice it is not always feasible. While some subject-matter experts (SMEs) can verbalize the direction the instruction should take, others are not able to provide detailed information this early in the development process. To an instructional designer, the content may be unfamiliar and additional information may be needed to formulate meaningful objectives. Thus, the task analysis element is placed in the instructional design plan preceding the element of instructional objectives.

Writing instructional objectives is a developmental activity that requires changes and additions as the instruction is developed. Sometimes it is not until the instructional activities are selected or evaluation methods stated that the "real" objectives for a topic are evident. Thus, your project may start with broadly defined objectives that you refine as development progresses. Our experiences have shown that designers often refine and modify the objectives as the SMEs refine their approach to instruction during the development process.

The Basis for Objectives

Objectives are based on the results of the task analysis and provide a refinement and implementation of the needs of and/or goals for a project. If you use only a needs assessment to define your problem, the objectives will relate directly to those needs. If you use a goal analysis, the objectives will reflect a refinement of the goals. There are two cases, however, when a discrepancy may exist between the goals or needs and the objectives. First, the SME who helps with the task analysis may have a better understanding of the problem and provide different content and focus. Second, the SME may simply take a different approach to solving the problem. In either case, when this discrepancy exists, you should verify the accuracy and validity of the objectives with the group that helped you with the goal analysis or identification of needs.

Instructional objectives identify information necessary to solve the performance problem. Deriving the objectives is a four-step process to be completed after the task analysis. These steps are as follows:

1. Review the task analysis and identify the essential knowledge, tasks (e.g., procedures), and attitudes the learner must master to solve the performance problem.
2. Group the task analysis in clusters with the goals or needs you have identified.
3. Write an objective for each of the goal statements or needs.
4. Write objectives for any additional information that is essential and that is not addressed by an objective.

Approaches to Objectives

Historically, instructional designers have insisted on the use of precise objectives (often referred to as Mager-style objectives) that evolved from programmed instruction. This approach is based on behavioral psychology principles that require the learner to demonstrate an *overt* response indicating mastery of the content. The Mager (1984c) approach was applied to writing objectives for all three domains of learning—cognitive, psychomotor, and affective. Recent trends in cognitive psychology, however, have prompted a reconsideration of the specification of objectives for each of the learning domains.

In the following sections, we describe how to write different styles of objectives. We begin with the behavioral and cognitive approaches to writing objectives in the cognitive domain. Then we describe how to write objectives for the psychomotor and affective domains.

WRITING OBJECTIVES IN THE COGNITIVE DOMAIN

There are two generally recognized approaches to writing objectives: behavioral and cognitive. The behavioral orientation is typically applied to writing objectives in all the domains, whereas the cognitive approach is best suited for the cognitive domain. The following sections focus on their application in the cognitive domain.

Behavioral Objectives

A behavioral objective is a *precise* statement that answers the question, "What behavior can the learner demonstrate to indicate that he or she has mastered the knowledge or skills specified in the instruction?" Ask yourself this question each time you start to formulate an objective; your answer will guide your efforts. To answer this question satisfactorily, you need to recognize that behavioral objectives consist of at least two essential parts and two optional parts.

Essential Parts.   Start with an action verb that describes the learning required by the learner or trainee:

> To name
> To operate
> To arrange
> To compare

Follow the action verb with the subject content reference that describes the content treated:

> To name *the parts of speech used in a sentence*
> To operate *a videotape recorder*
> To arrange *parts in order for assembly*
> To compare *points of view expressed on political issues*

Taken together, the action verb (e.g., to name) and the subject content reference (e.g., parts of speech used in a sentence) indicate what the student is to achieve.

Undoubtedly, you or the SME can easily choose the content for an objective. Selecting the appropriate action verb to describe the learning behavior required is the difficult part of writing objectives. For instructional objectives developed in the cognitive domain, a "shopping list" of verbs that express behaviors on each of the six levels in Bloom's taxonomy can be helpful (Table 5-5). These verbs can assist you in identifying (and giving attention to) the higher intellectual levels in your planning.

You should have little difficulty in deciding on the action verb for a psychomotor domain objective, since the skill to perform is usually directly definable.

Optional Parts.   You may feel that stating the action verb and the content reference completely expresses an instructional objective. Although these two components are adequate in many situations, sometimes it is desirable or necessary to include other parameters as part of the learning requirement. Such an objective is particularly important when the instruction has specific or minimum outcome requirements for proficiency. Objectives for such a competency-based program require two additional parts.

TABLE 5-5
Observable verbs for the cognitive domain

1. Knowledge		2. Comprehension		3. Application	
Recall information		Interpret information in one's own words		Use knowledge or generalization in a new situation	
arrange	name	classify	report	apply	operate
define	order	describe	restate	choose	practice
duplicate	recall	discuss	review	demonstrate	prepare
label	relate	explain	select	dramatize	schedule
list	repeat	express	sort	employ	sketch
match	reproduce	identify	tell	illustrate	solve
memorize		indicate	translate	interpret	use
		locate			

4. Analysis		5. Synthesis		6. Evaluation	
Break down knowledge into parts and show relationships among parts		Bring together parts of knowledge to form a whole and build relationships for new situations		Make judgments on basis of given criteria	
analyze	differentiate	arrange	manage	appraise	evaluate
appraise	discriminate	assemble	organize	argue	judge
calculate	distinguish	collect	plan	assess	predict
categorize	examine	compose	prepare	attack	rate
compare	experiment	construct	propose	choose	score
contrast	inventory	create	set up	compare	select
criticize	question	design	synthesize	defend	support
diagram	test	formulate	write	estimate	value

Note: Depending on the meaning for use, some verbs may apply to more than one level.

Level of Achievement. The performance standard or criterion indicates the minimum acceptable performance. It answers such questions as, "How well?" "How much?" "How accurate?" "How complete?" and "In what time period?" Here are ways in which the performance standard is stated:

In proper order
At least 8 out of 10 correct (or 80 percent correct)
With an accuracy of 2 centimeters
Within 3 minutes
Meeting the criteria stated in the manual

The following examples illustrate objectives with an action verb, content, and performance standard:

To arrange the six steps of water purification in proper order
To troubleshoot circuit problems with a correct solution rate of 90 percent

To measure a client's blood pressure within 5mm Hg accuracy as determined by the instructor

To design a display that received a rating of at least 4 relative to the criteria discussed in class

Conditions of Performance.   Conditions result from answers to questions such as, "Is specific equipment required?" "Is access to a certain book, chart, or other reference allowed?" "Are time limitations imposed?" and "Are other specific factors set as conditions for testing?" Conditions are resources necessary for establishing evaluation requirements. They specify the conditions under which the evaluation takes place.

The following statements exemplify instructional objectives, each of which includes a condition:

Using the hospital's floor map as a guide, locate all fire extinguishers and emergency exits on the floor with 100 percent accuracy.

Based on assigned readings, compare the cultures of two past civilizations, enumerating at least five characteristics of each.

Given the chart showing the normal growth rate of a redwood tree, predict within 15 percent accuracy the size of a tree over a five-year period.

Within a three-minute period, set up, zero in, and operate a multimeter tester.

Mager-style instructional objectives follow the form of the objectives illustrated in these examples. When appropriate, include either or both of the optional parts. When no performance standard is included, the assumption is that only a 100 percent correct response or performance is acceptable. Keep your statements simple and brief. Avoid including so much detail that the effort of writing the objectives becomes discouraging and the requirements seem overwhelming to learners and instructors.

An alternative approach for specifying behavioral objectives is the use of terminal and enabling objectives. A major objective for a topic or task is called a *terminal objective*. It describes, in behavioral terms, the overall learning outcomes expressed originally as the general purpose for a topic. More than a single terminal objective may be necessary for accomplishing a general purpose. Here are examples of terminal instructional objectives:

Topic: Fetal circulation
General purpose: To acquire knowledge and understanding of the anatomy and physiology of fetal circulation
Terminal objective: To describe the normal circulation pattern within a fetus

Topic: Renaissance and Reformation
General purpose: To understand the changes that took place in European civilization during the late Middle Ages
Terminal objective: To interpret the significant developments taking place as Europeans broke the continental bonds and established a world hegemony

Topic: The automobile distributor
General purpose: To clean and adjust the distributor for a smooth-running engine
Terminal objective: To service a distributor

The subobjectives that lead to accomplishing the terminal objective are referred to as *enabling,* or *supporting, objectives. Enabling objectives* describe the specific behaviors (single activities or steps) that must be learned or performed, often sequentially, to achieve the terminal objective. For the terminal objectives cited previously, the following enabling objectives are required:

Terminal objective: To describe the normal circulation pattern within a fetus
Enabling objectives:
1. To name the two types of blood vessels found in the umbilical cord
2. To locate the two shunts that are normal in fetal circulation
3. To label a diagram of fetal circulation, indicating differences in systolic pressure between the left and right sides of the heart

Terminal objective: To interpret the significant developments taking place as Europeans broke the continental bonds and established a world hegemony
Enabling objectives:
1. To identify economic developments that emerged in medieval Europe
2. To analyze the political, religious, social, and psychological forces that helped create the Reformation
3. To relate the intellectual and architectural accomplishments of the twelfth century to the foundations for the Renaissance

Terminal objective: To service a distributor
Enabling objectives:
1. To identify the four main parts of a distributor
2. To remove and clean the distributor cap
3. To remove and clean the rotor
4. To clean and install breaker points
5. To set breaker points

A Caution. When instructional designers first start to write objectives, they sometimes tend to write descriptions of what is to occur during the instruction and consider the statements to be instructional objectives (e.g., "To view a videotape on ecological safeguards," "To teach the student how . . . ," or "To read pages 45 through 70 in the text"). These statements are *activities;* they do not indicate learning outcomes. An instructional objective should focus on outcomes or products rather than on process. If you are not sure whether what you are stating is an objective, ask yourself, "Is this outcome what I want the learner to know or demonstrate after completing the topic or unit?"

Cognitive Objectives

Gronlund (1985, 1995) suggests an alternative approach to Mager's for writing instructional objectives in the cognitive domain. Both behavioral objectives and cognitive objectives specify learning as outcomes. Cognitive objectives, however, are stated in two parts. First is a statement of the general instructional objective. General objectives are stated in broad terms to encompass a domain of learning (e.g., comprehend, understand, apply, use, interpret, evaluate):

> Selects information using ERIC
> Understands the meaning of the terms used in the gas laws
> Interprets a graph
> Comprehends the meaning of a poem

These general statements indicate the overall outcome of the instruction. Like a behavioral objective, they focus on the products or outcomes of the instruction, not the process. Statements that include words such as *gains, views,* or *acquires* are indicators that the designer is focusing on the learning process instead of the outcomes. Thus, an objective written as "The learner will gain . . . " is focusing on the process and should be rewritten as "The learner interprets . . . " to focus on the outcome.

The second part of a cognitive objective is one or more samples of the specific types of performance that indicate mastery of the objective. Following are examples:

Selects information using ERIC
1. Finds an article on a given topic
2. Compiles a bibliography of related literature
3. Identifies narrower and broader terms for a search

Interprets a graph
1. Determines the group that sold the most
2. Determines the groups that were below average
3. Determines the year with the greatest number of sales

Conducts effective meetings
1. Prepares an agenda prior to the meeting
2. Arranges the room for effective communication
3. States the intended outcomes at the beginning of the meeting

Why use cognitive objectives instead of behavioral objectives? If we compare the cognitive objectives to Mager-type behavioral objectives, we find they both specify a student performance in specific, measurable terms. However, with behavioral objectives, the objective becomes the end rather than the means for instruction. Cognitive-style objectives overcome this problem by first stating a general objective (similar in structure to the terminal objective) to communicate the intent (e.g., "To interpret the graph"). A behavioral objective might oversimplify the intent by stating the outcome as "Identify the tallest bar on the chart." The resulting instruction from the behavioral objective, then, focuses on measuring the elements of the graph rather than interpreting it. The sample performances of the cognitive objective simply indicate behaviors that allow the teacher or instructor to infer that the learner has achieved the higher-level intent.

Behavioral objectives are particularly well suited for mastery learning instruction for which the learner must demonstrate specific behaviors to advance to the next level. For example, a course that stresses how to produce a specific report, such as sales by departments for a given month, might best be defined with behavioral objectives. These objectives will accurately describe the outcome, "The learner will print a report indicating sales revenue by department," which involves a repetitive task of entering the month and department name.

Cognitive objectives are well suited for describing higher levels of learning. For example, in a course that emphasizes labor negotiation skills, the designer might develop a cognitive objective to describe the outcome related to evaluating a contract offer: "The learner will comprehend the implications of an offer." The examples of behaviors related to this outcome could focus on specifics such as "calculating the cost of the contract to the company," "identifying possible counteroffers," and "determining long-range implications." Cognitive objectives can be written for all three domains of learning.

Expert's Edge

Legal Outcomes

One of my first projects as an instructional designer for the University of British Columbia's Department of Distance Education and Technology was the development of a new (not repurposed) web-based course on Online Mediation for the Dispute Resolution Program, Faculty of Law. The faculty member was an experienced classroom instructor, but new to web-based instruction. Nevertheless, she was open to new approaches and particularly wanted to look at problem-based learning (PBL) as a major learning strategy.

The main target audience for the course was second-year law students from the University of British Columbia and the University of Victoria. At the time when I began to work with her, the faculty member had only a rough idea of what the course structure might entail, but had a relatively solid understanding of the content and skills she wanted the students to learn. The content was to include such concepts as types of online dispute resolution available, online dispute resolution terminology, and issues in online dispute resolution, as well as a strong emphasis on such "practical" online dispute resolution skills as advocacy, rapport building online, and client/counsel communication.

At this stage, I decided the best course of action was to work with the faculty member to look carefully at her course learning outcomes. In my experience, most university faculty are well practiced in writing instructional objectives and, while they may not always be cognizant of the range of possibilities, they either come to a project with a preference or are bound by a faculty approach or existing curriculum document. In this case, the faculty member was open to suggestion, although opposed to the perceived narrowness and detail of performance objectives. Clearly, this was a situation that indicated the use of some sort of cognitive learning outcomes, but which of the many approaches and taxonomies would suit her needs?

This faculty member, like many educators, was most familiar with the general categories of Bloom et al.'s (1956) taxonomy and had developed an initial list using the six groupings: knowledge, comprehension, application, analysis, synthesis, and evaluation. Not surprisingly, the largest category was knowledge. This presented a problem since the whole point of the course was to teach the students to analyze a dispute and then decide on (or even design) an appropriate method of mediation, which they would then carry out (apply). There seemed to be insufficient focus on the "higher-order" learning outcomes she wanted the students to achieve.

What I decided to do was to continue to work with Bloom's taxonomy (in a slightly modified format as per the following), since she was comfortable with that approach. We examined and discussed the wording in her initial list and made modifications to it, including rewording some outcomes and switching them to "higher-level" categories. To complement this process, since she was open to rethinking her learning outcomes, we also looked over a couple of other taxonomies (e.g., the Iowa Department of Education's Integrated Thinking Model), which place designing, problem solving, and decision making—all-important skills for this course—at the top of the pecking order and which, it can be argued, subsume Bloom's process categories of analyzing and evaluating. While we didn't switch to a new taxonomy, we were able to use aspects of the other approaches to revise some of the initial outcome wordings to take into account these processes. As a result, I believe we were able to improve the range and breadth of what she wanted the students to learn from the course. We also used the new learning outcomes to guide us in developing instructional strategies appropriate to help them achieve these outcomes. Here is a sampling of what we came up with:

> *Remember*
> Recall the basic terminology for online dispute resolution (DR)
> Recall the options available for online dispute resolution (synchronous/asynchronous mediation, arbitration, blind bidding, etc.)
> *Understand*
> Explain the process of online mediation
> Interpret the issues raised by an Agreement to Mediate
> *Apply*
> Practice the skills required of an advocate in an online environment (reframing, paraphrasing, context building through documentary exchange, etc.)
> Apply client interview skills through conduct of live client interview and follow-up e-mail interviews

Analyze

Analyze a transcript of online mediation to identify strengths and weaknesses of advocates' approaches

Compare and contrast effectiveness of a variety of online DR processes in resolution of single dispute

Create

Recommend the choice of DR process for a client in specific circumstances based on integration of knowledge regarding process choice, client profile, legal and nonlegal factors raised by facts

Utilize existing information to develop a range of available options for other party

Evaluate

During online mediation, argue for client's preferred resolution

Assess arguments and offers of opposing counsel

Richard F. Kenny is an instructional designer with the Department of Distance Education and Technology and an adjunct professor with the Faculty of Education at the University of British Columbia, Canada. Rick works with members of such faculties as Agriculture, Education, Forestry, Law, and Nursing to design and develop web-based instruction. He also edits the *Canadian Journal of Learning and Technology*. Rick's research agenda focuses on the design and development of emerging technologies to foster higher-order thinking.

WRITING OBJECTIVES FOR THE PSYCHOMOTOR DOMAIN

Psychomotor skills are the most easily observed of the three domains. Objectives in this domain rely on the same four objective parts; however, the emphasis is often different. For example, the verb *demonstrate* is frequently used as the behavior. Explicitly stated conditions are often required for psychomotor objectives. For example, is the learner to use an electric drill or a manually powered drill, or are the ground balls thrown or hit by a batter? Similarly, psychomotor objectives are more likely to require specific criteria since 100 percent accuracy (e.g., all 10 shots in the bull's-eye) is often not expected from the novice. Thus, we might have a number of objectives ranging from hitting a large target by the end of the first practice to eventually scoring a specific number of points. Following are examples of behavioral objectives in the psychomotor domain:

Given five rounds of ammunition, the learner will shoot each round from 50 feet so that each hits within a 7-inch circle.

Given five rounds of ammunition, the learner will score a total of 30 points while firing from a distance of 50 feet.

Given two 15-inch straight needles and yarn, the learner will cast on 50 stitches of equal size and correct tension.

Time is often used with psychomotor objectives, but it may be difficult to determine whether time is a condition or a criterion in behavioral objectives. Let's examine two additional psychomotor objectives:

Students will run a quarter mile around a track in under 2 minutes.

Given a malfunctioning light switch, the student will correctly replace the switch in 30 minutes.

In the first objective, time (2 minutes) is a *criterion* because it is conceivable that some students are not capable of running a quarter mile in under 2 minutes. Thus, the time is a standard for measurement. The 30-minute time limit in the second objective is a *condition* because almost any physically able student will be capable of completing the task in less than 30 minutes.

To summarize, if the time factor is used to measure the performance, then it is a criterion for the objective. If the time factor is used to set a maximum time limit and there is another criterion (e.g., "correctly replace"), then time is a condition.

WRITING OBJECTIVES FOR THE AFFECTIVE DOMAIN

The affective domain encompasses more abstract behaviors (attitudes, feelings, and appreciations) that are relatively difficult to observe and measure. One method of developing objectives in this domain is to specify behaviors indirectly by inferring from what the instructor can observe. What a learner does or says is assumed as evidence of behavior relating to an affective objective.

Some behaviors in this area are difficult to identify, let alone to name and measure. How, for instance, do you measure an attitude of appreciating the importance of good nutrition or developing a positive relationship with company clients? Such attitudes are inferred only indirectly from secondary clues. When developing an affective objective, it is often useful to divide the objective into two parts. First, identify the cognitive component or "thought" that describes the attitude. Second, identify a behavior that when observed would represent the attitude. This behavior is then used to write the affective objective.

To measure an attitude about an activity, we must generalize from learner behaviors that indicate the student is developing or has developed the attitude. The following examples illustrate behaviors indicating a positive attitude:

The learner says he or she likes the activity.
The learner selects the activity in place of other possible activities.
The learner participates in the activity with much enthusiasm.
The learner shares his or her interest in the activity by discussing it with others or by encouraging others to participate.

If the instructional objective is "to appreciate the importance of good nutrition," accomplishment is demonstrated by the following behaviors:

Is observed eating only foods of high nutritional value (no junk foods or refined products)
Readily advises other people about the value of nutritious foods
Voluntarily reads books and articles describing good nutrition practices
Attends lectures and workshops presented by nutrition authorities

If the instructional objective is "to develop a positive relationship with company clients," evidence of accomplishment can be shown if the employee does the following:

Is prompt for appointments with clients

Calls each client by name, is courteous, and speaks in a friendly tone

Shows an interest in the client as a person by talking about matters other than business that are mutually interesting

Spends extra time with a client, as necessary

Provides requested information promptly

Admittedly, these examples are only indicative of the possible successful fulfillment of an attitudinal objective and do not measure it directly. Mager (1984a) calls these attitudinal objectives *approach tendencies* toward exhibiting a positive attitude to a subject or a situation. The learner's attitude is considered negative if he or she shows *avoidance tendencies*. Notice, however, that Mager's approach to affective objectives is very close to Gronlund's (1985, 1995) cognitive approach. They both begin with a general behavior and then proceed to specific example behaviors that the instructor uses to infer the presence of the attitude.

In the book *Goal Analysis*, Mager (1984b) suggests that if employees are to exhibit safety consciousness, they are expected to practice the following behaviors: "Report safety hazards; wear safety equipment; follow safety rules; practice good housekeeping by keeping the work area free of dirt and loose tools; encourage safe practice in others by reminding them to wear safety equipment; and so forth" (p. 46–47). This example is similar to a cognitive objective as it states a general purpose, safety consciousness, and then provides specific examples of behaviors indicating the practice of safety.

Gronlund's and Mager's approaches can help you refine ways of indicating attitudinal objectives and then setting a degree of measurement for them. (For additional help in identifying and writing affective domain objectives, refer to the work of Lee and Merrill [1972].) Table 5-6 is a list of verbs you may find useful as you state instructional objectives in this domain.

TABLE 5-6
Affective verbs

acclaims	cooperates	joins
agrees	defends	offers
argues	disagrees	participates in
assumes	disputes	praises
attempts	engages in	resists
avoids	helps	shares
challenges	is attentive to	volunteers

Realistically, we must recognize that there are many important objectives that cannot result in measurable outcomes. Eisner (1969) uses the term *expressive objectives* for those for which specific outcomes are not readily stated. These objectives identify situations for the learner. An expressive objective may allow for self-discovery, originality, and inventiveness, the result surprising both the learner and the instructor. For example, "To develop a feeling of personal adequacy in athletic performance" is an expressive objective. By stating such nonmeasurable objectives during planning, you can at least identify aspects of instructional goals that have personal or social importance and thus can make a start on deciding how to achieve them.

CLASSIFYING OBJECTIVES

The cognitive and affective domains comprise sequential hierarchies starting from low levels of learning or behavior and progressing through more intellectual or sophisticated levels. The psychomotor domain does not exhibit as consistent a sequencing pattern as do the other two domains.

These three domains are useful for determining the level of learning for each objective and for checking that the objectives are distributed across several levels rather than clumped as rote memory objectives. The next element of the design process is to use the objectives as a basis for developing the instructional strategies. We accomplish this task by classifying the objectives into a matrix that is then used to prescribe the instructional strategy. The three taxonomies we have just discussed are not well suited for developing instructional strategies for two reasons. First, an objective can often be classified into more than one level because the levels are not mutually exclusive. Second, the taxonomies do not provide prescriptive instructional strategies for each level. The following pages describe two different models for classifying objectives and then prescribing instructional strategies. The Mager and Beach (1967) model is particularly suited for classroom instruction, whereas the performance-content matrix provides a structured instructional design approach.

Mager and Beach's Model

Mager and Beach (1967) describe a performance classification approach in their book *Developing Vocational Instruction*. Objectives are classified into one of five categories or performance types and then ranked by difficulty (Table 5-7).

Objectives that require the learner to speak in a specific manner are classified as *speech performance* objectives. This category is limited to speaking; written verbal responses are not classified in this performance category. *Manipulation* is the execution of a psychomotor skill that can range from simple skills such as dialing a phone number to complex machine operations. Objectives requiring the rote memorization of information (e.g., listing two types of screwdrivers) are classified in the *recall* category. The *discrimination* category requires the learner to distinguish

TABLE 5-7
Mager and Beach's performance types

Objective	Performance	Learning Difficulty
1. When answering the phone, the salesperson will correctly identify the company and self.	Speech	Easy
2. Salesperson will correctly enter the customer's ID number into the computer.	Manipulation	Easy
3. Salesperson will identify to whom he or she transfers a customer with a problem.	Recall	Easy
4. Salesperson will determine shipping time based on zip code and package size.	Discrimination	Moderately difficult
5. When an article is out of stock, the salesperson will suggest an alternative item.	Problem solving	Difficult

between two objects (e.g., a Phillips-head and a flat-head screwdriver) or two events (e.g., a strike and a ball). Objectives that require the student to determine what to do are classified as *problem-solving* performances. Finally, each objective is classified as *easy, moderately difficult, difficult,* or *very difficult* to perform based on the instructional designer's observations during the task analysis and input from the SME.

Expanded Performance-Content Matrix Model

Merrill (1983) proposes another useful tool for classifying objectives in his component display theory. Although Merrill's performance-content matrix is not hierarchical like Bloom's taxonomy, it does provide a means of determining which type of instructional strategy to use to master the objective. The expanded model builds on Merrill's model to account for psychomotor, affective, and interpersonal tasks (Table 5-8) that are not included in Merrill's component display theory. Unlike Bloom's taxonomy, this model classifies types of content and performance as opposed to levels of learning. In addition, Bloom's model is descriptive in that it describes different levels of learning. Instructional design models must prescribe optimum instructional strategies for achieving an objective. Thus, like Merrill's model, the present model uses content categories that are then used to prescribe instructional strategies (see Chapter 7).

The content aspect of the matrix provides six categories for classifying objectives. Each objective is classified into one category. If the objective fits into two categories, it needs to be refined and stated as two separate objectives. The following paragraphs briefly review each of the content categories.

Fact. A *fact* is a statement that associates one item with another. The statement "Columbus was an explorer" associates the words Columbus and explorer. Learning that the symbol H represents hydrogen in a chemical equation is also a fact that associates H with hydrogen. Facts are memorized for later recall.

TABLE 5-8
Expanded performance-content matrix

Content	Performance	
	Recall	Application
Fact		
Concept		
Principles and rules		
Procedure		
Interpersonal		
Attitude		

Concept.   *Concepts* are categories we use for simplifying the world. It is much easier to refer to two-wheeled, self-propelled vehicles as bicycles than to remember the brand name of every bike. Examples of concepts are circle, car, box, woman, mirror, and tree. We can identify several different models of automobiles, but we classify each as a car just as we group maple, oak, and pine trees in the category of tree.

Principles and Rules.   *Principles* and *rules* express relationships between concepts. For example, "Metal expands when its temperature is increased" expresses a causal relationship between the concepts of metal and temperature. Similarly, "Providing reinforcement increases the chances the behavior will be repeated" expresses a relationship between learning (repeating a behavior) and reinforcement.

Procedure.   A *procedure* is a sequence of steps one follows to achieve a goal. Procedures can describe primarily cognitive operations such as solving a quadratic equation, an operation that involves both cognitive and psychomotor operations such as taking a voltmeter reading, and primarily psychomotor operations such as driving a nail. Procedures can also vary in difficulty from repetitive tasks (e.g., driving a nail) to problem-solving tasks (e.g., debugging a computer program).

Interpersonal Skills.   This category describes spoken and nonverbal (i.e., body language) interaction between two or more people. For example, an objective that describes the phone-answering skills of a telemarketing professional or the skills in making an effective presentation would be classified as *interpersonal skills.* Similarly, a course designed to improve the skills of managers interviewed on television by improving their posture and sitting habits to project confidence would be grouped in this category.

Attitude.   Objectives that seek to change or modify the learner's *attitude* are classified in this category. Affective objectives can vary from simply developing an awareness of different options to changes in attitudes that result in action, such as stopping theft of company materials.

The second part of the model is the performance specified in the objective. The behavior or performance specified in the objective is considered and then classified as either recall or application.

Recall.   Objectives that specify that the learner simply memorize information for later recall (e.g., "Name an explorer" "Define reinforcement") are classified as *recall* performance. Recall performance encompasses those behaviors at the lower levels of Bloom's taxonomy. Verbs such as *list, define,* and *name* are often cues of recall performance.

Application.   When the performance requires the learner to use or apply the information, the objective is classified as *application*. For example, an objective that requires the learner to demonstrate the use of reinforcement in a microteaching lesson would be classified as application. Verbs such as *demonstrate, discriminate,* and *solve* are cues that the performance requires an application of the content. Note that facts are always classified as recall because they cannot be applied.

Later chapters use this expanded performance-content matrix to prescribe instructional strategies to help the learner achieve the objective.

DIFFICULTIES IN WRITING OBJECTIVES

One reason many people shy away from stating precise objectives is that formulating them demands much thought and effort. Each objective should be unambiguous. It must communicate exactly the same thing to all learners and to other instructors and designers. Many instructors are not accustomed to such exactness in instructional planning. For too long we have based our teaching on broad generalizations, often leaving it up to the learner to interpret what we actually mean.

Not until the importance of objectives for an instructional program becomes apparent are instructors or designers willing to put sincere effort into preparing them. Then the difficulties and frustrations are taken in stride, and we gradually develop a habit and pattern for expressing as many of the desired outcomes of effective learning as possible in specific, meaningful terms.

PROS AND CONS OF WRITING OBJECTIVES

As you studied the content of this chapter, you no doubt considered your own feelings and attitudes relative to the importance of writing instructional objectives. Some designers and instructors readily accept the position taken in this book that it is important to write observable and measurable objectives whenever possible. Others have strong views against such specificity, believing that objectives are often unnecessary or that the important outcomes of a program do not lend themselves to objective statements. These latter individuals may feel that the more important long-term outcomes of an instructional program are hard to define and often unmeasurable.

This view should not be an either/or situation. Admittedly, most objectives we write relate to short-term goals, attainable during a course or training program. Some, however, may contribute to long-term goals, such as the development of analytical skills or decision-making abilities, over which the instructor has little or no control. These high-level objectives may not be fully measurable until years later. Therefore, it is reasonable at times to assume that certain objectives cannot be completely satisfied during the planned instructional program. Instructors and designers can do a follow-up evaluation after a course to determine learner competencies relative to such important long-term objectives.

If you would like to read a rationale that examines all aspects of this topic of objectives, Davies (1976) may be most helpful. He puts objectives in perspective, based on his review of literature and research in the field of curriculum design.

SUMMARY

1. A procedure for systematically planning instruction in which the specification of instructional objectives plays a key role has been described.
2. The objectives indicate what a learner is expected to do after completing a unit of instruction, and they are expressed in precise, unambiguous terms. We have provided both a strict behavioral approach and a more flexible cognitive approach to specifying instructional objectives.
3. Objectives are important to both learners and instructors. They help learners plan their study and prepare for examinations. They guide the instructor in planning instruction and devising tests.
4. Objectives are grouped into cognitive, psychomotor, and affective domains within which increasingly higher levels of intellectual aptitude, skill ability, and emotional behavior are recognized. The domains are closely related, since a single major objective can require learning in more than one area.
5. Behavioral objectives consist of an action verb and subject content reference; they may also include a performance standard and/or conditions. Cognitive objectives consist of a general objective and then samples of student performance.
6. Objectives for higher intellectual levels are more difficult, yet more important, to specify. Objectives in the affective domain are identified indirectly by inferring learner acceptance of an attitude from observable behavior.
7. Objectives are organized and sequenced by various methods to ensure that the more advanced objectives receive suitable attention. After the objectives are specified, they are classified into categories using one of the schemes presented. These classifications are then used to prescribe an appropriate instructional strategy.
8. The subject matter relating to instructional objectives as treated in this chapter provides the essential information to guide you in developing your own objectives and in assisting a subject-matter expert to write instructional objectives.

THE ID PROCESS

A list of instructional objectives and their classification in the expanded perform-ance-content matrix is the output for this step of the instructional design process. The objectives are derived from the task analysis and represent the major tasks, knowledge, and attitudes defined by the analysis. These objectives are the starting point for the design of the instructional strategies. However, as you design the strate-gies and develop the instruction you will often find the need for more details in your task analysis. This additional analysis and even the strategy design process can lead to a refinement of your objectives.

Once you have written your objectives, you can collect feedback from your SME and other instructional designers (see Chapter 12 for specific formative evalu-ation strategies). Your SME and other content experts can help you determine whether the objectives will support a solution for the performance problem. Other instructional designers can help you ensure that your objectives are appropriate for the task analysis and for solving the performance problem.

APPLICATION

1. Change the verb in each of the following phrases to one that is observable.
   a. The learner will understand . . .
   b. The learner will recognize . . .
   c. The learner will feel . . .
2. Write a cognitive objective for the following task: The customer service repre-sentative will calm an upset customer.
3. Classify each of the following objectives into the expanded performance-content matrix.
   _____ a. On a posttest following the completion of this instructional unit, the learner will state the inherent rate of the sinus node, atrioventricular node, and His-Purkinje system with 100 percent accuracy.
   _____ b. The system operator will remove the pH sensor.
   _____ c. Given a control panel, the system operator will identify the location of the override switch.
   _____ d. Given five black-and-white photographs of insects, the learner will correctly identify the three insects detrimental to corn.
   _____ e. Given a list of three insecticides and a list of five insects, the learner will correctly match the insect to the insecticide that kills or controls it.
   _____ f. The learner will list the four steps to reconcile a discrepancy in the piece count.
   _____ g. Given the hearing evaluation form and a patient, the learner will cor-rectly administer a hearing test.
   _____ h. Given a choice of various musical CDs, the student will listen to those from the Baroque period.

ANSWERS

1. Change the verb in the following phrases to one that is observable:
   a. The learner will *understand* (classify, discuss, identify, select, analyze, distinguish) . . .
   b. The learner will *recognize* (identify, select, categorize, indicate, locate) . . .
   c. The learner will *feel* (express, attempt, defend, share, participate in, choose) . . .
   (Note the problems of dealing with ambiguous verbs and attempting to find agreement on their meaning!)
2. Write a cognitive objective for the following task: The customer service representative calms an upset customer.
   (1) Listens to customer's complaint without interrupting
   (2) Asks appropriate questions to define customer's problem/concern
   (3) Assures customer complaint will be addressed
   (4) Demonstrates desire to help customer
   (5) Takes responsibility for helping customer
   (6) Maintains a balance between customer's request and company's interests
   (7) Keeps a log of the call
   (8) Uses questions to gather information before taking action
3. Classify each of the following objectives into the expanded performance-content matrix.
   a. Fact/Recall
   b. Procedure/Application
   c. Fact/Recall
   d. Concept/Application
   e. Fact/Recall
   f. Procedure/Recall
   g. Procedure/Application
   h. Attitude/Application

QUALITY MANAGEMENT

The quality check for objectives consists of two steps. First, you need to check each objective to determine that it is complete and adequately describes the intended outcome. The objectives should be concise to avoid misinterpretation. Behavioral objectives should include a verb and related content, conditions, and criteria. Cognitive objectives should have a general objective and adequate descriptions of learner performance. Second, determine whether the objectives are in alignment with your task analysis and goals. The objectives should represent the knowledge and skills identified in your task analysis. To avoid having a large number of objectives, you may need to write your objectives at a higher level of learning. Next, check your objectives against the goals and/or needs identified for the problem. The objectives should support the achievement of the goals and alleviation of the needs.

If there is a discrepancy between the objectives and the problem, then there are two courses of action. First, you can revise your problem and goals to more accurately reflect the problem. Second, you revise the task analysis and/or objectives to focus more on the problem and goals.

SAMPLE DESIGN PLAN

INSTRUCTIONAL OBJECTIVES

After several refinements, the task analysis is finally in a workable format. The time spent on the task analysis will pay off as I start writing the objectives. My sense is that the major domains represented in the task analysis are cognitive and psychomotor, so I'll look through the analysis with an eye toward those domains. Once I've identified the domains, I'll begin developing the objectives. I know from experience that the process of writing instructional objectives is developmental—it'll take a few rewrites and several glances back at the task analysis to get the objectives just right. Although I'm just starting to write the objectives, I want to start thinking about the strategies, so I'll include preliminary content/performance categories for each objective.

I'll write behavioral objectives for the first section of instruction because this section is based on a prespecified scenario (preparing to travel to a conference) for which I can control the outcomes. I'll write a cognitive objective for the second section because the process is more interpretive (the learners will define their own projects, goals, tasks, etc.).

1. Given a short description of a project, the learner will write a project goal in an acceptable format. *(Procedure/Application)*
2. Given a worksheet, the learner will list at least three tasks associated with the project goal. *(Procedure/Application)*
3. Given the priority/time-frame matrix and a list of tasks, the learner will accurately classify the degree of criticality for each task. *(Concept/Application)*
4. Given the priority/time-frame matrix, the learner will sequence the tasks according to due date. *(Procedure/Application)*
5. The learner will create a prioritized to-do list on a PDA. *(Procedure/Application)*
   a. Creates a to-do list
   b. Assigns items to a category
   c. Assigns a priority to each task
   d. Assigns a due date to tasks as appropriate

REFERENCES

Bloom, B. S., Englehart, M. D., Furst, E. J., Hill, W. H., & Krathwohl, D. R. (1956). *A taxonomy of educational objectives: Handbook I. The cognitive domain.* New York: McKay.

Davies, I. K. (1976). *Objectives in curriculum design.* New York: McGraw-Hill.

Eisner, E. W. (1969). Instructional and expressive objectives: Their formulation and use in curriculum. In W. J. Popham (Ed.), *Instructional objectives: An analysis of emerging issues* (pp. 13–18). Chicago: Rand McNally.

Gronlund, N. E. (1985). *Stating behavioral objectives for classroom instruction.* New York: Macmillan.

Gronlund, N. E. (1995). *How to write and use instructional objectives* (5th ed.). New York: Prentice Hall.

Heinich, R., Molenda, M., & Russell, J. D. (1993). *Instructional media and the new technologies of instruction* (4th ed.). New York: Macmillan.

Kibler, R. J. (1981). *Objectives for instruction and evaluation.* Boston: Allyn & Bacon.

Krathwohl, D. R., Bloom, B. S., & Masia, B. B. (1964). *A taxonomy of educational objectives: Handbook II. The affective domain.* New York: McKay.

Lee, B. N., & Merrill, D. M. (1972). *Writing complete affective objectives: A short course.* Belmont, CA: Wadsworth.

Mager, R. F. (1984a). *Developing attitude toward learning* (2nd ed.). Belmont, CA: Pitman.

Mager, R. F. (1984b). *Goal analysis* (2nd ed.). Belmont, CA: Lake.

Mager, R. F. (1984c). *Preparing instructional objectives* (2nd ed.). Belmont, CA: Pitman.

Mager, R. F., & Beach, K. M. (1967). *Developing vocational instruction.* Belmont, CA: Pitman.

Merrill, M. D. (1983). Component display theory. In C. M. Reigeluth (Ed.), *Instructional-design theories and models: An overview of their current status* (pp. 282–333). Mahwah, NJ: Erlbaum.

Designing the Instruction: Sequencing

GETTING STARTED

You work for a national telecommunication corporation that employs 2,000 people in 30 call centers around the country. These individuals sell the company's services, which range from simple telephone service, to voice mail, to 800 numbers, to Internet access. This group experiences a high turnover rate of approximately 30 percent a year. In 12 months, the company will install a new computer system that integrates all of the services into one system (as opposed to the 14 individual computer systems needed now for the various products). You are responsible for developing the training to teach this group the products the company offers and the process for determining the pricing of each product based on past or projected usage. There are several options for sequencing the content. For example, you could organize the sequencing of the products based on their appeal to the learner (interest) or their frequency of sales or inquiry from customers (e.g., residential long-distance service before voice mail). Or you could sequence them based on prerequisites such as 800 numbers before discussing the total small business package, which includes voice mail and 800 numbers. How would you sequence the information for the naïve and experienced learners?

"Can sequencing the content improve the learner's understanding?"

"What strategies are available to help me sequence a unit?"

"When do I determine the sequencing of the content?"

"What are the benefits of using a sequencing scheme?"

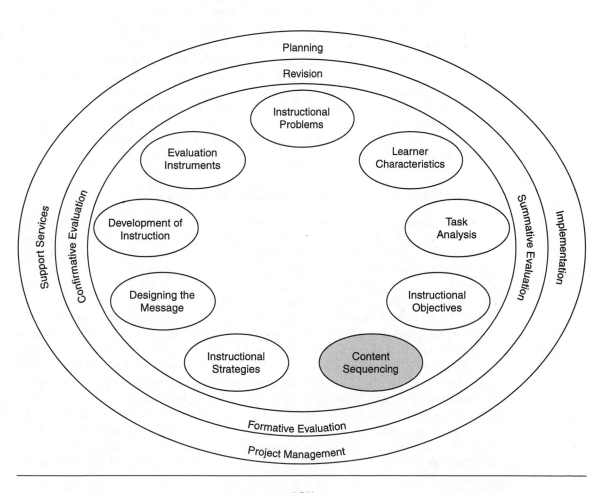

Once you have developed the objectives, you are ready to determine the optimum sequence for the instruction. As you completed the task analysis, you may have made mental notes as to how you might present the content. Instructional designers recognize that the sequence the subject-matter expert (SME) presented during the task analysis may not be the most appropriate sequence for learning the content. This chapter focuses on how to determine the most appropriate sequence for presenting the content related to each objective.

Sequencing is the efficient ordering of content in such a way as to help the learner achieve the objectives. For some objectives, the sequence is suggested by the procedure. For example, when teaching someone how to change a tire, it would seem more appropriate to teach where the tools are located before teaching how to remove the lug nuts. Other topics, however, have a less obvious sequence. A course on how to write a research paper has several possible sequences, all of which are equally effective. For example, one instructor might start with how to read a research paper, whereas another might first teach how to use the library.

There are several general methods of sequencing content. One well-known method is the prerequisite method (Gagné, 1985), which is based on a learning hierarchy that identifies skills that are dependent on other skills. The sequence is to teach the prerequisite skills first (e.g., how to sort checks before marking them as cleared). A second approach, described by Posner and Strike (1976), is a set of strategies for sequencing the instruction based on learning-related, world-related, and concept-related content. A more recent approach is one described by English and Reigeluth (1996) as part of Reigeluth's elaboration theory. This chapter focuses on two sequencing strategies: those prescribed by Posner and Strike and those prescribed by Reigeluth.

THE POSNER AND STRIKE SEQUENCING SCHEMES

We review three sequencing schemes proposed by Posner and Strike (1976). The first scheme, which is learning related, suggests ways of sequencing the content based on learner characteristics identified in the learner analysis. This scheme considers the difficulty of the material, its appeal or interest to the learner, prerequisite information, and the learner's cognitive development. Since this scheme is based on the needs of the learner, it seems appropriate that the initial sequencing of the unit of instruction follows these guidelines. The next two schemes, world-related and concept-related, recommend sequencing schemes based on the type of content treated in the unit. For example, the world-related scheme suggests sequencing based on spatial, temporal, and physical relationships identified in the content. Similarly, the concept-related scheme suggests sequencing based on the relationships between the concepts. After the initial sequencing based on learner characteristics, you must select a best-fit scheme for the content from either the world-related or concept-related schemes. Thus, if you are trying to sequence a series of related concepts (e.g., herbivores, carnivores, omnivores, and examples of each), the concept-related guidelines would be most appropriate for determining which concept to present first, second, third, and so forth. The following sections describe each of the sequencing schemes.

Learning-Related Sequencing

This strategy for sequencing content is based on five student-learning concepts (Table 6-1). First, there are identifiable prerequisites a learner must master before demonstrating a more complex task. For example, one needs to learn the alphabet before using a dictionary or encyclopedia or before arranging data alphabetically. The prerequisite skills and knowledge are identified in the task analysis. Second is teaching about the familiar or known before teaching about the unknown. When teaching a math unit on measurement in the United States, for example, you might begin with inch, foot, and yard measurement problems before teaching problems involving calculations with centimeters and meters. A third learning-related scheme is difficulty. Posner and Strike (1976) state that difficulty is determined by the fineness of the discrimination the learner must make, how quickly the procedure is executed, and the amount of cognitive processing required. Guidelines prescribe teaching the easier tasks first, such as spelling short words before longer words and replacing a button before sewing a seam. Similarly, a French horn tutor would first teach a student about intervals and then move to complex chords. Fourth is the sequencing of content based on interest. An introductory unit on LOGO programming might start with how to draw a design on the screen (high interest) before introducing structured programming techniques (lower interest). Fifth, the content is sequenced according to a development theory such as that of Bruner, Piaget, or

TABLE 6-1

Learning-related sequencing

Phenomenon	Example/Prescription
Identifiable prerequisite	Teach a skill required to perform another skill first Teach addition of whole numbers before teaching addition of fractions
Familiarity	Begin with the most familiar information and then progress to the most remote Teach about mammals in the surrounding area before teaching about mammals of another country
Difficulty	Teach the less difficult before the more difficult Teach how to complete a simple income tax form before teaching how to complete a form with itemized deductions
Interest	Begin with the topics or tasks that will create the most learner interest Teach a recruit how to fire a rifle before teaching how to clean it
Development	Ensure that the learner has reached the appropriate developmental level before teaching a task or topic Teach students to recognize the color green before teaching them how to read the word

Kohlberg. For example, following Bruner's theory, words *(symbols)* would be introduced only after the learner had the appropriate visual images *(icons)* related to the words.

Suppose a professor asks for help in redesigning a course in photography. The objectives might cover the basic operation of the camera, exposure control, depth of field, developing film, and producing prints. We might first sequence the content using learner interest by allowing the learners to shoot a roll of film using the exposure guide that comes with the film. Learners can enjoy immediate satisfaction with the hands-on experience. When we organize the content related to controlling the exposure, we would first teach the learner how to set the f-stop and shutter speed. Next, we would teach how to change the shutter speed and select the appropriate f-stop. Sequencing for the information on controlling exposure begins with the easiest step of simply setting a selected exposure and proceeds to a more difficult step of manipulating the shutter speed and f-stop to obtain different depths of field and to stop the action. Finally, we would teach how to print a picture before teaching how to improve the quality of a picture through techniques such as dodging and burning. This sequencing is based on the identifiable prerequisite of printing a simple picture before manipulating it.

A procedural analysis typically reveals a temporal sequence, whereas a topic analysis usually reveals a logical sequence. Although the sequence identified by the procedural analysis is usable in a unit of instruction, a more effective unit might result from a different sequence or combination of sequences. A detailed analysis of basic photography techniques might proceed from reading a light meter, composing a picture, manipulating lighting, and so forth. A teaching strategy might start with how to take a picture and then how to develop the film to increase the student's interest and motivation. Thus, basing the sequence first on interest rather than a logical sequence might heighten the learner's motivation for learning.

World-Related Sequencing

Suppose you are developing a unit of instruction for automobile salespeople on the features of a new car model. Do you start at the front of the car and move to the back in your presentation? Or do you begin by describing what the drivers see when they approach the car, then what happens when they enter the door, start the car, and so on? Or do you describe the different systems in the car, such as all the safety features, the electrical system, and the power system? Obviously, there are several different ways to organize and describe the features of the car for a sales training program. Sequencing the content by walking around the car and viewing it from a driver's perspective might be appropriate for salespeople learning the features so that they can point them out to prospective customers. Describing what the driver sees in sequence is probably most appropriate for the new owner. The third approach of describing the related systems is probably more appropriate for mechanics, who require and use a different conceptualization of a car. The sequencing strategy you select, then, depends largely on the characteristics and needs of the target audience.

Content that represents objects, people, and events is presented in a sequence that is consistent with the real world. Thus, we want a one-to-one correspondence between the sequence of the instruction and the sequence of the objects and events in the real world. Sequencing is typically done according to spatial relations, temporal relations, or physical attributes that occur in the real world (Table 6-2). A unit on a new car for salespeople might group the new features in sequence as they are found while walking around the car. Basing the organization on the physical layout of the car is referred to as *spatial organization*. A mechanic might be more interested in the individual components of each system (electrical, power, etc.). This grouping by related features is referred to as *grouping by physical phenomena*, which is the presentation of similar items together. Finally, a unit organized on an orderly sequence of steps, such as what the driver sees when approaching the car, entering the car, and then starting it, is based on a *temporal sequence*. Temporal sequences use a time line to sequence the content.

Once a sequence is selected, the content is presented in an orderly fashion according to the scheme. For example, if we were using a temporal organization for our new car owners, we would not begin with explaining how to adjust the radio. Rather, we would start with what the driver sees when approaching the car and continue to present the content in the sequence it would occur in the real world (e.g., opening the door, sitting in the seat, putting on a seat belt). Adjusting the radio would come sometime after the key is inserted in the ignition. A spatial organization might begin with the front bumper, then the engine, the tires, the front disk brakes, the door latches, and finally the trunk. The presentation sequence follows an orderly plan from left to right, top to bottom, and so forth. Table 6-2 describes the three sequences for world-related phenomena and a sample sequence using each.

Consider the sequencing of the *Oregon Trail* (1996) computer simulation of a wagon train trip. If we organized the simulation in alphabetical order (temporal), then the students would be searching for food at Chimney Rock *before* they loaded their wagons for departure on the trail in St. Louis, Missouri! A spatial sequencing based on the east-to-west travel along the trail makes much more sense for the computer simulation. A unit on types of rocks might organize the rocks according to

TABLE 6-2

World-related sequencing

Phenomenon	Example/Principle
Spatial	Left to right, top to bottom, north to south Describe a plant starting with the flower and moving toward the roots in sequence
Temporal	Historical; first, second, third, etc.; fast to slow When describing the mailing options at the post office, begin with the fastest and proceed to the slowest When describing how to give an insulin injection, describe the steps in sequence
Physical	Roundness, hardness, large to small, color, smoothness When teaching the different types of wines, group them by color (e.g., white, red, blush)

their hardness or softness (physical). The unit, then, might start with the softest rocks and progress to the hardest rocks. Such a sequencing scheme is based on naturally occurring physical attributes. Following a world-related scheme for sequencing provides a concrete organization that reflects the sequence of the content as it exists in nature.

Concept-Related Sequencing

Content can also be sequenced in a manner consistent with how we organize the world conceptually or logically. Posner and Strike (1976) present four schemes for sequencing conceptual content (Table 6-3). First is *class relations*, which groups things or events (i.e., concepts) that are similar. The recommended sequence is to teach the concept of the class first (i.e., personal computers) and then the individual class members. For example, a unit on computers might start with a description of the general concept of a computer (e.g., input, output, central processor) before moving on to specific types of computers (e.g., mainframe, mini, PC). In an instructor course on database programming, an instructor would begin by teaching the concept "database" before discussing specific types of databases such as hierarchical, relational, and multidimensional databases.

A second concept-sequencing scheme, *propositional relations*, prescribes teaching the relationship between propositions before teaching the proposition. An application of this principle is the sequence for teaching the relationship among volume, temperature, and pressure of an ideal gas (Boyle's law). A prescribed sequence might be to illustrate a variety of different volume, temperature, and pressure conditions to illustrate relationships between the three variables before teaching Boyle's law.

TABLE 6-3
Concept-related sequencing

Phenomenon	Example/Principle
Class relations	Teach characteristics of a class before teaching members of the class Teach concept of central tendency before teaching about mean, mode, and median
Propositional relations	Provide examples first, then the proposition Show students examples of metal expansion (cookie sheet, bridge on a hot day, etc.), and then explain that metal expands when heated
Sophistication	Begin with concrete or simple and then proceed to abstract or complex concepts Teach the concepts of mean, mode, and median before teaching analysis of variance
Logical prerequisite	Teach the logical prerequisite concepts first Teach the concept of the mean before teaching the concept of standard deviation

What Do Procedures, Chains, and Learners Have in Common?

Let's assume you are an instructional designer working on a particular instructional design project. You have completed many of the design tasks discussed in the chapters of this book including needs assessment, learner analysis, task analysis, and objective development. The primary goal that you identified for the students describes a procedural task. At some point in the design process you will have to decide how the instruction you design will be sequenced. Will the instructional sequence "start at the beginning" or "go from simple to complex"? Will the learners structure their own instructional sequence or will the instruction be sequenced using some other approach?

A classic approach to sequencing was described by Gilbert (1962) in his discussion of *mathetics*. Mathetics as a technology of instruction was a pioneering effort to systematically apply reinforcement theory in order to help students master instructional content and develop skills. A well-known aspect of mathetical procedures related to sequencing is that of "backward" chaining.

But first what is a chain? A *chain* is a procedure that requires the performance of a sequence of tasks including the condition that the performance of each task depends on the outcome of the previous task (Mechner, 1971). Classic examples of chains include learning how to tie your shoes, solving mathematical problems such as long division, or writing a computer program.

Let's consider the task of students learning to successfully use a word-processing system. In particular, the goal is to create and print a word-processing document. The "basic" tasks involved include loading the word-processing software, creating and naming a file, entering text and numeric information, editing the entered information, and printing the word-processing document. A typical instructional sequence for the word-processing task would be to order the tasks in the order listed. However, we could sequence differently using Gilbert's idea of "starting the students at the terminal acts of mastery." In the word-processing example, the first step in the instructional sequence would be printing the document. The next step would be editing the entered information and then printing the document. The next step in the instructional sequence is entering text and numeric information, editing entered information, and printing the information, and so on. The general idea is to start with the final goal and always make each new subtask lead directly to the goal. This mathetical procedure is referred to as *backward chaining* (Markle, 1969). It should be noted that the learner always goes forward through the performance sequence to the goal. The backward chaining only refers to the method used in the design process for sequencing the instruction. One argument for sequencing the instruction using backward chaining is that the learner always masters the terminal act in each step of the instructional sequence, and this type of sequencing helps learners maintain their motivation.

Gilbert, T. F. (1962). Mathetics: The technology of education. *Journal of Mathetics*, *1*, 7-73.

Markle, S. M. (1969). *Good frames and bad: A grammar of frame writing*. New York: Wiley.

Mechner, F. (1971). Complex cognitive behavior: The teaching of concepts and chains. In M. D. Merrill (Ed.), *Instructional Design Readings* (pp. 264-284). Englewood Cliffs, NJ: Prentice Hall.

Gary J. Anglin is associate professor and program coordinator of the Instructional Systems Design program at the University of Kentucky. He teaches courses in instructional design and technology and consults with private sector organizations. His current research interests are in the areas of visual learning and the design and delivery of distance-learning programs.

The third concept-sequencing scheme is to organize the content by sophistication. Examples of *concept sophistication* are the continuums of concrete to abstract and simple to complex. The prescription is to start with concrete, simple, or precise concepts and then proceed to abstract, complex, and imprecise concepts. For example, a chemistry instructor might start a unit with an explanation of a simple compound such as salt before discussing ionic bonding (concrete to abstract).

The fourth concept-sequencing scheme is *logical prerequisite*, which prescribes that concepts necessary to understand another concept be taught first. In chemistry, an instructor would need to teach the concept of a chemical reaction before introducing the concept of an enzyme that hastens a chemical reaction.

Suppose you are developing a unit on pests for a firm that specializes in pest management for the agricultural business. One of the objectives requires the learners to identify the different types of pests, including insects, plants, fungi, nematodes, and viruses. The unit might begin with a definition of pest (class relations) and then provide examples of the different types of pests (class members). The remainder of the unit might be organized by beginning with the simplest, concrete pests (e.g., weeds) and proceeding to the more complex and abstract types of pests (e.g., viruses, bacteria) based on the sophistication of the concepts. In the section on insects, an objective might require the learner to explain the relationship between the weather (temperature) and the developmental stages of insects. Before the learners read the section on this relationship, you would present information on the life cycle (e.g., egg, larva, pupa, and adult) of insects (logical prerequisite). Examples would then be organized showing the different life cycles of the insects in relation to the temperature. Finally, the learners would receive information about the relationship between temperature and insect development (propositional relations).

The sequence of a unit of instruction may use strategies from each of the three sequencing schemes—learning related, world related, and concept related—identified by Posner and Strike (1976). The actual decision is based first on the characteristics of the learner and then on the nature of the content.

ELABORATION THEORY SEQUENCING

To determine the sequence of the instruction, the elaboration theory makes a distinction between the types of expertise the learner will develop (English & Reigeluth, 1996). Content expertise describes instruction that will help the learner master a body of knowledge such as chemistry or management. Task expertise describes a unit that will help the learner become an expert at a task such as using a bow and arrow, completing a tax form, or solving a mathematical story problem. Let's examine the sequencing schemes for each type of expertise.

Content Expertise Sequencing

A conceptual or theoretical elaboration sequence is used for developing content expertise. The *conceptual sequence* arranges concepts according to their superordinate, coordinate, and subordinate relationships. For example, in a statistics course, a superordinate concept would be measures of central tendency. The coordinate concepts would be mean, mode, and median. Subordinate concepts would include scores and sum. A *theoretical elaboration sequence* organizes the content in much the same way a researcher might have followed to discover an idea. For example, when teaching Boyle's law in an introductory chemistry class, we might start with several observations of gases expanding when heated. Then, we might introduce learners to a computer-based animation that allows them to observe the pressure in a vessel as they increase and decrease the temperature. This sequence follows the recommendation by Reigeluth (1987) for starting with the readily observable and then proceeding to the more detailed and complex aspects of the theory or discovery.

Task Expertise Sequencing

The *elaboration theory sequence* for teaching tasks uses the simplifying conditions method. Sequencing for a task should start with the simplest task and proceed to the more complex task. For example, when training bank tellers, we might start with a simple task such as how to accept a deposit of cash into a savings account. Next, we might show the tellers how to check the balance of a checking account. After they know how to check the balance of an account, we could show them how to check the balance and then cash a check if there are adequate funds. Teaching these naïve learners how to assess a loan application or how to react in a robbery are more complex tasks and would come near the end of the training rather than at the beginning.

FROM OBJECTIVES TO SEQUENCING

Your task analysis will provide a general outline, whereas the classification of your objectives in the expanded performance-content matrix (see Chapter 5) will identify the types of content in your task analysis. Based on your content and performance, you can select a sequencing strategy for each objective. If your unit is primarily concerned with teaching a procedure (e.g., how to tie knots for fly fishing), you might use the same sequencing strategy for the total unit, such as arranging the notes from simple to most difficult and then presenting the steps in a temporal sequence.

SUMMARY

1. Once you have completed your task analysis and written the objectives, you are ready to begin designing the instruction by determining the most appropriate sequence for presenting the information.
2. Posner and Strike (1976) suggest three sequencing strategies based on how objects or events occur in the real world, concepts and their relationships to other concepts, and the interests and needs of the learner. Organizing the content according to one of these schemes provides a systematic method for presenting the content that is likely to match the learner's expectations.
3. The elaboration theory suggests sequencing content based on whether the learner is developing task expertise or concept expertise. Concept expertise sequencing presents the logical relationships between the concepts or presents the content in a sequence similar to what one might have used to discover the idea. Task expertise sequencing proceeds from the simplest to the more complex tasks.

THE ID PROCESS

The output of this step of the instructional design process is a sequencing of your objectives. If your unit is of sufficient complexity, you might use multiple sequencing strategies. For example, you might start with a few basic concepts sequenced by order of interest, then use a temporal approach for a procedure, introduce some additional concepts sequenced according to class relations, and finally end with a series of rules presented according to difficulty.

You will use your sequencing strategy to design the instructional strategies and finally as input for developing the instructional materials. The sequencing strategy creates a high-level outline that corresponds to the roman numerals I, II, III, IV, and so on of your task analysis.

APPLICATION

Assume that you have contracted with a paint store franchise to develop a training program for new employees on how to mix (e.g., tint) paints. Your task analysis has produced the following objectives:

> After completing this unit of instruction, the learner will correctly distinguish between a paint tint and a paint base.
> Given a painting problem, the learner will correctly select the correct type of paint base for a task.

Given a stock color, the learner will demonstrate how to select the appropriate amount of tint.

Given a tinted base, the learner will correctly demonstrate how to shake the paint.

Develop a sequencing strategy.

ANSWERS

There are several options for sequencing these objectives. We chose to sequence the fourth objective first (using interest as a guide) as it seems we are all fascinated by the mechanical shaker in a paint store! The remaining three objectives were sequenced according to a temporal plan, that is, the sequence performed or used.

Given a tinted base, the learner will correctly demonstrate how to shake the paint.

After completing this unit of instruction, the learner will correctly distinguish between a paint tint and a paint base.

Given a painting problem, the learner will correctly select the correct type of paint base for a task.

Given a stock color, the learner will demonstrate how to select the appropriate amount of tint.

QUALITY MANAGEMENT

Our quality check at this stage of the design process focuses on the objectives and task analsysis. First, as you sequence the objectives, you need to check each objective for clarity. Does it communicate the intended outcomes? Does the objective include the needed parts (i.e., verb and content, conditions, and criteria for behavioral objectives)? Is the objective measureable? Second, as you sequence the objectives, you can review the task analysis to ensure that it is adequate. That is, does the analysis include the required information for the sequencing strategy? For example, if you are using an identifiable prerequisite strategy, are those prerequistes identified in the task analysis?

SAMPLE DESIGN PLAN

SEQUENCING CONTENT—TEMPORAL RELATION

It wasn't difficult to decide on a temporal relation sequencing scheme for this instruction. The task analysis was quite procedural in nature, and attaining those objectives depends on proceeding through an orderly sequence of steps—tasks must be determined before subtasks, and so forth. I wanted the instruction to reflect the real world. There was some flexibility in when to introduce the priority/time-frame matrix. I could have introduced it right after the tasks were written, then regressed a bit to generating the subtasks, and returned again to the matrix. I decided against that, however, because I also wanted to stick close to the learning-related sequencing scheme of familiar to novel. So, I dealt with breaking down tasks into subtasks first, then on to the less familiar strategies of assigning criticality and due dates using the priority/time-frame matrix. The piece on using the PDA to prioritize project tasks was presented last for a couple of reasons: (1) learners needed a good understanding of how to prioritize and sequence tasks before using those features on the PDA, and (2) although the university provides every student with a PDA, using it still represents a level of novelty best left to the end of the instruction.

REFERENCES

English, R. E., & Reigeluth, C. M. (1996). Formative evaluation research on sequencing instruction with elaboration theory. *Educational Technology and Research Journal, 44,* 23–41.

Gagné, R. M. (1985). *Conditions of learning and theory of instruction* (4th ed.). New York: Holt, Rinehart and Winston.

Oregon Trail. (1996). [Computer software package.] Minneapolis: MECC.

Posner, G. J., & Strike, K. A. (1976). A categorization scheme for principles of sequencing content. *Review of Educational Research, 46,* 665–690.

Reigeluth, C. M. (1987). Lesson blueprints based on the elaboration theory of instruction. In C. M. Reigeluth (Ed.), *Instructional theories in action: Lessons illustrating selected theories and models.* Hillsdale, NJ: Erlbaum.

Designing the Instruction: Strategies

GETTING STARTED

You are developing an introductory course on management information systems (MIS) for a company. Your task analysis has identified three different types of databases *(concepts)* and information on how to determine which database is appropriate for the user's data *(rules)*. The next step is to design the strategies for teaching the concepts and rules.

The concepts include relational, hierarchical, and multidimensional databases. You have also identified a total of seven rules that will help a user determine which database is most appropriate for the task. In your task analysis, you have identified one excellent example of an existing database for each of the three that you will include in the unit. You also have two or more examples of each rule. How would you design the initial presentation and generative strategy for this instruction?

QUESTIONS TO CONSIDER

"What is the best way to teach a fact, a concept, a rule, a procedure, an interpersonal skill, or an attitude?"

"How can I make the instruction meaningful?"

"How can I teach an objective that focuses on interpersonal skills?"

"What is the best way to present the content so that each learner will master the objectives?"

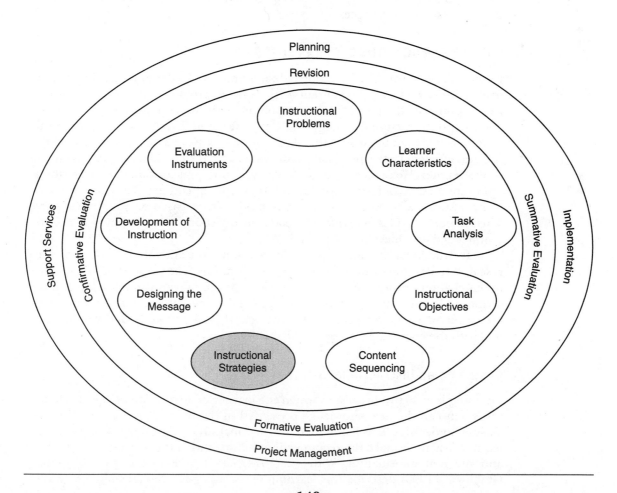

Decisions on the design of the instruction are made at two levels. The first decision is the *delivery strategy*, which describes the general learning environment. General learning environments can range from a typical lecture presentation to a highly interactive multimedia or web-based lesson. These strategies are often classified according to the *degree of individualization*. Individualized instruction presents the content (or objectives) to each student at an appropriate rate for the individual. Thus, one student might be on unit 1 while another student is on unit 5. A *group-paced approach* is the typical classroom lecture course with scheduled examinations that all students take at the designated times.

The second decision is the *instructional strategy*, which prescribes sequences and methods of instruction to achieve an objective. These prescriptions provide guidance on how to design instructional sequences, and they are generalizable to a number of delivery strategies. These prescriptions are determined by the type of content and performance specified in the objectives (see Chapter 5). This chapter presents instructional strategies for each cell of the expanded performance-content matrix presented in Chapter 5.

WHY INSTRUCTIONAL STRATEGIES?

Prior to this stage of the instructional design process, the designer has identified an instructional problem, the content to correct the problem, and objectives for the instruction. The design of the instruction includes the sequencing of the content and the preinstructional strategy (see Chapters 6 and 8). The next element in the process is to design the instructional strategies. Our primary goal is to design effective and efficient instruction that produces reliable results each time it is presented to the learner. We achieve this goal by developing prescriptions that describe an optimum method of instruction for different types of content. These prescriptions or heuristics are based on research; you modify them based on your experiences. This chapter provides heuristics to answer the question, "How do I present the content needed to achieve this objective?"

Instructional design uses findings from educational and psychological research to develop sound instructional applications. The prescriptions presented in this chapter provide a foundation on which you should add and develop new prescriptions based on new research and your experience with each. The prescriptions are based on a generative-learning (Wittrock, 1974, 1989) approach that is consistent with the constructivist view (Lebow, 1994).

Designing an Instructional Strategy

Learning is an active process in which the learner constructs meaningful relationships between the new knowledge presented in the instruction and the learner's existing knowledge. A well-designed instructional strategy prompts or motivates the learner to actively make these connections between what the learner already knows and the new information. Wittrock (1974, 1989) and others (Jonassen, 1985; Grabowski, 1996) describe this learning process as *generative learning*. The advantages of generative learning are the learner's deeper understanding and longer retention of what is learned.

Foundations for the Prescriptions

Craik and Lockhart (1972) suggest that a learner can process new information on a continuum that ranges from phonemic to semantic processing. For example, in one study a researcher might ask one group to read through a passage and put an X through every *e* on the page. She might tell a second group that they will have a test on the passage when they finish. The first group, the one marking the *e*s, would process the material at a *phonemic* level; that is, they are looking for *e*s and not reading for meaning. The second group will most likely read the material for a greater depth of meaning to achieve a higher test score (especially if they are offered a reward for the performance). They will try to relate the new material to what they already know. This second group is said to process the material at a *semantic*, or deeper, level of processing. This type of processing produces meaningful learning.

Processing the new information at a deeper level allows the learner to relate the information to several existing ideas and generate more meaningful relationships. Thus, stronger memory traces are created that make the information more resistant to forgetting. One of the goals of an instructional strategy, then, is to design the instruction so that the learner is motivated to generate or construct these meaningful relationships. The design should activate the existing knowledge structures (i.e., recall of prior knowledge) and then assist the learner in altering and encoding the new structures.

This cognitive approach to instructional design is different from the traditional *mathemagenic approach*, which attempted to control the learner by manipulating the instructional materials. The mathemagenic approach was first suggested by Rothkopf (1960, 1996). Its most frequent implementation was the insertion of adjunct questions either before or after a paragraph. The results with a mathemagenic approach were typically rote learning or very shallow levels of processing (Jonassen, 1985).

As an alternative to the mathemagenic approach, Jonassen (1988) identified four different information-processing strategies a learner can use to promote deeper processing. Designers can embed these strategies into the instruction to motivate the learner to process the new information in a meaningful way. Following are descriptions of the four strategies.

Generative Strategies

The four generative categories identified by Jonassen (1988) are recall, integration, organizational, and elaboration.

- The first, *recall*, is helpful for learning facts and lists for verbatim recall. Specific learning strategies that facilitate recall include repetition, rehearsal (e.g., mental practice), review, and mnemonics.

- The second type, *integration* strategies, are useful for transforming information into a more easily remembered form. Strategies that help the learner transform new content include *paraphrasing*, which requires learners to describe the new material in their own words, and generating questions or examples from the new information.
- The third type of strategy, *organizational*, helps the learner identify how new ideas relate to existing ideas. Sample strategies include *analyzing key ideas*, which requires the learner to identify the key ideas and then interrelate them; outlining; and categorizing. West, Farmer, and Wolff (1991) suggest the use of tables for categorizing and integrating new information (Table 7-1). In this example, the learner completes the table by describing the type of cut each blade makes as part of the integration process.
- The fourth strategy type is *elaboration*, which requires learners to add their ideas (elaborations) to the new information. Strategies that facilitate elaboration include the generation of mental images, creating physical diagrams, and sentence elaborations.

PRESCRIPTIONS FOR INSTRUCTIONAL STRATEGIES

The following prescriptions are useful as basic guides for developing instructional strategies to achieve each of the content-performance types in Table 7-2. This expanded content-performance matrix was first described in Chapter 5. Each instructional objective for a unit is classified into one of the cells based on the type of content the objective treats (fact, concept, principle, procedure, interpersonal skill, or attitude) and the type of performance the learner must demonstrate (recall or application). Prescriptions are provided for each cell or type of objective/performance to use in developing the strategies.

Recall performance relies on rote memorization of the content. For example, the learner would recall a fact, state the definition of a concept, state a rule, list the steps of a procedure, describe a type of interpersonal behavior (e.g., how to deal with a domineering individual), and state a previously described example of a behavior indicating an attitude. Application performance requires the learner to apply the content (e.g., concept, principle) to a new situation or problem. For

TABLE 7-1
Categorization table

Saw Blade	Type of Cut
Cross cut	
Rip	
Hollow ground planer	
Combination	

⬭ **Expert's Edge**

How to Fit 25 Days of Training into Three

The training team at Perfect Software Corporation (not its real name) had a problem: it was December 2000, and the rollout of PSC's new software system for collaborative workgroups was scheduled for February 1. On that date, all PSC field engineers would assemble at headquarters for their annual three-day Field Service Convention. The training team's mandate was to get all 175 field engineers trained in how to troubleshoot the new system.

Using the classical methods of job task analysis, the team had identified well over 200 troubleshooting procedures. Details of each procedure varied based on the way the software system was installed on a client's network of mainframes. The team could see the disaster coming: at the convention, they would have time to teach perhaps two dozen procedures, at most. Months of agonizing service problems would result, and the hotline would be overwhelmed with calls from field service technicians. Not a pretty picture!

I was called in to see if PLATO could help automate the training. But it soon became clear that a computer-based training solution teaching over 200 procedures would be overwhelmingly large and expensive and would take months too long to develop. There had to be a better way.

After a little dialog, a few additional facts emerged:

- The new system consisted of 10 major modules. Clients would install them on their mainframe networks in different ways.
- Almost all of the procedures involved failures or conflicts of communication between the modules.
- The field technicians were already certified network engineers, with experience in troubleshooting network problems.

The principles of problem solving, grounded in cognitive psychology, looked like they might apply here, I thought. One of these principles is that expert problem solving is the ability to manipulate a *mental model* of the system to predict what kinds of faults *could* cause the observed symptoms.

I reasoned that our instructional strategy should focus on the mental model, not the individual procedures. The strategy had three basic steps:

1. Teach the technicians the functions of each kind of system module and how the modules communicate when performing various tasks.
2. Point out that in a client's installation, any module could reside on any mainframe in a network, and more than one instance of a module was allowed in order to assure fast performance. In short, we would teach how the system worked normally.
3. Finally, we would give the technicians practice in manipulating their mental models of the system to predict probable causes of symptoms. In

other words, the technicians would be asked to predict and explain how and why the system behaves when it doesn't work. We would be careful to select a range of symptoms that would involve every kind of communication and every kind of communication fault possible for each communication. A few of the symptoms would be used as case studies to illustrate, and the rest would be used in practice and tests.

The team estimated that this training could easily be completed by the end of the second day of the conference. That would leave the third day for proficiency testing, certification on the new system, and remedial tutoring as needed.

Not only did this instructional strategy save training time, but also it solved another problem: the product was expected to evolve right up to product release, so the details of the more than 200 troubleshooting procedures were not stable. Visions of being overwhelmed by last-minute revisions to the training concerned the team. By emphasizing the basic structure of the system, however, last-minute training updates could be expected to be minimal. Since technicians could practice with a stand-alone real installation that could be "broken" as needed for training, training materials didn't need to include these details. Furthermore, it was likely that in the future, technicians could easily master product upgrades with *no* further procedure training: only a brief orientation to new features would be needed.

Rob Foshay is vice president for instructional design and cognitive learning for PLATO Learning, a major provider of instructional software solutions for adults and young adults. His 30 years of experience in educational technology have included teaching, technology management, instructional design, and human performance technology at the secondary and postsecondary levels, and in industry.

example, an application for a concept (e.g., herbivore) would be to identify new examples as either belonging to the class (e.g., a cow) or not belonging to the class (e.g., a lion). Application objectives for rules and procedures would require the learner to apply the rule or procedure to solve a problem, explain an instance, or

TABLE 7-2
Expanded performance-content matrix

Content	Performance	
	Recall	Application
Fact		
Concept		
Principles and rules		
Procedure		
Interpersonal		
Attitude		

complete a task. For example, we could ask the learner to list the steps for loading film into a camera (recall) or we could ask the learner to demonstrate how to load film into a camera (application).

The remainder of this chapter presents a series of heuristics based on the research literature. *Heuristics* represent a problem-solving strategy, rather than a set of rules, that allows for a flexible approach that you can modify with each new experience. Thus, we encourage you to develop your own set of heuristics to expand and modify based on experience and your interpretation of the research literature.

These prescriptions represent a number of heuristics based on behavioral and cognitive research for each of the content-performance matrix cells in Table 7-2. A prescription is designed for each of your objectives based on the type of performance (e.g., recall or application) and content and is included as part of the instructional design plan. Each prescription has a minimum of two parts: (1) a description of how the information is initially presented to the learner and (2) the generative strategy to increase the depth of processing. The initial presentation is a means of structuring the information in your task analysis for the learner in a form that facilitates learning. Design of the initial presentation must consider what information is needed (e.g., definitions, examples, cues, steps) to achieve the objective and how best to present it (e.g., model, pictures, narrative). The generative strategy incorporates one of the four groups of strategies identified by Jonassen (1985) to help the learner make the necessary connections between existing knowledge and the new knowledge.

Prescriptions for Teaching Facts

A *fact* is a statement of association between two things (e.g., "The earth is 92.96 million miles from the sun."). Facts can only be recalled—they have no specific application (see Table 7-2). If an objective is classified as factual content and the performance is recall, then the prescriptions in Table 7-3 describe how to present the fact to the learner for optimum learning.

For concrete facts, the initial presentation should provide the student with experience with the objects of the fact (see Table 7-3). For example, to teach the fact that tomato sauce is red, we might open a can of tomato sauce and let each learner see the color. When teaching abstract facts, the designer should first attempt to find a concrete representation of the fact (e.g., a picture or other artifact) for the initial presentation. To teach the learner that the capital of Indiana is Indianapolis, we might present a map of Indiana with only Indianapolis identified. The map forms a concrete representation of the fact.

Applicable generative strategies for learning facts are rehearsal–practice and the development of mnemonics (see Table 7-3). A *rehearsal–practice strategy* might involve covertly rehearsing by simply repeating the fact mentally, overtly practice writing the fact, or answering questions related to the fact. *Mnemonics* are devices that help recall facts. For example, photography students must often learn the primary colors and their complements (red–cyan, blue–yellow, and green–magenta).

TABLE 7-3
Example fact strategies

Factual Content	Example	Initial Presentation and Generative Strategy
Concrete facts	Macintosh apples are red.	Show a Macintosh apple and ask for the color. Allow for practice/rehearsal by showing the color and asking which apple is that color, or by naming the apple and asking for its color.
Abstract facts	The airport code for Memphis is MEM.	Show luggage tag with *MEM* and explain it indicates *Memphis*. Allow for practice/rehearsal by showing tag or the word *Memphis* and asking for the city or code.
Abstract facts	It's best to wear safety goggles when hammering.	Show students a picture or model of someone hammering and wearing safety goggles. Have student explain why this safety rule is important.
Lists	The lines of the musical staff are EGBDF.	Show a musical staff with each line labeled. Provide students with the mnemonic to practice, "Every Good Boy Does Fine."

A simple mnemonic (*red cars by General Motors*) will assist the learner in recalling the colors later. Mnemonics can be generated by the learner ("Can you think of a picture that will help you remember that cotton is the main export of Egypt?"), or the instruction can provide directions on how to use a mnemonic ("You can use the phrase, '*My very eccentric mother just sent us ninety parakeets*' to help you remember the order of the planets from the sun."). Another useful approach is elaborative interrogation (Woloshyn, Paivio, & Pressley, 1994), which asks the learner to explain why a fact is true. For example, if we are teaching students that they must wear safety goggles in the work area, we might ask them to explain why it is important for them to wear the goggles. Answering this question requires them to relate this new fact to knowledge they already know, which is a generative activity.

Let's return to our earlier example of wood fasteners (see Chapter 4) and assume that we are developing a unit of instruction for employees of a newly opened hardware store. One of the objectives is to teach the fact that most screws are made of steel. To teach this fact, the strategy might start with a steel screw followed by the statement that screws are made from steel. Our instructional strategy, then, gives the fact (screws are made from steel) and a concrete representation of the fact (the steel screw). Note that we are not teaching the concept of a screw; rather, we are teaching a fact of its composition. Our generative strategy might involve having the learner write this fact 10 times on a sheet of paper (practice) or explaining why screws are often made from steel (elaborative interrogation).

Prescriptions for Teaching Concepts

A *concept* is a category used to group similar ideas or things (e.g., jewelry) to organize knowledge. Performance for a concept can be either recall (e.g., state the definition of) or application, such as identifying new examples of the concept (see Table 7-2). Recommended recall strategies for a concept are the same repetition, rehearsal, review, and mnemonics used for a fact. The instructional strategies for application-type performance, summarized in Table 7-4, are described next.

The initial presentation of the concept includes the concept name, definition, and best example (Tennyson & Cocchiarella, 1986) that illustrates the category, such as a diamond ring for the concept *jewelry*. Additional examples of the concept are then presented to refine the category further (necklaces, bracelets, earrings, etc.), as are nonexamples of the concept (e.g., silverware, figurines). For abstract concepts such as in chemistry, models are often used to illustrate the different types of chemical bonds. Similarly, a number of Ping-Pong balls can be glued together to illustrate the concept of *hole* in a chemical structure.

If the purpose of the objective is simply to remember the concept (e.g., "define herbivore"), then the same generative strategies recommended for a fact are applicable to the recall of a concept. Students could use a rehearsal–practice strategy or develop a mnemonic to help them recall the definition of the concept.

Both integration and organization strategies are useful for facilitating generative learning of concepts for application. An integrative strategy might have the learners generate new examples and nonexamples of the concept by making two columns on a piece of paper and writing examples in one column and nonexamples in the other. Another integration strategy is practice in determining whether new instances are examples or nonexamples of the concept. For example, provide students with a tool catalog and have them circle examples of all the wrenches. Students would need to descriminate between wrenches and pliers, both of which are used to grip nuts and bolts. Organizational strategies include analysis of key ideas, categorization, and cognitive mapping. A strategy to induce the learners to analyze key ideas might ask them to identify the features (critical attributes) that define the concept. The instruction could direct the learner to use a categorization strategy by presenting the learners with a list of examples and nonexamples. The learners would identify those items that are examples. Finally, the instruction could encourage the learners to develop a cognitive map to determine how this new concept

TABLE 7-4
Example concept strategies

Concept Example	Strategy	Initial Presentation and Generative Strategy
Open-end wrench	Integration	Present the student with the concept name, definition, and best example of the concept. Provide the student with a catalog of tools, and ask the student to identify examples of open-end wrenches.
Box wrench	Organizational	Present the student with the concept name, definition, and best example of the concept. Ask the student to list the characteristics of a box wrench and compare the box wrench to other wrenches and pliers.

relates to concepts they have already learned. Table 7-4 provides examples of how a designer might use an integration and organizational strategy to design the instruction to teach two concepts.

Let's consider another objective from the training unit example on wood fasteners. The objective is to have the learners identify various types of screws. Our initial presentation would select the one best example (e.g., a flat-head wood screw) and present it as an example of a wood screw. The presentation would then include several variations of types (e.g., oval-head, round-head, and Phillips-head) and sizes of screws. Nonexamples could include bolts and sheet-metal screws.

An organizational strategy was selected from Table 7-4 for this objective because the intent of the objective was to have learners identify a screw if a customer needed a replacement for a stripped one or additional screws of the same or different size. Organizational strategies help the learner transform the new information into a more easily remembered form by having the learner classify new examples. This approach matches our objective of having the student identify examples of screws. Our instructional strategy, then, is to send the learners through the store and have them select 25 different packages of screws, which will require the students to actively process the content and classify each package as either a screw or a nonscrew.

Prescriptions for Teaching Principles and Rules

A *principle* or *rule* is a statement that expresses a relationship between concepts such as "The sum of the angles in a triangle is 180 degrees." Performance for learning a principle or rule can be either recall or application (Table 7-2). Principle application includes both explanation of the *effect* of the rule and prediction of *consequences* based on the rule.

There are two general approaches to principle and rule learning (Markle, 1969). The first, *rule–eg*, includes a statement of a rule followed by several examples. Using the rule–eg approach, the instruction begins with a statement of the rule or principle ("The sum of the angles in a triangle is 180 degrees."), and then provides several triangles with the angle measurements listed and summed. A second, more active learning approach is *eg–rule*, which provides the learner with several examples (the triangles with their angles summed) and asks the learner to generate the rule (Table 7-5).

If the purpose of the objective is simply to recall the principle or rule, the initial presentation strategy would be either an example or demonstration of the rule for the learner. The generative strategies are the same as those recommended for a fact. For example, the learner might employ a covert rehearsal strategy of repeating the rule or an elaboration strategy of explaining why the rule is true.

Integrative, organizational, and elaboration strategies can facilitate generative learning of principles and rules. Using an *integrative* strategy, the learners can paraphrase the principle using their own words or generate examples of different types of triangles, for instance, to illustrate the principle. An *organizational* strategy might

TABLE 7-5
Example principle and rule strategies

Rule Example	Strategy	Initial Presentation and Generative Strategy
Brush painting requires 1/3 more labor than spray painting.	Rule–eg and integration	State the rule and then show examples. Have the learner complete a table illustrating the required time for each painting method.
A higher gear-ratio is harder to pedal.	Eg–rule and integration	Have the student try pedaling three different gear ratios. Ask the student the relationship between the three gears. Have the learner complete a table indicating the relative effort needed to pedal each gear ratio.
Fusion welding is used when the base metal and weld metal colors must match.	Eg–rule and organizational	Show examples of fusion welding and bronze welding. Ask the student to generate the rule. Ask the student to identify the visual difference between the two. Have the student develop a decision tree for selecting the welding process.
Metal expands when heated.	Eg–rule and elaboration	Show an example of a cookie sheet warping in an oven. Ask the student to explain what has happened. Have the student explain why a bridge has expansion joints. Have the student predict the effect of temperature on the expansion joints.

include having the learners identify key components of the principle and then compare the principle to similar principles (e.g., the number of degrees in a square). An *elaborative* strategy might ask the student to develop a diagram that explains the principle. Another approach is to require the students to develop an argument (e.g., explain why something happened; Wiley & Voss, 1999).

Returning to our example unit on wood fasteners, we find that the next objective is a rule that a nail should be driven through the thinnest piece of wood into the thicker piece. The student will use this rule to explain to customers how to select the size of the nail. Table 7-5 illustrates the use of the rule–eg and eg–rule initial presentation strategies and the use of integration and elaboration generative strategies. The fourth suggestion, eg–rule and elaboration, was selected since this strategy is most similar to the job performance condition of explaining this principle to the customer. An elaboration strategy encourages the learner to add more information to the content, which makes the content meaningful.

The initial presentation of the rule will show several mocked-up pieces of wood nailed together. The learners are then asked to identify which piece of wood to drive the nail into first (eg–rule). An alternative would be to have the learners nail several thin and thick pieces of wood together to observe the results. The *generative* strategy (elaborative) asks the learners to draw a diagram for a customer to explain how to nail a 1″ × 6″ × 6′ fence piece to a 2″ × 4″ fence rail.

Prescriptions for Teaching Procedures

A *procedure* is a sequence of steps the learner performs to accomplish a task such as threading a needle or solving a calculus problem. Like concepts and principles, the performance for a procedure can take the form of recall or application (see Table 7-2). Recall performance requires the learner to list or describe the steps of the procedure, while application requires the learner to demonstrate the procedure. The prescriptions for procedures are summarized in Table 7-6. The following sections describe the strategy design for cognitive procedures and psychomotor procedures.

Cognitive Procedures.   The initial instruction is the demonstration or modeling of the procedure. Since cognitive procedures are not directly observable, we must find a means of representing the procedure for the learner. Worked examples (Table 7-7) are one method used to teach cognitive procedures such as solving a math problem (Sweller & Cooper, 1985; Van Gerven, Paas, van Merriënboer, & Schmidt, 2002; van Merriënboer, 1997). The worked example shows each step of the problem-solving process. A learner studies the problem by working through each step of the example. Then, similar example problems are presented for practice.

If the purpose of the objective is simply to recall the procedure, the initial strategy would be an example. The generative strategies (e.g., recall, rehearsal of step names, mnemonics) are the same as recommended for a fact. For example, you might suggest a verbal mnemonic to help the learner remember either the steps or possibly a rule associated with a step. The generative strategy for an application performance involves two steps. First, the learner must either paraphrase the procedure or use an elaboration strategy to embellish the processes. Second, the

TABLE 7-6
Example procedure strategies

Procedure Example	Strategy	Initial Presentation and Generative Strategy
Removing and installing piston rings	Demonstration, organization, elaboration, practice	While watching a videotape of the process, students are encouraged to take notes on each step. After the videotape, students are encouraged to develop a mental image of the positioning of the piston ring expander for removing and installing the rings. Then, they are encouraged to practice the procedure on an engine.
Calculating the amount of paint needed to paint a house	Demonstration, organization, elaboration, practice	Students are presented with a worked example that illustrates how to calculate the amount needed using the square footage of the house and coverage of the paint. Learners are then encouraged to paraphrase the steps for doing the calculation. Last, they are given three examples and asked to calculate the needed paint. When they complete an example, they compare their work against a worked example of the problem.

TABLE 7-7
Worked example

Problem: In baking a cake, the baker must combine 4 parts of flour with 1 part of milk. This particular cake will use 16 cups of flour. How much milk needs to be added?

Solution: Let's make 4 the number of cups of milk that are needed. It is the unknown quantity. Now let's summarize the problem information in a table.

	Recipe	Baker's Cake
Flour	4 parts	16 cups
Milk	1 part	y cups

Note that to solve the problem, we need equal ratios of milk to flour. Thus,

$1/4 = y/16$

$16 = 4y$

$4 = y$

The baker needs 4 cups of milk.

---

instruction must provide the learner with practice in applying the procedure. In a classroom, the instructor can provide feedback, whereas model answers or checklists for feedback are provided in a self-paced environment.

Psychomotor Procedures. The initial strategy for psychomotor procedures also involves modeling or demonstration of the task. For tasks involving psychomotor skills, the demonstration may need to have motion (e.g., a live demonstration or a videotape), or a series of still pictures may be adequate. Motion is often required for complex psychomotor tasks or when teaching psychomotor tasks to naïve learners. A skilled individual such as an experienced car mechanic may find a series of still pictures (see Figure 8-4) adequate to learn a familiar procedure (e.g., replacing the brake pads on an automobile). A naïve learner who is unfamiliar with the basic skills may find a more realistic demonstration, such as a videotape or streaming video, more beneficial because it helps develop a model for executing the task. The initial learning for a psychomotor procedure is enhanced by encouraging the learner to develop mental images of the procedure and by adding verbal labels to the steps (Anshel & Singer, 1980; Bandura & Jeffery, 1973).

Again, the generative strategy involves two steps. First, the learner is encouraged to develop a mental image of the procedure, paraphrase the procedure, or elaborate on the steps of the procedure (e.g., connecting cues or decisions to each step). Second, the learner is encouraged to practice the procedure. Feedback can be provided by an instructor, samples for comparison, or a checklist. If the objective is recall performance, then the generative strategies (e.g., recall, rehearsal of step names, mnemonics) are the same as those recommended for a fact.

The sample wood fastener unit has an objective of converting the length of a nail given in pennies to inches. The initial presentation is a worked example that illustrates the steps (Table 7-8). The generative strategy involves two steps: (1) ask the learners to paraphrase the procedure, and then (2) provide the learner with five problems to solve. The learners will then compare their answers with a worked example of each problem for feedback.

Prescriptions for Teaching Interpersonal Skills

Interpersonal skills deal with the development of communication skills. Performance for interpersonal skills is either recall or application, with a primary emphasis on application (see Table 7-2). The strategy for interpersonal objectives, based on Bandura's (1977) social learning theory, involves four steps. The first step is the initial instruction that presents the model to the learner. Models of the interpersonal behavior (e.g., how to coach an employee who has difficulty working with other team members) are usually presented as live demonstrations or role plays, videotapes, or printed scenarios. As part of the observation process, the learner's attention may need to be directed to identify key steps of the behavior as a generative activity (Table 7-9).

The second step is for each learner to develop verbal and imaginal models of the behavior. A *verbal model* is derived from the key steps—the process (e.g., modeling) can be paraphrased, or a cognitive map can be developed showing the relationship between the steps. The *imaginal model* is developed either by offering the learner an image (e.g., "Remember how the manager focused the employee's attention on the primary issue?") or by directing the student to develop an image of the behavior.

Third is providing for *mental rehearsal* (covert practice) in executing the skill. Strategies for mental rehearsal can include examples or case studies presented in print or on videotape that prompt the learners to determine how they would respond.

Fourth is *overt practice*, which can include role plays involving two or more learners. Some environments might allow the development of interactive programs that present a situation, allow the learners to select a response, and then show the effects of the response.

If the purpose of the objective is simply to recall the interpersonal skill, the initial strategy would be a videotape or role play. The generative strategies (e.g., rehearsal of the step names, practice in reciting the names, mnemonics) are the same as those recommended for a fact.

The sample unit on wood fasteners includes a unit on sales techniques. One of the unit's objectives is for the student to demonstrate how to greet a customer correctly. The first step of the strategy is for the learner to view a videotape in which an

TABLE 7-8
Wood fastener worked example

Problem: Determine the length in inches of a $9d$ (penny) nail.

Solution: Divide the penny size by 4 and add 0.5 inch.

$$9d \div 4 = 2.25 \text{ inches}$$
$$2.25 + 0.5 = 2.75 \text{ inches}$$

TABLE 7-9
Example interpersonal skills strategies

Interpersonal Skill Example	Strategy	Implementation
Facilitate a group problem-solving meeting	Model	Show students a videotape of a facilitator demonstrating the appropriate behaviors for a group.
	Verbal and imaginal models (organization)	Have students identify the key behaviors and when they are used.
	Mental rehearsal (elaboration)	Provide students with several instances, which require the application of a facilitative behavior, and ask them to imagine how they would react.
	Overt practice	Provide opportunities for each student to facilitate a group as part of a role play.

expert demonstrates how to greet a customer. During a second viewing of the tape, words describing each of the steps for greeting a customer (e.g., making eye contact, smiling, verbal greeting) are superimposed on the video image to cue the student.

The second step is for the learner to develop the verbal and imaginal models. After viewing the videotape, students are asked to paraphrase the process (verbal model). Next, learners are directed to imagine themselves working in the wood fastener department when a customer approaches them. They are then told to visualize the scenario in their minds as to how they would greet the customer (imaginal model).

Mental rehearsal, the third step, is accomplished by presenting the learners with three scenarios with different situations (e.g., you are stocking new screws, you are busy with another customer) and asking them to imagine how they would greet the customer. For the fourth step, the learners are divided into pairs and directed to role-play the different roles of the customer and sales associate as overt practice.

Prescriptions for Teaching Attitudes

An *attitude* consists of a belief and associated behavior or response. The strategy for teaching (changing) attitudes is similar to the strategy for interpersonal objectives. Both are based on Bandura's (1977) social learning theory. The prescription for attitudes is to model the behavior, develop the verbal and imaginal models, use mental rehearsal, and provide for both covert and overt rehearsal (Table 7-10).

The last objective for our sales associates' training concerns an attitude that all nails need to be weighed accurately. If the purchase weighs more than marked, then the store loses money; if the package weighs less than measured, then the customer loses. (Students learned how to weigh the nails in an earlier unit.) The strategy employs the same four steps used for interpersonal skills.

TABLE 7-10
Example attitude strategies

Attitude Example	Strategy	Implementation
Discussion of work projects with others may be giving away proprietary information.	Model	Have two students role-play a casual conversation between two individuals from two different companies in which each describes a problem he or she is having with a work project.
	Develop verbal and imaginal models (organization)	Have students identify the type of information exchanged.
	Mental rehearsal (elaboration)	Provide students with several instances in which they might inadvertently give information away and ask them to imagine how they would react.
	Overt practice	Provide opportunities for each student to practice the appropriate behaviors.

In the first step, the instructor models how the exact weight of the nails is recorded on the sales slip. Second, the learner identifies the consequences of over- and undercharging the customer (verbal model) and imagines the consequences of each action (imaginal model). Third, the learner practices the imaginal model. Fourth, the learner practices the behavior of weighing the nails with an emphasis on marking the sales slip accurately.

S U M M A R Y

1. To design effective instruction, the designer must concentrate on how to present each individual objective in a manner that will help the learner achieve the objective. Designing the instructional strategies is probably the most crucial step in the process and can contribute the most to making the instruction successful. Unfortunately, however, the design of the instructional strategies is often the most neglected step of the instructional design process.

2. Instructional strategies begin with determining the content and performance type of each objective using the expanded content-performance matrix. This classification of the objectives helps the designer identify how the learner is to perform the behavior specified in the objective and the type of content the learner must master. Specific strategies are then prescribed for each cell of the content-performance matrix.

3. There are six categories of content. Facts are associations that learners recall. Concepts are categories learners use to classify similar things or events, such as circles or strikes in baseball. Principles and rules are relationships between two concepts, such as "metal expands when heated." Procedures are are sequences of steps a learner must follow to accomplish a task. Interpersonal skills describe

spoken and nonverbal communications. Attitudes are predispositions we have toward an object, such as wearing safety goggles when using power equipment.

4. Each prescription involves two components. The first component is the initial presentation of the content for the learner. Our preferred form is direct, purposeful experience (concrete) with the content. Typically, the prescriptions recommend either hands-on learning experiences or the use of visuals or representations for abstract ideas.

5. The second component of the prescription is a generative strategy to make the content meaningful and to encourage active processing by the student. The generative strategies include recall, integration, organization, and elaboration. These strategies are then embedded—that is, made a part of the instructional unit—so as to encourage the student to respond actively.

6. The prescriptions presented in this chapter form the basis of a set of heuristics for designing instruction. Each designer should attempt to modify and expand these heuristics based on experience.

7. The following steps describe how to design your instructional strategies:
    a. Review each objective and determine in which cell it best fits in the performance-content matrix.
    b. Refer to the appropriate table of prescriptions in this chapter and select an initial and generative strategy.
    c. Develop the instruction, which consists of the initial presentation and the generative strategy.

THE ID PROCESS

The instructional design product from this step of the process is the strategy design for treating each objective. The instructional strategies provide a guide for developing the instructional materials presented in the sequence you specified in Chapter 6. You use the initial presentation component to direct the development of the basic information for the objective. The generative strategy component provides the active learning aspect of the instruction. Consider the instructional strategy as a blueprint for developing the unit. It should allow you flexibility for creatively presenting the information interestingly, motivationally, and effectively. Designing the instructional strategy requires that you integrate your creative skills with the science of instructional design to create an approach that will help the learner understand and learn the content and skills. Interesting strategies that have the flavor of a real-world application can not only motivate the learner, but make the instruction exciting.

APPLICATIONS

As part of your job, you have been asked to review the design document for a course on decision making. Your review of the objectives for the course indicates that the learners will demonstrate how to use data to make decisions. Several of the objectives focus on different types of decisions (e.g., costs, sales, forecasting) the learners will need to make using available data. As you review the instructional materials, you realize that all the strategies are focused on memorizing either the steps for decision making or memorizing the types of data that are available for managers.

What would you recommend to improve the effectiveness of the instructional strategies in this course?

Your technology company has recently hired a number of young professionals "to pave the way of the future" in information technology. The wise old CEO (she is 31 years old) is genuinely interested in all her employees. Since everyone is paid an excellent salary, she feels that the young staff should be educated in proper investment strategies so they can have a comfortable life. She has *personally* asked you to design an investment-training program and has hired a personal financial consultant as your subject-matter expert.

One of your tasks is to teach about bonds, mutual funds, and stocks. What type of strategy would you design to teach this information?

ANSWERS

There is an obvious discrepancy between the performance described by the objectives—decision making—and the instructional materials, which are using strategies to help the learner memorize the decision-making steps and other information. We assume that the client has already agreed with the problem-solving focus of the objectives. A different set of instructional strategies that will support the development of the decision-making skills is needed. A closer analysis of the objectives would likely indicate that we could classify them as concept, rule, or procedure with application-level performance. Once we have correctly classified the objectives, we can select the appropriate instructional strategies that will develop application performance rather than recall performance.

Bonds, mutual funds, and stocks are concepts. We would select a concept-application strategy so that the employees could identify each type of investment. Our initial presentation would include the name of the concept (e.g., bond), the definition provided by the SME, and a best example of the concept. We would use an integrative strategy that asks the learner to identify new examples of each concept from various investment web sites. This instruction would address the current instructional goal—understanding the facets of investment options. Subsequent units, if required by additional training goals, might then address applications, such as choosing between investment options and buying and selling stocks.

QUALITY MANAGEMENT

The first question to ask is whether the instructional strategies *really* support the development of the behaviors specified in the objectives. The first application problem (i.e., the decision-making course) illustrates instructional strategies that do not support the development of the objectives. Your quality check should compare the strategies against the objectives to determine whether your instruction will develop the appropriate knowledge and skills. Consider, for example, a series of objectives that focus on teaching troubleshooting skills at the application level. The instructional strategies, however, focus on memorizing faults and steps for troubleshooting. This mismatch between the objectives will not help the learners achieve the objectives. If your objectives accurately reflect what is needed to address the problem, then the instructional strategies must be revised. It is more time- and cost-efficient to correct these mistakes now, rather than *after* the materials are developed. The second question to ask is whether the objectives, content, and instructional strategies address the instructional problem you have identified. We are always amazed at how different individuals attempt to influence our design process and begin to move us away from our original purpose. When this deviation occurs, it is often because we have accepted personal viewpoints on what should be included rather than remaining focused on the problem and the instruction needed to solve the problem. This final check of the alignment of your task analysis, objectives, and instructional strategies is needed *before* you begin development of the instructional materials. Changes at this stage are relatively inexpensive compared with major revisions of developed materials. Last, review your instructional strategies and the sequencing. Is the logic of the sequencing still appropriate now that you have designed the instructional strategies? If not, make the needed changes in the sequencing prior to beginning the development work.

SAMPLE DESIGN PLAN

INSTRUCTIONAL STRATEGIES

The objectives are written and I'm ready to design the instruction. Finally, I can fit in the strategies and assessments that have been swimming around in my mind since doing the task analysis. For me as a designer, this is the sweet spot. This is the point in the instructional design process where I can be creative; this is where I can draw on my background in learning theory and instructional design theory to give this instruction some genuine learning power.

All along I have planned for the instruction to be self-paced in a paper or .pdf file format. Furthermore, these concepts aren't too difficult, and, coupled with the opportunity for learners to work independently, this troubles me a bit. I'm concerned that some learners may be tempted to rush through the instruction and miss the opportunity to deeply process these concepts. I'll have to be certain that the strategies reflect authentic time-management problems; adding relevance to the activities should keep the learners motivated as well as strengthen this design. I also decided to drop the first objective; I think those definitions will work better as a pre-instructional strategy than as an instructional objective.

Objective 1

Given a short description of a project, the learner will write a project goal in an acceptable format. *(Procedure/Application)*

Initial Presentation.   A step-by-step description will be used to describe how to write a goal. The examples will be presented within the context established by the preinstructional strategy.

Generative Strategy.   First, the learner will be asked to describe how to write a good goal statement. Second, the learner will be asked to write a goal for three different scenarios.

Objective 2

Given a worksheet, the learner will list at least three tasks associated with the project goal. *(Procedure/Application)*

Initial Presentation.   The process of breaking two travel goals into tasks will be illustrated.

Generative Strategy.   First, the learner will paraphrase the process for identifying tasks. Second, the learner will identify tasks for two different goals.

Objective 3

Given the priority/time-frame matrix and a list of tasks, the learner will accurately classify the degree of criticality for each task. *(Concept/Application)*

Initial Presentation.   The process for classifying tasks according to criticality will be illustrated using the examples developed for the travel example.

Generative Strategy.   First, the learners will paraphrase the process for classifying the priority of tasks. Second, using the project worksheet, the learner will classify project tasks in an example according to criticality by writing the number one (1) beside essential tasks, the number two (2) beside important tasks, and the number three (3) beside noncritical tasks.

Objective 4

Given the priority/time-frame matrix, the learner will sequence the tasks according to due date. *(Procedure/Application)*

Initial Presentation.   The process for using the priority/time-frame matrix to classify birthday-party-planning tasks according to due date will be provided.

Generative Strategy.   First, the learner will summarize the steps for classifying tasks by due date. Second, on the project worksheet, the learner will classify each of the travel project tasks according to due date by writing the word *today* beside tasks that must be done today, *tomorrow* beside tasks that must be done tomorrow, *in one week* beside tasks that must be done within one week, and *specific date* beside tasks that require a specific due date.

Objective 5

The learner will create a priortized to-do list on a PDA. *(Procedure/Application)*

Initial Presentation.   An example of how to create a prioritized task list will be presented with screenshots taken from a PDA.

Generative Strategy.   First, the learner will describe the key steps of creating the prioritized list on a PDA. Second, the learner will use the travel example and create a prioritized class list on a PDA.

REFERENCES

Anshel, M. H., & Singer, R. N. (1980). Effect of learner strategies with modular versus traditional instruction on motor skill learning and retention. *Research Quarterly for Exercise and Sport, 51*, 451–462.

Bandura, A. (1977). *Social learning theory.* Englewood Cliffs, NJ: Prentice Hall.

Bandura, A., & Jeffery, R. W. (1973). Role of symbolic coding and rehearsal processes in observational learning. *Journal of Personality and Social Psychology, 26*, 122–130.

Craik, F. I. M., & Lockhart, R. S. (1972). Levels of processing: A framework for memory research. *Journal of Verbal Learning and Verbal Behavior, 11*, 671–684.

Grabowski, B. L. (1996). Generative learning: Past, present, and future. In D. Jonassen (Ed.), *Handbook of research for educational communication and technology* (pp. 897–918). New York: Macmillan Library Reference USA.

Jonassen, D. H. (1985). Generative learning vs. mathemagenic control of text processing. In D. H. Jonassen (Ed.), *Technology of text: Vol. 2. Principles for structuring, designing, and displaying text* (pp. 9–45). Englewood Cliffs, NJ: Educational Technology Publications.

Jonassen, D. H. (1988). Integrating learning strategies into courseware to facilitate deeper processing. In D. H. Jonassen (Ed.), *Instructional designs for microcomputer courseware* (pp. 151–182). Hillsdale, NJ: Erlbaum.

Lebow, D. (1994). Constructivist values for instructional systems design: Five principles toward a new mindset. *Educational Technology Research and Development, 41*, 4–16.

Markle, S. (1969). *Good frames and bad: A grammar of frame writing.* New York: Wiley.

Rothkopf, E. Z. (1960). The concept of mathemagenic activities. *Review of Educational Research, 40*, 325–336.

Rothkopf, E. Z. (1996). Control of mathemagenic activities. Generative learning: Past, present, and future. In D. Jonassen (Ed.), *Handbook of research for educational communication and technology* (pp. 879–896). New York: Macmillan Library Reference USA.

Sweller, J., & Cooper, G. (1985). The use of worked examples as a substitute for problem solving in learning algebra. *Cognition and Instruction, 2*, 59–89.

Tennyson, R. D., & Cocchiarella, M. J. (1986). An empirically based instructional design theory for teaching concepts. *Review of Educational Research, 56*, 40–71.

Van Gerven, P. W. M., Paas, F. G. W. C., van Merriënboer, J. J. G., & Schmidt, H. G. (2002). Congitive load theory and aging: Effects of worked examples on training efficiency. *Learning and Instruction, 12,* 87–105.

van Merriënboer, J. J. G. (1997). *Training complex cognitive skills.* Englewood Cliffs, NJ: Educational Technology Publications.

West, C. K., Farmer, J. A., & Wolff, P. M. (1991). *Instructional design: Implications from cognitive science.* Englewood Cliffs, NJ: Prentice Hall.

Wiley, J., & Voss, J. F. (1999). Constructing arguments from multiple sources: Tasks that promote understanding and not just memory for text. *Journal of Educational Psychology, 91,* 301–311.

Wittrock, M. C. (1974). A generative model of mathematics learning. *Journal of Research in Mathematics Education, 5,* 181–197.

Wittrock, M. C. (1989). Generative processes of comprehension. *Educational Psychologist, 24,* 345–376.

Woloshyn, V. E., Paivio, A., & Pressley, M. (1994). Use of elaborative interrogation to help students acquire information consistent with prior knowledge and information inconsistent with prior knowledge. *Journal of Educational Psychology, 86,* 79–89.

CHAPTER 8

Designing the Instructional Message

GETTING STARTED

You have worked diligently on an instructional project, including creating the design of the graphics and printed page. At the last minute, your manager decides that your project is just the thing to showcase the training department. He makes arrangements for you to meet with a production house that will transform your document into something to rival a *National Geographic* publication, at least in looks. During your first meeting with the graphic designers, you explain your design scheme with the headings, indentations, and your use of bold and italic text, stressing their importance for communicating the structure of the text. You also stress the importance of keeping the graphics very simple so as not to confuse the learner with too much detail. The graphic designers agree and promise to follow your suggestions.

Two weeks later you receive the page proofs from the production house. After a cursory examination, you can find absolutely no trace of the original structure that you conveyed to the graphic designers. In addition, the artists have turned your carefully crafted drawings into balloon-style cartoons, which detract from the potential dangers of working with the high-voltage electrical equipment. In fact, the unit looks more like a comic book than a copy of *National Geographic* magazine. Having seen the invoice included with the work, you wonder if you should mention the problems to your manager. Assuming that you have your anger and surprise under control, how would you approach this problem and correct it?

"What is the best way to introduce the content to a learner?"

"What is the best way to implement your instructional strategies?"

"How can you cue the learner to the most important information?"

"Should you use pictures with your instruction?"

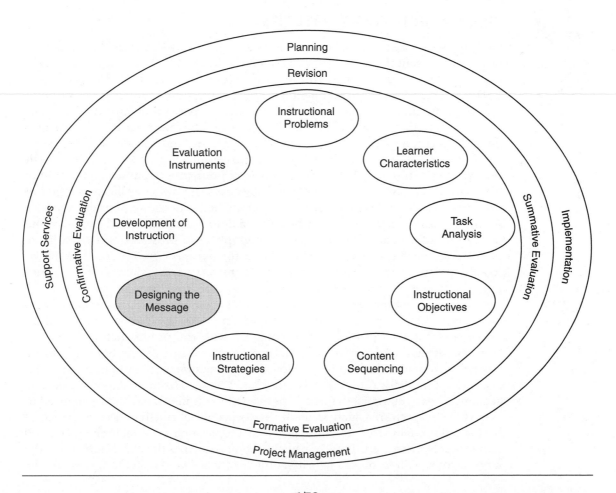

Thus far, we have focused on defining the problem and content, defining the characteristics of our audience, specifying the objectives, and designing the instructional strategies. The next step is to prepare the instructional materials by translating the instructional design plan into a unit of instruction. Translating the plan into an effective instructional unit requires more than simply "writing" the instruction. Effective instruction is developed through carefully structuring and presenting the materials that both engage the learner and signal the learner to the important points. Now that we have determined the content and strategies for the instruction, we must shift our focus to the design of the message (Fleming, 1993).

In this chapter, we divide this message design process into three sections. First is the *preinstructional strategy*, which is a technique for preparing the learner for the instruction. Second are strategies for *signaling* the structure of the text through words and typography. Third is discussion of the use of pictures and graphics in your instructional materials.

PREINSTRUCTIONAL STRATEGIES

Once the sequence for the instruction is established, the designer can begin to focus on how to present the information. Each unit of instruction begins with some form of an introduction that prepares the learner for learning the task. Hartley and Davies (1976) identified four different methods of preinstructional strategies for introducing an instructional unit—the traditional written paragraph introduction (i.e., overview) plus three alternative approaches. Each of the four preinstructional strategies has specific applications for use in creating a better introduction for the unit.

The first preinstructional strategy is a *pretest*, which is a set of questions directly relevant to the instruction. The second type of preinstructional strategy is a set of *objectives*, which often simply restate the objectives the designer has developed or presents them as goal statements describing the behavior the student must master. A third technique is the *overview*, which is similar to a summary. Unlike pretests and objectives, an overview is written as a paragraph(s) of prose rather than a list of items. The fourth preinstructional strategy is the *advance organizer*, which is similar to an overview but written at a higher level of abstraction. A variation of an advance organizer is the *graphic organizer*, which uses a graphic to illustrate the content.

Table 8-1 summarizes the applications and prescriptions derived from Hartley and Davies (1976) for each of these strategies. The "Function" column describes the instructional purpose we want to accomplish with the preinstructional strategy. "Content Structure" describes the nature or length of the content. Some topics are labeled as loosely structured (e.g., "How to sell a vacuum cleaner") because there is not one set method. A highly structured topic (e.g., "How to balance a checking account") has a set of well-defined steps that are easily identified and recognized by experts. A subject area such as math that is primarily rule-based is described as having a dominant structure, as opposed to a topic such as visual literacy, which is more loosely structured. The "Learner" column describes the characteristics of the target audience in terms of maturity or intelligence. The last column, "Task Attrib-

TABLE 8-1

Preinstructional strategies

Strategy	Function	Content Structure	Learner	Task Attributes
Pretests	Alert student to what is expected	Length of the instruction is relatively short and loosely structured	Above-average IQ, older, or more mature learners	Learners should have some familiarity with the content if the questions are to be meaningful.
Behavioral objectives	*Precisely* inform the student of what is expected	Used to preface a passage of fewer than 2,500 words[1]	Middle-ability students	Works best with traditional methods such as lectures.
Overviews	Prepare the learners for the learning task	Little or no structure	Lower-ability students	Facts.
			Higher-ability students	Concepts.
Advance organizer	Conceptual framework needed to clarify content for learner	Should have a dominant structure	Above-average ability, maturity, and sophistication	Factual information.

[1]Klauer (1984).

utes," identifies the learning conditions best suited for this preinstructional strategy. The following sections provide guidelines for developing each type of preinstructional strategy.

Pretests

A pretest used as a preinstructional strategy differs from a pretest used to assess the learner's prior knowledge (see Chapter 10). When used as a preinstructional strategy, a pretest is designed to heighten the student's awareness of the content by serving as cues to the key points. These cues will help the learner identify and focus on the main ideas in the unit of instruction. Pretests work best when the instructional time is relatively short, allowing the learner to remain focused on the questions. Answers are typically not provided to the pretest questions, since the answers are derived from the instructional materials. (Additional guidelines for developing pretest questions are provided in Chapter 10.)

The following pretest might be used with a chapter on measures of central tendency:

Think about the following questions as you read this unit.

1. What are three measures of central tendency?
2. When is it appropriate to use each of the measures?
3. What are the steps to follow when calculating the mean?

Each question is open-ended and serves to make the learner aware of three main points in the chapter. The designer does not expect the learners to answer the questions (if they can, they may not need to complete the unit). Instead, the questions should direct the learner to the key areas identified by the questions.

Pretest Guidelines

1. A preinstructional pretest should be relatively short so as not to delay the start of the instruction.
2. Typically, the questions are open-ended and answered mentally to stimulate the student to think about the answer as he or she reads the content.
3. If there are several objectives for the unit, the pretest items can be a sampling of the objectives rather than an item for each.

Objectives

The use of behavioral objectives has been the subject of much research in recent years (Jegede, 1995; Klauer, 1984; Klein & Cavalier, 1999; McNeil & Alibali, 2000). Davies (1976) has suggested that objectives may even be superfluous with highly designed materials such as computer-assisted instruction and other instructional design products. Another issue is whether students actually know how to use objectives for learning. Klauer's analysis found that learning directions and questions were more effective than specific (e.g., Mager-style) objectives. One possible explanation was that the learners were better able to interpret and understand the implications of the learning directions and questions because they were presented in simpler sentences. Although the general trend continues to be the use of objectives as a preinstructional strategy, the research results suggest they are not as effective for promoting student learning as once thought. However, research and practice strongly support the use of objectives by instructional designers and teachers when designing instruction. And, if learners see over time that test items are directly linked to objectives (see Chapter 11), the orienting influences of the objectives should greatly increase.

Here is an example of the use of objectives as a preinstructional strategy for a unit on job aids:

At the end of this unit, you will

- describe the difference between a job aid and a unit of instruction,
- determine when a job aid might be more appropriate than training, and
- design a job aid.

Objective Guidelines

1. Use a statement that clearly indicates the behavior the student needs to master rather than including the condition and criteria (cf. Klauer, 1984).
2. If there are several objectives for the unit, create more general statements to keep the list shorter than seven items long. Too many objectives will

place too many requirements on working memory, resulting in confusion rather than mastery of the material.

3. Write the objectives in a style the learner can understand (e.g., "At the end of this unit you will . . . " as opposed to, "At the termination of the instructional presentation, the learner will be able to . . . ").

4. Objectives are less effective with units of instruction that are longer than 2,500 words (Klauer, 1984). Researchers theorize that it is too difficult for learners to remember the objectives and the content for lengthy passages. As a result, the effectiveness of the objectives as a preinstructional strategy is decreased.

Overviews

Overviews and advance organizers are often referred to synonymously, although they are quite different. Overviews are written at the same level of abstraction as the unit of instruction and simply serve to introduce the student to the central themes. Overviews are most often identified as an introduction because they are written as prose. The following is an example of an overview for a unit on job aids:

> A *job aid* is a step-by-step guide for performing a task on the job. Job aids are often used for complex tasks or infrequently performed tasks. An example of a task is the instructions on a pay telephone for making different types of long-distance calls. Although most individuals making such calls have received instruction on the task, the task is performed so infrequently that a job aid is used to prompt the user for the steps to perform.

The "Getting Started" section of each chapter in this textbook is an overview for the chapter.

Overview Guidelines

1. There are three general approaches to an overview. The first is simply to provide a summary of the content. The second is to pose a problem that the unit will help the learner solve (e.g., finding a discrepancy in your bank account). The third approach is to describe how the content will help the learner (e.g., this unit will help you develop job aids).

2. An overview should be relatively short (e.g., less than one page). A longer overview places an extra burden on the learner's short-term memory, which can interfere with the actual learning task.

Advance Organizers

An advance organizer is written at a higher level of abstraction and serves to provide a conceptual framework to increase the meaningfulness of the content. This conceptual framework is hypothesized to make it easier for the learner to grasp the new material. There are two forms of advance organizers. If the learner is familiar with the content, then a *comparative* organizer is used that compares the new content with what the learner already knows. If the learner is unfamiliar with the content, then an *expository* organizer is used that incorporates relevant information the learner already knows.

The following comparative organizer is from a study by Glover, Bullock, and Dietzer (1990). Notice how the authors compare the idea of model testing to the development of a car using a model car.

> Many scientific advances are the result of testing models that describe natural phenomena. Scientific models are similar in some ways to the models with which we are all familiar. For example, a model car represents a real car but is easier to manipulate and study than the real car. Consider how a car easily can be put into a small wind tunnel to test the means by which the car's form allows it to slip through the air. By testing the model car, engineers can quickly and inexpensively test many possible forms of new cars before settling on one. On the next several pages you will read more about how astronomy uses models. (p. 296)

Advance Organizer Guidelines

1. State ideas in general terms that learners can understand and remember.
2. Ideas presented should be inclusive of the content covered.
3. If the learner is unfamiliar with the content, use an expository advance organizer. Expository organizers include relevant information the learner already possesses and compares this known information to the new information in the instruction.
4. If the learner is somewhat familiar with the content, use a comparative organizer to compare the new idea to known ideas.

The selection of a preinstructional strategy should be based on the factors in Table 8-1. The process is one of finding the best fit among the function, content structure, target audience, and task attributes.

MESSAGE DESIGN FOR TEXT

An instructional unit—whether a textbook, printed manual, computer-based instruction, or videotape—is an artifact of the design process that will endure (Simon, 1981). This artifact represents the interface or interaction between the learner and the instructional materials. In Simon's terms, the artifact will serve its purpose if it is appropriate for the learner. Thus, our task as designers is to create an appropriate interface between the instructional materials and the learner. One part of this process is to design the message so that it is communicated effectively. In this section, we consider how we can design the message by manipulating the text (e.g., structure of the writing) and the typography.

After analyzing science textbooks, Chambliss and Calfee (1989) concluded that there are three critical design elements essential to good printed instruction.

First is a set of distinctive elements such as words or typography that signal the structure of the text to the learner. For example, in this book the words at the beginning of each chapter signal the structure of the text through an overview and a series of questions. The headings signal the structure of the chapter, and italics is used to signal key words or phrases. Second is the coherence of the text structure that aids the organization and recall of information. We can affect this structure by using redundancy and familiar text. Third, there must be a match between the content and the learner's background if the learner is to comprehend the text. Other research also supports the notion that we can affect cognitive processes by designing the message (Britton & Gülgöz, 1991; Jonassen, 1982; Mannes, 1994; Schraw, Wade, & Kardash, 1993). Similarly, Wiley and Voss (1999) suggest that the amount of information learners retain from the instruction is dependent on the *considerateness* of the text. Let's examine how we can manipulate or structure the text to communicate the schema or topic structure to the learner.

Signaling the Text's Schema

When learners are presented with a signal that identifies the text's structure, they can use this information to form a model of expectations that will aid comprehension (Mannes, 1994). As the learner encounters new information, this information is placed within the existing model. The preinstructional strategies described in the first part of this chapter are one means of signaling the overall structure of the text. Another approach is to alert the learner to specific information within a paragraph or section of the material. For example, how can you alert the reader that six different tools are needed to complete a task, or that a particular paragraph will compare RAM memory to ROM memory?

Armbruster (1986) identified five common text structures that a designer can use to signal important text for the learner:

- *Lists of items or ideas*, which are in no significant order. Examples of lists in instructional materials could include the clothing you would need to take on a raft trip or the instruments needed to extract a tooth.
- *Comparisons* or *contrasts* of ideas or objects. In a science textbook we might contrast the differences between a planet and a moon. Similarly, a course on corporate finance might compare two methods of cost accounting.
- *Temporal sequences* connected by time or specific sequences. The steps for testing and replacing an automobile battery or for solving a quadratic equation are examples of temporal sequences of events.
- *Cause and effect structures*, or *explanations*. These describe the relationship between two ideas or events. That is, one idea or event is explained as a result of the second. For example, an economics text explains the relationship between consumer demand and price. An instructional unit on crude oil production explains the relationship between well-pipe diameter and maximum flow rate through the pipe.

- *Definition* and *example* structures. These are used to teach concepts by defining the concept and then offering examples of it. An example concept in a biology textbook is a capillary. Similarly, a concept in a database management training manual is a relational database.

Once the designer has identified the different topic structures in the instruction, the task is one of signaling these structures to the learner. These signals do not add new content to the text; rather, they provide emphasis to the structure or message the designer wishes to convey (Meyer, 1985). There are two methods for signaling these structures. First is through explicit statements that alert the learner to the structure. For example, we have signaled this list of two items by first mentioning that there are two methods, and then by starting the sentences with *first* and *second*. Second is through typographical conventions that signal the structure through change. Examples of typographic signals are the use of boldface, italics, and spacing (e.g., indenting and vertical space).

Explicit Signals

Probably the most common method of explicit signaling is through the use of what Meyer (1985) calls *pointer words*. These words, such as "There are two methods . . . ," alert the learner to what to expect in the following sentence, paragraph, or chapter. By combining Meyer's pointer words with Armbruster's (1986) content structures, we can create a table of explicit signals (Table 8-2) used as part of the message design process.

This list provides a general guide for how you can manipulate your text information to provide signals to important points for the learner. It is important that you use signals wisely and not overload the learner. Using too many signals on a page, whether in printed or electronic text, can result in too much distraction, with the learner failing to identify what is important. A second method for signaling the structure of the text is through the use of typography.

Typographical Signals

With the increased availability and ease of use of desktop publishing, the instructional designer now has greater control over the use of typographical signaling. We can use typography to signal the structure of the text by identifying changes in topic, and we can signal important words, phrases, and ideas by making them different from the surrounding text. Let's examine how we can use headings, layout, and typographical variations to signal the learner.

Headings.   Authors use headings to signal the change of ideas and to provide the learner with a picture of how the materials are organized. The use of headings to signal changes of topics is even prominent in electronic documents. The tags used to create web pages for the World Wide Web provide six different levels of headings for a web page document (Figure 8-1).

TABLE 8-2
Explicit signals

Text Structure	Example	Signaling Words[1]
Lists	*The following* items are essential for a weeklong raft trip . . . Humans *have five* senses. *First is* . . .	*First, second, third, etc.; subsequent; another*
Comparisons or contrasts	A sole proprietorship is a business that is owned by one individual and typically managed by the owner. *In contrast,* a corporation is owned by a few to several thousand individuals and is incorporated under the laws of one of the fifty states. A prime number is divisible by itself and 1, *whereas* a composite number is divisible by at least one other whole number in addition to itself and 1.	*But, in comparison, however, while, to differentiate, a distinguishing*
Temporal sequence	Hold down the Command key *while* pressing **S** to save the document. *Finally,* switch the main breaker to on and close the fuse box door.	*Beginning with, after, next, then, first, second, etc.*
Cause and effect	*If* the application works properly with the extensions off, *then* there is probably a conflict with an extension. *One result* of increased recycling is the development of new industries to convert these items into new products.	*Consequently, as a result, if/then, the reason, one explanation*
Definition and example	Assets are items or resources of value that are owned by an individual or business. *Examples of* assets include cars, buildings, homes, furniture, and computers. Hibernation is a period of inactivity in cold-blooded animals. Animals that hibernate *include* snakes, rodents, and bees.	*For example, include, another*

[1]See Meyer (1985) for a detailed list.

Headings are key words or short phrases that identify the content of the sections of text information. We have found that most instructional materials need two or three levels of headings. A heading level corresponds to the different levels in an outline you might use for writing a paper. For example, first-level headings would correspond to the points listed as roman numerals I, II, III, and so forth. Second-level headings would refer to the A, B, and C points under each of the roman-numeral headings. The third level of headings would correspond to the points under the 1, 2, and 3 points under the A, B, and C headings.

FIGURE 8-1
Using headings as signals

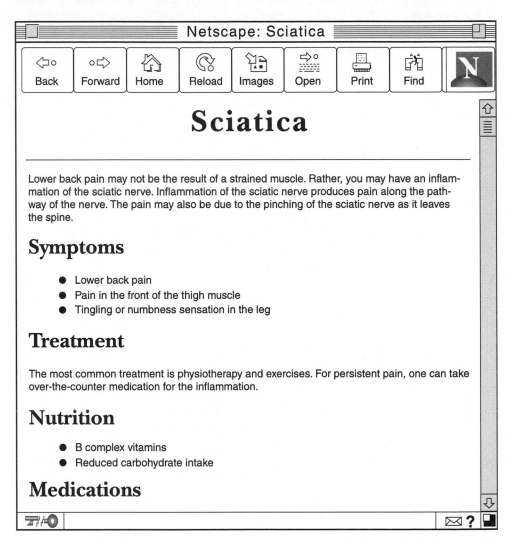

Each level of heading has a different typographical design. For example, in an early edition of this book, the manuscript, the first-level headings were 18-point boldface type centered on the line. The second-level headings were left justified (i.e., flush against the left margin) and in 14-point boldface type. Finally, the third-level headings were the first few words of a paragraph and were printed in boldface. This style is one that is similar to the method used when writing articles for publication using the American Psychological Association's *Publication Manual* (1994) and works well for manuscripts or documents that are desktop published.

To design headings for instructional materials, we suggest that you start with the objectives for the unit. Often, the objectives can function as the first level of headings. The second-level headings will signal the major ideas or steps needed to achieve the objectives. For complex content, you may want to also add a third level of heading that identifies specific ideas, tasks, or concepts in the unit. Next, you will need to select a typographical style that signals the heading. If you look through a number of books, magazines, and instructional materials, you will find a variety of styles used to identify the various levels. Your style should be easily recognizable by the learner. For example, using subtle changes in type size (e.g., 14-, 12-, and 10-point) with left-justified headings might be a unique typographical design, but may be confusing to the learner. Again, we prefer a design based on the APA *Publication Manual* with minor variations used to create a unique design. A unique approach that does not signal the changing level of headings for the learner is likely to result in ineffective communication of the structure of the information.

If a graphic designer designs your materials, you may want to meet with this individual before you start creating your materials and seek his or her input on the design. In some instances, you may not have any decision-making authority on the typographical design of the final document. For example, a textbook author seldom has any input in the actual typographical design of the book. Yet, an instructional designer working in industry may have total control. Similarly, many graphic designers and editors are requesting that authors (including instructional designers) use a style template that assigns a specific style to text and graphics in a document. The graphic designer can then take the disk copy of the manuscript and easily create a layout on a microcomputer by assigning different typographical styles (e.g., boldface, italics, type size, and spacing) to the document. This process can greatly reduce the production process and cost of the materials.

Layout.   A designer can also use the layout of the page to signal structure of the information. For example, you can divide the page into vertical spacing and horizontal spacing, which graphic designers refer to as "white space." By increasing the number of lines or *points* between a heading and the previous and next paragraphs, you can emphasize the heading. Similarly, you can indent a list of items from the left margin to signify that the items are grouped together.

Typographical Variations.   Another means of signaling the structure of the information is by varying the type—adding boldface, italics, or a change in type size—which creates a difference in the pattern of the page. Out of curiosity, the human eye is drawn to this difference. Thus, type variations are used to signal important words and new information. There are three factors to consider when using typographical variations. First, using too many variations on a page can overwhelm the reader, making it difficult to determine what is important. Second, the use of a single variation must be consistent throughout your materials. For example, you should not use boldface to identify new terms in one chapter of a book and then switch to italics in another chapter. Decide on how you will use a variation, if any, before you start writing, and then be consistent. Third, the mixing of different typefaces or fonts on a page requires an understanding of concord and contrast in typography. Designers who lack experience in typography should avoid mixing typefaces and should rely primarily on the use of boldface, italics, and size variations of one type font to signal the structure of the text.

◯ Expert's Edge

Improving the Clarity of the Abstracts of Journal Articles

In my research on designing instructional text, I focus on three questions:

- What does the original text look like? (A question of layout.)
- How easy is it to understand? (A question of language.)
- How effective are the changes that I make to the original? (A question of evaluation.)

I use these three questions for improving all kinds of texts (see Hartley, 1994). Here, for illustrative purposes, I am concerned with the abstracts (summaries) of journal articles. Such abstracts are typically published immediately following the title and the author's name in a journal article. They are also printed separately in journals of abstracts and in computer-based retrieval systems.

Journal abstracts are difficult to read and to write. Authors have to summarize several pages of complex text in about 100 to 200 words. Readers have to be able to extract information easily from the text in order to decide whether they want to read more of the article in question.

How can these aims be achieved? Let me consider my three questions.

- *Layout?*   An abstract is usually printed in a single block paragraph and in a smaller type size than the main body of the text. We can improve upon this by (1) opening up the paragraph into its constituent parts and (2) printing it in a larger type size.
- *Language?*   We can make abstracts easier to follow by giving them standard structures together with simpler vocabulary and grammar. When abstracts have the same format readers can access the text more easily, and authors do not omit any relevant information.
- *Evaluation?*   We can assess the effectiveness of changing traditional abstracts to structured ones by using computer-based measures of reading difficulty, asking readers to find information in the texts, and by asking readers and authors for their preferences.

The following figures show before and after examples of the results of applying considerations arising from the first two questions. Figure 1 shows an original abstract. Figure 2 shows a suggested revision. Data obtained in response to question 3 show that, compared with Figure 1, the abstract in Figure 2 is longer but more informative, is slightly easier to read, and is preferred by readers. Similar results have been found in other more substantial studies (e.g., Hartley & Benjamin, 1998).

It is often assumed that automatic teller machines (ATMs) are inherently easy to use and require no training. However, there is evidence to suggest that ATM users do experience difficulty when learning to use the system. The purpose of the present study was to conduct an in-depth analysis of ATM usage by older adults. Our approach consisted of telephone interviews followed by structured individual interviews. The goals were to understand the problems encountered by ATM users, to determine how ATMs might be better designed, and to assess the training needs of individuals. The phone interview data provide information about the relationship between age, gender, and ATM usage within the adult sample, as well as information about why some people choose not to use ATMs. The structured interview data provide a more in-depth view of the concerns of both users and nonusers and information about training needs. The training and design implications of the results are discussed (Rogers et al., 1997).

Figure 1 An original abstract reproduced with permission of the authors. Note the small type size and the block paragraph.

Background. It is often assumed that automatic teller machines (ATMs) are easy to use. However, the evidence suggests that many people experience difficulties learning to use ATMs.

Aims. The aim of our study was to conduct an in-depth analysis of how older people use ATMs. We wished to understand the problems of ATM users, to determine how ATMs might be better designed, and to assess the training needs of individuals.

Method. We first interviewed by telephone 100 people (aged on average 72 years), and we then asked 24 of them to take part in more detailed individual interviews.

Results. The phone data provided information about relationships between age, gender, and ATM usage, as well as information about why some people choose not to use ATMs. The interview data provided a more in-depth view of the concerns of both users and nonusers and provided information relevant to training needs.

Comment. The participants reported a number of problems that could be corrected with design improvements and that would benefit all users, not just older ones. The results also indicated that older populations could benefit from training in using ATMs.

Figure 2 A revised version of the abstract shown in Figure 1. Note the larger type size, the revised layout with its subheadings, and the slightly simpler language. More information is also given about the method and the findings.

These three general questions, then, can be used in a variety of contexts. They can be asked, for example, of text summaries (as presented in this textbook), of small details in particular situations—like warnings, cautions, or special notes—and, indeed, of all training or textbook materials. There are useful research findings to consider with respect to all three questions and their interactions (e.g., see Schriver, 1997).

References

Hartley, J. (1994). *Designing instructional text* (3rd ed.). East Brunswick, NJ: Nichols Publishing.

Hartley, J., & Benjamin, M. (1998). An evaluation of structured abstracts in journals published by the British Psychological Society. *British Journal of Educational Psychology, 68,* 443-456.

Rogers, W., Gilbert, D. K., & Cabrera, E. F. (1997). An analysis of automatic teller use by older adults: A structured interview approach. *Applied Ergonomics, 28* (3), 173-180.

Schriver, K. A. (1997). *Dynamics in document design: Creating texts for readers.* New York: Wiley.

James Hartley is professor of psychology at Keele University in the United Kingdom. He has worked extensively in the field of designing instructional text for over 30 years.

PICTURES AND GRAPHICS IN INSTRUCTION

The final consideration is the use of pictures and graphics in instruction. Considerable research (e.g., Anglin, Towers, & Levie, 1996; Levie & Lentz, 1982) and books (e.g., Willows & Houghton, 1987) are devoted to the study and use of pictures in instruction. In this section, we describe the effectiveness of pictures in instructional materials, the functions pictures can serve, and some general design considerations for using pictures for instruction.

Effectiveness

There is a general consensus that illustrated text is conducive to learning the related text information. Pictures help readers learn the text information that was illustrated (Levie & Lentz, 1982). The pictures neither helped nor hindered the learning of textual information that was not duplicated in the illustrations. Pictures are particularly helpful when used to show spatial relationships described in the text (Peeck, 1987). For example, in a text describing the relationship between the position of the moon relative to the earth and sun during a lunar eclipse, a picture of these spatial relations would benefit the reader. Pictorial representations are also beneficial when used to illustrate abstract material and the main ideas in the text. However, no one type of information benefits more from illustrations than another.

Extensive research on the effectiveness of different types of illustrations was the subject of much of Dwyer's (e.g., 1970, 1972) work. A series of his studies focused on the use of photographs, realistic drawings, and simple line drawings in instruction. He concluded that if the learner has limited time for viewing the illustration, such as in an externally paced presentation like a videotape or lecture, then a simple line drawing tends to be most effective. If the learning environment is self-paced, then the learner is more likely to take advantage of the details in a more realistic picture such as a photograph. However, there is always the possibility that the learner may focus on inappropriate parts of an illustration with too much detail.

Simply placing an illustration in the instruction, however, does not guarantee that the learner will examine the illustration and gain any benefits. Directing the learner's attention to the illustration through prompts such as "examine the difference . . ." are not always effective (Peeck, 1987). Researchers, however, have had more success when the learner interacts with or studies the illustration (Dean & Kulhavy, 1981; Winn & Holliday, 1982). For example, the designer might require the learner to label parts of a diagram or picture, answer questions about the picture, or trace and study a picture. A balance is needed between the picture and the activity, as overprompting the learner is also detrimental to learning from a picture (Winn & Holliday, 1982).

The Function of Pictures

One can examine almost any textbook with pictures and often see a variety of styles (e.g., simple to complex, black and white or color, line drawings, or color drawings). Upon a more careful examination of the pictures and prose, one can identify pictures that serve different functions in a textbook. Levin (1981) has identified five different learning functions that pictures can perform in text. He also suggests that these functions are not equal in their effects on learning. Following is a summary of his categories with examples of how you might use each in designing instructional materials.

Decoration. Pictures at the beginning of a chapter often serve no other purpose than to decorate and to signal that a new chapter is about to start (Figure 8-2). From a publisher's standpoint, the inclusion of these pictures increases sales by making the text appealing. An instructional designer might view the pictures as motivational for the student. Graphic designers also use decorative pictures in the text to "break up" the page so that it is appealing to the reader. The general idea is that a full page of text is threatening to the reader. Decorative pictures have no direct connection to the text information.

Representation. When a picture is used to represent people, tools, things, or events in the text or other media, it may be classified as *representational*. These pictures illustrate a major portion of the important textual information (Figure 8-3). For example, a designer might use two pictures in a science text to illustrate the

FIGURE 8-2
Decorative picture

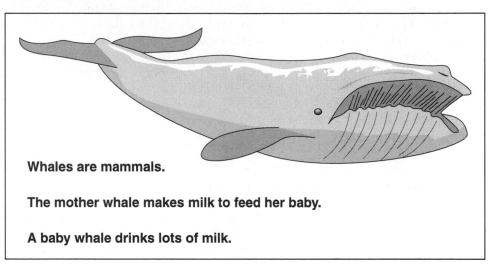

Whales are mammals.

The mother whale makes milk to feed her baby.

A baby whale drinks lots of milk.

difference between rotation and revolution of a planet. Representational pictures provide a concrete reference for verbal information, which makes the information easier and more meaningful to the learner. These pictures are often used in children's books to illustrate poems, fairy tales, and stories. They are also used in technical training materials to illustrate new ideas.

Organization.   If you have ever purchased a car repair manual or tried to use your VCR's instructions, you have probably seen a series of pictures that performed an *organizational* function. Designers can use pictures, such as step-by-step, how-to pictures, to provide a framework for the text (Figure 8-4). The pictures in a manual on how to program a VCR or set up an answering machine provide a map or path for completing the process. In many cases, the pictures provide more information than the few words associated with each picture. Pictures that perform an organizational function are not limited to procedural tasks. They are often used to describe the various attributes or features of an object (e.g., a new car) or a concept (e.g., a tornado).

Interpretation.   Pictures that help learner understanding of difficult or abstract information are classified as performing an *interpretation* function (Figure 8-5). Carefully selected pictures can add comprehensibility to a passage by providing visual interpretation of the content. For example, a science book that uses pictures to explain Ohm's law by comparing it to the flow of water or that compares the heart to a water pump is an example of uses of interpretative pictures. According to

FIGURE 8-3
Representational picture

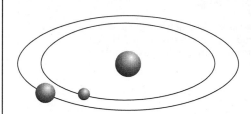

Planets orbit the sun. We can also say that planets revolve around the sun. All the planets revolve around the sun in the same direction. The time it takes a planet to revolve around the sun is known as one year on that planet.

Planets also spin or rotate on their axes, which causes day and night. If we were to draw an imaginary line through the center of the earth, we would call it an axis. The earth spins or turns on this axis. The planets all rotate on their own axes at different speeds. The earth rotates on its axis once every 24 hours.

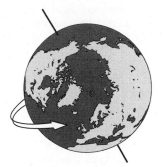

Levin, Anglin, and Carney (1987), the distinction between the representation, organization, and interpretation functions is one of the underlying mechanisms (i.e., how the picture is used). Representational pictures add concrete representations to familiar information. Organizational pictures add coherence to easy-to-process material. Interpretative pictures, on the other hand, provide added comprehensibility to difficult or abstract materials.

Transformation.   Pictures that provide the learner with a mnemonic learning aid perform a *transformation* function (Figure 8-6). Transformational pictures are useful in passages that require the memorization of facts by providing the learner with a visual anchor for recalling the fact. A transformation picture often combines concrete images to help the student recall an abstract idea.

Using Pictures in Instruction

The decision to use pictures in instruction is influenced by three factors. The first and most influential is to enhance learning. Second is the availability of the picture or illustration. Third is the cost of reproducing the materials with the added pictures. We have examined the first factor in the previous sections and now address the last two factors.

FIGURE 8-4
Organizational picture

The Surgeon's Knot

The surgeon's knot is used to tie different diameter lines. Although it is not a very neat knot, it is very strong and easy to tie. It can be used to add tippet to the end of your line. This is especially useful when modifying your line to imitate dry flies, and when you want to do it quick, use the surgeon's knot.

Lay the new line parallel to the end of the leader, so that the lines overlap about four inches.

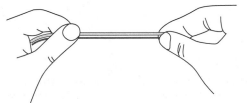

Make an overhand knot by forming a loop, bringing the tippet and leader around and through the loop. Keep the strands together.

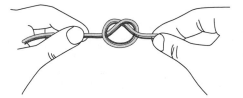

Bring the same double strand around and through the loop once more, forming a double overhand.

Wet the knot, and then tighten by pulling all four ends to set the knot. Apply equal tension to both sides as you pull. Trim the tag ends as close as possible.

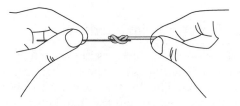

FIGURE 8-5
Interpretative picture

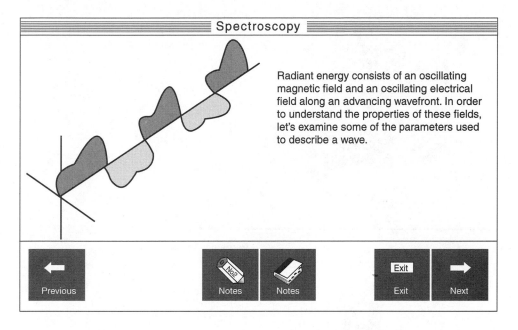

Availability.   With the advent of desktop publishing, computer-based instruction, and multimedia productions came the introduction of new technologies and processes for incorporating pictures and illustrations in instructional materials. For our purposes, we will classify pictures into three categories—original art, clip art, and photographs.

Original art is typically drawn by the instructional designer, artist, or graphic artist. The work can be a simple pen-and-ink line drawing, a watercolor, or a computer drawing. Original art requires someone with the artistic ability to render the picture. Computer drawing and drafting programs make it relatively simple for an individual with limited artistic ability to produce an illustration. More complex illustrations require more expertise. Thus, the use of original art can substantially increase the cost of your materials.

Clip art is widely available on CD-ROM for most computer platforms. A designer can find a wide variety of photographs and line art (e.g., line drawings). Some of the materials are available for little or no royalty costs, and any royalty paid is often less than the cost of creating an original drawing. One problem with clip art is that it is generic and may not fit a designer's needs without some alteration. Also, the art may be outdated, depicting, for example, computers that are several years old or different from those used in the designer's organization. However, for those with limited artistic ability and limited access to a graphic artist, clip art provides a viable alternative.

FIGURE 8-6
Transformation picture

 $= \mathbf{PV}$

Perpetual Annuity Formula

$$\frac{A}{i} = PV$$

A = amount of money
i = interest
PV = Present Value

Designers have the option of hiring a photographer to take specific *photographs,* purchasing stock photographs, or selecting photographs from a CD-ROM. Again, CD-ROM photographs are often generic in nature and may not fit the specific need. Digital cameras have made it relatively easy for a designer to take a picture and incorporate it into the instructional materials whether they are distributed on paper or electronically via computer. The quality of the photograph depends upon the skill of the individual taking the picture.

Cost of Reproducing.   The cost of reproducing the instructional materials is the final factor that influences the use of pictures in instructional materials. The cost of reproducing pictures is seldom a factor when the materials are distributed electronically such as in computer-based instruction, web publishing, or on CD-ROM. Typically, cost is only a factor when a large number of pictures require additional disks. Cost, however, is often a factor when preparing print materials that use either color and/or photographs.

Accurate reproduction of photographic images typically requires the use of the printing process (e.g., offset printing) as opposed to photocopying. Before a photographic print can be reproduced, it must be converted to a screened image, which is an additional cost. Each photograph must be individually screened and prepared for printing. Digital photographs do not require this process and may produce an acceptable photocopy.

Black-and-white line drawings add no additional cost to the duplication of materials. These drawings can be scanned into a computer and included with text or simply pasted in if they are clip art or computer drawings. Documents composed of only text and line drawings can be reproduced by photocopying or offset printing. The addition of color either for text or drawings will add cost for any method of reproduction.

SUMMARY

1. Once you have completed the design of your instructional strategies, you are ready to concentrate on how to present the information. In this chapter, we have described how to create a preinstructional strategy to focus the learner's attention on the instruction, how to signal different aspects of the instruction through words and typography, and, finally, how to use pictures to enhance learner understanding. This message design process provides a means for effectively communicating your instructional strategies.

2. There are four types of preinstructional strategies—pretests, objectives, overivews, and advance organizers—you can use to introduce the learner to the content. Each strategy performs different functions and works with different content structures (see Table 8-1).

3. You can enhance the communication of your instructional message by signaling the text's structure to the learner. Signaling can take the form of explicit pointer words, such as "There are two methods . . . ," or typographical signals, such as boldface or italics.

4. Pictures can provide concrete references for abstract terms presented in the text. Pictures can provide a decoration, representation, organization, interpretation, or transformation function in the text.

THE ID PROCESS

The outcomes for this chapter include two different products. First is the preinstructional strategy, and second is the message design plan.

The preinstructional strategy product includes two parts. First is the rationale for the selection that is based on Table 8-1. Your rationale should describe the best fit among the function, content structure, learner, and task attributes. As you develop this rationale, you will need to consider the results of your learner analysis, task analysis, and goal analysis. As you make your decision, you will need to consider which of the variables (e.g., function, content structure, learner, or task analysis) has the most weight for the project. Second is the design of the preinstructional strategy. This activity will result in the first page or part of your instructional unit. You need to design this strategy so that it accurately reflects the function of the preinstructional strategy you have selected. As you design and write the strategy, keep your audience in mind so that you write it at the appropriate level that will appeal to the learner.

The message design product is a plan and a template for the unit. A good place to start is by examining your task analysis and identifying the text structures shown in Table 8-2. After identifying these structures, you can make notes as to the signal words and typographical signals you can use to alert the reader. This stage is also a good time to identify any pictures you will need and make arrangements for clip art, an illustrator, or a photographer. The second part of the message design is a word-processing template that defines the various styles for headings, text, lists, and so forth. Templates are an excellent method for providing consistency across multiple units of instruction or when more than one designer is working on a project.

APPLICATIONS

Assume that you are working for an energy company that has assigned you to develop the training for an in situ uranium-mining operation. You are responsible for developing training as prescribed by the federal government. Failure to design and offer the training can result in legal action.

One of the first tasks you are directed to complete is how to dispose of contaminated water that is spilled from one of the injection wells that pumps the water into the uranium veins. The mining engineers as well as the field operators have traditionally ignored such spillage and simply let the water seep back into the ground. The unit you are developing requires proper disposal activities that run counter to field practices. Failure to dispose of the contaminated water and contaminated soil in a proper manner can result in substantial fines.

Given this information, which preinstructional strategy would you select for your instruction? Explain your rationale.

The sales personnel and company representatives for your plastics manufacturing company have requested that they have dial-up access to the sales server so that they can retrieve data from the field or from home. Management has refused the request for several years, but has finally agreed to provide access through a national Internet provider.

As senior instructional designer, you are assigned the task of preparing a three-hour lab-based course on how to access the server through standard and cellular telephone communication as well as how to log on to the server.

Which preinstructional strategy would you select for your instruction? Explain your rationale.

ANSWERS

One primary factor in designing the uranium-mining unit and the preinstructional strategy is the audience. The prospective trainees are using an unacceptable practice and may see this unit as a "waste of time." Thus, we can make a strong argument that the function of this strategy should precisely inform the learner of what is expected. Behavioral objectives would perform this function. Similarly, we might consider an overview that prepares the learner for the task. Our overview might take the form of a case study that describes the legal problems of a company that ignored the proper disposal methods.

The learners in the second example are familiar with the task (task attribute) of using the server, and the process is highly structured. Learners will range from low to high ability as well as low to high maturity. The function of the task will probably guide your decision for selecting either an objective or overview as your preinstructional strategy.

The new unit provides you with an opportunity to develop instruction for a highly motivated audience. Access to the sales information could lead to increased sales, which could result in increased income for the audience. The learners in the audience have used the data on the company server, so they are familiar with part of the task. They are not familiar with dial-up procedures.

The procedure is highly structured and the audience is middle to high ability. The task is straightforward and will be short in duration. Given the workshop/lecture format of the instruction, the length of the instruction, and the motivation of the learners, objectives would be a good choice for the preinstructional strategy. An advance organizer is also a viable choice given the dominant structure and the need to memorize the individual steps.

QUALITY MANAGEMENT

The first quality check is to determine whether the preinstructional strategy you have selected represents the best fit between your learners and instruction. You can use Table 8-1 to determine whether you have the best match. As you develop your preinstructional strategy, keep your focus on the learners and consider what will help them prepare for the instruction.

The second quality check focuses on the message design of the unit. First, make sure that you have selected illustrations that properly illustrate the instruction. Are the illustrations accurate? Are they legible when reproduced? Have you obtained copyright clearance or paid the royalty if required? Second, as you edit your materials, try to identify the different text structures listed in Table 8-2 and then use the appropriate signal words to alert the learners. Third, check your headings. Do they convey the structure of the text? Can the reader easily identify the different headings? Are the headings distinct from one another and from the text?

SAMPLE DESIGN PLAN

PREINSTRUCTIONAL STRATEGY—OVERVIEW

I will introduce this unit with an overview that presents the learner with a realistic problem involving setting priorities. The learner will read a brief account about a disorganized businessperson who has only two weeks to prepare to attend an educational technology conference in Boston and who requires the assistance of a time-management expert to create a context.

I chose an overview because these are high-ability students who need to learn the concepts of prioritizing tasks as well as the procedures. Presenting only the objectives in the preinstructional strategy would probably be less meaningful to them. I could have used an advance organizer in the form of a concept map, but this content is just not that difficult or unfamiliar to warrant an advance organizer.

REFERENCES

American Psychological Association. (1994). *Publication manual of the American Psychological Association* (4th ed.). Washington, DC: American Psychological Association.

Anglin, G. J., Towers, R. L., & Levie, H. (1996). Visual message design and learning: The role of static and dynamic illustrations. In D. Jonassen (Ed.), *Handbook of research for educational communication and technology* (pp. 755–794). New York: Macmillan Library Reference USA.

Armbruster, B. B. (1986). Schema theory and the design of content-area textbooks. *Educational Psychology, 21,* 253–267.

Britton, B. K., & Gülgöz, S. (1991). Using Kintsch's computational model to improve instructional text: Effects of repairing inference calls on recall and cognitive structures. *Journal of Educational Psychology, 83,* 329–345.

Chamblis, M. J., & Calfee, R. C. (1989). Designing science textbooks to enhance student understanding. *Educational Psychologist, 24,* 307–322.

Davies, I. K. (1976). *Objectives in curriculum design.* New York: McGraw-Hill.

Dean, R. S., & Kulhavy, R. W. (1981). The influence of spatial organization in prose learning. *Journal of Educational Psychology, 73,* 57–64.

Dwyer, F. M. (1970). Exploratory studies in the effectiveness of visual illustrations. *AV Communication Review, 18,* 11–15.

Dwyer, F. M. (1972). *A guide to improving visualized instruction.* State College: Pennsylvania State University, Learning Services Division.

Fleming, M. (1993). Introduction. In M. Fleming and W. H. Levie (Eds.), *Instructional message design: Principles from the behavioral and cognitive sciences* (pp. ix–xi). Englewood Cliffs, NJ: Educational Technology Publications.

Glover, J. A., Bullock, R. G., & Dietzer, M. L. (1990). Advance organizers: Delay hypothesis. *Journal of Educational Psychology, 82,* 291–297.

Hartley, J., & Davies, I. K. (1976). Preinstructional strategies: The role of pretests, behavioral objectives, overviews, and advanced organizers. *Review of Educational Research, 46,* 239–265.

Jegede, O. J. (1995). An investigation of student's disposition to the use of objectives in distance learning materials. *Educational Research, 37,* 293–304.

Jonassen, D. (1982). *The technology of text.* Englewood Cliffs, NJ: Educational Technology Publications.

Klauer, K. J. (1984). Intentional and incidental learning with instructional texts: A meta-analysis for 1970–1980. *American Educational Research Journal, 21,* 323–339.

Klein, J. D., & Cavalier, J. C. (1999). Using cooperative learning and objectives with computer-based instruction. Proceedings of selected research papers presented at the National

Convention of the Association for Educational Communications and Technology, Houston, TX, February 10–14, 1999.

Levie, W. H., & Lentz, R. (1982). Effects of text illustrations: A review of research. *Educational Communications and Technology Journal, 30,* 195–232.

Levin, J. R. (1981). On the functions of pictures in prose. In F. J. Pirozzolo & M. C. Wittrock (Eds.), *Neuropsychological and cognitive processes in reading* (pp. 203–228). New York: Academic Press.

Levin, J. R., Anglin, G. J., & Carney, R. N. (1987). On empirically validating functions of pictures in prose. In D. M. Willows & H. A. Houghton (Eds.), *The psychology of illustration: Volume 1. Basic research* (pp. 51–85). New York: Springer-Verlag.

Mannes, S. (1994). Strategic processing of text. *Journal of Educational Psychology, 86,* 577–588.

McNeil, N. M., & Alibali, M. W. (2000). Learning mathematics from procedural instruction: Externally imposed goals influence what is learned. *Journal of Eduational Psychology, 92,* 734–744.

Meyer, B. J. F. (1985). Signaling the structure of text. In D. J. Jonassen (Ed.), *The technology of text,* vol. 2 (pp. 64–89). Englewood Cliffs, NJ: Educational Technology Publications.

Peeck, J. (1987). The role of illustrations in processing and remembering illustrated texts. In D. M. Willows & H. A. Houghton (Eds.), *The psychology of illustration: Volume 1. Basic research* (pp. 114–151). New York: Springer-Verlag.

Schraw, G., Wade, S. E., & Kardash, C. A. (1993). Interactive effects of text-based and task-based importance on learning from text. *Journal of Educational Psychology, 85,* 652–661.

Simon, H. A. (1981). *Sciences of the artificial* (2nd ed.). Cambridge, MA: MIT Press.

Wiley, J., & Voss, J. F. (1999). Constructing arguments from multiple sources: Tasks that promote understanding and not just memory for text. *Journal of Educational Psychology, 91,* 301–311.

Willows, D. M., & Houghton, H. A. (Eds.). (1987). *The psychology of illustration: Volume 1. Basic research.* New York: Springer-Verlag.

Winn, W. D., & Holliday, W. G. (1982). Design principles for diagrams and charts. In D. Jonassen (Ed.), *The technology of text,* vol. 1 (pp. 277–299). Englewood Cliffs, NJ: Educational Technology Publications.

CHAPTER 9

Developing Instructional Materials

GETTING STARTED

You have spent almost nine months working on a business economics course for your international consulting company. The vice president of your division believes that this course will provide a significant revenue stream for your company. Your manager said that your design plan was a model for future projects—"The task analysis was very thorough, you have a good grasp of the learners, and your instructional strategies were creative." You now have to prepare the instructor's manual and the student's manual. The instructor's manual will include fairly detailed lecture notes and exercises. The student's manual consists of an outline for the lectures, readings, and problems that are done either before or after the lectures. You are responsible for writing *every* word in the manual. Where will you start?

QUESTIONS TO CONSIDER

"How do I use the design plan to develop the instruction?"

"What guidelines can I follow when 'writing' the instruction?"

"What makes good instruction from the learner's perspective?"

"Shall I do role playing somewhere in this unit since my students are likely to benefit from such an activity?"

"Are there alternatives to having an instructor lecture?"

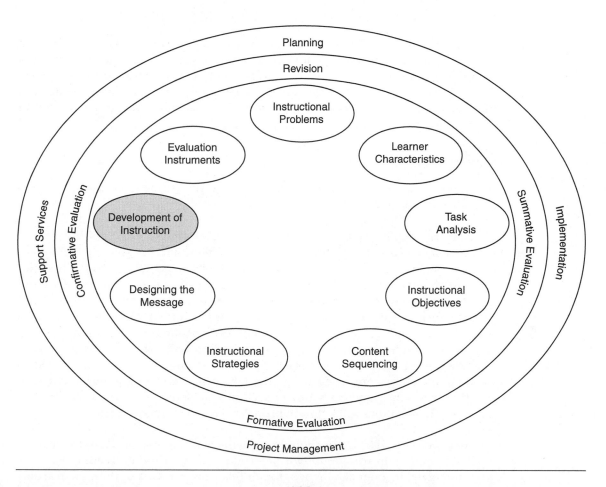

Once the instructional strategies are designed (see Chapter 7), the instructional designer is ready to start developing the instruction. This task is the process of translating the design plan into instruction. An instructional designer can choose from a wide variety of formats for the instruction, ranging from a simple printed manual to a videotape to a multimedia unit that includes full-motion video, coaching, and immediate feedback. The common feature of almost all instruction is text. Each medium offers a different challenge and opportunity for the designer. However, there are many principles that apply to the development of the instruction regardless of the medium used to deliver it to the learner.

This chapter has two main sections. In the first section, we discuss some heuristics for developing the instruction with an emphasis on print-based materials. The second section of the chapter focuses on three different instructional delivery methods: group presentations (e.g., lectures), self-paced instruction, and small-group activities.

STARTING THE DEVELOPMENT OF THE INSTRUCTION

How do we craft effective, exciting, and motivating instruction using our instructional design plan? Instruction does not need to be dry and pedantic like that of a technical manual. Although we would not expect the instruction to be as captivating as a mystery novel, we would expect it to be more exciting and interesting than instructions on how to assemble a gas grill. Let's examine how to get started in developing the instruction.

Staying Focused

As you develop the instruction, it is important to stay focused on solving the performance problem.

Objectives.   Make sure the objectives support the resolution of the instructional need. Each objective should address either content or skill that will help the learner improve performance related to the problem. Similarly, the instructional strategies you have designed should support the mastery of the objectives. Now is an excellent time to review the strategies and make sure each strategy supports the content and performance specified for the objective in the expanded content-performance matrix. One common error is to have an objective classified as application-level performance when the strategy is designed to develop only recall. For example, the objective might state that the learner will calculate how much paint is needed to paint the walls of a room. The strategy, though, focuses on helping the learner *memorize* the steps rather than *apply* the steps. Thus, a quick review of your strategies and objective classifications will help you maintain a focus on the problem.

Learner Analysis.   Next, you should review the learner analysis. First, the learner analysis should help you identify or determine the appropriate reading level for your audience. If you make the text too difficult to understand, then the learners may fail to complete the instruction. If it is too simple, they may be bored and tend to ignore it or feel that the information is unimportant. It is unlikely you will know the exact average reading level of your audience; however, you should be able to determine a typical range of abilities. Once you start developing the materials, you can use a readability index included with some word processors to judge and modify the level of your materials (see Figure 9-1).

Second, you can use the learner analysis to determine the learners' familiarity with the content and technical terms. If you were designing the introductory unit in a computer repair course, could you use the terms *ROM, RAM, SCSI, parallel port,* and *modem* without first defining them? If you had recruited your learners from a high school that also offers a network administrators' certificate and has extensive computer resources, then your learners might be familiar with the terms. If you recruited your learners from a group of students at a high school with very limited computer resources, then your learners might not be familiar with the terminology. Assuming that your learners know too much can result in instruction that is too difficult.

Third, understanding the audience's background can help you select an appropriate context for examples used in the instruction. For example, when describing a computer port to computer-naïve students, you might use an analogy

FIGURE 9-1
Readability Index

Readability Statistics	?	X

Counts	
Words	2582
Characters	14743
Paragraphs	35
Sentences	135

Averages	
Sentences per Paragraph	5.1
Words per Sentence	18.8
Characters per Word	5.5

Readability	
Passive Sentences	20%
Flesch Reading Ease	25.6
Flesch-Kincaid Grade Level	12.0

OK

of a phone jack or electrical outlet. Similarly, our designer in the "Getting Started" scenario might need to use a variety of examples for different industries or parts of the country. Using an auto-manufacturing plant as an example for teaching the students how to calculate the return on investment might work for learners in Michigan. For learners in Texas, a more appropriate context might be an oil industry example.

HEURISTICS FOR DEVELOPING INSTRUCTION

Each time we develop instructional materials, we learn something new. This approach is the heuristic process described in Chapter 1. We modify existing heuristics and we add new heuristics as we learn what works and what does not work. These heuristics are general rules we can apply to the design process. The following discussion provides several heuristics that will help you develop a unit of instruction.

Make It Concrete

The positive benefits of learning from concrete materials have been well established by Paivio (1971, 1986). Unfortunately, because text materials are often abstract, learners may have difficulty in understanding the ideas the author wants to convey. We might initially think that the best way to make instruction concrete is to add a picture. Carter (1985) suggests that carefully crafted words have their benefits, "If a picture is worth a thousand words, a good concrete example is worth at least several hundred words of further definition and explanation" (p. 151). As designers who may slip into the mode of an author while developing materials, we may easily be seduced by the idea that abstract presentations are better for our learners and a necessary part of learning. Research, however, suggests that a mix of abstract and concrete information increases both the learner's interest and recall of the information (Sadoski, Goetz, & Fritz, 1993).

What Is Concrete?   *Concrete words* are those that readily create a mental image for the learner. For example, the word *truth* is considered abstract because it does not bring to mind an image. The word *house,* though, is concrete because our minds easily conjure an image of a house. Similarly, sentences can be abstract or concrete. Sadoski et al. (1993) give the example, "The traditional customs fascinated the tourists" (p. 292) as *abstract* because the subject, *traditional customs,* is abstract (e.g., not something represented by a single picture or image). In contrast, the subject of the sentence "The tribal marriage customs fascinated the tourists" (p. 292) is concrete and is more likely to be remembered by the reader.

Making Text Concrete.   There are three ways to make instructional text concrete and thus more comprehensible. First is the use of illustrations (see Chapter 8). Drawings, graphics, graphs, and photographs provide a *referent* or an image for words. By providing this image for the learner, we can make the text more concrete.

Simply adding a picture to the text, however, is typically not adequate. You will need to direct the learner's attention to the picture with words such as, "Note the roundedness of the upper edge . . ." or through some interaction such as, "Label the three points subject to stress on the chassis in Figure 9."

Second, we can create concrete text through the use of concrete words, shorter words, and active sentences. Simple words tend to increase the readability of the text, making it easier to comprehend. Active sentences as opposed to passive sentences are easier to understand. For example, "The pointer should be aimed at the 2 o'clock position" is more difficult to comprehend than "Move the pointer to the 2 o'clock position." Given the passive text, our learner might stand before the control panel for hours waiting for the pointer to move to the 2 o'clock position!

The third method is to use ample examples to illustrate the ideas (Carter, 1985). Interspersing examples of the abstract ideas can add concreteness to the text. For example, consider the paragraph with the heading "What Is Concrete?" Notice how we used examples of abstract and concrete words and sentences to explain concrete text. The research does not advocate removing all abstract ideas from instructional materials. Rather, these abstract ideas need elaborations in the form of pictures, concrete text, and examples to improve learner's comprehension.

Control the Step Size

If you have read a research article, especially in an unfamiliar area, you may have found it difficult to follow the literature review. The reason is that the authors are typically writing for individuals who are familiar with background information and they make large jumps between ideas. These jumps or transitions are referred to as *step size*. Researchers assume that readers of their articles have the background knowledge and can follow the logic leading to the new study. As a result, the naïve reader may find it quite difficult to read the article because of a lack of prior knowledge. As designers, we can control the step size of our instruction.

There are two strategies for controlling step size. First, use *consistent terminology* throughout the instruction. For example, do not refer to the *mesh screen* in step 1 and then refer to it as the *filter* in step 4. Select one term and use it consistently throughout the instruction. Second, *make explicit references* back to what the learner has previously learned. You can use the references when transitioning from one unit to the next and from one idea to the next idea. Simple statements such as, "Remember examining the mesh screen of the filter in step 1? If it was dirty, you can now remove it and clean it." Or, "Yesterday we examined how to use a predefined formula in Excel." Using consistent terminology and providing references to prior learning provide contextual cues to the learner. These cues make the new information easier to comprehend by providing a context or frame of reference.

Step size can vary for different audiences. A small step for one group might be a large step for another group (Fleming & Levie, 1978). Having an appropriate learner analysis can help you determine the appropriate step size for your target audience.

Use Appropriate Pacing

When we think of pacing, we often think of how fast the lecturer is speaking. Pacing, however, also refers to text materials. *Pacing* is a function of the number of examples, problems, interactions, or exercises presented with an idea. Designers can control the pacing of the instruction by varying the number of examples and/or problems in the instruction. If we were to create a map of a unit of instruction, a fast-paced unit would look like the map at the top of Figure 9-2. A unit that has several examples (bottom of Figure 9-2) would have a slower pacing. The fast-paced unit might define the first concept and then immediately define a second concept. To slow the pacing of this unit, the designer might add one or more examples of the first concept.

For example, a unit begins by introducing the concept "rectangle" by defining it. Then, the concept "square" is introduced. To reduce the pacing of this unit, we might add several examples of rectangles *after* we define the concept. Then, we could introduce the concept of square and provide examples of squares. After these examples, we could further reduce the pacing by presenting to the student a mixture of five rectangles and five squares. The student is directed to place an X in each square.

Increasing the "distance" (see Figure 9-2) between two ideas *slows* the pacing. Selecting an appropriate pacing is a function of the learner's prior knowledge, general ability, and the difficulty of the material. For novel and/or difficult material, a slower pacing can provide the learner with adequate time and support to develop an understanding. For reviews or less difficult material, a faster pace may be necessary to maintain the learner's interest.

Maintain Consistency

Using consistent terms throughout a unit can aid learner understanding. An editor will often direct you to create a style guide *before* you start writing. One part of this guide is a listing of terms/words you will use. For example, will you spell *email* as "E-mail," "email," or "e-mail"? Consider a unit where the spelling "E-mail" is used at the beginning to describe how to communicate with people within the company,

FIGURE 9-2
Illustration of pacing

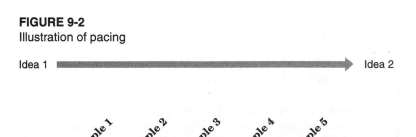

and then the spelling "e-mail" is used during discussion of communication to and from a mailing list. Your learner might incorrectly assume that "E-mail" is a term describing internal company e-mail and "e-mail" is a different form of communication that is used with mailing lists.

Consistent terminology is important when preparing instructional materials for technical areas. Naïve learners are easily confused by similar terms. Referring to a covering as a "port cover" in one paragraph and the same object later as the "lower access" can lead to confusion. Although it is not always possible to use familiar terms, instructional designers should strive to use consistent terms to reduce the cognitive load on and confusion of the learner.

Use Cues

Our last heuristic focuses on the use of cues in the instruction. As you completed your task analysis, you may have identified different cues that either make the process easier or that are essential. For example, when explaining how to splice two electrical wires, the SME would probably indicate that before cutting the wires, they first need to be checked to determine whether they have power. Or a learner might need to "turn the indicator until the arrow is at the 12 o'clock position." Developing the instruction includes identifying the cues and then accurately communicating them to the learner. We might cue the learner to "*First* turn off the electricity and check for voltage."

In Chapter 8 we describe several methods for cueing the learner using words (e.g., first, second) and using typographical conventions such as boldface and italics. Combining signaling with the cues will help the learner both identify the cue and increase the probability that it will be recalled (Lorch & Lorch, 1996; Lorch, Lorch, & Inman, 1993).

PUTTING PEN TO PAPER OR FINGERS TO KEYBOARD

Tweaking the instructional design plan, identifying another cue, or coming up with just one more example must end sometime, and the writing must start. There will come a time when each refinement to the design plan becomes less and less productive. As a designer, you need to identify this stage of diminishing returns long before the returns are minuscule and recognize the signal to start developing the materials. In this section, we provide some final guidelines for translating your design plan into instruction.

Preinstructional Strategy

If you have followed the model presented in this text, you have already designed and developed your preinstructional strategy. Once you have completed the title page for a manual, the opening logo for the video program, or the *splash* (opening) screen for the multimedia program, you are ready for the preinstructional strategy.

The preinstructional strategy is the learner's first contact with your unit of instruction. Start your unit by copying the preinstructional strategy (e.g., just the overview, pretest, objectives, or advance organizer) from your design documentation and pasting it into your unit.

Your next step is to address each of the objectives according to your sequencing plan. You will present the initial presentation and then the generative strategy for the first objective, then the initial presentation and generative strategy for the second objective, and so on until you have completed the unit of instruction.

Initial Presentation

The initial presentation for an objective provides the learner with the information needed to achieve the objective. Each initial presentation in your design plan includes a brief plan for how to present the information. For example, the initial presentation of a concept will include the concept name, definition, and best example. Your task analysis will include this information.

During the development of the initial presentations, you may identify a need to vary the step size or pacing. You can include summaries or refer to specific ideas presented earlier to reduce step size. To increase step size, you can reduce or remove redundancy and transitions. Similarly, you can vary the pacing by adding or removing examples and elaborations.

The initial presentation will include the cues to signal the learner to critical information. Signals in the initial presentation include those that indicate critical information such as cues or lists of items, the use of headings to identify the content structure (e.g., Tools Needed, Safety Precautions, Steps, Definition, Example), and headings that signal the structure of the unit (e.g., Introduction, Practice, Application). Signaling the intent will influence not only how much is remembered, but also the type of knowledge that is learned (Anderson & Armbruster, 1985).

Generative Strategy

The generative strategy creates an active learning opportunity for the learner. Implementing the strategy from the design plan provides the learner with the guidance and chance to relate the new information to existing information by generating new linkages. Thus, it is essential that the initial presentation provide the learner with the appropriate information to accomplish this task.

Once the learners have completed the generative strategy, how will you provide them with feedback? One effective approach used with the audiotutorial method (Postlethwait, Novak, & Murray, 1972) is to present the learner with the instructor's answer after the learner completes one of the embedded exercises. Other research has also demonstrated that providing the learners with an expert's paraphrase is an effective strategy (Johnsey, Morrison, & Ross, 1992). Generative strategies differ from the more traditional strategies, such as mathemagenic activities (Rothkopf, 1996) that typically have a single correct answer. Responses to generative strategies, such as asking the learner to paraphrase or generate questions, do not have clear-cut right and wrong answers. Thus, any feedback should include directions to the learners that they should compare their responses to that of the expert to identify differences.

Transitions

As you finish the development of one objective and start the next, you may want to include a transition. Transitions can help reduce the step size or jump from one idea to the next for the learner. Similarly, you can use a transition to alert the learner that the instruction is moving to a new idea. Transitions can be a single sentence at the end of the previous section or one at the beginning of the next section. You can also create short paragraphs that help the learner transition from one idea or objective to the next. The following is an example of a transition.

> Now that you have completed the installation of the Ethernet card and installed the software, we are ready to modify the operating system so that we can share a folder and a printer connected to the computer.

This transition refers back to the section the learner has just completed (installation) and shows how the completed steps are related to the next section, modifying the operating system. When you prepare a transition, avoid the trap of providing extensive summaries that overwhelm the learner.

Developing the instruction may seem like a daunting task to both novice and experienced instructional designers. We can simplify this task if we consider our design plan as a blueprint of our outline for the unit of instruction. By developing the instruction to follow the instructional design plan and addressing each objective, the development process becomes a manageable task. Developing the materials is a combination of following the instructional design plan and using a good dose of creativity.

Cognitive Load

Many introductory psychology courses introduce students to the "magic number 7 plus or minus 2" (see Miller, 1956). The basic conclusion from this rule is that learners can remember between five and nine items at one time. As instructional designers, we concluded that when giving the learner a list of items to memorize, such as airport codes, we should design our strategy so as to present only five to nine codes at a time rather than a list of two or three hundred codes at one time. While this heuristic is an important guideline, Sweller (1999) and his associates, who have researched the cognitive load placed on the learner during instructional tasks, have suggested other factors to consider. In this section, we examine the application of cognitive load theory to the design of instructional materials. First, we examine the learning process. Second, we define two types of cognitive load. Third, we examine how we can manage cognitive load as we develop our materials.

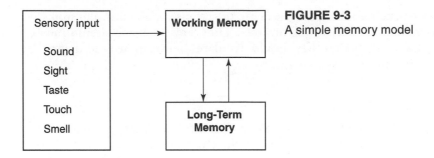

FIGURE 9-3
A simple memory model

The Learning Process.   As you read or watch television, three important process take place. First, you must attend to or be aware of the information coming from your senses. Second, you can then process the information or transform it into another form so that you can easily encode it so that you will remember it for future recall (see Figure 9-3). These processes occur in working, or short-term, memory. Information held in working memory will only remain there for a few seconds unless we refresh the information by rehearsal. For example, you might use the phone book to look up the phone number for the pharmacy. As you walk across the room to the phone, you keep repeating the phone number in your memory to keep it from fading from working memory. Most often we are trying to remember a seven-digit number such as 555-1212. But what if we needed to call another country and the number was 5475-4329? The additional number and unusual pattern would require us to expend extra effort to remember the phone number as we walked across the room. We have developed a schema that helps us recognize 555-1456 as a telephone number; more precisely, it is probably a local telephone number since it does not have an area code preceding the seven digits. When we use our schema to organize or recognize a seven-digit number, we can easily remember it for a few short seconds. The foreign number, 5475-4329, does not match our schema for phone numbers and requires extra effort to remember. This extra effort is the mental effort or cognitive load we must expend to remember or process the number.

As instructional designers, we need to be concerned with the cognitive load we place on learners as they work with the materials we have designed. How can we control the effort the learner must expend to process the information?

Two Types of Cognitive Load.   Most of us have found that some subjects are easy whereas others are difficult. Some topics such as the elements in chemistry are easy to memorize. We can create a list and start memorizing O for oxygen, S for sulfur, C for carbon, and so forth. Each element is learned by itself and the learning task has little dependence on learning the other elements. Sweller (1999) refers to this content as having little element interactivity. Other tasks require us to grasp several elements and consider the relationships between them before we can understand the content. For example, in microeconomics we must understand fixed costs and variable costs to understand the concepts of total costs and marginal costs. Memorizing the definitions of each term would not contribute to our understanding of total or marginal costs. Similarly, we must go beyond memorizing the variables for calculating acceleration (acceleration = [Final rate – Initial rate] / time) and understand the meaning of each element to understand the concept of acceleration. These two examples identify content that has a high degree of interactivity; that is, we must understand the different parts and their relationships to gain an understanding. The first type of cognitive load, instrinsic load, is determined by the interactivity of the elements of the content. As designers, we have no control over the interactivity. If there is a high degree of interactivity, between the elements, then there will be a high intrinsic cognitive load. If there is low interactivity, such as learning the chemical elements, then the intrinsic cognitive load will be low.

In contrast is extraneous cognitive load that is introduced in the design or layout of the instructional materials. We *can control* the extraneous cognitive load imposed on the learner by careful use of instructional design and message design elements. For example, consider the task of teaching a student how to calculate the area of a trapezoid. To calculate the area you must add the two bases, then divide by 2, and multiply by the height. We can simply the process further by providing a formula: area = $([b_1 + b_2]/2)h$. Since the intrinsic cognitive load for the calculating acceleration and the area of a trapezoid is high, we want to avoid introducing or increasing the extraneous cognitive load. We can significantly reduce the cognitive load required to understand this calculation by providing a diagram (see Figure 9-4). The diagram provides the learner with a concrete reference for the terms in the formula, thus reducing the need for the student to use working memory to make those transformations. Instead, the student can focus on the calculation process.

As designers, our task is twofold. First, we must recognize content that has a high intrinsic cognitive load. Second, we must use appropriate instructional design and message design strategies to reduce the extraneous cognitive load imposed on the learner by our designs. The following paragraphs describe four ways of controlling cognitive load.

Goal-Free Effect.   When faced with a novel problem, learners often use a means-ends analysis to solve the problem. That is, they determine what is known, then try to find the shortest path to the solution of the problem. This approach is often

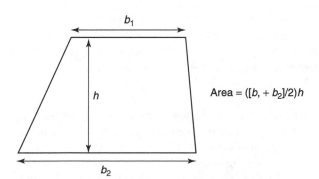

FIGURE 9-4
Using illustrations to reduce
cognitive load

Area = $([b, + b_2]/2)h$

highly efficient and effective for solving problems; however, Sweller (1999) suggests that it is not the best approach for *learning* how to solve problems. When learning how to solve a problem, the learner needs to develop a schema, such as one we have for determining the area of a rectangle so that we can apply it to determining the area of our yard in order to purchase the correct size bag of fertilizer. As we learn how to make this calculation, we learn to recognize elements such as length and width so that we can determine the area. The means-ends analysis does not help us understand the relationship between the elements (e.g., length and width) nor does it help us automate the calculation process. This approach also increases the intrinsic cognitive load for the learner. Sweller suggests that we incorporate goal-free problems to reduce the cognitive load. For example, when presented with the problem in Figure 9-5, the learner would focus on finding the value of *C*, whereas finding the value of *B* becomes a subgoal. However, if we add the statement, "Determine the value of as many variables as you can," the learner will take a different approach, which also reduces the cognitive load. That is, the learner first sees that she can substitute 3 for the value of *A* and then determine the value of *B*. Then, the learner sees that the value of *B* can be substituted in the next equation to determine the value of *C*. According to Sweller, this goal-free approach reduces the cognitive load and allows the learner to develop a problem-solving strategy.

$$A = 3$$
$$B = A + 4$$
$$C = B + 5$$

FIGURE 9-5
Means-ends analysis problem

Worked-Example Effect.   If you developed a math anxiety in your early years, you probably felt the return of the same anxiety when you first opened a statistics textbook. You were ready for the instructor to introduce a math-related topic, provide an example, and then expect you to solve a similar problem. Again, you were faced with trying to determine what steps were required to arrive at the correct answer. In recent years, we have seen considerable research (Kalyuga, Chandler, & Sweller, 2000, 2001; Paas & van Merriënboer, 1994; Sweller, 1999; Tuovinen & Sweller, 1999) on the use of worked examples. The worked example illustrates how to solve the problem by presenting each individual step rather than just the problem and final solution step. A sample worked example is presented in Table 7-7. The worked examples direct the learners' attention to the steps of the process and reduce the cognitive load needed to transform the steps in the presentation of a more traditional math example.

Split-Attention Effect.   If you have ever tried to follow instructions for replacing spark plugs, installing a graphics card in a computer, or installing a zipper, then you have probably experienced a split-attention effect. "How to" and textbooks often unintentionally create layout that increases the learners' cognitive load when trying to learn tasks. This effect is created when an illustration is introduced into the text.

Typically, the learner must divide his attention between the text and the graphic to comprehend the material. Figure 9-6 illustrates a passage that has introduced a split-attention affect and then how we corrected the problem to reduce the cognitive load imposed on the learner. In the first example, the learner must split her attention between the text and the labels (i.e., A, B, and C) on the drawing, which requires more cognitive effort than the second example, in which the text explanation and the graphic are integrated. The second example results in a reduction of cognitive effort required for understanding the text. We can prevent extraneous cognitive load by integrating our text and graphics rather than keeping them separated, as in the first example.

FIGURE 9-6
Split-attention effect

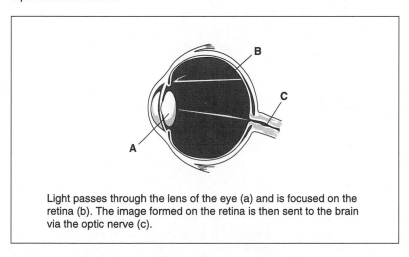

Light passes through the lens of the eye (a) and is focused on the retina (b). The image formed on the retina is then sent to the brain via the optic nerve (c).

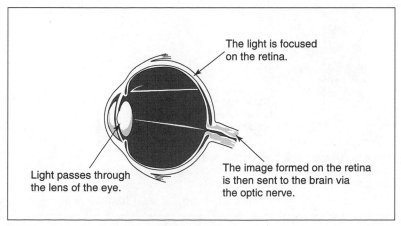

The light is focused on the retina.

Light passes through the lens of the eye.

The image formed on the retina is then sent to the brain via the optic nerve.

Redundancy.   While correcting a problem that creates a split-attention effect, you might decide that if text integrated with an illustration is good, then keeping the similar information in the text should further enhance the instructional quality of the materials. Sweller (1999), however, has found that repeating the same information in both the illustration and text creates a redundancy effect that actually increases the cognitive effort to process the information. The learner must pay attention to both the text and the graphic source, resulting in less working memory available to process the information. Figure 9-7 illustrates the redundancy effect. The information should be presented either in the graphic or in the text rather than in both.

During the design and development phase, the instructional designer needs to identify strategies for reducing the cognitive load of the instructional materials. The four effects—goal free, worked example, split attention, and redundancy—provide examples of ways cognitive load can be increased as well as strategies for decreasing it. The effort might require working closely with a graphic artist since the integration of text and graphics is not a traditional method used in the layout and design of materials.

FIGURE 9-7
Redundancy effect

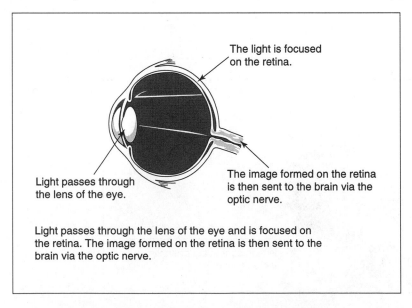

Expert's Edge

Helping the Learner Comprehend

Some time ago, we noticed that our students were often overwhelmed by the abundance of irrelevant hits that was generated by their scientific literature search activities and were amazed by the results of an expert searching for literature using different databases and Boolean operators. As a result of this observation, we realized that searching for scientific literature is a complex task for which we might have a training problem. A quick analysis of the task and a closer look at the current training practice revealed that the task consisted of many interactive elements. The training focused on isolated elements and almost immediately began with authentic search assignments. From our experience as "cognitive" instructional designers, we knew that high element-interactivity material is highly cognitively demanding and difficult to understand. Although the elements can be learned individually, meaningful learning or deep understanding can only commence if the learner is able to attend to the important aspects of the presented material, mentally organize it into a coherent cognitive schema, and integrate it with relevant existing knowledge.

To tackle this training problem, we used the four-component instructional design (4C/ID) approach (Van Merriënboer, 1997). With its heavy reliance on cognitive load theory (CLT) (Sweller, Van Merriënboer, & Paas, 1998), the methodology is especially suitable to developing training for these complex cognitive tasks, which, without the appropriate instruction, may easily impose a high burden on the cognitive system of the learner. CLT is concerned with the development of innovative instructional methods that efficiently use people's limited cognitive-processing capacity in order to stimulate meaningful learning.

Although 4C/ID considers authentic learning tasks as the driving force for learning, it acknowledges that the intrinsic load of these tasks in combination with the load caused by the manner in which the information is presented may hamper learning. When the load is necessary and enhances learning, it is referred to as *germane load*. After a thorough task analysis, use the following techniques to manage the cognitive load.

Organization of Learning Tasks in a Simple-to-Complex Sequence of Task Classes

To prevent the excessive cognitive load that is typically associated with authentic tasks, learners will typically start working on learning tasks that represent relatively simple versions of the whole task. They progress toward tasks that represent more complex versions of the whole tasks as their expertise increases. Cognitive load is optimized because at any time in the training program learners receive tasks that are challenging to them but never too demanding on their cognitive capacities. The intrinsic aspects of cognitive load can be reduced by this simple-to-complex sequencing.

Task classes are used to define these simple-to-complex categories of learning tasks. The basic idea is to use a whole-task approach in which the first task class refers to the simplest version of whole tasks that experts encounter in the real world. For increasingly more complex task classes, the assumptions that simplify task performance are relaxed. The final task class represents all tasks, including the most complex ones that professionals encounter in the real world.

For example, some of the task factors that determine how complex it is to perform the scientific literature search skill are (1) the clearness of the concept definitions within the domain, (2) the number of articles written about the topic of interest, and (3) the number of search terms and Boolean operators needed to identify the topic of interest. Using these factors, we can define the simplest task as a category of learning tasks in which the concepts are clearly defined, with only few search terms, and which yields a limited amount of relevant articles. In contrast, the most complex task class is defined as a category of learning tasks for which concept definitions within the domain are unclear and searches require many terms and Boolean operators in order to limit relevant articles. Additional task classes of an intermediate complexity level can be added in between by varying one or more of the task factors.

Timing of Supportive and Prerequisite Information

From a cognitive load perspective, the distribution of essential information over a training program and the timing and the format of presentation to students is critical. In many contemporary training programs, all information is provided before practice starts and is presented in a manner that unnecessarily increases extraneous cognitive load. The 4C/ID model takes this problem into account by making a distinction between supportive and prerequisite information and by prescribing how, when, and where in the program it should be presented.

Supportive information is helpful to the learning and performance of the variable aspects of learning tasks. It can be information that describes how a learning domain is organized and therefore allows for reasoning in that domain. It can also be information that describes the way problems in a domain may be effectively approached and therefore guides problem solving. To keep the load resulting from the presentation of supportive information within manageable proportions, the supportive information within a 4C/ID training program is connected to task classes and evenly distributed across the whole training program.

Prerequisite information is conditional to the learning and performance of the consistent aspects of learning tasks. It consists of step-by-step knowledge that exactly describes how consistent skills need to be performed. This information is always applied in the same manner. Once a learner has mastered a consistent skill, the declarative information of how the skill is performed (e.g., procedures for selecting and filling in search fields) is no longer necessary. We can decrease the extraneous load imposed by organizing the consistent skills (i.e., how to fill in search fields) in small units or information displays and presenting it precisely when learners need it (just in time) during their work on the learning tasks.

Part-Task Practice to Automate Consistent Skills

Learning tasks are designed in such a way that they primarily promote knowledge construction for the performance of the variable aspects of the to-be-learned complex skill. However, in some cases the use of repeated practice in order to automate the consistent aspects of the skill is needed. For example, in complex literature searches a learner has to formulate search queries in which many search terms are combined with Boolean operators (e.g., learning *and* psychomotor) to decrease the otherwise large amount of hits. The cognitive load resulting from performing this consistent skill might be so high that learners have no cognitive resources available to organize the different literature search problems. As a result, the learning of the whole skill is disrupted. Repeated short isolated practice sessions are used to automate the performance of the consistent skill and to free up cognitive resources to cope with the variable aspects of the learning task.

High Variability of Practice within Task Classes

The learning tasks within the same task class are sequenced in a randomized order so that each next learning task differs from the previous one. High variability is known to promote meaningful learning by stimulating learners to compare the solutions to the different learning tasks and to abstract more general knowledge for solving a wide range of problems. So, high variability of learning tasks is used as a technique to increase germane cognitive load.

Learner Support

To compensate for the increased germane load that is created by the high variability of learning tasks, a task class will typically start with learning tasks having a large amount of learner support. As learners acquire more expertise in working on the learning tasks, learner support is gradually decreased until learners are practicing with no support at all. One popular way to realize the reduction in extraneous load is by providing the substantial scaffolding of worked examples initially, followed by completion problems and then full problems. Each of these problem forms may provide product and/or process support. Product support is provided by giving more or less of the solution to the problem that the learner has to solve in the learning task. Process support is also directed to the problem-solving process itself. Full process support can be provided as a modeling example in which the learner is confronted with an expert who is performing a literature search and simultaneously explains why the task is performed as it is.

References

Sweller, J., van Merriënboer, J. J. G., & Paas, F. (1998). Cognitive architecture and instructional design. *Educational Psychology Review, 10*, 251-296.

Van Merriënboer, J. J. G. (1997). *Training complex cognitive skills: A four-component instructional design model for technical training.* Englewood Cliffs, NJ: Educational Technology Publications.

Fred Paas is senior educational technologist at the Educational Technology Expertise Center of the Open University of the Netherlands. His interests include research and development with a main focus on the instructional control of cognitive load in the training of complex cognitive tasks.

Marcel de Croock is an assistant professor of educational technology at the Educational Technology Expertise Center of the Open University of the Netherlands. He is currently involved in the development of computer-based tools for the design of personalized training for complex skills. His research interests include transfer of training, cognitive load and learning, training of troubleshooting skills, and adaptive computer-based learning environments for complex skills.

The next section of this chapter focuses on three different instructional delivery methods: group presentations (lectures), self-paced instruction, and small-group activities. Examples of each method are described, followed by a discussion of the method's strengths and limitations.

GROUP PRESENTATIONS

In the group presentation or lecture method, the instructor tells, shows, demonstrates, dramatizes, or otherwise disseminates subject content to a group of learners. This pattern can be utilized in a classroom, an auditorium, or a variety of locations through the use of radio, amplified telephone, closed-circuit television transmission, interactive distance television, or satellite communication (teleconferencing).

While lecturing, the teacher may include media materials, such as transparencies, recordings, slides, video recordings, or multimedia presentations, either singly or in multi-image combination. These activities illustrate the one-way transmission of information from instructor to learners, often for a set period of time (generally a 40- to 50-minute class period). In small classes there may be some degree of two-way communication between teacher and learners, but most frequently, learners are passively listening and watching.

Strengths

The benefits of choosing a group presentation method to accomplish certain learning objectives include the following:

- A lecture format is familiar and conventionally acceptable to both instructor and learners. This method is the most common form of instructional delivery.
- Lectures can often be fairly quickly designed since the instructor is familiar with the material and will make the actual presentation. The designer often works with the subject-matter expert to provide the instructor with a list of objectives and a topic outline with the unwritten agreement that the instructor will follow the outline. The assumption is that the instructor can make

the necessary strategy decisions. This strength is a particular advantage when instruction is needed to address a critical, short-term need.

- A lecture places the instructor in direct control of the class and in a visible authority position. For some instructors and in many teaching contexts, these factors are advantageous for achieving the objectives.
- Large numbers of learners can be served at one time with a lecture. The group is limited only by the size of the room; thus, lectures can be highly economical.
- As instructional needs change, a presentation can be easily modified by deleting content or adding new content just before or even during the delivery. Also, the presentation can be easily adapted for a specific group of learners (e.g., made longer or shorter, more or less difficult).
- Lectures are a feasible method of communicating when the information requires frequent changes and updates or when the information is relevant for only a short time period, such as the implementation of a new travel policy.
- A good lecture can be motivating and interesting for the students.

Limitations

The group presentation method of instruction suffers from the following limitations:

- Learning is typically very passive, involving listening, watching, and taking notes, with little or no opportunity for exchanging ideas with the instructor.
- To maintain learners' attention during a presentation, the lecturer needs to be interesting, enthusiastic, and challenging.
- When an instructor lectures, demonstrates, shows a video, or otherwise presents subject content to a class of learners, the assumption is made that all learners are acquiring the same understanding, with the same level of comprehension, at the same time. They are forced to learn at a pace set by the teacher. Thus, lectures are not adaptive to individual differences.
- If questioning is permitted, instruction stops and all learners must wait until the question is answered before the presentation can proceed.
- In a large lecture class, it is difficult for the instructor to receive individual feedback from learners pertaining to misunderstandings and difficulties encountered during the presentation. Thus, some learners may leave the class with incorrect learning.
- A presentation may be inappropriate for teaching psychomotor and affective objectives, as these objectives typically require some form of practice or active learning environment.
- A large-group presentation may vary from presentation to presentation. Thus, the consistency of information and topics covered may not be the same for any two groups. This problem is particularly relevant when the training needs to be consistent, such as when teaching policies or procedures.
- Students who have difficulty with auditory learning will be at a disadvantage throughout the presentation.

Applications

There are specific situations and times at which a presentation to a group of learners is most valuable:

- As an introduction, overview, or orientation to a new topic
- To create interest for a subject or topic
- To present basic or essential information as common background before learners engage in small-group or individual activities
- To introduce recent developments in a field, especially when preparation time is limited
- To provide such resources as a one-time guest speaker, a video, or other visual presentation that can most conveniently and efficiently be shown to the whole group at one time
- To provide opportunities for learners to make their own presentations as reports to the class
- As a review or summary when the study of the topic or unit is concluded
- To teach a large group of learners in a highly economical manner

Guidelines for Effective Lecturing

Keep in mind that learning is enhanced when learners are actively involved. Therefore, it is important to develop a plan for including learner participation activities when lecturing. Also, to facilitate learners' understanding of the material, lectures should be clear and well organized. We recommend the following components:

- *Active interaction with the instructor.* Prepare questions to use at various points during the verbal presentation; encourage or direct learners to answer and enter into discussion with the instructor. Decide on places to stop a presentation (often at the conclusion of a section or the end of information presented on a concept), and ask questions to measure understanding and encourage discussion.
- *Note taking.* Encourage note taking by learners so that they will actively work with the material. Notes taken in the students' own words are useful in producing meaningful learning rather than rote memorization.
- *Handouts.* Consider preparing structured notes on topics requiring the learner to (1) fill in an outline of content (e.g., structured notes), (2) complete diagrams that accompany visuals used in the presentation, (3) write replies to questions, (4) solve problems, and (5) make applications of content and concepts as the presentation proceeds. Learners can also complete self-check exercises or quizzes of the content presented. The key is to stimulate active processing of the information. For this reason, detailed notes are generally not recommended, since they eliminate the need for the students to generate their own. Other forms of handouts include slides from a multimedia presentation such as PowerPoint that allows you to print three slides per page with room for notes.

- *Other mental activity.* Encourage thinking by helping learners verbalize answers mentally to rhetorical or direct questions that you or another learner pose. You can also ask learners to formulate their own questions relating to the materials for use in follow-up, small-group sessions.
- *Terminology.* Use clear terminology and meaningful examples to illustrate concepts.
- *Organization.* Organize the lecture by constructing an outline. Bring the outline (or note cards) to the presentation and talk "from" it rather than reading it verbatim (a guaranteed painful experience for listeners). Unless you are very accomplished as a lecturer and highly familiar with the presentation, do not try to speak extemporaneously; a frequent result is a disorganized and rambling presentation.
- *Enthusiasm.* Show enthusiasm and interest in your subject.
- *Format.* A standard model (adapted from Slavin, 1994) is as follows:
  1. Orient the students to the topics (an outline, story, or overview).
  2. Review prerequisites.
  3. Present the material in a clear, organized way.
  4. Ask questions.
  5. Provide independent practice.
  6. Review and preview.

Distance Education as a Special Application

As telecommunications technology becomes more advanced and cost-effective, distance education is receiving increasing attention as an instructional delivery system. As Simonson (1995) points out, although few students prefer to learn at a distance relative to being in the same room with the instructor, there are times when the convenience of distance education outweighs other factors. Keegan (1996) identifies two categories of distance education. According to his definition of distance education, the learner and the instructor are separated in time and space for the majority of the course. Examples include correspondence courses, broadcast television courses, and web-based courses. The second category is for those delivery systems such as interactive distance television that separate the learner and instructor in space but not time. That is, all the students must meet at the same time, but in different locations. He labels this category as virtual education rather than as a form of distance education. In the typical virtual education setting, there is a host classroom or studio in which the instructor actually presents the instruction. Remote sites contain one or more video monitors, TV cameras, or microphones, along with other, optional equipment (e.g., a fax machine) permitting the two-way transmission of voice, video images, written communications, and computer animations and simulations. In essence, the students at the remote site can hear, see, and interact with the instructor as he or she presents material in real time. Naturally, differing degrees of instructor-to-student interaction are possible depending on the number of remote sites to which the instruction is transmitted. Another type of distance education is one using the Internet to deliver the instruction. Instruction offered via the

Internet can take many forms, ranging from web pages to mailing lists. Students can interact in real time in chat rooms or asynchronously by posting to bulletin boards or forums. Various websites also provide software and hosting services for instructors who want to create either web-based resources for their classes or a web-based course (e.g., www.blackboard.com). Another form of Internet-based instruction is asynchronous learning networks (ALNs) that have many features common to the personalized system of instruction (discussed later in the chapter). Descriptions of ALN courses can be found at www.aln.org. Today, it is not unusual for a distance education course to include a mix of media or delivery systems. For example, PBS's teleWEBcourses include a weekly broadcast video program, web-based activities, and a textbook. Similarly, campus courses often make use of web-based instruction through applications such as Blackboard, allowing a blend of traditional and distance education delivery systems.

Strengths.   Distance and virtual education have additional strengths beyond the traditional classroom lecture and self-paced instruction for both training and education environments as follows:

- Students can "attend" a class without going to campus.
- Very large audiences situated miles apart can potentially be served.
- Quality communications equipment at the host site can transmit professional-level, multimedia presentations.
- Unlike conventional video presentations, students can experience instruction as it happens, thus permitting updates, announcements, and the spontaneity of live events.
- Unlike conventional instructional television, students can interact with the instructor by asking questions or making comments.
- Students can study and complete course activities anytime, anywhere.

Weaknesses.   There are also weaknesses associated with distance education that one would not encounter in a traditional classroom. These weaknesses are as follows:

- Depending on the sophistication of the telecommunications system and other resources, the quality of the video and/or audio transmission may be inferior to a presentation given in the same room (e.g., video images that are not well synchronized with the sound may be distracting to learners; layout of room may limit viewing of monitors).
- Despite the two-way communication capabilities, interactions between individuals at the host and remote sites are more constrained and less fluid than those taking place in the same room. Because such interactions interrupt the main presentation or are difficult to follow aurally and visually, students may lose interest in the instruction.
- The hardware requirements for some distance education delivery systems may prove too expensive for some organizations.

- Students working independently in a distance course lack a pacing mechanism, such as a weekly lecture, and may fall behind.
- Students in distance education courses tend to have a higher dropout rate than students attending campus courses.

Guidelines for Effective Learning.   The following heuristics can help you plan an effective distance education lesson.

- Consider the cost of delivering the instruction and use distance education selectively where it fits special instructional conditions and needs (i.e., enables you to reach learners who are geographically dispersed).
- At the remote site, use multiple monitors rather than a single monitor where appropriate to achieve greater closeness between students and the presentation (Gopalakrishnan Jayasinghe, Morrison, & Ross, 1997).
- At the host site, favor an eye-level rather than high-angle camera position to increase eye contact by the presenter (Gopalakrishnan Jayasinghe et al., 1997).
- Carefully balance the amount of two-way communication permitted so that appropriate opportunities for interactivity are provided without compromising the pace or continuity of the lesson.
- Where appropriate, integrate multiple media (e.g., professional-quality videos or software presentations) to increase variety and impact, so that the distance instruction is more interesting than watching essentially a TV-type lecture.
- Provide a means for students to contact the instructor, and then provide a response in a reasonable time frame.
- Provide detailed feedback on assignments.
- Materials must be designed in a way to create a guided-didactic conversation (Holmberg, 1983). In distance education, the teaching (i.e., design of the instruction) and the learning (i.e., when the student studies the materials) are often separated by weeks or even months. Keegan (1996) suggests that we need to reintegrate the teaching and learning acts that were separated due the design of the materials prior to their delivery to the students. That is, design the instruction to engage the learner with the content so that it is actively processed rather than passively read.

SELF-PACED LEARNING

Self-paced learning has received the most attention in instructional design. As the principles of learning indicate, much evidence supports the belief that optimum learning takes place when a student works at his or her own pace, is actively involved in performing specific learning tasks, and experiences success in learning.

Self-paced learning methods are also called *individualized learning* or *self-instruction*. While these terms may have different meanings, the important features for the learner are responsibility, pacing, and successful learning based on specific learning objectives and a variety of activities with accompanying resources.

Most frequently, the instructor selects the learning objectives and sets the requirements learners must follow. A "true" individualized learning or learner-controlled program would require the design of separate objectives and learning activities for each learner according to that individual's own characteristics, preparation, needs, and interests. Implementation of such a system usually requires a computer-managed instructional system to track the progress of each student and to select the appropriate objectives. Self-paced instruction, however, can occur at several different levels. Classic models from the literature are mastery learning (Block, 1971) at the precollege level and the Personalized System of Instruction (PSI) at the college level (Keller & Sherman, 1982). In school contexts, comparable approaches are sometimes referred to as *continuous-progress grading*, in which students' evaluations depend on the number of units they complete in a given time period (Slavin, 1994).

Drawing from these models, a quality self-paced learning program includes the following specific features:

- Learning activities are carefully designed to address specific objectives. A typical self-paced unit is organized into comparatively small, discrete steps, each one treating a single concept or segment of content. The size of the steps can vary, but it is essential that they are carefully sequenced.
- Activities and resources are carefully selected in terms of the required instructional objectives.
- The learner's mastery of each step is checked before he or she proceeds to the next step. Therefore, it is necessary to require the learner to demonstrate mastery of the content.
- The learner then must receive immediate confirmation of mastery of the objectives. With each success, the learner confidently advances to the next step.
- When the learner has difficulty understanding the material or fails to master the objectives for a unit, further study may be necessary, or the learner may ask the instructor for help. Thus, the learner is continually engaged in active learning and receives immediate feedback.

Most objectives in all three domains can be treated through some form of self-paced learning activities. In some learning environments, the instructor and students may feel more secure using a mixture of self-paced and group-paced instruction (see the description of audio-tutorial instruction). The instructor and designer must determine the most appropriate delivery method for each of the objectives. In some situations, background and factual information might be assigned to a self-paced mode to ensure that all learners have mastered the basic information. Then, the group presentation (lecture) can build on this foundation. In another situation, the lecture might provide the background material, and some form of individualized instruction treatment would help the learners achieve the higher-level objectives. The instructor can then work with individual students who have difficulty mastering the material, while the faster learners can proceed to the next unit. Today, the greater emphasis being placed by educators on cognitive theory and self-constructed knowledge has altered thinking that self-paced units must be highly rigid in content and linked to highly specific mastery criteria. That is, units that are project-based and discovery-oriented would certainly represent desirable types of self-paced instruction (e.g., using the Internet as an information source for creating a classroom exhibition on world-renowned natural history museums).

Strengths

Evidence suggests that in many situations, learners participating in self-paced learning programs work harder, learn more, and retain more of what is learned than do learners in conventional classes. Self-paced learning offers a number of unique advantages as an instructional method:

- Both slow and advanced learners can complete the instruction according to their own abilities and under appropriate learning conditions.
- The self-reliance and personal responsibility required of learners by a self-paced learning program may carry over as habits to other educational activities, job responsibilities, and personal behavior.
- Increased attention by instructors can be given to the individual learner.
- The activities and responsibilities of an instructor involved in a self-paced learning program change because less time is spent in making presentations and more time is devoted to addressing learners in group sessions, consulting with individuals, and managing the learning environment.
- While major approaches to self-paced learning are not always immediately cost-effective, as the lessons and resources are employed over time with additional classes, the cost of a program can be reduced appreciably. (For a consideration of program costs and measuring program efficiency, see Chapter 12.)
- The information presented to each learner remains consistent (i.e., each learner receives the same basic ideas) over time, which reduces variations caused by lectures presented on different days.

Limitations

There are also some limitations to self-paced learning that make it less suitable for some environments:

- There may be a lack of interaction between instructor and learners or among learners if a self-paced program is the sole method of instruction in a course. Therefore, it is important to plan for periodic instructor–learner, small-group activities as appropriate.
- If a single-path, lockstep method is followed, learning can become monotonous and uninteresting. On the other hand, open-ended (discovery-type) projects may allow for too much divergence in what learners experience and accomplish.

- Lack of self-discipline combined with procrastination can result in delaying the completion of required study by some learners. Many learners must develop new habits and patterns of behavior before they are successful in self-paced learning. Setting deadlines (weekly or monthly) within which learners can adjust to their own study pace is often required and beneficial for some learners.

- The self-paced method often requires cooperation and detailed team planning with the faculty involved in the course. Also, coordination with other support services of the organization (facilities, media, reproduction, etc.) may become necessary or even critical. Such an effort is in contrast to the usual single-person operation characteristic of conventional teaching.

- More preparation and expense is typically involved in developing self-paced units compared with lecture presentations.

Guidelines for Effective Learning

A self-paced unit typically includes a great deal of active learning. If existing materials (e.g., textbook, films, videotapes) are adapted, then the designer needs to develop materials to encourage active learning. These materials can include study guides, worksheets, and exercises. The Keller Plan (PSI) is a good example of how an instructor can adapt existing materials for use in an individualized program.

Since individuals learn at different rates, there should be time to study when it is convenient for them and also time in which to pace themselves. Individuals may want to linger over some material and speed through that which they understand quickly. A preferable way to plan for individualized learning is to start with a variety of materials serving the objectives and then plan more than one instructional sequence to provide for differences among individual learners. Depending on preparation and need, some learners may take the fast track, even skipping ahead and using few materials before concluding their study. Other learners may require a slower track that contains a greater number of concrete illustrations or examples, more review exercises, or even smaller segments of subject content with a repetition of explanations in different contexts. A designer needs to include a management system into the course design to accommodate these learners.

Individuals also differ in how they prefer to learn (see Chapter 3). Some learners respond best to visual materials, whereas others work better with printed resources or hands-on experiences. Therefore, it may be advisable to collect or prepare a variety of materials to treat a set of learning objectives and then allow each learner to select a preferred way to study. For example, if an objective requires the operation of a piece of laboratory equipment, the program for mastering this objective may include printed instructions, a set of still photographs, a short film or videotape, and the equipment. One learner may choose to begin with the video demonstration and then go immediately to practice with the equipment; another learner might prefer to read the instruction sheet and then examine the still pictures before attempting to practice; a third might go immediately to the equipment and learn in a trial-and-error fashion.

By recognizing that active participation is a key element for learning, instructional planners can design a variety of experiences for learners. These can range from a carefully structured program that allows learners to proceed at their own pace to one that gives individuals virtually complete freedom and responsibility for choosing their own activities and materials according to their own learning styles or preferences.

Examples

Following are descriptions of several procedures for implementing self-paced learning. They range from the use of simple, prepared materials to adaptations of commercial materials to systematically planned, full-scale programs.

Learner Contracts.   The learner enters into an agreement with the instructor to achieve acceptable objectives, often by completing a project in exchange for rewards (credit points, participation in special activities, or free time). Either the teacher suggests resources or the learner takes responsibility for deciding what to do to achieve the objectives and carry out the project.

Textbooks/Worksheets.   At times, to effectively study the content of textbooks or other printed resources used as an integral part of a course, learners may need guidance when their reading or language skills are limited. First, objectives are developed from the textbook content. Second, a worksheet directs the study of text chapters and provides review exercises, questions, and other activities. Third, a self-check test or a project to apply the content may be provided at the conclusion of each chapter review. After completing this work, a learner will be better prepared to participate in class work requiring both understanding and application of the textual content.

Computer-Based Instruction.   A computer-based instruction (CBI) unit offers several options. It can offer a drill-and-practice routine to improve associations such as math facts, a tutorial to present new information, or a simulation that allows the learner to manipulate a system and observe the results. Some CBI programs are adaptive. One type of adaptation is through branching and presentation of information based on the learners' performance. A second form of adaptation is through the use of personalized information (e.g., learner's birth date, best friends, favorite food) in the examples and problems (Dorsey-Davis, Ross, & Morrison, 1991).

Audiotape/Worksheets.   With audiotapes and worksheets, a learner reads information, refers to diagrams or other visuals, solves problems, and completes other activities under the direction of the instructor's voice on tape. The recording provides directions, information, explanations of answers, and other "tutorial" assistance.

The tape/worksheet combination is often developed to treat specific course topics for which other instructional materials may not exist or which require a unique approach. Tapes that contain the instructor's voice are typically a personal, often informal method of presenting course material in an interesting way. The audiocassette tape and worksheet combination form a compact package that learners can conveniently use wherever or whenever they choose.

Visuals/Guide Sheets.   Visuals with a guide sheet may be used when learners need directions or instructions to operate equipment, carry out a process, or complete a precise activity. Visuals in either still or motion-picture form can guide learners through the steps necessary for completing a specific task.

A careful task analysis of the steps is a necessary prerequisite to developing a guide sheet. When visuals are combined with printed guide sheets that summarize an operation or provide other necessary factual or supplemental information, a complete self-instructional package on a topic can result.

Multimedia Packages.   As the name implies, a multimedia package consists of several types of media resource materials that are used concurrently or sequentially in a self-paced learning situation. A package usually treats a single topic within a course. It can best provide the instruction for topics that require the realism of photographs or the symbolism of diagrams along with verbal explanations.

Commercially prepared multimedia packages are available in several formats: slides or a set of filmstrips with correlated audiocassettes and printed materials; a videocassette or motion picture film and printed materials; an interactive CD-ROM; and an interactive videodisc. The materials may include combinations of readings, worksheets, illustrations, animations, and real-time demonstrations. In addition, equipment and tools may be part of the kit with which the learner carries out performance activities.

As part of these packages, a syllabus or guide should describe (1) the learning objectives of the package, (2) the directions for use, and (3) the methods for evaluating how well the utilization of the package satisfies the instructional objectives.

Self-Instructional Modules.   The self-instructional module is a package that treats a single topic or unit of subject content. It includes a study guide containing all necessary information for a learner to proceed through the assigned material. Important components of a module are (1) carefully stated directions; (2) instructional objectives; (3) descriptions of activities and exercises (often with alternative choices so that a learner may select a preferred method of study); (4) a list of resources; and (5) one or more tests, with answers, so the learner may check progress in learning.

The module may refer the learner to other resources in the library or lab. Activities are not necessarily limited to the study of written materials alone. Video and audio media resources are often used to augment, clarify, or enhance printed information. A series of self-instructional modules may constitute an entire course or be used as part of a course to cover topical areas. Study time for individual modules may vary from less than an hour to a day or more of work.

The personalized system of instruction and audio-tutorial method were two highly successful self-paced instructional approaches. They are still used to some degree today and are still very successful. We are including them in this discussion since they offer good ideas for developing new approaches or creating adapations for other delivery methods.

Personalized System of Instruction (PSI).   The PSI method of self-paced learning (developed by psychologist Fred Keller [Keller & Sherman, 1982] and often called the Keller Plan) is an approach that may be applied to a complete course. Most frequently, it is based on a textbook with study units consisting of readings, questions, and problems. Instructional resources need not be limited to only written material. Other media of a visual and/or audio nature may be incorporated. It is also a method that can be adapted to web-based instruction for a distance education course.

    After studying and completing prescribed activities for each unit of material, a learner reports to a course proctor to be tested on the unit of instruction. The complete test is immediately graded by the proctor (usually a learner who previously completed the course successfully), who then shows the results to the learner. With satisfactory accomplishment of the test (often a competency-level requirement of 80 to 90 percent), the learner proceeds to the next chapter or unit. If the specified level of learning does not result, the learner studies the material again and takes another form of the test when ready.

    This procedure is repeated until the learner achieves success on each unit. Thus, completion times vary among learners. Where course completion time must be fixed (e.g., in a semester), grades may be based on the number of units completed. While some study is undertaken individually, not all learning has to occur in isolation. Some instructors meet with a class or small groups of learners to conduct special lectures and discussions. In addition, the contact between individual learners and proctors, for the purpose of evaluation and immediate feedback, can encourage further study. Although these days the Keller Plan is less frequently used as a comprehensive, intact design than it was in the 1970s, its basic elements offer viable strategies for self-paced instruction that can be adapted for use in a variety of contexts.

Audio-Tutorial Method.   Another complete, systematic approach to a self-paced learning course is the audio-tutorial method, designed by the botanist Samuel N. Postlethwait (Postlethwait, Novak, & Murray, 1972). The process usually includes three major components: (1) a large group meeting of the whole class, usually weekly, for a number of purposes—introducing a new topic, presenting a guest speaker, showing a film, or administering an examination; (2) self-paced learning activities in a learning lab appropriate for the course; and (3) group discussion sessions in which learners may ask questions, make reports, and engage in other forms of interaction.

    A study guide is prepared that contains learning objectives, activities, exercises, and self-check tests. Audiotapes are used during the self-paced learning period to lead the learner through the learning experiences. The recording is not a lecture. The instructor's voice on the tape provides some information, tutorial guidance, and directions for the learner. Activities directed by the tape may include completing readings in books and from articles, studying visual materials, completing worksheet questions, and performing laboratory work as appropriate. The tape also provides the learner with answers as feedback on learning. The instructor or a teaching assistant usually is available in the learning lab to assist learners and answer questions. As with the Keller Plan, the audio-tutorial method is more likely to be seen today in adapted forms, all involving, in some way, self-paced completion of audiotaped lessons as primary or supplementary instruction. Similarly, the audio-tutorial model can serve as a basis for developing a distance education course that might include PowerPoint presentations (e.g., study guide) with streaming audio, chat rooms for small group discussions, and forums for larger group discussions. Laboratory exercises could be either web or CD-ROM animations or experiments.

A Planning Checklist

If you are developing a self-paced program, the following checklist of questions for evaluating your planning may prove useful:

1. Is the program adaptable to the characteristics of learners who have different cultural and ethnic backgrounds?
2. Are learners who need remedial help identified before they start on a unit or module?
3. Are learners allowed to skip ahead if they already show competencies in part of the topic being treated?
4. Are low-level cognitive knowledge and psychomotor skills mastered before requiring higher-level learning experiences and practical applications of subject content?
5. Is adequate attention given to affective objectives? That is, are learners developing positive attitudes toward the subject or its applications?
6. Are options provided so that a learner may select learning experiences and resources?
7. Are learners permitted or encouraged to progress at their own rates?
8. Do learners have opportunities for checking their progress as they proceed through a program?
9. Do learners have opportunities to share their learning or otherwise interact among themselves and with the instructor?
10. Do instructors consult with or assist individual learners and small groups?
11. How will self-pacing for the particular unit impact other activities in the course?

Changing Roles

Finally, as a planning team designs a self-paced learning program, the instructors involved should recognize that not only are they changing their methods of instruction, they also must change their own roles in working with learners. These changes can become both stimulating and more demanding. Some of the changes that can be anticipated are these:

- Freedom from routine teaching of basic facts and skills
- More time spent with individual learners in diagnosing their difficulties, giving help, and monitoring their progress
- More opportunities to interact with learners on higher intellectual levels concerning their problems, interests, and uses of the subject content
- More time required for preparing, gathering, and organizing materials for use by learners
- More time required to orient and supervise aides, tutors, proctors, and other assistants

SMALL-GROUP FORMATS

In the small-group teaching/learning format, teachers and learners, or learners themselves, work together in groups of 2 to 10 or so individuals to discuss, question, pursue problems cooperatively, and report. This approach provides students an opportunity to synthesize the content and improve their communication skills.

Strengths

Small-group formats have the following strengths:

- A small-group format can engender synthesis of content by allowing individuals to discuss materials, share ideas, and problem solve with others.
- Learners acquire experiences in listening and oral expression through reacting to others' ideas and presenting their own. The more able learners can strengthen their own learning by explaining points or principles to other learners (also known as "peer teaching").
- By listening to students' discussion in a small-group session, an instructor can gain an increased awareness of the successes or shortcomings of various phases of an instructional program as well as obtain suggestions from learners for revisions.
- Small-group sessions promote active learning.
- Learners develop social skills by working with others.

Limitations

Small-group learning may have the following drawbacks:

- Students need to complete the assigned readings before the small-group activities so that they will be ready to participate.
- Instructors who are not prepared or who are inexperienced with small-group activities may fall back on lecturing for their own security or may provide too much input at the expense of the discussion.

- Careful planning of group composition and management is required to create an atmosphere that encourages all group members to participate.
- Individual groups require feedback on their progress and prompting to keep them on task.
- Students are not trained instructors; thus, the group activities should be used to supplement rather than replace other forms of instruction (lecture or individualized).
- Logistics of providing space for small groups and the expense associated with the additional rooms may prohibit the use of this approach.

Formats

A number of different techniques are available to encourage and provide for interaction within small groups. These eight techniques are useful in both large-group and self-paced formats.

Discussion.   Discussion is the most common form of face-to-face teaching in which facts, ideas, and opinions can be exchanged. As learners think about a subject under discussion and present their views, learning can take place on higher intellectual levels (specifically, analysis, synthesis, and evaluation) than is possible solely with the recall of information.

Discussions can take three forms:

1. Instructor-directed discussion is characterized by questions posed by the instructor and answered by individual learners. Such a format provides for a limited exchange of ideas within the group.
2. Group-centered discussion allows for a free-flowing exchange of ideas without the controlling influence of the instructor. Cooperation between participants provides their own direction and control of the pace. This method is open ended, as the discussion can go in any number of directions depending on learner interactions and reactions.
3. Collaborative discussions often focus on solving a specific problem. The instructor has neither a dominant nor a passive role but serves as a resource person and also as a contributor. All participants share decision-making responsibilities and are obliged to accept and integrate the ideas presented and to critically evaluate alternative solutions. This method is the most difficult form of discussion to implement; it is best used after a group has experience with the previous two forms of discussion.

Panel Discussion.   In the panel discussion, three to six qualified persons (from the community or a professional group) present information or their views on an assigned topic in front of the class. The individuals may represent different viewpoints, various interest groups, or special experiences. Learners may research topics and serve on the panels themselves to present their findings. Following the presentations, learners in the class are encouraged to ask questions of the panel members.

Guided Design.   The guided-design method, developed by Charles E. Wales (Wales, Nardi, & Stager, 1987) of West Virginia University, focuses on developing the learners' decision-making skills as well as on teaching specific concepts and principles. Learners work in small groups to solve open-ended problems that require them to gather information (outside of class), think logically, communicate ideas, and apply steps in a decision-making process. Learners are required to look closely at each step in the decision-making operation, apply the subject matter they have learned, exchange ideas, and reflect on solutions developed by others. The instructor acts as a consultant to the class.

Case Study.   In a case study, learners are provided with detailed information about a real-life situation. All related circumstances, issues, and actions of persons involved are carefully described. Learners must study and analyze the situation as presented. They decide what was done correctly and what mistakes might have been made in terms of principles and accepted practices in their field of specialization. During discussion, each person must explain, justify, and defend his or her own analysis of the case situation. This method is widely used in the business management field.

Role Playing.   Role playing involves the spontaneous dramatization by two or more persons of a situation relating to a problem. The incident might have to do with interpersonal relations or an operational problem within an organization. Each person acts out a role as he or she feels it would be played in real life. Other learners or trainees observe the performance and then, when the performance ends, discuss the feelings expressed and actions observed. This process promotes an understanding of other persons' positions and attitudes as well as the procedures that might be used for diagnosing and solving problems.

Simulation.   Simulation is an abstract representation of a real-life situation that requires a learner or a team to solve a complex problem. The instructor creates aspects of the situation that are close to reality, and the learner must perform manipulations, make responses, and take actions to correct deficiencies or maintain a proper status. Many simulations are computer controlled, such as a mock-up simulator of an airplane cockpit for pilot training. The simulator allows the instructor to set up appropriate conditions that require specific responses by the trainee. The participants become deeply involved, undergoing the same stress and pressures they would experience in reality. The instructor discusses and evaluates the results of the activity with the learners.

Games.   Games are formalized simulation activities. Two or more participants or teams compete in attempting to meet a set of objectives relating to a training topic. The game takes place under a set of rules and procedures, with information being provided that requires decision making and follow-up actions. The subjects of most instructional games are typical real-life situations as related to a training topic. Periodically, the results are evaluated by the instructor, other learners, or a group of judges. A wide variety of prepared games is available for use in many areas of instruction.

Cooperative Learning.   Cooperative learning is a specific type of group activity that attempts to promote both learning and social skills by incorporating three concepts (Slavin, 1995) into the instruction: (1) group rewards, (2) individual accountability, and (3) equal opportunity for success. Consideration of these components suggests that cooperative learning must be carefully planned and systematically implemented. It is much more than assigning learners to groups and telling them to "tutor each other" or complete a project.

Two major forms of cooperative learning involve having students work in groups to (1) help one another master material and (2) complete a project, such as a written report, presentation, experiment, or artwork. In both situations it is desirable to follow these guidelines:

- Limit group size to three to five students.
- Compose groups so that they are heterogeneous in ability level, gender, and ethnicity.
- Carefully plan the activities with regard to room arrangement, task materials, and time frame.
- Establish some reward (recognition or something tangible, depending on the age level of the learners) to motivate the groups.
- Ensure that everyone in the group has a specific task with which he or she can succeed with appropriate effort. Otherwise, shy or lower-ability students may defer to others and not benefit from the activity.
- Teach the lesson using an instructor presentation or appropriate individualized approach; use cooperative learning as a supplement for review, practice, remediation, or enrichment.
- Monitor and assist the groups as needed.
- Base grades as much as possible on individual group members' personal contributions or achievement; use the group reward as the means of recognizing the group's success.

Cooperative learning has proved very successful in research studies. Several models, such as Student-Teams Achievement Divisions, Co-op Co-op, Cooperative Controversy, and Jig Saw, have become quite popular in recent years. Also consider that the way cooperative learning is designed may depend on the conditions of instruction. In a computer-based learning context, for example, the lack of sufficient computers for all students may necessitate employing some form of cooperative groupings. However, the availability of space around the computers may further dictate how many students can work together at the same time.

As Sherman and Klein (1995) recently demonstrated in a research study, strategies for making cooperative learning more effective may be integrated with the main instruction. Specifically, they designed a computer-based unit to cue students working in groups to perform various interactive cooperative activities (e.g., "Yulanda, explain to Gerry why the first statement below is an example of an observation, but the second statement is not."). Their findings indicated that both learning interactivity and achievement increased relative to a noncued condition. For more ideas on cooperative learning, the books by Slavin (1995) and Johnson and Johnson (1986) should be valuable in suggesting alternative approaches and outlining implementation procedures.

SUMMARY

1. The development of the instruction materials is the implementation of the instructional design plan. Designers must consider how to accurately convey the information to the learner in a manner he or she can comprehend. During the development process, the designer should keep a focus on the problem and objectives to ensure the instruction supports the resolution of the problem.
2. There are two types of cognitive load. Intrinsic cognitive load is a function of the content and is highest when there is a high degree of interactivity between the elements. Extraneous cognitive load can be increased or decreased through the design and layout of the instructional materials.
3. The three patterns we have examined—presentation to class, self-paced learning, and small-group interaction activities—provide the framework for delivering a variety of instructional formats. As you consider the selection of methods, the following important questions should be asked:
   a. Is there subject content or other material that can best be uniformly presented to all learners at one time?
   b. Is there subject content that learners can better study on their own, at their individual paces?
   c. Are there experiences that would best be served by discussion or other group activity, with or without the instructor being present?
   d. Is there need for individual learner–instructor discussion or consultation in private?

   In considering these questions, the planning team should consider some degree of balance among the three delivery patterns.
1. Although the large-group presentation format is still the most widely accepted method in schools, it keeps learners in a generally passive mode and may not be cost-effective in training contexts where learners are geographically dispersed or highly varied in experiences and training needs. Distance learning is gaining popularity as a mode for reaching many learners located at remote sites.
2. In business, many companies are switching to a self-paced delivery format to reduce travel costs and time away from the job and to increase the efficiency of the instruction. Greater access to computers by businesses and schools is making self-paced instruction more practical and potentially more powerful.

3. In many situations, there are no clear-cut divisions among the three patterns. A presentation to a regular-sized class can incorporate questions and discussion. A self-paced learning period may be supplemented periodically with tutorial interaction as one learner helps another or as the instructor replies to a trainee's question. Combining orientations to fit instructional conditions and individual needs is a sensible approach that can potentially yield benefits much greater than could be attained by using any one method alone.

THE ID PROCESS

Developing the instructional materials gives the instructional designer an opportunity to test the design plan. The "testing" process, formative evaluation, is explained in Chapters 10 and 12. You can use these procedures to test some of your materials as you develop them and then make modifications to improve their effectiveness.

Developing instructional materials is very similar to writing an article or a book; however, we designers have one advantage. It seems that many of our high school English teachers always tried to convince us to create a *complete* outline before beginning to write an essay. The design plan is a very detailed outline of the content and structure of the instructional materials. By following this outline, we are more likely to produce an effective unit of instruction.

APPLICATION

The city police department requests the development of a training unit to teach officers a new protocol for testing drivers for possible intoxication. The officers work three different shifts a day, have rotating days off, and must appear in court on short notice. Thus, you cannot select one day that everyone or even every officer on a specific shift will attend the training. The department also hires approximately 20 new officers a year. Your contextual analysis reveals that the department does not have computers for delivering computer-based instruction. What type of approach would you suggest for the instruction?

ANSWER

The officers' schedule makes it difficult to offer a group-paced course. Another factor against a group-paced course is the need to train the 20 new officers each year. Given these constraints, a self-paced approach appears to be most viable. A computer-based unit that simulates the testing process and the equipment would make an excellent choice; however, the department does not have computer resources. One option is to offer the instruction individually with printed materials, and then use pairs or small groups for simulations on the actual equipment.

QUALITY MANAGEMENT

Managing the cognitive load imposed by the instructional materials consists of two activities. First, the designer must make sure that unnecessary cognitive load is not created through poor designs that create a split-attention effect or redudancy. Second, the designer can use goal-free problems, worked examples, and integrated text and graphics to reduce the cognitive load imposed by the materials.

During the development process, the designer needs to regularly check to make sure the materials are supportive of the objectives. It is easy to fall into a mode of writing instruction rather than following the design plan if the designer is overly familiar with the content. As the material is developed, the designer should check to make sure it is presented in a concrete manner and add examples and illustrations as needed. Once the first draft is prepared, you can check the flow of the instruction while paying particular attention to step size and pacing. Last, check to make sure the initial presentation and generative strategy are implemented for each objective.

REFERENCES

Anderson, T. H., & Armbruster, B. B. (1985). Studying strategies and their implications for textbook design. In T. M. Duffy & R. Waller (Eds.), *Designing useable texts* (pp. 159–177). Orlando: Academic Press.

Block, J. H. (Ed.). (1971). *Mastery learning: Theory and practice.* Englewood Cliffs, NJ: Prentice Hall.

Carter, J. F. (1985). Lessons in text design from an instructional design perspective. In T. M. Duffy & R. Waller (Eds.), *Designing useable texts* (pp. 145–156). Orlando: Academic Press.

Dorsey-Davis, J. D., Ross, S. M., & Morrison, G. R. (1991). The role of rewording and context personalization in the solving of mathematical word problems. *Journal of Educational Psychology, 83,* 61–68.

Fleming, M., & Levie, W. H. (1978). *Instructional message design: Principles from the behavioral sciences.* Englewood Cliffs, NJ: Educational Technology Publications.

Gopalakrishnan Jayasinghe, M., Morrison, G. R., & Ross, S. M. (1997). The effect of distance learning classroom design on student perceptions. *Educational Technology Research and Development, 45,* 5–19.

Holmberg, B. (1983). Guided didactic conversation in distance education. In D. Stewart, D. Keegan, & B. Holmberg (Eds.), *Distance education: International perspectives* (pp. 114–122). London: Routledge.

Johnsey, A., Morrison, G. R., & Ross, S. M. (1992). Promoting generative learning in computer-based instruction through the use of elaboration strategies training. *Contemporary Educational Psychology, 17,* 125–135.

Johnson, D. W., & Johnson, R. T. (1986). *Learning together and alone.* Englewood Cliffs, NJ: Prentice Hall.

Kalyuga, S., Chandler, P., & Sweller, J. (2000). Incorporating learner experience into the design of multimedia experience. *Journal of Educational Psychology, 92,* 126–136.

Kalyuga, S., Chandler, P., & Sweller, J. (2001). Learner experience and efficiency of instructional guidance. *Educational Psychology, 21,* 5–23.

Keegan, D. (1996). *Foundations of distance education* (3rd ed.). New York: Routledge.

Keller, F. S., & Sherman, J. G. (1982). *The PSI handbook: Essays on personalized instruction.* Lawrence, KS: International Society for Individualized Instruction.

Lorch, R. F., & Lorch, E. P. (1996). Effects of organizational signals on free recall of expository text. *Journal of Educational Psychology, 88,* 38–48.

Lorch, R. F., Lorch, E. P., & Inman, W. E. (1993). Effects of signaling topic structure on text recall. *Journal of Educational Psychology, 85,* 281–290.

Miller, G. A. (1956). The magical number seven, plus or minus two: Some limits on our capacity for processing information. *Psychological Review, 63,* 81–97.

Paas, F. G., & van Merriënboer, J. J. G. (1994). Variability of worked examples and transfer of geometrical problem-solving skills: A cognitive-load approach. *Journal of Educational Psychology, 86,* 122–133.

Paivio, A. (1971). *Imagery and verbal processes.* New York: Holt, Rinehart and Winston.

Paivio, A. (1986). *Mental representations: A dual coding approach.* New York: Oxford University Press.

Postlethwait, S. N., Novak, J., & Murray, H. (1972). *The audio-tutorial approach to learning.* Minneapolis: Burgess.

Rothkopf, E. Z. (1996). Control of mathemagenic activities. In D. Jonassen (Ed.), *Handbook of research for educational communication and technology* (pp. 879–897). New York: Macmillan Library Reference USA.

Sadoski, M., Goetz, E. T., & Fritz, J. B. (1993). Impact of concreteness on comprehensibility, interest, and memory for text: Implications for dual coding theory and text design. *Journal of Educational Psychology, 85,* 291–304.

Sherman, G. P., & Klein, J. D. (1995). The effects of cued interaction and ability grouping during cooperative computer-based science instruction. *Educational Technology Research and Development, 43,* 5–24.

Simonson, M. (1995). Does anyone really want to learn at a distance? *Tech Trends, 40,* 12.

Slavin, R. E. (1994). *Educational psychology* (4th ed.). Needham Heights, MA: Allyn & Bacon.

Slavin, R. E. (1995). *Cooperative learning: Theory, research, and practice.* Englewood Cliffs, NJ: Prentice Hall.

Sweller, J. (1999). *Instructional design in technical areas.* Camberwell, Victoria: ACER Press.

Tuovinen, J. E., & Sweller, J. (1999). A comparison of cognitive load associated with discovery learning and worked examples. *Journal of Educational Psychology, 2,* 334–341.

Wales, C. E., Nardi, A. H., & Stager, R. A. (1987). *Thinking skills: Making a choice.* Morgantown, WV: Center for Guided Design.

CHAPTER ⟨10⟩

The Many Faces of Evaluation

GETTING STARTED

You are asked by a school system to evaluate a new health sciences program that it has purchased to teach "healthy habits" to elementary schoolchildren. Before you design the evaluation, you first determine what questions the school system is trying to answer. Because the program is "complete" as purchased and implemented (i.e., it cannot be easily modified), summative rather than formative evaluation is desired. But the program hasn't been used enough to justify conducting a confirmative evaluation. The teachers and administrators involved with the program indicate that, aside from issues concerning cost and training requirements, their main interest is with the effects of the program in increasing positive attitudes and knowledge about healthy practices.

To increase the validity of your findings, you decide to use multiple data collection instruments, including a teacher survey and interview, student interview, parent interview, student attitude survey, and a test of student learning of health principles. For the last two measures (attitudes and learning), you also arrange to assess control students who attend similar schools as the program students. In constructing the test of learning, you create some criterion-referenced sections to determine the percentage of students who have mastered particular program objectives. One performance-based section asks students to demonstrate treatment for minor cuts using actual first-aid materials. You also create some norm-referenced sections especially designed to compare program and control students on knowledge and application of key health principles. Your synthesis of results from these multiple data sources will form the basis for conclusions about the effectiveness of the program for achieving the district's objectives in the health education area. A member of the school board, however, asks why the evaluation contains "so many things." What would you say to defend the use of multiple measures? What would you concede to be disadvantages?

QUESTIONS TO CONSIDER

"How can I determine whether this course is teaching what it is supposed to?"

"What are some ways to measure the accomplishment of performance skills besides observing a person at work on a job?"

"When is it appropriate to use a performance test instead of an objective test?"

"The questions on this test don't relate to the objectives the teacher gave us at the beginning of the unit. Shouldn't they?"

"Should I pretest my students? If so, how can that information be used to improve instruction?"

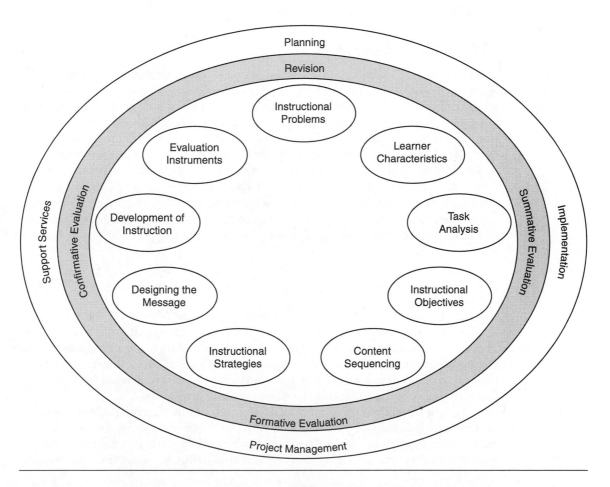

As reflected by these questions, evaluating learning is essential in the instructional design process. After examining learner characteristics, you identified instructional objectives and selected instructional strategies to accomplish them. Now, finally, you must develop the testing instruments and materials to measure the degree to which learners have acquired the knowledge, can perform the skills, and exhibit changes in attitudes as required by the objectives.

In this chapter we examine the purposes and major forms of evaluation and important concepts concerning the role of evaluation in the instructional design process. In Chapter 11, we focus on specific procedures for constructing different types of tests and instruments to evaluate student learning. Before we begin, however, here is a quick overview of terminology. In these chapters, we use the term *evaluating* to refer to the process of using measurement or assessment to make judgments about something. Is the training unit achieving its goals? Has the trainee attained the criteria required, for instance, for licensing as a day care van driver? We use the terms *measuring* and *assessing* interchangeably to denote the systematic collection of data about programs or people.

PURPOSES OF EVALUATION

As just stated, evaluation is used for the purposes of making judgments about the worth or success of people or things (e.g., lessons, programs, projects). Before initiating an evaluation, you must determine its goals. The overall goal in training and educational settings is to determine student success in learning. But will the evaluation results be used primarily for improving how the course is taught or for identifying the effectiveness of the course? Will the results be used to judge a course that is being developed, has just been completed, or has been offered for some time? These varied interests clearly go hand in hand, but the nature of the evaluation approach employed is likely to differ depending on which is assigned greater importance. Specifically, depending on the stage of the instructional design process, one of three types of evaluation will become most useful—the *formative, summative,* or *confirmative* approach.

Formative Evaluation

Even the most talented and conscientious designer is not likely to develop the "perfect" lesson or course the first time through. What seems excellent as a concept or idea may not work as well as planned when actually put to use in the classroom. Formative evaluation thus becomes an important part of the instructional design process. Its function is to inform the instructor or planning team how well the instructional program is serving the objectives as it progresses.

Formative evaluation is most valuable when conducted during development and tryouts. It should be performed *early* in the process, before valuable time and resources are wasted on things that aren't working. If the instructional plan contains weaknesses, they can be identified and eliminated before full-scale implementation.

Expert's Edge

But Did They Get Their Money's Worth?

Recently, Kmart Corporation needed to take numerous initiatives to improve competitiveness in the retail field. Among the initiatives was the use of new learning technologies for training. The training management team determined that the "buddy system" used to train new hires in register skills could no longer meet the demand and that they were going to use technology to accelerate a change in training methods. But what were the benefits of this change?

A four-year plan for conversion of existing register-skills training to a computer-based training (CBT) format was adopted with an embedded evaluation plan to determine effectiveness and return on investment (ROI). The computer-based training approach was adopted with the following projected benefits:

- Increased flexibility across and within stores
- Reduced delivery costs
- Consistency of application and administration
- Reduced employee training time
- Greater skill development

A comprehensive evaluation plan was devised that included measures before, during, and following implementation. Key measures for data collection included training time savings, learning gains, register productivity improvements (e.g., minutes per customer, transaction voids, number of overrides), team member turnover reduction, store usage figures, and increases in the customer satisfaction measurement index. A set of general guidelines was developed to assure that various levels of management reviewing the progress of implementation accepted the resulting evaluation data. These guidelines included the following:

- Verifying measures with field and operations staff
- Defining measures and data sources up front
- Using conservative figures (when such options existed)
- Focusing on change management interventions
- Allowing an eight-month to one-year lag for initial reporting

ROI calculations typically provide a snapshot in time that may not provide an accurate picture during the implementation. We decided to use a "rolling ROI" that was calculated at different time periods to provide a truer picture of the impacts. In general, ROI can be applied to projects for which the following conditions are in place: (1) the projects are of longer duration (more than one year); (2) training is tied to organizational objectives or change; and (3) there exists significant management support and interest. On the other hand, ROI data analysis might be questioned when senior management is skeptical of the value of training, training is required to break the "not invented here" syndrome, the "bean counters" (financial staff) demand hard evidence, or the CEO asks for the data (it is probably too late!).

During the first six months of the rollout, 37 stores participated in an in-depth pilot study to determine bugs in the implementation process, including training materials, technical computer support, job aids, and ease of computer usage by trainees. The second six months involved the participation of a total of 197 stores throughout the United States. The third phase, during the next 18 months, was implementation in all of Kmart Super K stores (the large superstores) and about one-third of the Big K stores (regular Kmarts) for a total of about 650 stores. The fourth phase, over the final 18 months, included all 2,161 stores in the United States and Puerto Rico.

Because stores participating in the four phases were included at various stages of implementation, CBT stores could be compared with non-CBT stores for any given time period. Variables such as differences in region, economic environment, and size were controlled during the implementation. In addition, baseline quantitative data could be collected on all key measures for any given time through the use of an enterprise-wide data collection system. A comprehensive data collection system with key and control variables was available for analysis.

Initial results for the first year of implementation showed that approximately 40,000 training hours were saved, CBT trainees had 6 percent higher productivity, and there was less turnover during the first 90 days of employment. The ROI calculation for this first year was a very conservative 126 percent. During the second year, it was determined that the turnover data was maintained in the CBT stores, there were 10 percent fewer overrides, and checkouts were 13 percent faster. These data together with the reduction in training hours resulted in an ROI calculation of about 400 percent.

Overall conclusions drawn by training management and reported to senior operations management showed that register trainee performance demonstrated significant improvements in that trainees were both faster and better (fewer errors). The impact on turnover was significant—much more than what was originally projected. The only downside was the failure to show any demonstrated impact on the customer service index. It was suggested that this measure was too "global" in nature and was beyond the control of direct impact of register operators.

Dale C. Brandenburg is research professor and director of workplace education and training at Wayne State University. He has over 30 years of experience in needs assessment, training evaluation, technical training strategy, and the impacts of technology deployment on workforce issues with an emphasis on manufacturing and advanced technology organizations.

Test results, reactions from learners, observations of learners at work, reviews by subject-matter experts, and suggestions from colleagues may indicate deficiencies in the learning sequence, procedures, or materials.

Formative evaluation is quality control of the development process. Starting in Chapter 2, we have included a section titled "Quality Management"—a formative evaluation step during the design of the instruction. This section in each chapter includes suggestions on how to evaluate your progress as you design a project. The suggestions provide guidelines for determining whether you are focused on the original problem and whether the instruction you are developing would solve the problem you identified.

Formative testing and revision (and retesting and further revision, if necessary) are important for the success of an instructional design plan. They should relate not only to the suitability of objectives, subject content, instructional strategies, and materials but also to the roles of personnel, the use of facilities and equipment, the schedules, and other factors that together affect optimum performance in achieving objectives. Remember, the planning process is highly interactive—each element affects other elements.

Keep in mind that both instructional designers and instructors need to use formative evaluation. For designers, the usual focus is the effectiveness of materials. Thus, if students perform poorly, the conclusion will be that the *materials*, not the students, are at fault (Hellebrandt & Russell, 1993, p. 22). For instructors, the focus will be placed on the students. If students don't perform up to expectations and the effectiveness of instruction has been previously demonstrated, the conclusion will be that the *students*, not the materials, are at fault.

The following questions might be used by designers to gather data during formative evaluation:

1. Given the objectives for the unit or lesson, is the level of learning acceptable? What weaknesses are apparent?
2. Are learners able to use the knowledge or perform the skills at an acceptable level? Are any weaknesses indicated?
3. How much time did the instruction and learning require? Is this acceptable?
4. Did the activities seem appropriate and manageable to the instructor and learners?
5. Were the materials convenient and easy to locate, use, and file?
6. What were the learners' reactions to the method of study, activities, materials, and evaluation methods?
7. Do the unit tests and other outcome measures satisfactorily assess the instructional objectives?
8. What revisions in the program seem necessary (content, format, etc.)?
9. Is the instructional context appropriate?

We more closely examine the procedures for conducting formative evaluations in Chapter 12. For now, consider the purposes of the formative approach in comparison to those of an alternative orientation—summative evaluation.

Summative Evaluation

Summative evaluation is directed toward measuring the degree to which the major outcomes are attained by the end of the course. Key information sources are therefore likely to be the results of both the unit posttests and the final examination for the course. In addition to measuring the effectiveness of student or trainee learning, summative evaluations also frequently measure the following:

- Efficiency of learning (material mastered/time)
- Cost of program development
- Continuing expenses
- Reactions toward the course or program
- Long-term benefits of the program

Long-term benefits may be determined by following up on learners who complete the program to discover whether and when they are using the knowledge, skills, and attitudes learned. (Summative evaluation receives full attention in Chapter 12.) As for formative evaluation, instructional designers focus summative evaluations on the effectiveness of materials, whereas instructors focus them on the effectiveness of students.

Confirmative Evaluation

Suppose that you've developed a training unit to teach the accounting staff of a company how to use a new billing system. The unit was subjected to continuous formative evaluation, and appropriate revisions were made at each stage of the design process. Summative evaluation further confirmed that the training unit was effective in preparing employees to use the system accurately and efficiently. Everyone seems happy in the accounting department until it is realized over time that employees are making numerous mistakes and reacting negatively toward the software system. You investigate by conducting a follow-up evaluation. Your findings reveal that increasing numbers of customers are paying for purchases through automatic bank withdrawals, a type of transaction that was not sufficiently addressed in the initial training. The evaluation also yields a number of useful suggestions by the accounting staff for how other aspects of the training could be strengthened to provide better preparation for actual job tasks.

The type of evaluation performed in the preceding example is called *confirmative evaluation*. It was originally introduced by Misanchuk (1978) based on the rationale that evaluation of instruction needs to be continuous and, therefore, extend beyond summative evaluation. Similar to formative and summative evaluations, confirmative evaluations rely on multiple data-gathering instruments, such as questionnaires, interviews, performance assessments, self-reports, and knowledge tests (Moseley & Solomon, 1997). Of special interest to the confirmative evaluator are questions such as these:

Do learners continue to perform correctly over time?
Do materials still meet their original objectives?
How can clients' needs be best met over time?

If improvements are needed in the training or materials, how can they be made most effectively?

If the instruction isn't working as well as it did originally, what are the reasons?

Should the instruction be continued as is?

Should it be revised?

Should it be terminated?

RELATIONSHIP AMONG FORMATIVE, SUMMATIVE, AND CONFIRMATIVE EVALUATIONS

At this stage, you probably have noted some similarities as well as differences among formative, summative, and confirmative evaluations. Let's now take a closer look at similarities and differences between these components in addressing different evaluation needs.

The Role of Instructional Objectives

For all three evaluation approaches, what is evaluated is determined directly by instructional objectives. If one objective, for example, is to teach trainees how to file an accident report correctly, then assessing how well they do this task becomes an essential part of an evaluation regardless of whether the primary interest is to improve the instruction *(formative)* or judge its effectiveness after completion *(summative)* or over time *(confirmative)*. If improving student attitudes toward the accident-reporting process is not an instructional goal, there will be little rationale for including an attitude measure (although, as we will see, attitude assessments can be valuable in interpreting why particular objectives are or are not achieved successfully).

Instructional objectives, however, provide only part of the basis for determining evaluation objectives. Broader educational or training goals may suggest looking at "summative" impacts of instruction on personnel, administration, resource allocation, and cost-effectiveness (see Chapter 12). As is discussed later, analyzing *processes* of instruction (e.g., instructional strategies, teaching methods, student behaviors, or student feelings) becomes especially important in conducting formative evaluations to describe how well particular course features are operating. Confirmative evaluation, like summative evaluation, examines all training impacts, but it takes place some time after the completion of instruction and usually in the actual performance environment (i.e., at the workplace).

Key idea: All three types of evaluation are driven by instructional objectives and goals.

Multiple Data Sources Equal Increased Information

Because most units of instruction have multiple objectives with different focuses, all three evaluation approaches require varied sources of outcome data. Examples include measures of knowledge, skills, behaviors, attitudes, and completion time, as well as information about the instructional delivery, learning activities, resources, teacher characteristics, and so on. The more the designer knows about the instruction and its outcomes, the more confidently he or she can make conclusions and recommendations. Generally speaking, there is a greater need for multiple data sources in formative evaluations, since the interest is not only to determine the effectiveness of particular elements but also how to improve those that are not working as planned. Similarly, if trainees or materials are not maintaining expected standards over time, the confirmative evaluator will want to determine the causes of the problem and possible remedies.

> Key idea: All three types of evaluation (but especially formative) typically require multiple data sources.

Processes and Products

Formative evaluation asks, "How are we doing?" Summative evaluation asks, "How did we do?" Confirmative evaluation asks, "How are we still doing?" To answer these questions, different types of measurement orientations are needed. Specifically, formative evaluation emphasizes the measurement of outcomes as instruction evolves (or "forms"). Interest is as much with process as with product. Summative evaluation stresses measurement of criterion outcomes that occur at the end of instruction. Interest is more with products than with processes. Confirmative evaluation stresses the measurement of criterion outcomes that occur after the instruction has been completed for some time. Its interest is, therefore, the long-term maintenance of products.

> Key idea: Formative evaluation gives equal attention to processes and products. Summative and especially confirmative evaluations give greater weight to products.

Time of Testing

For formative evaluations, testing is important at all phases of instruction—pretesting (before), embedded testing (during), and posttesting (after). Although all three types of testing may be used in both summative and confirmative evaluation, posttesting is clearly the most critical and the main basis for forming conclusions about the instruction. (In the final section of this chapter, we examine uses of pretesting in more detail.) Confirmative evaluation, however, should generally include repeated posttesting to monitor performance over time.

> Key idea: Formative evaluation gives equal attention to pretesting, embedded testing, and posttesting. Summative and confirmative evaluation give greater weight to posttesting.

When to Evaluate

Formative evaluations are most valuable before instruction is fully developed, when it is inexpensive to make changes. They are also most valuable when used in a continuous manner, at different phases of the design process. As is discussed more fully in Chapter 12, some common modes of formative evaluation are *connoisseur-based (expert) review, one-to-one trials, small-group testing,* and *field testing.* All of these are used to refine instruction at different developmental stages. Summative and confirmative evaluations, in contrast, are designed to examine the effectiveness of completed versions of instruction. Summative comes after the instruction is first used, but before sustained implementation, whereas confirmative is used after implementation has occurred and the design has been used for a reasonable time (usually at least six months to a year)

RELATIONSHIP BETWEEN EVALUATION AND INSTRUCTIONAL OBJECTIVES

The broad purpose of evaluation is to determine to what extent the objectives of the instruction are being attained. The assessments used to inform the evaluation should therefore have a direct relationship with the objectives. In the case of knowledge testing, some authorities even suggest that as soon as a subject content list and the details of a task analysis are first completed, you should immediately write examination questions relating to the content. In turn, the questions can be reworded as instructional objectives. This procedure may seem to be a backward way of planning, but it points to the importance of relating evaluation directly to instructional objectives.

Usually, once you are satisfied with the extent and completeness of the instructional objectives, you are ready to develop ways for evaluating them. For accomplishing this, two key ideas are crucial. First, obtain a good match between types of assessment instruments and types of objectives. Second, consider using several data sources to gain as complete a picture as possible about the degree of learner attainment of each objective and the processes involved. Remember, not all instructional objectives lend themselves to direct, precise measurement leading to a simple "success/fail" answer.

Matching Measures to Objectives

In Chapter 5 we discuss the fact that various forms of objectives are useful for describing different types of learning outcomes—for instance, cognitive objectives for knowledge, psychomotor objectives for skills, and affective objectives for attitudes. To complete the cycle, those objectives, coupled with the evaluation goals, in turn suggest certain types of measures. Finding the measures that best fit each objective is an important evaluation task. Note the following real-life examples, for which such fits could be seriously questioned:

- A corporate training course on group leadership skills included objectives that were nearly all performance- or skill-based. For example: "The student will distribute an agenda for the meeting." Yet, the sole assessment measure employed was a 25-item multiple-choice knowledge test administered as a pre- and postassessment! Not surprisingly, students "significantly" improved their scores across the two testings (after all, they were taught new material). Should the course be viewed as successful in meeting its objectives?

- A college professor assessed achievement on the midterm and final exams of a history course by asking students to list the "major developments" that led to the Vietnam War. Scoring was based on how closely the students' listings matched the one given in class; these assessments accounted for about 85 percent of the final course grade. Does this evaluation approach appear valid given instructional objectives that emphasize analysis and synthesis of historic events?

- A department chairman wanted to evaluate the effectiveness of teaching in a certain core course. Toward the end of the year, he scheduled sessions in which he would visit a class, dismiss the instructor for 20 minutes, and ask class members to react in a group discussion to the teaching methods and teacher qualities. Was he likely to obtain an accurate picture of teaching effectiveness in that course?

The answer to the questions in all three illustrations is a definite no. Inappropriate instruments were employed in each situation. For the corporate training evaluation, improvement on the knowledge test says little about trainees' abilities to perform the desired skills. Similarly, verbatim recall of historical facts from a listing appears to be a trivial, lower-level measure of learning in the history course. Finally, although the department chairman was on the right track by employing student attitudes as a data source, the specific measure used (a group discussion) likely would generate invalid results because students may feel pressured and self-conscious about speaking openly in front of a group and the department chairman.

Suggested Measures for Alternative Outcomes

Suggested instrument selections for assessing different types of instructional outcomes are provided in Figure 10-1. For now, we simply identify the instruments and save discussion of the procedures for developing them for Chapter 11. Keep in mind that the ultimate choice of evaluation measures depends on a variety of factors other than what is considered in an ideal sense to be most desirable and valid. These factors include costs, time, skill required for test administration, instrument availability, and accepted practices in the educational or training context concerned.

FIGURE 10-1
Various evaluation instruments for different outcomes

A. Knowledge

Data Sources: **Objective Tests**

Objective test questions have one correct answer and thus can be easily ("objectively") graded.

1. Multiple choice
Example: *Which state is the farthest west in longitude?*

    a. Hawaii
    b. California
    c. Alaska
    d. Washington

2. True-False
Example: *In the sentence "The boys enjoyed the movie," the subject is "movie." (T/F)*

3. Matching
Example: *Match the choice in column B that describes the term in column A.*

A	B
Mean	Midpoint
Mode	Most frequent score
Median	Variability
	Average

Data Sources: **Constructed-Response Tests**

Constructed-response tests require the learner to generate ("construct") responses to questions. Thus, alternative answers and/or solution strategies are usually possible.

1. Completion (fill-in-the-blank)
Example: *Instructional objectives that describe the use and coordination of physical activities fall into the _____ domain.*

2. Short essay
Example: *Define formative and summative evaluation and describe two ways in which they might differ procedurally.*

3. Long essay
Example: *Discuss the purposes of instructional evaluation. Using an example lesson or course, describe the considerations or steps that would be involved in such evaluations with regard to (a) planning, (b) implementation, and (c) interpretation and dissemination of results.*

4. Problem-solving
Example: *Complete the following math problem, showing the correct formula, your work, and the solution.*

Four electricians install 1,327 outlets in 70 apartments. What is the average number of outlets in each apartment?

(continues on next page)

FIGURE 10-1 (*continued*)
Various evaluation instruments for different outcomes

B. Skills and Behavior

Data Sources: 1. Direct testing of performance outcomes

Example: *A test of tying different types of knots used in sailing*

2. Analysis of naturally occurring results

Examples: *Number of accidents, attendance, sales increases, etc.*

3. Ratings of behaviors based on direct observation

Example: *Rate teacher clarity on a five-point scale.*

4. Checklists of behavior based on direct observation

Example: *Check each safety precaution exhibited by trainees while wiring circuits.*

5. Ratings or checklists of behavior based on indirect measures

Example: *Peer evaluation of the student's communication skills while dealing with clients*

6. Authentic tests

Example: *Portfolios or exhibitions that display students' work in meaningful contexts.*

C. Attitudes

Data Sources: 1. Observation of instruction

Examples: *What percentage of the students is attentive? How frequently does the typical student participate in class discussion? Do students appear to enjoy the lesson?*

2. Observation/assessment of behavior

Examples: *How many plays do students attend following an arts appreciation course? What percentage of students enroll in Algebra II following completion of Algebra I?*

3. Attitude surveys

Examples: *Ratings of instructor preparedness, lesson difficulty, clarity, and organization, open-ended evaluation by hospital patients of the bedside manner of the nurses who cared for them*

4. Interviews

Examples: *What appear to be the strengths of the instruction? Why? What appear to be the weaknesses? Why?*

VALIDITY AND RELIABILITY OF TESTS

Once you have determined the types of measures for assessing objectives, selecting or developing the instruments becomes the next major task. Whichever route is taken, it is important to ensure that those instruments possess two necessary qualities: validity and reliability.

Validity

Attention was previously given to the validity of testing when the necessity for a direct relationship between instructional objectives and assessment items was indicated. A test is considered valid when it specifically measures what was learned, as specified by the instructional objectives for the unit or topic.

In Chapter 5 we describe the benefits of developing a performance-content matrix that relates objectives to learning levels. One way of ensuring a high degree of test validity is to devise a second table of specifications that relates test items to objectives. Such a table can serve two purposes. First, it helps verify that outcomes at the higher learning levels (application, analysis, synthesis, and evaluation) receive adequate attention. Second, it shows the number of questions needed for measuring individual instructional objectives or groups of related objectives. These frequency values reflect the relative importance of each objective or the proportion of emphasis it is given during instruction.

Table 10-1 indicates the nature and number of test questions for instructional objectives in a knowledge-based unit. Table 10-2 relates the number of test items to the instructional objectives on a task involving different cognitive levels and psychomotor performances. By designing such tables, you can be reasonably certain you will test for all instructional objectives and give each the proper amount of attention.

Although validity is typically associated with knowledge tests, it has the same importance for all types of assessment measures. The key idea is that the test assesses what it is supposed to measure. Thus, course attitude surveys need to measure reactions to the course (and not primarily instructor popularity or some other incidental variable); performance tests need to assess processes and outcomes relating to the skills or competencies of concern; observations of instruction need to describe events and impressions that accurately capture what occurred when the instruction was delivered.

Validity is not always easy to measure or quantify. Several different types exist and are discussed in most measurement texts (e.g., face, content, predictive, concurrent, and construct validity). The two most important types for the instructional designer are face validity and content validity, which both involve judgmental processes. *Face validity* is supported by the judgment (often by an expert panel) that the measure appears ("on the face of it") to assess the measure of interest. *Content validity* is similar to face validity but typically involves a more specific examination of individual items or questions to ensure that each "content domain" is appropriately

TABLE 10-1
Specifications relating number of test items to learning objectives on cognitive levels

Topic: Community Services for the Elderly						
Objective	Knowledge	Comprehension	Application	Analysis	Synthesis	Evaluation
1. Recognize misconceptions and superstitions about the elderly.	3					
2. Differentiate between facts and opinions about physical and social behaviors of the elderly.		2				
3. Describe attitudes toward the elderly as practiced by various ethnic groups.		2				
4. Locate information relative to community programs for the elderly.		4				
5. Classify community organizations according to types of services offered for the elderly.				2		
6. Develop a plan for judging the value of individual community programs for the elderly.					3	
7. Assess the merits of a community program for the elderly.						2
8. Given a hypothetical or real situation, analyze the needs of a senior citizen and recommend one or more community programs.			4			

addressed. For example, a final achievement exam that draws 90 percent of its items from only one out of four primary course units would have questionable content validity. Tables of specification (see Tables 10-1 and 10-2) are especially useful in making content validity judgments.

Reliability

Reliability refers to a test's ability to produce consistent results whenever used. If the same learners, without changes in their preparation, were to take the same test or an equal form of the test, there should be little variation in the scores. Certain procedures can affect the reliability of a test:

TABLE 10-2
Specifications relating number of test items to learning objectives on cognitive levels for psychomotor performance

Task: Measuring Electrical Values in Series Circuits				
Objective	**Knowledge**	**Comprehension**	**Application**	**Psychomotor**
1. List symbols used to identify components in an electrical circuit.	2			
2. Recognize the makeup of a complete series circuit.		3		
3. Identify a series circuit in a schematic diagram.		1	2	
4. Assemble a series circuit on a board using component parts.				2
5. Set up and adjust a multimeter for measuring each of three electrical values.				1
6. Measure and calculate voltage, current flow, and resistance in a series circuit.			3	3

- The more questions used relating to each instructional objective, the more reliable the test will be. If only one question is asked about a major objective or an extensive content area, it can be difficult to ascertain whether a learner has acquired the knowledge or guessed the correct answer. (See the previous procedure for developing a specification table relating the number of test questions to the objectives.)
- The test should be administered in a standardized way. If more than one person directs testing, similar instructions must be given to each group of individuals who take the test over a period of time.
- Everyone should be tested under the same conditions so that distractions do not contribute to discrepancies in the scores.
- Testing time should be the same length for all learners.
- Possibly the most important factor that can affect test reliability is the scoring method, especially when marking an essay test or judging performance on a rating scale. Despite attempts to standardize how different persons score tests, criteria can be viewed in various ways, and variations are unavoidable. The less subjective the scoring, the more reliable the test results will be. As is discussed in Chapter 11, ensuring adequate reliability has been the main challenge for instructors using performance assessments (e.g., evaluating students on the quality of their oral reports) and authentic measures (e.g., portfolios showing the students' work in mathematics over the last six weeks).

There are a number of different methods for assessing reliability:

- The test–retest method correlates students' scores on two different administrations of the same measure.
- The parallel forms method correlates scores on similar ("parallel" or matched) tests taken at different times.
- The split–half method correlates students' scores on half of the test with those on the other half. (The split should be every other item, rather than the first versus the second half, to ensure similar content and difficulty.)
- Internal consistency reliability is comparable to performing all unique split–half correlations. High internal consistency means that different test items are measuring the same abilities or traits. Popularly used formulas such as KR 20 and coefficient alpha are described in basic educational measurement texts and can be easily run by most computer-based statistical packages.

Relationship between Validity and Reliability

A final question to consider is the relationship between validity and reliability. Does validity require reliability? Does reliability require validity? The answers to these two questions are yes and no, respectively.

For an assessment to be valid, it must be reliable. Think about it: how could a test measure what it is supposed to if the scores vary from testing to testing (without any change in testing conditions or learner states)? On the other hand, you could have reliability without validity. For example, an instructor might attempt to assess students' ability to design lessons by giving them a 50-item true/false test on learning theories. The scores might remain consistent from one testing to the next, but they would hardly reflect instructional design skills, the outcome of major interest.

STANDARDS OF ACHIEVEMENT

Suppose you have completed planning your evaluation. Not only have you identified the types of measures needed, but you also have outlined the domains to be assessed and the amount of weight to be given to each one to establish high content validity. Before you develop the actual tests, there is another decision to be made—how to judge achievement.

Two standards of achievement can be applied when interpreting test scores and assigning grades: relative or absolute. Understanding each standard, as well as its particular implications within the instructional design process, is an important part of evaluation.

Relative Standards

In most conventional educational programs, the performance of one learner is compared with those of other learners in the class. A test based on relative standards indicates that one learner has learned more or less than other learners have, which results in a relative rating of each learner within the group. The rating does not necessarily signify the level of proficiency of any learner in the group with respect to a specific standard of accomplishment.

For example, assume that scores on an 85-point test range from 44 to 73. The instructor would assign grades, starting with the 73 score as the highest A. It might then be decided, for example, to have about 7.5 percent of the learners receive a grade of A, 17.5 percent a B, 50 percent a C, 17.5 percent a D, and 7.5 percent an F (see Figure 10-2). This approach is called a *normal distribution,* or "grading on the normal curve." Grades are assigned in a relative or normative fashion. Note the characteristics of the normal distribution. It is symmetric (you can fold it in half); the *mean* (average), *mode* (most frequent score), and *median* (halfway point or fiftieth percentile) are identical and positioned in the exact middle of the distribution; and the frequency of scores decreases as you move from the middle to the extremes of the distribution in either direction. Many human characteristics (height, weight, and intelligence) tend to be normally distributed. Note, however, that normal distributions facilitate the use of (but are not required for) norm-referenced grading. Regardless of the distribution, the critical element is that people are being compared with one another rather than against a standard.

Norm-referenced scoring, grading, and reporting conventions are therefore designed to convey these comparisons. But, under norm-referenced systems, it cannot be assumed, for example, that a learner who received an A this year in Biology 101 is comparable in achievement to another learner who received an A in the same course last semester. The high grades convey that both students did well relative to their classmates, but they do not indicate which specific competencies or skills the students have mastered.

Standardized scores, such as those for the American College Testing (ACT), Stanford Achievement Test (SAT), and Graduate Record Examination (GRE) exams, also illustrate norm-referenced scores. Perhaps the type of relative score with which you are most familiar is percentile scores. If you know that Micah scored at the eighty-ninth percentile on the geometry final, what have you learned? Essentially, you know that Micah performed well, surpassing close to 9 out of 10 of his classmates. What you do not know from that information alone is how he did in terms of his actual score (number or percentage correct) or types of learning demonstrated.

FIGURE 10-2
Grading on a normal curve

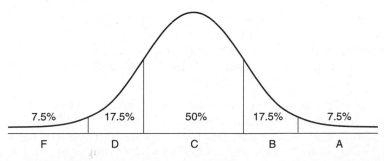

Norm-referenced testing procedures are important in comparing the overall accomplishments of individuals or a class with established local, state, or national norms. They are also useful when the purpose of evaluation is to select individuals who stand out from the group (at the high or low extremes) for special programs. For example, there seems to be a good reason to want one's heart or brain surgeon to be someone who not only passed all the competencies but also excelled in the knowledge and skills required relative to other medical students. Because of this property, norm-referenced testing may not fit well with plans to make instruction and resulting learning effective for the great majority of learners in a class or training program.

Absolute Standards

In many instances, the primary goal of our instructional design is to have as many learners as possible reach a satisfactory level of achievement. Therefore, learning outcomes must be measured against a specific standard rather than a relative standard. The *specific standard* is the criterion specified by the instructional objectives. Criterion-referenced testing includes the measurement of how well each learner attains the required level of comprehension and competence specified for each objective. This degree of achievement is independent of the performance of other students.

The terms *competency-based instruction, performance-based instruction,* and *mastery-based instruction* are used interchangeably with *criterion-referenced instruction.* These methods identify a program that provides experiences intended to bring most learners to a satisfactory level of proficiency in learning or performing a task that will be measured by testing. When criteria are set and learners successfully meet them, the concept of *mastery learning* is realized. This goal partly justifies giving increased attention to self-paced learning methods and providing more than one opportunity for a learner to restudy, self-test, and then be retested until the mastery level is attained.

There is concern about the emphasis on mastery learning in some programs. While it is successful when identifiable competencies are required (e.g., in the training of dental technicians or airline pilots), some people fear that use of conventional letter grading (A-B-C-D-F) will lead to "grade inflation" and lower academic standards. In a well-designed and properly executed instructional program, each learner could attain mastery of each topic and receive an A. Students are especially likely to obtain high grades when the learning situation satisfies a combination of the following conditions:

- The learner group has been carefully selected on the basis of ability.
- Each learner is highly motivated to learn.
- Learners have received excellent prerequisite training.
- Instruction has been carefully prepared, pretested, and proven to be effective.

On the other hand, mastery can be accepted as attainment of minimum or essential knowledge and skills at a reasonable competency level (e.g., an 80 percent performance standard), which may guarantee a B or C grade (or possibly a P for pass or credit). Then, to reach a higher level, or an A grade, additional accomplishments may be required, such as answering 95 to 100 percent of the posttest questions correctly or achieving optional objectives and engaging in additional activities. If a number of performance levels above the acceptable minimum is set, each learner could be permitted to choose a goal on the basis of his or her capabilities, background, and motivation. This procedure is similar to the contract concept used in some educational programs.

Measurement Issues

In comparing norm-referenced and criterion-referenced testing and grading methods, a final matter should be emphasized. First, in the norm-referenced approach, tests are constructed so that expected learner attainment levels are purposefully spread out to achieve high, average, and low scores. In measurement terms, the key concern is that items *discriminate* (differentiate) among learners. Given this goal, what item-difficulty level (proportion of learners answering correctly) would provide maximum discrimination? The answer is 0.50—an item that is answered correctly by half the examinees and missed by half. Note, by comparison, that an item that is answered correctly or missed by 100 percent of the examinees provides *zero discrimination*. In most normative instances, we would not want a test to consist exclusively of items having 0.50 difficulty (nor would our students or trainees be very happy about that). Some easier items should be included to increase motivation and morale.

In the criterion-referenced method, test items are included as relevant to the required standards. The results clearly indicate what a learner has learned and can do. Assuming that training has been effective, you would expect and probably want most students to demonstrate mastery. Items with difficulty levels of 0.80 or higher would therefore be desirable in the criterion-referenced situation.

In summary, guiding and assessing learners to help them accomplish their objectives is a normal procedure in criterion-referenced measurement and mastery learning. This orientation fosters cooperation among learners. The norm-referenced approach, on the other hand, emphasizes competition, resulting in differentiation among learners based on achievement levels.

Standards versus Conventional Measurement

In K–12 contexts, controversy has been generated in recent years regarding the use of norm-referenced versus criterion-referenced tests. Perhaps you remember taking norm-referenced standardized achievement tests, such as the Iowa Test of Basic Skills (ITBS), the Scholatic Achievement Test (SAT), or the California Achievement Test (CAT), when you were in school. These tests involved answering multiple-choice questions in language arts, mathematics, and other core subjects, under strictly controlled conditions. In many school districts, school means on the standardized tests are published in the local newspaper and interpreted by the public and often by district and state administrators as indicators of the success of the individual schools. Needless to say, these conditions typically create a high-stakes testing environment in which teaching to the test, coaching, and sometimes even cheating may occur in the quest to raise scores (Haladyna, Nolen, & Haas, 1991; Taylor, 1994).

The advantage of standardized objective tests is high reliability of measurement. On the other hand, a growing number of educators have questioned the validity of the scores for reflecting students' ability to apply the knowledge and skills they have learned (Shepard, 2000). These concerns have given rise to national efforts to develop standards of achievement that focus on demonstrations of higher-level learning (e.g., writing essays, solving problems, participating in debates) rather than simple recall of knowledge. You may remember from Chapter 5 that a traditional behavioral-type instructional objective might read something like, "Given a familiar topic and 30 minutes' time, the student will write a 500-word essay on that topic containing no grammatical errors and fewer than five errors of spelling or punctuation." A language arts content standard in the same area, however, might read, "The student will write a persuasive essay that shows a clear sense of purpose and audience and that uses language forms accurately, clearly, and appropriately." Associated benchmarks for that standard would then specify what students should know and be able to do at developmentally appropriate levels (e.g., for a ninth-grader: "introduces and clearly states a position," "supports main points by relevant and accurate information," "clearly conveys the main points of the opposing argument").

The standards approach shares some similarities with Gronlund's (1985, 1995) cognitive objectives (see Chapter 5) in the sense of operationally defining a generally stated outcome (the standard) in terms of more specific competencies (the *benchmark*). The main difference is that objectives tend to be more narrow and unit-specific, whereas standards delineate an entire curriculum, quite possibly for all subjects and all grades in the school system. Associated with content standards are *performance standards*, which specify the criteria for assessing student achievement at different skill levels (e.g., for exiting primary grades, intermediate grades, middle school, or high school). These assessments are criterion-referenced in nature and employ tasks requiring relatively realistic or "authentic" demonstrations of skill and knowledge. An example would be requiring students to test a hypothesis in science by performing a simple experiment. This approach contrasts with reading about an experiment and answering multiple-choice questions about it, as on a norm-referenced achievement test. What is the advantage of the performance assessment? Clearly, it is increasing external validity (realism) and orienting instruction toward meaningful learning. The disadvantage, however, is the difficulty of scoring such performances reliably for both everyday feedback and formal grading, such as report cards. (We return to the reliability issue in Chapter 11.)

What does the standards movement mean for instructional designers? Designers working with schools using standards-based curricula will need to link instructional material directly to those standards and benchmarks (as they would with conventional objectives). Although lower-level learning (e.g., memorizing facts and dates) will still be required, greater emphasis than in the past will be placed on teaching such knowledge as a natural part of performing more complex, real-world tasks (e.g., learning history facts by completing a project on the Civil War, learning punctuation through reading and writing). Assessments will also need to be integrated with learning activities such that students demonstrate what they know and can do through portfolios, exhibitions, and projects (see Chapter 11 for more discussion). For classroom teachers, instructional design skills (formal or otherwise) will likewise become increasingly valuable as they attempt to address standards by creating meaningful performance-based tasks to replace traditional seatwork and drill exercises. This trend is already being evidenced in contemporary school reform programs (Stringfield, Ross, & Smith, 1996).

STUDENT SELF-EVALUATION

Successful learning is enhanced when individuals receive feedback on how well they are learning as instruction takes place. This can be accomplished by allowing learners to grade their own short tests at the end of a unit or set of learning activities. The results indicate to them whether the material has been learned satisfactorily or whether further study is needed.

By completing such self-check tests, learners can individually evaluate progress, recognize difficulties or confusion in understanding, and review material prior to taking the instructor's test covering the same objectives. This procedure can better ensure learner preparation for and success with the unit posttest.

Pretesting

Up to this point, we have discussed different approaches to evaluation, assessment, and measurement instrument selection. Our final focus in this chapter is the question of when and how to use pretests as part of the evaluation design.

Suppose you want to begin a strenuous swimming, cycling, or running program. What is advisable to do before starting? Having a physical examination seems necessary to ensure that your body is prepared for rigorous exercise. A similar practice is important in the instructional process. Specifically, pretesting is used to assess learners' entry skills for a course or a particular unit of study.

Pretesting serves two important roles in the instructional design process. One role has two functions: (1) to assess the learner's preparation to study the course or topic, and (2) to determine which competencies for the course or topic the learner may have already mastered. The second major role is to measure the degree of improvement after instruction is completed.

Testing for Prerequisites

A prerequisite test determines whether students have appropriate preparation for starting a course or studying a topic. For example:

- Can junior high school students perform basic arithmetic at a level that qualifies them to start learning algebra?
- Is an apprentice entering a furniture-manufacturing training program competent in using such machines as a table saw, a belt sander, and a router?

Refer to the listing of subject content for the topic or the analysis of the task to be taught (Chapter 4) as well as your learner analysis (Chapter 3). Enumerate the required competencies that a learner should have before starting this phase of the program. From the list, develop appropriate methods, such as those in the following list, to gather information about necessary prerequisite knowledge and abilities:

- Paper-and-pencil tests (sometimes standardized tests in fundamental areas such as reading, writing, mathematics, chemistry, or physics)
- Observations of performance and rating of competencies exhibited by learner
- A questionnaire to determine learner background, training, and experiences
- Review of learner's previous or related work
- Talks with supervisors or other persons with whom the learner has worked

The results of this prerequisite testing will indicate which learners are fully prepared to start studying the topic, which need some remedial work, and which are not ready and should therefore start at a lower level. Do not assume that grades in previous or related courses necessarily indicate the degree of readiness for a learner to be successful in a program. The objectives of courses taken elsewhere may be quite different from what you interpret them to be by reading the titles or descriptions of those courses. Do your own prerequisite evaluation of each learner's preparation.

To determine learners' previous experience with a topic, you might use a pretopic questionnaire or even an informal, oral questioning of the class (e.g., "How many of you have ever used an ohmmeter?") instead of a formal test. Have learners reply with a show of hands. For mature learners, a questionnaire, in which each learner indicates his or her level of skill or knowledge for all items to be studied, will go further than the few questions of a pretest.

Testing for Improvement in Performance

A second reason for pretesting is to determine the degree to which learners improve in critical competencies as a result of the instruction. Since the accomplishment of instructional objectives is measured by the evaluation test for each objective, some authorities recommend using the actual evaluation test (or a modified form of it) for both pretesting and final evaluation (the posttest). In this case, the amount of learning is determined from the gain in scores between pretesting and posttesting. An illustration of this is shown in Figure 10-3. Note that large gains are indicated for objectives 1, 5, and 7, whereas only small improvements occurred for objectives 3 and 8.

If the final examination is too detailed for use as a pretest, select only the most important or representative test items. Do not test only the easiest (often knowledge-level) or the most difficult (higher cognitive levels) objectives. Maintain a fair balance.

FIGURE 10-3
Using pretests and posttests to determine improvements in performance

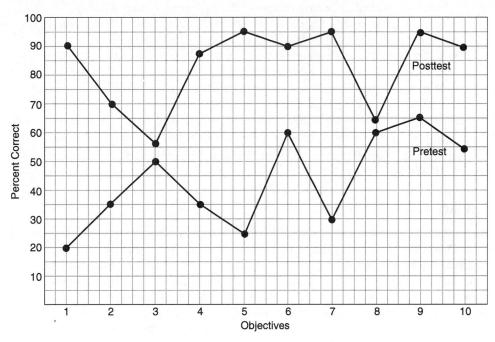

Benefits of Pretesting

For the more traditional group instruction situation, in which learners move together through all teacher-controlled activities, pretesting may have limited value for adapting instruction to individuals. The instructor may discover a range of preparation within the group. Not much can be done to provide for the differences among learners other than to recommend some remedial work while the instruction moves ahead as planned. If some learners show on the pretest that they already are competent with some of the content to be treated in the class, they most often still have to sit through the regular instruction. Only infrequently does a concerned instructor adjust assignments to accommodate these learners.

If you plan to individualize or provide for self-paced learning, then pretesting will be important for the following reasons:

- It determines learners' readiness for the program by alerting each of them to what they do and do not know about the topic.
- It indicates to both learners and the instructor the point at which to begin the program or complete remedial (or lower-level) course work before starting the program.

- It may motivate learners to study the topic by arousing their curiosity and interest as they read pretest questions or otherwise experience what they will be learning (a preinstructional strategy; see Chapter 8).
- It informs learners of what will be treated during study of the topic so that they realize what will be required of them (see Chapter 8).
- It indicates the testing methods the instructor will use in the final examination since there is a close relationship between pretest and posttest.
- It provides baseline data for determining learner growth in learning by comparing scores on pretest and posttest.
- It provides formative evaluation information useful to help the instructor modify parts of the course or program (adding or eliminating objectives and/or activities) so that the program can start at the point of learner readiness.

Whether or Not to Pretest

Given the advantages of pretesting, you may believe that pretests are always desirable. This is not the case. Disadvantages of pretests are that they take time away from instruction, involve extra work in creating the tests, may cue the learner to concentrate on certain things (while neglecting others), and may produce negative feelings. The last point seems the most critical. When learners have little background in the topics to be taught and therefore are likely to perform at a very low level (e.g., by making random guesses) on the pretest, there is little point in administering a pretest. Without useful performance information, anxiety or frustration may result. In light of these concerns, when you do pretest, be sure that learners understand the purpose. Explain clearly why the pretest is being given and that it in no way counts toward grades.

S U M M A R Y

1. Evaluation is used to provide information about the success of a course or unit of instruction.
2. One general category of evaluation is formative, which focuses on instructional processes and outcomes during development, tryout, and the progression of the course.
3. Summative evaluation assesses the degree to which instructional objectives have been achieved at the end of the course.
4. Confirmative evaluation assesses the degree to which instructional objectives are being achieved over an extended period of time after the course.
5. Whatever evaluation approach is used, there must be a direct relationship between instructional objectives and assessment measures. Multiple data sources are particularly valuable in providing a more accurate and comprehensive picture of a particular outcome than any single measure could provide.

6. For assessing knowledge, both objective tests (completion, multiple-choice, true/false, and matching) and constructed-response tests (short essay, long essay, and problem solving) may be used.

7. For assessing skills and behavior, recommended measures are direct testing of performance, analysis of naturally occurring events, ratings and checklists of behavior, and performance testing.

8. Attitudes are commonly assessed by observing instruction, observing behavior, using rating scales, surveying, and interviewing.

9. A test has a high degree of validity if it measures the behavior or trait specified by the instructional objectives. Test scores have a high degree of reliability if they remain consistent from one testing to the next. To be valid, a test must be reliable.

10. Relative standards of evaluating achievement are reflected in norm-referenced grading in which people are compared with one another, often for selection purposes.

11. Absolute standards are reflected in criterion-referenced grading, in which performance is judged relative to established criteria, regardless of how other learners score.

12. An emerging form of criterion-referenced testing in K–12 schools is standards-based assessment. These tests ask students to demonstrate the application of knowledge and skills by performing authentic, real-world tasks.

13. Student self-testing allows learners to check their own learning level as they progress through a program.

14. Pretesting is used to determine how well prepared a learner is to start an instructional program or a specific unit. Pretests are also useful in providing a baseline performance from which to judge the degree of improvement resulting from the instruction.

THE ID PROCESS

Evaluation is an essential component of instructional design. Contrary to the beliefs of some inexperienced designers, evaluation is not something that occurs only at the "back end" of a project, after the unit of instruction has been completed. Nor is it conducted only one time. Rather, evaluation is a continuous process that should occur early in a design process and then be repeated at different phases.

Determine your evaluation approach early in the process of planning the overall instructional design (see Chapter 1). You will want to include formative evaluation as the instruction is developed, summative evaluation after it is completed, and perhaps confirmative evaluation as it is being implemented over time. Whether you have the opportunity to conduct confirmative evaluations may depend on your involvement with the course or instructional unit after it has been delivered to your clients. In negotiating with clients about instructional design projects, it is important to educate them about the need for continuous evaluation for supporting quality development of the instruction and quality control over its implementation. Sufficient funds must be allocated to support the immediate and long-term evaluation functions.

Early in the planning process, you need to decide who will conduct the evaluation. Depending on budget and the complexity of the design project, you or members of the design team may be able (or need) to conduct the evaluation, or outside experts may be judged more suitable. External evaluators may add cost to the project, but they bring expertise in instrument design and validation, data analysis, and reporting. They also add credibility and objectivity because they are not personally involved in the project's success. Internal evaluators (design team members), however, are experts in the project and can directly benefit by collecting evaluation data firsthand. In our experiences, we have often used a combination of internal and external people to collaborate on the evaluations, especially for formative purposes.

Part of the evaluation planning should also include deciding how often evaluations need to be conducted and at what critical times. Several formative evaluations will probably be needed. Although summative evaluation is formally conceived as a one-time process—to make a judgment about a project's success—in reality, the distinction among formative, summative, and confirmative evaluations often becomes blurred. That is, if you conduct a summative evaluation and the instruction is judged "unsuccessful," do you just scrap it? Suppose it could be easily fixed following simple suggestions from some trainees whom you interview in your "summative" evaluation? If the revisions are then made, was the previous evaluation summative or formative?

Based on the preceding discussion, here are some key points to consider for including evaluations in the ID process:

- Educate stakeholders about the need to support and use continuous, long-term evaluation.
- Devise your evaluation plan early in the planning process.
- Begin evaluations early in the design process.
- Determine where internal evaluators (design team members) versus external evaluators might be used, given the type of evaluation, budget, and complexity of the project.
- Consider designing all evaluations (summative, too!) so that they yield data for improving the instruction, not only for judging it.

APPLICATIONS

A design group has developed a training course for basketball referees who work youth games for the park commission in a large city. The course meets five nights for three hours and includes, as main components, a manual on basketball rules, a software program on refereeing hand signals, classroom lectures on rules and techniques, and simulated practice sessions. The main objectives of the course address the preparation of trainees in three areas: (1) knowledge of the rules, (2) working games, and (3) interactions with players, coaches, and spectators.

You have been hired to evaluate the completed program. What basic approach and data-gathering methods would you use in a summative evaluation?

ANSWERS

A summative evaluation is intended to examine instruction after its completion. The primary focus is whether instructional objectives are being achieved. Thus, outcomes resulting from the course rather than learners' reactions to the course are the main concern. Given the objectives of the refereeing training course, three outcomes need to be assessed. We suggest the following possible strategies, although you may have proposed reasonable alternatives. You be the judge (i.e., a self-evaluator).

One objective deals with knowledge of rules. This outcome might be addressed by administering, at the end of the course, a comprehensive written posttest that includes both simple knowledge items ("How many fouls is each player allowed?") and higher-order thinking items ("A player with the ball calls time-out while in the air before landing out of bounds. What is the call?"). Test items should be carefully developed and validated.

A second objective deals with performance in working games. For this objective, a random sample of 25 trainees who successfully completed the course are evaluated by experts while refereeing a game. The experts are given checklists of specific behaviors to observe (use of correct hand signals, calling of defensive fouls and offensive fouls, etc.) as well as rubrics (see Chapter 11) for making a global categorization of overall performance ("highly skilled," "skilled," "acceptable," "weak," etc.).

A third objective deals with the trainees' interactions with coaches, players, and spectators. This objective can also be evaluated as part of the observation of the trainees' working game. Also, 10 randomly selected trainees might be interviewed and asked to react to scenarios in which they would be refereeing and someone from one of the three target groups reacted to them in a certain way (e.g., a parent continually yells during the game that the referee is blind and unfit to be refereeing).

As a summative evaluator, you also have to interpret the data to support a conclusion about each objective. It is likely that on each measure, some trainees will perform at a high level, whereas some will perform poorly. Making an overall judgment requires synthesis of the multiple data sources relative to what is viewed as acceptable standards in each outcome area (i.e., what is an "acceptable" knowledge score or performance score?).

REFERENCES

Gronlund, N. E. (1985). *Stating behavioral objectives for classroom instruction.* New York: Macmillan.

Gronlund, N. E. (1995). *How to write and use instructional objectives* (5th ed.). Upper Saddle River, NJ: Prentice Hall.

Haladyna, T. M., Nolen, S. B., & Haas, N. S. (1991). Raising standardized achievement test scores and the origins of test score pollution. *Educational Researcher, 20,* 2–7.

Hellebrandt, J., & Russell, J. D. (1993). Confirmative evaluation of instructional materials and learners. *Performance and Instruction, 32,* 22–27.

Misanchuk, E. R. (1978). Beyond the formative-summative distinction. *Journal of Instructional Development, 2,* 15–19.

Moseley, J. L., & Solomon, D. L. (1997). Confirmative evaluation: A new paradigm for continuous improvement. *Performance Improvement, 36,* 12–15.

Shepard, L. A. (2000). The role of assessment in a learning culture. *Educational Researcher, 29*(7), 4–14.

Stringfield, S. C., Ross, S. M., & Smith, L. J. (1996). *Bold new plans for school restructuring: The New American Schools Development Corporation designs.* Mahwah, NJ: Erlbaum.

Taylor, C. T. (1994). Assessment for measurement of standards: The peril and promise of large-scale assessment reform. *American Educational Research Journal, 31,* 231–262.

CHAPTER ⬭ **11**

Developing Evaluation Instruments

GETTING STARTED

You have just finished designing a training unit for computer repair technicians working for a large aviation company. At this point, you want to add an evaluation component both to assess trainee skills and to evaluate the effectiveness of the instruction. Because a main emphasis of the unit is learning the specific components and terminology for the computer systems employed, you first create an objective test featuring 125 multiple-choice questions and 25 short-answer questions (e.g., "List the main hardware components of the employee workstations."). However, correctly applying rules and using proper protocol are also critical outcomes. For this area, you simulate five scenarios (e.g., "computer freezes," "slow response time," "no access to Internet," "cannot save to disk," and "doesn't allow password access") to which trainees will be asked to react via open-ended responses ("What would you do here?"). Next, you develop a ratings instrument, using rubrics defining four categories of skill level, to evaluate each trainee during an actual problem situation. Finally, you create a brief open-ended survey to collect feedback from the trainees regarding the effectiveness of the training unit. Would portfolios possibly be useful here as well? What is your reaction to the overall evaluation strategy? Is it likely to provide useful data? Why or why not?

"How do instructional objectives dictate the selection of evaluation methods?"

"What type of test should I use to measure comprehension rather than simple memorization?"

"How can I assess what students like and don't like about the instruction?"

"If it is not practical to assess skills in real-life situations, are there any alternative ways of assessing performance?"

"How should portfolios be evaluated?"

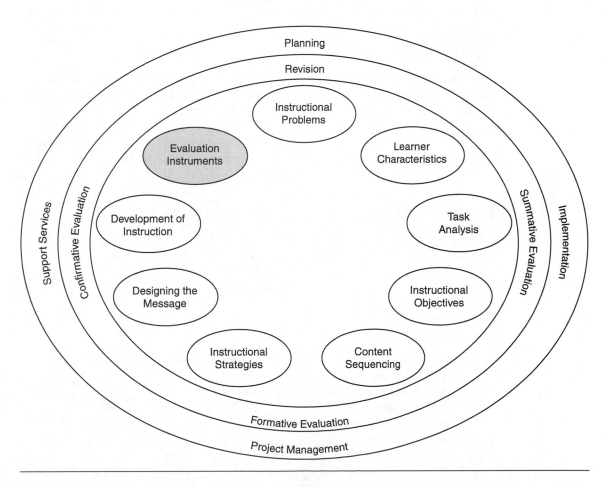

In Chapter 10 we discuss the purposes of evaluation in training and education and major principles relating to designing and conducting evaluations. As the opening questions suggest, we now turn to the more specific topic of constructing instruments to address each evaluation interest. Begin the process by asking questions such as these:

- What measures are likely to provide the most valid assessment of learning outcomes?
- Is using a particular measure complicated or precluded by practical constraints (cost, time, accepted practices)?
- What are appropriate procedures for constructing the selected measures and analyzing results?

Reexamine the first question concerning the types of measures needed. To answer it, classify the learning outcomes according to whether they deal primarily with knowledge, skills and behavior, or attitudes. We work with this scheme, as we do in Chapter 10, to identify and discuss alternative measures relating to each category.

TESTING KNOWLEDGE

The acquisition of relevant knowledge is central to most instructional programs. Pilots, for example, need to know principles of aeronautics before attempting to fly planes, doctors need to learn medical facts and concepts, and teachers require procedures for classroom management and grading (as well as expertise in the subjects they teach). Given the importance of knowledge in the learning process, assessing it becomes a critical part of instructional evaluations. This area mainly concerns the cognitive domain of instructional objectives.

The Relationship between Evaluation and Instructional Objectives

A direct relationship between instructional objectives and test items must exist. Thus, it is customary to derive test items directly from the objectives. You may recall from Chapter 5 that two recognized approaches to writing objectives are behavioral (what the learner must do to master the specified knowledge is precisely stated) and cognitive (general outcomes and specific behavior samples are described). The verb component of both of these types of objectives indicates possible forms that test items should take. Here are some examples:

To identify or recognize: Choosing an answer in an objective-type test item (see types in following discussion)

To list or label: Writing a word or brief statement

To state or describe: Writing or speaking a short or lengthy answer

To solve or calculate: Writing or choosing a solution or numerical answer

To compare or differentiate: Writing about a relationship or choosing an answer that shows a relationship

To operate or construct: Rating the quality of performance or product against criteria

To formulate or organize: Writing a plan or choosing an order of items relative to a plan

To predict or judge: Writing a description of what is expected to happen or choosing from alternative decisions

While some variation in interpreting the verb's meaning is inevitable, these examples illustrate the close relationship that is necessary between an instructional objective and a test item. A student should anticipate being tested on the same type of learning or behavior indicated by the objective, and the verb in an objective alerts the student to the content that is particularly important to study.

Most cognitive-domain objectives are evaluated by various types of paper-and-pencil tests grouped into two categories: objective and constructed response. Some instructional objectives might preferably be measured by one type of test rather than another. You should therefore become familiar with the considerations that can influence your choice. Let's look at the features of each of the commonly used types of tests. (For further help with formulating properly stated test questions, see the references at the end of this chapter.)

Objective Tests

Individuals scoring objective test items in the cognitive domain can easily agree on the correct answer; hence, the term *objective test* is used. This category includes questions for which the student must recognize and select an answer from two or more alternatives or respond to prepared statements. Typically, no writing, other than marking an answer, is required. Objective-type tests are of three major types: multiple choice, true/false, and matching.

Multiple Choice.   Multiple choice is the most useful and versatile type of objective testing. It consists of a *stem,* which is a question or an incomplete statement, plus the *alternatives,* which consist of a correct answer and several incorrect answers called *distractors.* Typically, it is best to use from three to five alternatives. More than five may stretch the test developer's creativity for devising reasonable options while increasing the reading demands on the student.

Multiple-choice items can be written at all levels of Bloom's taxonomy. Thus, compared with true/false and matching items, they can more easily test higher-order learning, including conceptual reasoning. You will probably find them to be somewhat limited, however, especially compared with essay questions, for testing synthesis and evaluation, the two highest levels in the taxonomy.

Here are examples of multiple-choice questions on the first four levels of the Bloom taxonomy:

1. Knowledge
   How does cardiovascular death rank as a killer in the United States?
   a. First
   b. Second
   c. Fifth
   d. Tenth

2. Comprehension
   When the temperature of a moving air mass is lower than that of the surface over which it is passing, heat transfer takes place vertically. This principle results in which designation for the air mass?
   a. k
   b. w
   c. A
   d. P
3. Application
   An operator can be expected to drill six holes a minute with a drill press. What is the amount of time required to drill 750 holes?
   a. 3 hours, 14 minutes
   b. 2 hours, 30 minutes
   c. 2 hours, 5 minutes
   d. 1 hour, 46 minutes
4. Analysis
   Examine the sample photographic print. What should you do to correct the condition shown?
   a. Use a different grade of paper.
   b. Expose the paper for a longer time.
   c. Develop the paper for a longer time.
   d. Use dodging to lighten shadows.

Multiple-choice tests have two advantages: (1) that of measuring a variety of learning levels and (2) that of being easy to grade. They have the disadvantages, however, of testing *recognition* (choosing an answer) rather than *recall* (constructing an answer), allowing for guessing, and being fairly difficult to construct.

Some novice developers think that the best multiple-choice item is one that is "tricky" or complex. Actually, the key to writing valid items is to make the item as clear and straightforward as possible. The purpose is to test learning, not reading skill, mind reading, or puzzle solving. Here are some guidelines for writing multiple-choice items, with examples of both poor and good questions (an asterisk denotes the correct answer):

1. Make the content meaningful relative to the instructional objectives. Do not test trivial or unimportant facts.
   Poor: Skinner developed programmed instruction in _____.
   a. 1953
   *b. 1954
   c. 1955
   d. 1956
   Better: Skinner developed programmed instruction in the _____.
   a. 1930s
   b. 1940s
   *c. 1950s
   d. 1970s

2. Reduce the length of the alternatives by moving as many words as possible to the stem. The rationale is that additional words in the alternatives have to be read four or five times, in the stem only once.

   Poor: The mean is _____.

   *a. a measure of the average
   b. a measure of the midpoint
   c. a measure of the most popular score
   d. a measure of the dispersion of scores

   Better: The mean is a measure of the _____.

   *a. average
   b. midpoint
   c. most popular score
   d. dispersion of scores

3. Construct the stem so that it conveys a complete thought.

   Poor: Objectives are _____.

   *a. used for planning instruction
   b. written in behavioral form only
   c. the last step in the instructional design process
   d. used in the cognitive but not the affective domain

   Better: The main function of instructional objectives is _____.

   *a. planning instruction
   b. comparing teachers
   c. selecting students with exceptional abilities
   d. assigning students to academic programs

4. Do not make the correct answer stand out as a result of its phrasing or length.

   Poor: A narrow strip of land bordered on both sides by water is called an

   _____.

   *a. isthmus
   b. peninsula
   c. bayou
   d. continent

   (Note: Do you see why *a* would be the best guess given the phrasing?)

   Better: A narrow strip of land bordered on both sides by water is called a(n) _____. (The same choices as in the preceding question would then follow.)

   Poor: In Bloom's cognitive taxonomy, analysis involves _____.

   a. memorizing
   b. valuing
   c. understanding
   *d. breaking down knowledge into parts and showing the relationship between the parts

   Better: In Bloom's taxonomy, analysis involves _____.

   a. memorizing information verbatim
   b. learning to value something
   c. understanding the meaning of material
   *d. breaking a whole into parts

5. Avoid overusing *always* and *never* in the distractors. Students who are good test takers quickly learn to avoid those choices.

6. Avoid overusing *all of the above* and *none of the above.* When *all of the above* is used, students can eliminate it simply by knowing that one answer is false. Or they will know to select it if any two answers are true. When *none of the above* is the correct answer, the student leaves the question having recognized what is not true but may still not know the correct answer. For example:

    The capital of Tennessee is _____.

    a. Birmingham

    b. Atlanta

    c. Albany

    *d. None of the above

    Some designers routinely add *all of the above* or *none of the above* when they run out of ideas for good distractors. A better strategy might be to include fewer choices rather than to use these two options indiscriminately.

7. Questions phrased in a positive direction are generally preferred over those phrased negatively.

    Negative stem: Which of the following is false?

    Positive stem: Which of the following is true?

    Negative stems may be good choices in some instances, but use them selectively. One disadvantage of such items is that the correct answer is a noninstance rather than the actual response to be learned (see number 6). Also, students may have more difficulty when interpreting negative phrasing. Underline, capitalize, or italicize the *not* to make sure that the student notices it.

8. Randomly select the position of the correct answer. This guideline is probably the easiest to follow, but we suspect that many instructors rely instead on making these selections subjectively. The problem is that they may have unintentional biases in favor of certain response positions. Consequently, students may learn, for example, that alternative *a* is a better guess than alternative *d* in Mr. Tessmer's class.

True/False Items.   True/false test questions are presented as statements that the learner judges as correct or incorrect. Only content material that lends itself to "either/or" answers should be written in this format. Consequently, the range of content that can be tested is fairly narrow, often limited to factual information.

True/false tests have the advantages of being fairly easy to write and very easy to grade. Their disadvantages are that they test recognition rather than recall, allow for a high probability (50 percent) of guessing the correct answer, and limit assessments to lower levels of learning (knowledge and comprehension). Some guidelines for true/false testing are as follows:

1. Be certain that the statement is entirely true or entirely false.

Poor: A good instructional objective will identify a performance standard. (True/False) (Note: The correct answer here is technically *false*. However, the statement is ambiguous. While a performance standard is a feature of some "good" objectives, it is not necessary to make an objective good.)

Better: A performance standard of an objective should be stated in measurable terms. (True/False) (Note: The answer here is clearly true.)

2. Convey only one thought or idea in a true/false statement.

Poor: Bloom's cognitive taxonomy of objectives includes six levels of objectives, the lowest being knowledge. (True/False)

Better: Bloom's cognitive taxonomy includes six levels of objectives. (True/False)

Knowledge is the lowest-level objective in Bloom's cognitive taxonomy. (True/False)

3. Unless there are special circumstances, use true/false questions sparingly.

The 50 percent guessing probability is a major disadvantage of this type of item. This factor, along with the limited levels of learning that can be assessed, make true/false, in general, less desirable than other testing forms.

Strategies for reducing these weaknesses are (1) requiring learners to write a short explanation of why false answers are incorrect and (2) incorporating third or fourth choices such as opinion (as opposed to fact)—"sometimes, but not always true," "cannot be resolved," and the like (see McBeath, 1992, for additional discussion and examples). Note that in the first case, we are converting the standard true/false question into a type of short-answer item; in the second case, it is being converted to a three- or four-alternative multiple-choice item. We might therefore consider whether we would have been better off in the first place with using alternatives to true/false testing.

Matching Items.   Matching items are a specific form of multiple-choice testing. They require the learner to identify the relationship between a list of entries in one column with a list of responses in a second column. A matching test is highly appropriate when each listing forms a category of related items (e.g., state capitals, chemistry elements, levels of Bloom's taxonomy). It is most suitable for testing ability to discriminate between

- definitions and terms,
- events and dates,
- achievements and people,
- descriptions or applications and principles, and
- functions and parts.

The main advantage of a matching test is that a large amount of material can be condensed to fit in less space on a page than would be required for multiple-choice testing of the same content. By your careful selection of terms, students have substantially fewer chances for guessing correct associations than on multiple-choice and true/false tests. A disadvantage of matching tests is assessing recognition rather than recall and lower levels of learning (knowledge).

Here are examples of matching tests:

A. In column I are descriptions of geographic characteristics of wind belts. For each statement, find the appropriate wind belt in column II. Answers may be used more than once.

Column I	*Column II*
1. Region of high pressure, calm, and light, baffling winds	a. Doldrums
2. The belt of calm air nearest the equator	b. Horse latitudes
3. A wind belt in the Northern Hemisphere	c. Polar easterlies
4. The belt in which most of the United States is found	d. Prevailing easterlies
	e. Prevailing westerlies

B. Select a lettering device in column II to carry out the task in column I. Answers may be used only once.

Column I	*Column II*
1. Making a thermal transparency quickly	a. Soft lead pencil
2. Preparing a transparency directly on clear acetate	b. Broad-tipped felt pen
3. Quick lettering for a paste-up sheet	c. Fine-tipped felt pen
4. Producing colored lettering for a poster	d. Mechanical pen
5. Preparing titles, without equipment, to be photographed as slides	e. Dry pen
	f. Photocopying
	g. Word-processing software

Following are some guidelines for constructing matching tests:

1. Limit the number of items to a maximum of six or seven. It becomes very confusing for learners to try to match a greater amount.
2. Limit the length of the items to a word, phrase, or brief sentence. In general, make the items as short as possible.
3. Provide one or two extra items (distractors) in the second column. Their inclusion reduces the probability of correct guessing. This also eliminates the situation that may occur in equal-sized lists, where if one match is incorrect, a second match must also be incorrect. Note from examples A and B that this "double-jeopardy" limitation can also be removed by allowing answers to be used more than one time.

Constructed-Response Tests

The major limitation of objective-type tests is that learners are not required to plan answers and express them in their own words. These shortcomings are overcome by using constructed-response tests. The requirements of such tests may range from a one-word response to an essay of several pages. An important advantage of constructed-response tests is that high-level cognitive objectives can be more appropriately evaluated. The main disadvantage, as will be seen, is obtaining reliable scores.

Short-Answer Items. Short-answer items require a learner to supply a single word, a few words, or a brief sentence in response to an incomplete statement or a question. The terms *fill in the blank* or *completion* are also used in referring to this type of constructed-response question.

As a category of tests, these items fall between objective types and essay questions. Since the expected answers are specific, scoring can be fairly objective. Another advantage, and a similarity to multiple-choice items, is that they can test a large amount of content within a given time period. A third advantage is that these items test recall rather than recognition.

On the other hand, short-answer items are limited to testing lower-level cognitive objectives, such as the recall of facts (knowledge level), comprehension, or the application of specific information. Also, scoring may not be as straightforward and objective as anticipated. Here are examples of short-answer test questions:

1. The type of evaluation designed to assess a program as it develops or progresses is called _____ evaluation.
2. Guessing is considered the greatest problem for which type of objective item?
3. List the four types of reliability defined in your text.
4. Define *criterion-referenced testing*.

The most important guideline for writing short-answer items is to word them so that only one answer is correct. Otherwise, scoring will become more subjective, and, when grades are at issue, arguments with students will become more frequent.

Poor: The first president of the United States was _____. (two words) (Note: The desired answer is George Washington, but students may write "from Virginia," "a general," "very smart," and other creative expressions.)
Better: Give the first and last name of the first president of the United States: _____.

Essay Questions. Essay questions are most useful for testing higher levels of cognitive learning. In particular, instructional objectives emphasizing analysis, synthesis, and evaluation can be measured effectively when learners are required to organize and express their thoughts in writing. A "short" essay, which may be restricted to a few paragraphs or a single page, typically requires a highly focused response. A "long" essay allows the learner more opportunity to express and defend a point of view. The trade-off, of course, is that the more expansion or divergence allowed, the more difficult the grading. (We return to the grading issue shortly in discussing advantages and limitations of essay tests.) Among the advantages are these:

- They are relatively easy to construct, taking less time than does the design of a comparable objective-type test.
- They require learners to express themselves in writing, a verbal skill that is highly important for students at all levels to develop.
- They are superior to objective tests for assessing higher-order learning, such as application, analysis, synthesis, and evaluation.
- They provide instructors with considerable information about learners' understanding of the content taught.

Disadvantages of essay tests include these:

- Because students will have time to write only a few essays, a limited number of concepts or principles relating to a topic can be tested.
- If the questions asked are not focused, students may stray off the topic or misinterpret the type of response desired. Scoring becomes more difficult and unreliable as a result.
- Because of the subjective nature of grading essay tests, attention by instructors to "style over substance" may result in a learner with good writing skills receiving higher grades than his or her knowledge of the subject warrants. Similarly, a student who is a poor writer will be at a disadvantage.
- Time required for different learners to complete an essay test will vary greatly.
- Much time and care must be taken when grading so as to be as objective as possible and avoid making personal judgments about individual learners.

Here are examples of essay questions:

1. Prepare a hypothetical route weather forecast from your station to a location 500 miles away. Assume that a winter cold front exists at the beginning of the forecast period halfway between the two locations, with squall lines and icing conditions below 12,000 feet MSL. Make reference to the general situation, sky conditions and cloud base, visibility, precipitation, freezing level, winds aloft, and other factors you deem important. (20 points)
2. In your judgment, what will be the most difficult change to which human society will have to adapt in the twenty-first century? Support your position with reference to at least three utopian objectives and their significance for the future. (15 minutes maximum; 2-page limit; 20 points)

Guidelines for constructing essay tests are as follows:

1. Make the questions as specific and focused as possible.
   Poor: Describe the role of instructional objectives in education.
   Discuss Bloom's contribution to the evaluation of instruction.

Better: Describe and differentiate between behavioral (Mager) and cognitive (Gronlund) objectives with regard to their (1) format and (2) relative advantages and disadvantages for specifying instructional intentions.

2. Inform students of the grading criteria and conditions. Will spelling count? How important is organization? Are all parts of the essay worth the same number of points? Can a dictionary be used? Do dates of historic events need to be indicated? Unless you specify the criteria, students may perform poorly simply because they do not know what type of response you expect. Also, keep in mind that certain criteria may be less relevant to evaluation needs. It may thus be desirable to derive separate scores for various criteria.

3. Write or outline a model answer. Essays are difficult to grade reliably. Incidental qualities such as length, handwriting, vocabulary, and writing style can all influence the overall impression and divert attention from the content. Writing a model answer makes it easier to focus on content, assign points to key concepts included, and grade more objectively and reliably.

4. Do not give students a choice of essays; have all respond to the same questions. All essay questions are not created equal. If one student selects a biology question on, say, cell division, while another selects a question on oxidation, they are essentially taking two different tests. Also, when students are given a choice, they can adapt the test to their strengths in the process.

5. Grade essays "in the blind," that is, without knowing the writers' identities. As noted already, the subjectivity involved in evaluating essays can reduce reliability. When you grade an essay knowing the identity of the writer, you may be swayed by an individual's prior performance and attitude. To reduce this effect, have students write their social security number (or some other code) instead of their names on their answer sheets. True, you may identify some individuals by handwriting or other telltale signs (purple ink, smudges, etc.), but you'll have enough doubt about most papers to make blind scoring worthwhile.

6. When multiple essay questions are required, evaluate a given question for all students before scoring the next essay. It is challenging enough to obtain reliable scores while concentrating on one question at a time; jumping around from question to question will complicate the scoring task immensely.

Problem-Solving Questions. Like essays, problem-solving questions are well suited to evaluating higher-level cognitive outcomes such as application, analysis, and synthesis. Another advantage is that such questions are generally easy to construct. The main disadvantage, as you probably have anticipated, is scoring. In some instances, the problem will have a single correct answer that can be derived in only one way. Scoring those answers is easy. The other extreme is a situation in which there are alternative solution approaches and possible answers. An example would be statistically describing and interpreting a set of test scores. A high class performance

Expert's Edge

Three Blind-Grading Principles . . . See How They Run

In the next few paragraphs, I would like to describe three principles that constitute a "blind-grading" procedure that I employ in one of the classes I teach. For many years, I have employed these principles when I grade student responses to a series of essay questions that are part of two take-home open-book exams I administer. Moreover, I have recently started to use the blind-grading technique to grade student responses to some open-ended questions I ask them to do for homework. Indeed, I feel that this method could be effectively employed in grading student responses to a wide variety of questions or assignments for which there is no one "correct" answer.

The principles I describe here certainly were not developed by me. I am sure that they have been described in many textbooks on measurement and testing. Nonetheless, I hope that this account of how an instructor (me!) has actually employed such principles may encourage you, and/or the instructors you will be working with, to employ these methods.

The first basic principle is that when I assign papers to my students, I ask them to not put their names on their papers. Instead, I ask them to simply list their student identification number on the back of the last page of their responses. Because students do not list their names, I am usually unaware of who wrote a particular paper. Not knowing this information allows me to be much more objective when grading papers. By not knowing who wrote a particular paper, my grading is not influenced by factors that might otherwise affect my grading—factors such as how often the student participates in class and the quality of his or her in-class comments. Personality factors, such as how much I like a student or how likely it is that the student will complain about the grade he or she receives, also cease to be issues. As easy as it may be for us to think that the aforementioned factors do not affect how we score an exam, I would bet that in many cases, these factors do have some influence. Indeed, I would wager that in many cases instructors are influenced by these factors, but are unaware of this fact. By scoring papers without knowing who wrote them, the chances of being influenced by such factors are greatly diminished, although not totally so (there may be a tendency to guess who wrote a particular paper, a tendency I am usually able to beat into submission).

The second principle I adhere to is that I grade each student's response to one question before I grade any student's response to the next question. By doing so, I am able to keep the same criteria clearly in mind as I review each student's answer to that particular question. Moreover, although in most cases I judge student responses in light of some specific criteria I have in mind (or have specified in writing), I am better able to judge how good (or bad) an answer to a question may be by comparing it with another answer to the same question. I know to many individuals this practice might appear to be antithetical to the principles of criterion-referenced testing, but I don't agree. I believe that in most of the cases when we are grading open-ended responses for which there is no one right answer, a certain degree of subjectivity comes into play; in other words, our criteria are rarely so well-defined as to rule out all subjectivity. In such instances, I believe we may be better able to judge the quality of a response to a question after having read several other responses to the same question, or after having reread a model response from a previous semester.

Another advantage of reading everyone's response to one question before reading anyone's response to the next question is that it lessens the likelihood of a halo effect. That is, it lessens the likelihood that how you judge a student's response to one question will be influenced by how you judged his or her response to a previous question. I further ensure that the halo effect will not occur by requiring my students to start their responses to each essay question on a new page. When I finish grading a student's response to one question, I record the student's grade on the last page of his or her response to that question, then turn to the first page of the next response and place the student's paper aside with the others I have already graded. When I have graded all of the students' answers to the first question and begin to grade their answers to the next one, all of their papers have now been turned to a page that gives me little, if any, clue as to how well any of the students responded to the first question. Thus, I greatly reduce the likelihood of my grading being influenced by a how well or poorly a student responded to the previous question.

The third principle I adhere to is closely related to the second one. When I complete grading students' answers to one question and begin grading their answers to the next question, I change the order in which I grade the papers. I usually do this by randomly shuffling the papers, or reversing the order in which I reviewed the papers when I graded student answers to the previous question. By changing the order in which I grade papers, I lessen the likelihood that a student will benefit from, or be hurt by, some idiosyncrasy in the way I score papers as I move from grading the first to last response to a given question. For example, it may be that as I review a series of responses to a question, I get more critical as I proceed through that set. If so, then the student whose paper is graded last will be at a disadvantage. Again, one may think that if the criteria for judging responses have been clearly identified, then the order in which a series of responses is reviewed should have no influence how an individual paper is judged. However, after many years of experience, I have found that no matter how carefully I identify the criteria I will use, my judgment of an individual response is often influenced, at least to some small degree, by the other responses I have read. I believe this circumstance is likely to be more common than many adherents of criterion-referenced testing are inclined to admit. If my opinion is correct, then by changing the order in which you grade students' responses, you are likely to lessen the impact of this phenomenon.

In summary, when I administer essay exams, the three principles I adhere to when grading those exams are the following:

1. Grade each exam without knowing who wrote it.
2. Grade all of the answers to one question before grading any of the answers to the next question.

3. When moving from question to question, change the order in which papers are graded.

I have employed these principles for many years and have found that they really enable me to grade students' responses much more objectively. Moreover, many of my students have indicated how much they appreciate my use of these methods. In conclusion, these techniques have worked very well for me and my students, and I believe they will work just as well for you and those you work with. I hope you will give these techniques a try.

Dr. Robert Reiser is a professor in the Instructional Systems program in the Department of Educational Psychology and Learning Systems at Florida State University. Dr. Reiser has written four books and more than 40 journal articles in the field of instructional design and technology. His most recent book, which was published in 2002, is *Trends and Issues in Instructional Design and Technology* (edited with John V. Dempsey).

(based on the mean) in the eye of one analyst may appear mediocre to another (who focuses on the median or some other property of the results).

Following are some examples of problem-solving questions:

1. One worker can build 5 benches in 1 day. For a particular job, 20 benches are needed in 1 day's time. How many workers need to be assigned to this job? Show all work and circle your final answer.
2. You are given a beaker that contains one of the five chemical solutions used in previous laboratory exercises. Describe a procedure that you would use to positively identify the particular solution and rule out the other alternatives. (Be sure to list each major step in your procedure.)

Here are some guidelines for constructing problem-solving items:

1. Specify the criteria for evaluation. For example, indicate whether students should show their work in addition to the final answer.
2. Award partial credit or give a separate score for using correct procedures when the final answer is incorrect. On many problems, a careless error may result in a wrong answer, even though the work shown conveys full understanding of the problem.
3. Construct a model answer for each problem that indicates the amount of credit to be awarded for work at different stages.

Remember that regardless of which type of test you employ (multiple-choice, essay, problem-solving, etc.), the key concern is that it provides a valid measure of performance. In the case of objective tests, validity will mostly depend on the appropriateness of the content tested and the clarity of the items. For constructed response tests, an additional element becomes the reliability of scoring. The guidelines provided here for the different constructed-response modes should be helpful toward that end.

TESTING SKILLS AND BEHAVIOR

In evaluating skills and behavior, we examine overt actions that can be directly observed. Frequently, the target behavior is some type of performance reflecting how well a trainee or student can carry out a particular task or a group of related tasks. Some examples are as follows:

- Using a power saw to cut boards of different thickness
- Doing a dance step for 10 repetitions without error
- Debugging a computer program so that it runs effectively
- Giving a speech that incorporates the "10 speaking skills" taught in a course
- Leading a group to resolve a conflict successfully

The standards of performance are judged according to the requirements of the instructional objectives and should be the same as those covered during instruction. Accordingly, each of the preceding general goals would need to be broken down into more precise descriptions of expected performance. Prior to testing, the learner should have had sufficient opportunities to practice and apply the skills to be able to demonstrate the learning. If so, he or she should be prepared to complete the test successfully.

Expert's Edge

The Proof Is in the Pudding, or Is It in How You Make the Pudding?

A large company we shall call Info Avenue is in an interesting and highly profitable business. It acquires sensitive, unpublished information from and about other companies—for which it pays nothing—and subsequently sells the information to customers. Obviously, this business relies heavily on the skills of Info Avenue employees who acquire this information; without their success, there is no product to sell. However, extracting this information is difficult; strong interpersonal, interviewing, and selling skills are required.

Because this job is so critical and difficult, Info Avenue had invested in extensive instruction to train new hires in how to perform this role. The instruction included weeks of self-study and coordinated follow-up with supervisors who were to perform important coaching and feedback functions for these employees. The investment in the training was so substantial and concern for verifying competence among these employees was so high that Info Avenue also wanted a good performance assessment tool. The instrument was to be used to screen new hires for competence before they were released to go into the field and begin interacting with organizations and collecting information. Performance assessment was planned to occur during a large, national meeting convened for this purpose.

When we were called by Info Avenue to assist with the development and validation of this performance-assessment instrument, we knew this would be a challenging project. However, we assumed that the challenges would be largely technical in nature. After all, this appeared to be among the "softest" of "soft skills." It was apparent that these competencies could not be assessed using multiple-choice test questions: a performance test was essential.

Performance tests actually have two components: the observation support tool, usually a rating scale or checklist; and the observer or rater. For performance tests to work and to be legally defensible, the rating scale must reflect job-related competencies (a validity issue), and the raters must be consistent in their use of the scale (a reliability issue). Both aspects require serious attention from the test developer.

The rating scale development began with a job analysis drawing on the expertise of those within the company who were knowledgeable about how the information-gathering position is best performed. We drafted the tool, and then an iterative process of review and revision began. The tool was piloted with a sample of raters, and its content validity (job relatedness) was documented by subject-matter experts. So far, so good.

The next technical hurdle was training the Info Avenue raters to use the observation tool. Even the best rating instruments or checklists can seldom be used consistently by untrained raters. Unfortunately, this part of performance testing is often overlooked. The good news is that training raters to score performances reliably—even soft skills performances—is easier than most people think. Interestingly, the process follows the same general pattern as a concept lesson. In other words, competent performance becomes a concept that the raters must master at the comprehension level: they must become consistent with one another in classifying previously unseen instances of the performance as examples or nonexamples of competent performance.

The process for training the raters generally looks like this:

- Create sample cases of performance that reflect competent and typically incompetent performance.
- Bring the raters together.
- Review the rating scale or checklist.
- Present the model-case competent performance for rating.
- Compare ratings and discuss any discrepancies.
- Present a "far-out" nonexample.
- Compare ratings and discuss discrepancies.
- Present nonexamples including "near-in" nonexamples, compare ratings, and discuss until discrepancies disappear.
- Present final trials to calculate interrater reliability for documentation.

Following this process, we were able to bring the Info Avenue raters to acceptable levels of interrater reliability in one morning session. Info Avenue was delighted with the assessment. It proceeded to implement the training for new hires and scheduled the nationwide testing session at the culmination of the training period.

The day of the testing session turned out to hold a major insight regarding the implementation of sound and rigorous testing in an organization. The assessment process worked beautifully and the vast majority of new-hire candidates passed the test. However, *all* those who did not pass were from one region in the southeastern United States. The candidates from that region were obviously less well prepared than they should have been, and all of them were under the supervision of the same regional training manager. It quickly became apparent that the problem was with this regional manager. In the process, the test—designed to assess new-hire competence—had shed unflattering light on management. Higher management, fearing embarrassment within middle management, suddenly announced that Info Avenue had "only winners" within its ranks and that the testing session would henceforth be regarded as a "coaching opportunity" rather than a performance evaluation.

And so it is with well-constructed, valid performance assessments. They often turn up performance problems elsewhere besides among the test takers. We now consider learning outcomes assessment more than simply a step in the instructional design process: it is truly *organizational* change. And the better the test, the more profound the change is likely to be, since much comfort is sometimes found in error and uncertainty. Be ready.

Sharon Shrock is professor of instructional development and evaluation at Southern Illinois University, where she is coordinator of Graduate Programs in Instructional Design and Technology. She has consulted with a number of global corporations in developing criterion-referenced assessment systems. She is first author of the award-winning book, *Criterion-Referenced Test Development: Technical and Legal Guidelines for Corporate Training and Certification.*

Bill Coscarelli is professor of instructional technology at Southern Illinois University and co-author of *Criterion-Referenced Test Development: Technical and Legal Guidelines for Corporate Training and Certification.* Dr. Coscarelli has been an active testing consultant. He is a former editor of *Performance Improvement Quarterly* and is a past president of the International Society for Performance and Improvement.

Preliminary Considerations

When preparing to evaluate performance, look for answers to the following questions:

1. Will process, product, or both be evaluated? When a learner performs a task, the confidence, care, and accuracy with which he or she carries out the procedures usually are important. This is a measurement of the process portion of the task, which may include elements such as these:
   - Following a proper sequence of actions or steps
   - Performing detailed manipulations
   - Using tools or instruments properly
   - Working within a specified time period

   Product evaluation focuses primarily on the end result or outcome of the effort. Attention is on the quality and possibly quantity of a product, or on the final action that results from applying the process. The evaluation of most tasks includes both process and product components.

2. What constraints or limitations should be recognized when planning a performance evaluation? The conditions under which a task is normally performed should be considered before developing the test. Such elements as the following can help you decide whether to use a realistic or a simulated testing situation:

   • Size and complexity of the task
   • Cost for materials or services required
   • Human safety factors
   • Time needed for testing

   Other matters that need attention when deciding on the method of testing include the following:

   • The required place for testing
   • Necessary or specialized equipment
   • Instruments, tools, and supplies needed
   • The required involvement of other persons

3. Will the testing conditions be simulated or realistic? By considering the various factors indicated in the answer to the previous question, you can be prepared to decide whether the test can be conducted under realistic conditions or, if this is impractical, whether it can be handled in some abbreviated or simulated fashion. The simulation should be as job-like as possible to serve as a valid measure of performance.

Today many of those involved in K–12 education are placing increasing emphasis on assessing student performance in addition to student's recall or recognition of content. Performance assessments are frequently confused with authentic assessments, even though they do not mean the same thing. *Authentic assessment* involves the student demonstrating the performance in a real-life context (Meyer, 1993). In your opinion, would going on a field trip, returning to class, and then writing an essay in a one-hour class period be an authentic assessment of writing? Probably not, since the conditions for the writing performance are contrived. A more authentic context would be one in which, similar to a journalist given an assignment and a deadline, the students have a day or two in which they can use a variety of resources (e.g., school or community library, Internet, textbooks) to generate the written report.

The instructional designer should also keep in mind that assessment is not only useful for measuring the outcomes of instruction. Another valuable contribution is enhancing the process of learning. As Lorie Shepard (2001) suggests, building meaningful "formative" assessment into instructional units can be extremely helpful to the learner. Shepard favors authentic performance measures that build learner motivation, require student self-assessment, and promote the transfer of knowledge in contrast to, say, merely inserting a few multiple-choice items in different sections of a lesson.

Whether the testing takes place under realistic or simulated conditions, an evaluator should give consideration to recording the performance on videotape. With this procedure, evaluation of a performance can take place at a later time and may involve the learner in the review. Depending on the evaluation needs and conditions, one or more of the alternative measures described next may be used.

Types of Skill/Behavior Assessments

Direct Testing.   For certain types of performances, it may be feasible to test the student or trainee directly to determine level of skill. The primary focus is on products (final outcomes), but examining processes (actions that lead to the products) will also be of interest in most situations.

Examples
> Keyboarding speed and accuracy
> Operating equipment
> Marksmanship
> Assembling parts
> Using a hammer
> Drawing geometric shapes

Procedure.   The first step in developing the test is to review the instructional objectives and details of the task to be evaluated. Then use the following procedure:

1. Review the task analysis (Chapter 4) for the task, and identify the steps or specific procedures of the task that constitute the criteria to be judged. Establish the proficiency level that will be accepted (as indicated by the performance standard component of the objective).
2. Plan how the performance will take place, including its location and the application of the procedure.
3. List the equipment, tools, materials, and printed resources to be made available.
4. Consider any special matters like safety and other persons needed.
5. Write the instructions that direct the actions of the learners during the test.

For example, in evaluating nursing trainees' skills at taking blood pressure, a designer might establish the standard of achieving an accuracy level averaging 95 percent proximity to experts' readings on 15 patients. Trainees perform in a simulated examining room where they are scheduled at 30-minute intervals; given instructions, the equipment, and volunteer patients needed; and tested under controlled conditions (e.g., with proper safety precautions and sanitary conditions).

Because the scores obtained will be reflective of each individual, it is highly important to establish appropriate conditions of testing to ensure that the scores are valid. For example, it would hardly seem appropriate to assess taking blood pressure in a noisy room with insufficient lighting.

Analysis of Naturally Occurring Results.   Certain skills or behaviors may be evaluated as products of activities naturally performed in realistic contexts. By assessing these products, the evaluator obtains a direct measure of the objective in question, without having to develop instruments or collect new data.

Examples

> Number of absences from school
> Number of traffic citations received this year
> Sales volume during the second quarter
> Verbal score obtained on the Graduate Record Exam
> Courses selected for the spring semester

As with direct testing, the score by itself reflects the target performance (or behavior), which thus makes the validity of that score the key concern. For example, if the measure of interest was sales volume in a given month, an evaluator would want to be sure that nothing unusual happened during that period to change outcomes that would normally occur. Weather, student illness, or special conditions in the business could have unanticipated effects in this regard. Similarly, following their completion of a driver's safety course, students may receive very few traffic citations, but the main reasons for their increased "driving success" may be local sales on radar detectors and the city's cutback on traffic officers. The evaluator, therefore, must make sure that the available data are valid indicators of performance associated with the instruction.

Analysis of naturally occurring events is especially useful for confirmative evaluations. Recall from Chapter 10 that the purpose of confirmative evaluations is to examine the effectiveness of instruction over an extended time. Available data, such as quantity of sales, number of patient complaints, and percentage of trainees passing the certification examination, provide a practical and cost-effective basis for judging the stability of instructional outcomes over time. Depending on needs and resources, supplementary measures may also be desired.

Procedure

1. Based on the instructional objectives for the instruction, identify any relevant results (behaviors or products) that naturally occur as the individual performs his or her job or normal activities.
2. Arrange to obtain the results. (Permission from the student and/or other individuals, such as supervisors or administrators, will often be be required.)
3. Ensure that the results reflect representative performance/behavior. If conditions seem unusual (e.g., a bad month for sales), increase the time frame to include additional data collection periods.

Ratings of Performance.   In many situations, especially when the process component of performance is to be evaluated, it becomes necessary for the instructor or other qualified judge to observe learner actions and rate them in terms of the necessary criteria.

Examples

Speaking ability
Applying colors in a painting
Technical skill in a gymnastics routine
Interpersonal skills
Carpentry ability in building a deck

The ratings are commonly made using one of the following instruments.

Checklists. A checklist can be used to determine whether sequential steps in a procedure or other actions are successfully performed. The evaluator indicates yes/no or done/not done for each element. A checklist, however, does not allow assessments to be made of quality of performance. An example of a checklist is shown in Figure 11-1.

Rating Scales. With a rating scale, special values can be assigned to each element of a performance. Only behaviors that can be observed and rated reliably should be included in a rating scale. A numerical scale is commonly used. It consists of standards from low to high, such as these:

0	1	2
Unacceptable	Acceptable with corrections	Acceptable

1	2	3	4
Poor	Fair	Good	Excellent

Using descriptive terms is recommended to differentiate and clarify the meaning of the individual rating categories. It would make little sense, for example, to ask

FIGURE 11-1
Checklist for task: Dry-mount a picture

Skill	Performed (Yes/No)
1. Plug in press.	_____
2. Set press at 225 degrees.	_____
3. Plug in tacking iron.	_____
4. Set tacking iron on *high*.	_____
5. Wait for press to each temperature before use.	_____
6. Dry picture in press.	_____
7. Dry cardboard in press.	_____
8. Tack dry-mount tissue to back of picture.	_____
9. Trim picture and tissue together.	_____
10. Align picture on cardboard.	_____
11. Tack tissue under picture in two corners.	_____
12. Seal picture to cardboard in press for 10 seconds.	_____
13. Remove and immediately cool mounting under weight.	_____

an observer to rate a manager's "leadership skills" given only a rating scale of 1 to 10. What would a 10 indicate? How would a 4 differ from a 5? Without clearer definitions, the ratings will be completely arbitrary and unreliable. Depending on the situation and the descriptors used, rating scales may be *norm referenced,* with which learners are judged in comparison to each other, or *criterion referenced,* with which they are judged relative to the acceptable standards for performance. Here is an example of a norm-referenced descriptive rating scale:

1	2	3	4	5
Unsatisfactory	Below average	Average	Above average	Superior

An important limitation of rating scales can be any personal bias an evaluator may have in preferring one learner over another for any number of reasons. Also, careful attention is required to discriminate each level of performance from the others on a scale; thus, limiting rating scales to three to five levels is usually advisable. Training of evaluators is also strongly encouraged to standardize their measurements.

In addition to evaluating the process component of a skill, a rating form should be used to judge the quality (and quantity) of a resulting product. Such factors as these may be included:

• General appearance of product
• Accuracy of product details (shape, dimensions, finish)
• Relationships between components or parts (size, fit, finish, color)
• Quantity of products produced during a time period

Figure 11-2 illustrates a rating scale that includes both process and product evaluations.

Before the rating instrument is used, it should be tried out with a sample of two or three persons from the potential learner group or equivalent. This trial allows checking for (1) the learner's clear understanding of the testing procedure, (2) the effectiveness of each part of the instrument, and (3) the required length of the testing period for each learner. Also, if more than one evaluator will use the scale, the procedure must be standardized so that each person making a judgment grades similar performances equally. That is, interrater reliability (consistency) must be established.

Rubrics. A newer evaluation approach involves the use of rubrics to judge the quality of performance. In contrast to a conventional rating scale, a *rubric* is intended to give a more descriptive, holistic characterization of the quality of students' work. Specifically, where multiple rating items might be used to evaluate isolated skills in a complex task (see Figure 11-2), the rubric represents a general assessment of the overall product. In designing and using a rubric, the concern is less with assigning a number to indicate quality than with selecting a verbal description that clearly communicates, based on the performance or product exhibited, what the student knows and is able to do. Thus, rubrics can be highly informative and useful for feedback purposes. On the other hand, the need to develop distinct

FIGURE 11-2
Rating scale for using direct instruction

Procedure	Rating			
	Poor			Excellent
1. Introduces objectives	0	1	2	3
2. Gives overview	0	1	2	3
3. Reviews prerequisites	0	1	2	3
4. Shows enthusiasm	0	1	2	3
5. Uses clear examples/explanations	0	1	2	3
6. Asks appropriate questions	0	1	2	3
7. Keeps students on task	0	1	2	3
8. Provides sufficient independent practice	0	1	2	3
9. Provides review	0	1	2	3
10. Closes lesson effectively	0	1	2	3
11. Summary rating	0	1	2	3

categories and meaningful verbal descriptions makes them challenging to develop and to score reliably. Figures 11-3 and 11-4 illustrate rubrics used, respectively, in evaluating writing in grades K–1 and at the secondary-school level. Note that these types of assessments are much more informative about students' skill levels compared with receiving simply a letter grade or numerical score. To the extent that standards-based education continues to gain acceptance, we can expect to see rubrics becoming increasingly pervasive as an evaluation and feedback tool.

Anecdotal Records.   An *anecdotal record* is an open-ended instrument for evaluating performance in a narrative fashion. An outline-type form containing behaviors to be observed is prepared. In addition to a description of performance, interpretations of what was done along with recommendations for improvement may be included in such a record. The written record should be made while observing the performance, or brief notes should be taken and then expanded on the record form immediately after the evaluation session.

Examples

> Observing a student teacher
> Attending a presentation given by a student who has completed a public speaking course
> Spending a day in an office to evaluate how a manager interacts with her employees

Procedure

> 1. Develop a general set of guidelines to focus your observations according to the objectives of the evaluation. (The guidelines may be modified over time as considered appropriate.)

FIGURE 11-3
Rubric used in evaluating writing in grades K and 1

Holistic Evaluation Scale (K and 1)
5   Focused to starter sentence; story structure is recognizable; contains successful attempts in sentence construction (i.e., capitalization, punctuation, etc.)
4   Focused to starter sentence; story structure is recognizable but contains little evidence of sentence mechanics
3   Some words are recognizable; may or may not have mechanics; has connection with starter sentence, but little story development
2   Some words are recognizable; no connection with starter sentence; no mechanics and little story content
1   No recognizable words, mechanics, or story content

Note: Created by Michele Woodward. Used with permission.

2. Determine whether the observation will be prearranged or unannounced. The advantage of the prearranged visit is ensuring that the observation can be done at a particular time and that your appearance will be accepted. The advantage of the unannounced visit is observing events as they naturally take place, without special preparation (to impress an observer). Regardless of the orientation used, permission to observe from school or company officials will most likely be required.

3. If you want to use a tape recorder or video camera, be sure to obtain approval from the individual(s) being observed as well as from school or company authorities.

4. Take brief notes during the observation. Expand the notes on a record form as soon after the observation as possible.

5. Make additional observations if needed. The more observations, the more complete and accurate the information obtained. The disadvantage is the time involved and possible disruption caused by the visits.

For example, two months after trainees complete a corporate training course on group leadership, the evaluator contacts them to identify times when they will be leading a group on the job. A prearranged visit is then coordinated with a given trainee, and permission is obtained to tape-record the session. The evaluator arrives at the meeting early and sits in the back of the room to be unobtrusive. The trainee introduces the evaluator to the group members at the beginning of the meeting and tells them her purposes for being there (and tape-recording the meeting). The evaluator carefully observes the trainee's behavior during the meeting and takes notes, which she later expands. Following the meeting, she decides that the observation produced sufficient information and that a second one with this trainee will not be needed. She decides, however, to observe several other trainees to compare the results.

Descriptive evaluation is time-consuming and often impractical with large numbers of learners. As with rating scales, a degree of subjectivity can easily, and

FIGURE 11-4

Rubric used for evaluating writing at the high school level

Score	Content	Organization	Expression	Mechanics
4	Focus is clear and on a limited topic; ideas are developed and supported with concrete details; evidence of consideration of possibilities and complexities of the issue	Strong introduction; transitions between paragraphs help tie information together; strong conclusion	Varied sentence structure; use of vivid language; tone is consistent with text; audience and purpose clearly defined; individual voice present	Use of standard grammar and punctuation; correct spelling
3	Focus may be clear but ideas developed minimally; no consideration for complexity of an issue	An introduction but may not be strong; transitions made between paragraphs; conclusion but may not be strong	Appropriate use of language and diction; tone is consistent with text; audience clearly defined; no individual voice	Same as 4
2	Focus there but predictable; ideas not developed; no complexity	May lack either an introduction or conclusion; few or illogical use of transitions	Simple, clear diction; lacks a sense of voice, may use inappropriate tone for audience at times	A few mechanical errors
1	No clear focus; little or no development of ideas	Lacks introduction; series of unrelated paragraphs	May use inappropriate or incorrect language; no sense of audience	Numerous mechanical errors which interfere with reading

Note: Created by Michele Woodward. Used with permission.

often unknowingly, find its way into an evaluation report. But when carefully prepared, with reference to a number of tasks over a period of time, an evaluator can gather valuable cumulative data on the performance of an individual. Similarly, by observing a sample of former trainees performing on the job, the evaluator can make more informed judgments about the adequacy of the instruction that the observed individuals received.

Indirect Checklist/Rating Measures.   In some instances, it is not feasible for the evaluator to observe the behavior directly. Sometimes the problem is cost. For example, in a course designed to teach individuals how to make more effective presentations at conferences and meetings, it may prove too expensive for the evaluator to attend the presentations of enough former students to make valid judgments about their performances. Or it might prove too costly to observe teachers to determine how well they are applying classroom management skills taught in a recent workshop.

In other situations, direct observations are impractical. Common examples are courses designed to help people improve social interactions, interpersonal skills, employee relations, and the like. The difficulty is that, short of following an individual around during the day, the evaluator cannot be present when typical situations requiring such skills arise. And, if the evaluator were present, the situations would probably become unnatural or artificial as a direct result. For example, suppose you and your friend started arguing about whose turn it was to pay for lunch. Would you respond in a "natural" way if an evaluator were there specifically to observe your behavior? Probably not.

If direct observations or assessments of behavior are not practical, the next best option might be to seek parallel information from individuals who are present when former students typically demonstrate the criterion skills. One source of data might be reactions from the former students themselves regarding the effectiveness of training for developing certain skills. Figure 11-5 displays items from such a survey. This instrument was administered to former students several months following their completion of a corporate training course on making effective presentations. Individuals were asked to rate the helpfulness of specific course features for improving the quality of presentations that they subsequently made. Instrument development essentially involves identifying, from the course objectives and materials, the criterion performance and the enabling (or component) skills involved. The skills/behaviors are then listed for evaluation by students using a conventional rating scale format.

Another indirect measure would be ratings or checklists submitted by individuals who work or interact with the former students in situations in which the target skills are likely to be exhibited. Figure 11-6 illustrates this type of instrument, as employed in the presentation skills evaluation referred to earlier. The instrument was developed by identifying component and criterion skills for the course. The skills were then listed with accompanying five-point rating scales for judging frequency of practice by the student, as observed by the respondent. In the actual evaluation (Morrison & Ross, 1991), respondents were managers, peers, and subordinates who worked with corporate trainees who completed the presentation skills course.

FIGURE 11-5
Job-based survey

Skills	Degree of Use		
	Not at all	**Some**	**A great deal**
Reducing nervousness before presenting	☐	☐	☐
Reducing nervousness while presenting	☐	☐	☐
Improving planning	☐	☐	☐
Improving organization	☐	☐	☐
Improving interruptions	☐	☐	☐
Maintaining proper pacing	☐	☐	☐
Using visual aids	☐	☐	☐
Responding to questions	☐	☐	☐

Note: Copyright 1991 The Dow Chemical Company. Used with permission.

FIGURE 11-6
Job application survey

Item	Always	Most of the time	Sometimes	Never	Does not apply
1. This individual uses overhead transparencies or other visuals to communicate ideas.	☐	☐	☐	☐	☐
2. This individual uses overhead transparencies to summarize main ideas.	☐	☐	☐	☐	☐
3. It is evident that this individual has spent time preparing and rehearsing the presentation.	☐	☐	☐	☐	☐
4. This individual uses graphs or pictures to emphasize the points he or she wishes to make.	☐	☐	☐	☐	☐
5. This individual begins a talk with a statement of the purpose and expected outcome to focus the audience's attention.	☐	☐	☐	☐	☐
6. This individual emphasizes the main points of the presentation.	☐	☐	☐	☐	☐
7. It is easy to follow the logic in this individual's presentations.	☐	☐	☐	☐	☐
8. This individual uses personal examples or analogies to explain a point.	☐	☐	☐	☐	☐
9. This individual identifies the benefits of implementing the presented idea.	☐	☐	☐	☐	☐
10. This individual arranges the room appropriately (e.g., seating, temperature, overhead projector) before the participants arrive.	☐	☐	☐	☐	☐
11. The presentations this individual makes have the appropriate level of detail needed for the audience.	☐	☐	☐	☐	☐

Note: Copyright 1991 The Dow Chemical Company. Used with permission.

Portfolio Assessments.   Performances frequently culminate, by design, in the creation of tangible products. Examples include paintings, essays, poems, musical compositions, and pottery. The nature of these products changes over time as a function of the student's experience and of the situation. Thus, examining only one sample (e.g., an essay on Thomas Jefferson written in a composition class) may provide a very limited view of the skills acquired from a composition class.

Portfolios represent a form of "authentic testing," which, as described in Chapter 10, is an assessment of performance in realistic contexts (Mullin, 1998). As described by Arhar, Holly, and Kasten (2001), portfolios are "a carefully selected, constructed, and narrated collection of work pertaining to a special topic" (p. 21). As a result, the teacher and the student can examine actual work products together to determine effort, improvement, ability, and quality. In the same manner, portfolios can also be used to illuminate strengths and needs in the instruction itself.

Procedure

1. Involve students in selecting samples of their work for the portfolio.
2. Update the portfolios over time so that improvements or changes in the quality of the work may be noted.
3. Based on instructional objectives, identify criteria for judging the work. For example, for evaluating a portfolio of writing samples, such criteria might include organization, expression, use of a topic sentence, correct grammar, and spelling.
4. Identify the evaluation mode. Possible modes, which may be used separately or in combination, would include checklists (yes/no), rating scales (e.g., poor, average, superior), rubrics, and comments (e.g., "shows good effort, but lacks fundamentals").

By examining group results for different criteria at various times of the year, the designer can obtain useful information about how effectively skills are being applied. For example, it may be found that carpentry students' early work evidences very poor routing skills, but later products show high proficiency in this area.

Just as there are different types of objective tests or rating scales, portfolios can take varied forms. Anderson (1994) describes four formats she has used in working with elementary schoolchildren:

- *Showcase:* Presents the student's "best" work while emphasizing self-assessment, reflection, and ownership
- *Evaluation:* Presents representative work to be evaluated on the basis of showing movement toward a specific academic goal
- *Process:* Asks students to reflect on work produced over time for the purpose of developing points of view on their long-term learning process and subject synthesis
- *Documentation:* Presents work that represents academic accomplishment for presentation to parents, other students, or school administrators

Portfolios potentially offer clear advantages over objective testing for assessing complex skills. But do they provide accurate assessments of student performance? Research on portfolio use suggests inconsistency across studies regarding this issue (Herman & Winters, 1994). Suppose that you were evaluating a high school student's portfolio in a science class. What factors might compromise the validity of the score you assign? One could be the high subjectivity of judgments being made. A second could be how the student's products (also called *artifacts*) were selected (do they represent best or typical work?). A third might be the extent to which the student did the work independently. A fourth could be the limitations of using fairly restricted scales (see Figures 11-3 and 11-4) to judge quality of performance on complex tasks.

Compared with objective testing, portfolios provide a means of obtaining a richer, more meaningful impression of what students are able to achieve, but perhaps at the risk of some measurement precision. By using each type of test to its best advantage, evaluators and designers can increase the depth and range of information obtained about student learning.

Exhibitions.   For some types of instruction, the culminating products are best displayed in a special type of performance before an audience. These performances, commonly called *exhibitions,* are characterized by being public and requiring many hours of preparation.

Examples

>   Reciting poetry
>   Playing an instrument
>   Singing
>   Acting
>   Giving a speech
>   Performing a gymnastics routine

Procedure.   Evaluating exhibitions requires using procedures comparable to those used for portfolios and shares similar advantages and disadvantages of objective testing. Typical procedures might include the following:

1. Identify skill behaviors and criteria based on instructional objectives.
2. Develop instruments such as checklists, rating scales, rubrics, or some combination thereof to evaluate the performance.
3. Use criterion-referenced measurement by focusing on how well the student has attained the desired level of competence for each skill.
4. Add comments to explain certain ratings, describe noteworthy events, and convey overall impressions of the performance.

ATTITUDES

Just as it is a challenging task to write affective-domain objectives, much planning and thought are required to assess individuals' feelings and attitudes toward instruction. Feelings, values, and beliefs are very private matters that cannot be measured directly. Attitudes can be inferred only through a person's words and behaviors.

The problem of evaluating attitudes is further compounded by two factors. First, a response expressed by a learner on an attitudinal survey may be stated so as to be socially acceptable, regardless of the individual's actual feelings. Therefore, true sentiments may not be conveyed. Second, outcomes of the most important objectives in a course may not become evident until some time after the course is completed, which thus makes it impossible to measure an attitude at the end of the study time for a unit or course. We sometimes hear students say something like, "I hated that course and old Dr. Brazle's lectures when I took it, but it really helped me in Algebra II."

In spite of these limitations, there can be benefits from attempting to determine, at the conclusion of a unit or portions of an instructional program, whether it satisfied attitudinal objectives. At the same time, student attitudes provide formative evaluation data regarding how positively different aspects of the course instruction are perceived.

Two Uses of Attitude Assessment

We commonly find two general categories of attitude assessments in formative, summative, and confirmative evaluations: evaluating instruction and evaluating affective outcomes. These approaches are similar in their basic methods and instruments employed (e.g., questionnaires, interviews, rating scales). What distinguishes them is their focus—the instruction itself or desired affective outcomes of the instruction.

Evaluating the Instruction.   In this approach, the interest is in determining how students or trainees react to the instruction they have received—what they like or do not like and their suggestions for improving it. The instruction, not the learner, is the focus. Exemplary evaluation questions are these:

- Was the course material well organized?
- Did you have sufficient time to learn the material?
- What suggestions do you have for improving the manual?

Evaluating Affective Outcomes.   In the second approach, the learners and their feelings toward certain ideas or behaviors are the focus. Of particular interest may be measuring how much attitude changes as a direct result of the instructional program (a pretest–posttest design). For example, prior to a dental hygiene workshop, only 13 percent of the enrollees (practicing dentists) agreed that working with gloves is an important hygienic practice. Following the workshop, the agreement rate increased to 87 percent, which suggests that the workshop was successful in promoting that view. Other examples:

- Nurses' attitudes toward showing empathy to patients
- Employees' feelings about tardiness and absenteeism
- Police officers' attitudes toward using force in stopping crime
- Students' interest in visiting museums
- Home builders' attitudes toward using cypress wood as a siding

As we will see, regardless of whether the focus is on attitudes toward the instruction or attitudes toward behaviors and practices, a variety of data collection methods is available.

Observation/Anecdotal Records

Just as observation is useful for evaluating performance (see pp. 288–291), it can provide a valuable source of information about student attitudes. Observation is often carried out by the instructor while learners are at work in their normal study or activity area. The instrument for recording what is observed can be a simple questionnaire, a rating scale, or an open-ended form on which descriptions and comments are made as in an anecdotal record.

What you focus on during an observation will depend on the evaluation objectives. Normally, there will be interest in how students react to the instruction—what holds their interest, what loses it, and the like. Relevant attitudes will thus be conveyed in observable behaviors such as attentiveness, *affect* (e.g., smiling, nodding in agreement, laughing), and *engagement* (taking notes, answering questions, raising hands, etc.). Exemplary items that might be included in an observer rating scale are the following:

Student Attitude	Low	Some	High
Interest in lesson	1	2	3
Attentiveness to lesson	1	2	3
Active engagement	1	2	3
Positive affect (smiles, laughter)	1	2	3

Assessment of Behavior

Students may smile frequently and be very enthusiastic about the instruction but not transfer their feelings about what is learned outside of class. Consider, for example, a college-level art appreciation class that is intended to increase students' knowledge and interest in music, art, and theater. Although students might like the class very much, few may increase their attendance at concerts, exhibitions, or plays. Positive attitudes toward instruction do not necessarily transfer to the subject, at least to the extent that behavior is changed.

The most powerful type of instrument for assessing behavioral changes would be direct observation of learner activities. For example, we may find that 60 percent of Ms. Leyton's Algebra I students elect to take Algebra II, whereas only 10 percent of Mr. Petza's students make that choice. A clear implication (assuming similar class makeups) is that Ms. Leyton's course is more successful in producing positive attitudes toward algebra. Similarly, it may be found that 40 percent of the nurses in a particular health care facility voluntarily attend a workshop on cardiopulmonary resuscitation (CPR) methods compared with a 10 percent rate for nurses in a neighboring facility.

You could probably think of many examples for which such direct observation or measurement would be very impractical. After all, we cannot easily follow students around to see what they do after class (e.g., how many visit the local art museum this month). In those cases, the best alternative is to construct a brief questionnaire that asks students to supply this information.

Questionnaire/Survey

Probably the most common means of assessing attitudes is through questionnaires or surveys. Such instruments may include two types of items: (1) open-ended questions to which the learner writes answers and (2) closed-ended questions with a number of fixed responses from which learners choose the answer that best reflects their opinion. A variation of this latter type consists of a longer list of alternatives from which the learner checks interesting or important choices or rates the alternatives on a numerical scale.

The decision to use open-ended or closed-ended items (or some combination of the two) may depend on the time available to tabulate the replies. The open-ended type provides data that are time-consuming to analyze but may be more valuable in conveying learners' feelings and the reasons for them. Closed-ended questions are quicker and more reliable (objective) to process but limit the depth and detail of expression. Examples of open-ended and closed-ended questionnaires are provided at the conclusion of this section.

A rating scale is a modification of the questionnaire on which the learner replies to a statement by selecting a point along a scale. The scale may be composed of two points (yes/no), three points (e.g., agree/no opinion/disagree), or up to five points (e.g., very often/quite often/sometimes/hardly ever/never). A commonly used scale is the five-point Likert-type scale consisting of "strongly agree, agree, undecided, disagree, and strongly disagree." Here are some guidelines for writing questionnaire and survey items:

1. Limit the number of rating scale points to a maximum of five or six. People usually have difficulty making finer discriminations. The younger the age group, the more restricted the choices should be. For example, in surveying first-grade students about their interest in reading, a simple yes/no scale should probably be used. A comparable survey for sixth-graders might use a three-point scale of "agree, uncertain, disagree." For high school students, a five-point scale would be an option. The more scale points, the greater the amount of information that will be obtained, but the greater the chances of confusing the respondent.
   Poor: Rate the organization of the course on a 10-point scale, where 1 = Very poor and 10 = Very good.
   Better: Rate the organization of the course on the following five-point scale, where 1 = Superior; 2 = Slightly above average; 3 = Average; 4 = Slightly below average; 5 = Inferior.

2. Use verbal descriptors to define numerical rating points. Examples are as follows:
   Rate the enthusiasm of clerical employees in the automotive division.

Low		Average		High
1	2	3	4	5

   Rate the difficulty of the mechanical assembly for you.

Very easy	Somewhat easy	Average	Somewhat difficult	Difficult
1	2	3	4	5

3. Use rating points that are clearly separable and nonoverlapping.
   Poor: How often do you play sports?

Never	Occasionally	Sometimes	Often	Frequently
1	2	3	4	5

Better: How often do you play sports?

Rarely/never	Sometimes	Frequently
1	2	3

Note that even in the last case, the meaning of "sometimes" and "frequently" may be ambiguous to students. Is twice a week "sometimes" or "frequently"? It would therefore be preferable to define these categories objectively, such as rarely (less than once a week), sometimes (once or twice a week), and frequently (more than twice a week).

4. Use clear and concrete language to express the idea to be rated.
   Poor: There is adequate equipment in the office.
   Better: I have the equipment that I need to do my office work.
   Poor: The instructional strategy employed was beneficial.
   Better: The teaching method used was helpful to me in learning the material.
5. Express only a single idea in each item.
   Poor: I like working with my clients and my coworkers.
   Better: I like working with my clients.
   I like working with my coworkers.

Interview

An interview allows learners to discuss their reactions toward instruction in more detail than can be done on a survey or questionnaire. The questions can be structured or unstructured. A structured interview has the advantage of being more controllable with regard to time and content. An unstructured interview, on the other hand, may provide an opportunity to probe more deeply to clarify learners' responses as well as to follow up on unanticipated responses that may yield new insights. The disadvantages are loss of control and increases in time. It is generally valuable to tape-record interviews, but be sure that the interviewee approves of this. Also, for objectivity, the interviewer should be a person not affiliated with the instructional program.

Another important decision is whether to conduct interviews with individuals or with groups. We have found both to be valuable, but the choice of one over the other may depend on the respondents' comfort with each other and sensitivity about the issues. A question such as, "Is Ms. Hanley a good boss, in your opinion?" may create quite a bit of reticence in a group setting. On the other hand, group interviews may be much more lively and informative than individual interviews because of respondents' interactions with one another and offerings of diverse perspectives. For further descriptions of the various instruments, including their benefits and limitations, see the references for this chapter.

Examples of questionnaires, rating scales, and an interview guide appear in Figure 11-7.

FIGURE 11-7
Sample questionnaires, rating scales, and interview guide

Questionnaire (Open-ended)

1. What is your general reaction to this topic? Comment specifically on the content treated, the way it was taught, your participation, and any other aspects that you feel are relevant.

2. In your opinion, what was the greatest strength of the teaching approach used for learning the material on this unit?

Questionnaire (Closed-ended)

Select the response on each item that best reflects your reaction.

1. Learner interest

   a I feel this topic challenged me intellectually.
   b. I found the material interesting but not challenging.
   c. I was not stimulated very often.
   d. I do not feel the topic was worthwhile.

2. Topic organization

   a. I could see how the concepts on this topic were interrelated.
   b. The instructor attempted to cover only the minimum amount of material.
   c. I didn't know where the instructor was heading most of the time.

Rating Scale

1. Did you have any difficulty or trouble operating the equipment?

   _____ No   _____ Yes   Comment:

2. How do you rate the self-study activity as a learning experience?

0	1	2	3	4
Waste of time	Slightly useful	Satisfactory	Good	Excellent

3. How demanding was the format used in the experimental unit compared with that in a conventional unit?

   _____ More demanding   _____ About equal   _____ Less demanding

4. Indicate your feeling about the value of wearing goggles for safety on your job:

1	2	3	4	5
No value				High value

Interview Guide

1. What is your reaction to the value of the unit you have just completed?

2. How would you rate the amount of assistance that the instructor and the assistants provided you outside of the discussion sessions?

   _____ None   _____ Low   _____ Some   _____ Sufficient   _____ Excellent

   Comments:

3. Do you feel the criteria adopted by your instructor for assigning letter grades in this unit were fair to you? If not, why not?

4. What suggestions do you have for improving the activities you completed for this topic?

S U M M A R Y

1. The selection or development of evaluation instruments begins with a reexamination of the evaluation questions and the types of outcomes they assess: knowledge, skills and behavior, and/or attitudes.
2. Critical to the assessment of cognitive outcomes is the matching of test items to the level of learning specified by objectives.
3. Objective tests, such as multiple-choice, true/false, and matching, have the advantage of being easy to grade. The disadvantage is their restriction to assessing recognition learning and relatively low levels of learning.
4. Short-answer tests have the advantage over multiple-choice tests of assessing recall rather than recognition. Other constructed-response tests, such as short-answer, essay, and problem solving, have the advantage of assessing higher levels of learning (application, analysis, and synthesis) but the disadvantage of being difficult to grade reliably.
5. Evaluations of performance frequently focus on both process (the behaviors that lead to an outcome) and product (the outcome).
6. Alternative means of assessing skills and behavior are direct testing, analysis of naturally occurring events, ratings of performance, anecdotal records, indirect checklist/rating measures, portfolio assessments, and exhibitions.
7. Attitudes cannot be directly measured but must be inferred on the bases of learners' verbal reports and behaviors. Common means for assessing attitudes are anecdotal records, observation of behavior, questionnaires, and interviews.

THE ID PROCESS

The evaluator of instruction needs to first and foremost put the cart *behind* the horse by using course objectives (and associated evaluation questions) as the foundation for selecting evaluation instruments. Novices oftentimes apply the reverse process by selecting attractive or convenient instruments first and then "force fitting" the evaluation questions to the resultant data. If the questions focus on knowledge, objective tests might be appropriate. If the focus is application or synthesis, then constructed-response or problem-solving tests might be the best choice. If the focus is on performance, then direct or indirect testing of actual skills might be preferred.

In addition to the evaluation questions, practical constraints such as available resources, accessibility to trainees and testing contexts, and costs must be considered in developing evaluation instruments. A small design project with a limited budget may not be able to support on-the-job assessment of trainees by external evaluators.

A third factor is the type of evaluation. Formative evaluations tend to make greater use than summative or confirmative evaluations of measures that deal with attitudes and behaviors associated with receiving the instruction. The latter types of evaluations, in turn, place greater focus on measures of learner knowledge and skill.

Whatever types of instruments are selected and developed, all must be properly validated and administered correctly. An old expression used by computer programmers is "garbage in, garbage out." The same applies to evaluation. Any weak link in the chain, such as a poorly constructed multiple-choice test or an unreliable performance-rating process, can result in incorrect decisions being made about the instruction.

Because learning and performance are complex processes, experienced evaluators avoid putting all their eggs in only one or two baskets. Multiple evaluation instruments provide a richer and more reliable (triangulated) impression of instructional outcomes.

APPLICATIONS

Given your known expertise in developing evaluation instruments, other designers frequently come to you with their questions. Here are several about which they would like your ideas today:

1. I am evaluating a training unit for Eagle Department Store employees on dealing with customer complaints. Most of the training involves simulated practice with instructor feedback. What type of testing approach (e.g., multiple-choice versus performance) should I emphasize and why?
2. I am evaluating a training unit that teaches automobile service technicians how to use new computer-based diagnostic equipment. Should I use portfolios as my primary evaluation instrument?
3. I am evaluating employee reactions to the "refresher training" courses at Airways Express, a large package-delivery company. The climate is fairly tense in this company because of downsizing. Should I use individual or group interviews?

ANSWERS

You might have replied to each question as follows:

1. Given that the training mostly involves practicing skills, it doesn't seem as if using multiple-choice or other objective-type testing would be very appropriate. Rather, you would want to focus on setting up practice situations either in simulated or real contexts. In a simulated context, particular scenarios might be created by actors to rate trainees on their reactions. In a real context, trainees would be rated based on how they react to situations that naturally arise. Other possible measures would be analysis of naturally occurring events (e.g., customer commendations or complaints about the trainee) and an indirect checklist or ratings by those who work with the trainees.
2. Portfolios would *not* appear a good choice as a *primary* measure. The service technicians are performing very specific functions in using the computer equipment. It is unlikely that portfolios would provide a practical or reliable indicator of such skills. Direct or indirect performance testing would be preferred.
3. Individual interviews would typically be preferred because of the negative climate; that is, the employees may be reticent about expressing their feelings in front of their coworkers.

SAMPLE DESIGN PLAN

Objective 1

Given a short description of a project, the learner will write a project goal in an acceptable format.

Test Items.   For each of the following scenarios, write a concise goal statement.

Objective 2

Given a worksheet, the learner will list at least three tasks associated with the project goal.

Test Items.   The learner will list four tasks for a goal statement.

Objective 3

Given the priority/time-frame matrix and a list of tasks, the learner will accurately classify the degree of criticality for each task.

Test Items.   The learner will classify a set of seven tasks according to criticality by writing each in the appropriate priority/time-frame matrix cells.

Objective 4

Given the priority/time-frame matrix, the learner will sequence the tasks according to due date.

Test Items.   The learner will classify four tasks according to due date by writing each in the appropriate priority/time-frame matrix cells.

Objective 5

The learner will create a prioritized to-do list on a PDA.

Test Items.   The learner will select a course project from his or her own course work and will create a prioritized task list using a PDA.

REFERENCES

Anderson, R. S. (1994). *Using portfolios in K–2 classrooms.* Unpublished manuscript, University of Memphis, TN.

Arhar, J. M., Holly, M. L., & Kasten, W. C. (2001). *Action research for teachers.* Columbus: Merrill Prentice Hall.

Herman, J. L., & Winters, L. (1994). Portfolio research: A slim collection. *Educational Leadership, 52,* 91–98.

McBeath, R. J. (1992). *Instruction and evaluation in higher education: A guidebook for planning and learning.* Englewood Cliffs, NJ: Educational Technology Publications.

Meyer, C. A. (1993). What's the difference between authentic and performance assessment? *Educational Leadership, 51,* 39–40.

Morrison, G. R., & Ross, S. M. (1991, October). *Evaluation report for presentation skills: Final report for Dow Chemical USA.* Memphis, TN: Memphis State University.

Mullin, J. A. (1998). Portfolios: Purposeful collections of student work. In R. S. Anderson & B. W. Speck (Eds.), *Changing the way we grade student performance: Classroom assessment and the new learning paradigm* (pp. 79–88). San Francisco: Jossey-Bass.

Shepard , L. A. (2001). The role of assessment in a learning culture. *Educational Researcher, 29* (7), 4–14.

CHAPTER 12

Using Evaluation to Enhance Programs: Conducting Formative and Summative Evaluations

GETTING STARTED

You receive a contract from a software firm to evaluate a series of computer-based instructional units for teaching high school geometry. The units are still in draft stage, with the expectation that they can be revised based on the results of the evaluation. Using the eight-step model (see Figure 12-1), you determine the purposes of the evaluation, conduct an analysis of the audience, identify issues (questions and objectives), determine available resources, identify the evidence that will be needed, specify and implement data-gathering techniques, conduct the data analysis, and write and present reports of the findings. To address the main interests of the stakeholders (the software developers), you decide to employ small-group trials in which students work through the materials, give "think-aloud" reactions and other feedback, and take unit achievement tests. You also use two subject-matter experts (SMEs), three high school geometry teachers, and one computer-based instruction (CBI) design expert to give impressions of the accuracy and quality of the content and user interface. Based on qualitative and quantitative analyses of the multiple data sources, you prepare a report detailing results and making specific recommendations for improving various parts of the units. One of the managers in the software firm criticizes your evaluation for "failing to prove whether the units actually increase learning." She further wants to know why you didn't use a control group. How would you respond to the manager's concern?

"At what stage of instructional development does formative evaluation begin?"

"How can formative evaluation results be used to improve instruction?"

"How can an instructional designer provide evidence that systematic instructional planning does pay off?"

"What is the actual cost of an instructional program?"

"How can a training program be valuable if it doesn't directly produce income for the company?"

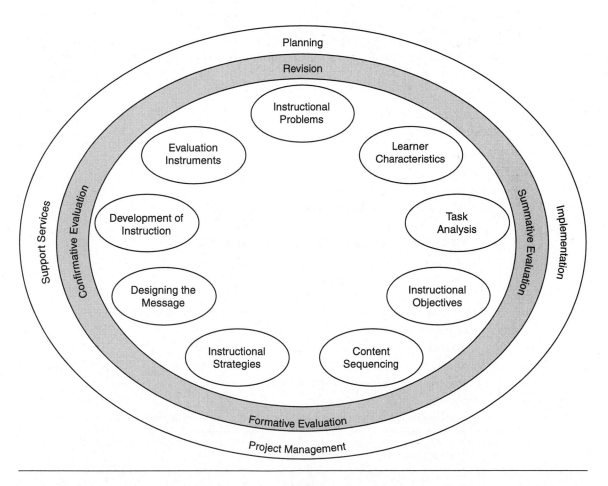

In Chapter 10, we differentiated between the three broad categories of evaluation—formative, summative, and confirmative—used by instructional designers. Now that you have a better understanding of the functions of evaluation as well as instrument construction, we turn to the procedures for conducting each type of evaluation.

A BASIC MODEL FOR FORMATIVE EVALUATION

Formative evaluations are used to provide feedback to designers for making course improvements. These evaluations take place as instruction is "forming," and thus they precede the development of the final version of the instructional unit or course. As is true for the design of instructional material, formative evaluations must be carefully planned to be effective. To help structure the evaluation planning, Gooler (1980) suggests the eight-step approach summarized in Figure 12-1. Each of the steps is examined next.

Purposes

The first step in conducting the evaluation is to determine its purposes: are the purposes to improve the materials, determine time requirements, or satisfy administrative requirements of the corporation or institution? Perhaps the most important

FIGURE 12-1
Steps in planning formative evaluations

- **Purpose**
  Why is the evaluation being conducted?
- **Audience**
  Who are the target recipients of the evaluation results?
- **Issues**
  What are the major questions/objectives of the evaluation?
- **Resources**
  What resources will be needed to conduct the evaluation?
- **Evidence**
  What type of data or information will be needed to answer the evaluation questions?
- **Data-gathering Techniques**
  What methods are needed to collect the evidence needed?
- **Analysis**
  How will the evidence collected be analyzed?
- **Reporting**
  How, to whom, and when will the results of the evaluation be reported?

Note: Adapted from D. D. Gooler (1980), "Formative Evaluation Strategies for Major Instructional Development Projects," *Journal of Instructional Development, 3,* 7–11.

question is whether an evaluation is really needed. Suppose, for example, that you are asked to evaluate a multimedia unit on basic electricity. After questioning the course administrators, you discover that the unit cannot be changed without the software being rewritten. You further determine that there are no available funds to pay for new programming. While there still may be good reasons for doing a formative evaluation, you certainly seem justified in questioning its purpose at the front end. That is, if the evaluation results cannot be used to make changes, is this really the best time for an evaluation to be performed?

The purposes of the evaluation are usually defined through consultation between the evaluator and the stakeholders of the course or program. As the name implies, stakeholders are individuals who have a "stake" or vested interest in the instruction. They might include company or school administrators, course vendors, training professionals, and/or teachers or trainers.

Audience

An additional part of the initial planning is to determine the intended audience(s) for the evaluation results. Will they be managers, teachers, course developers, or a combination of several groups? Depending on who the primary audience is, different types of information will probably be collected and reported. Clearly, instructors will be better able to use evaluation results dealing with the delivery of instructional material than results on the readability of the study guide; the study guide author, however, would have the opposite need. The key target audience(s) will usually be identified in the initial discussions with key stakeholders.

Issues

As is the case for designing instruction, specifying objectives provides the foundation for the evaluation process. Now that you know the overall purposes of the evaluation (step 1) and the primary audience (step 2), what specific questions need to be answered? Is there an interest in student attitudes, learning gains, or the quality of certain materials? Once defined, the evaluation objectives determine what information sources (data collection instruments) and analyses are needed to answer the questions of interest. Evaluation objectives may be written as questions or statements. Examples using the question structure are as follows:

- After receiving the instruction, can students correctly enter the data into the spreadsheet?
- Which exercises in the recycling unit do students find most understandable and least understandable?
- Do students perceive the diagrams to be helpful?
- On average, how long does each practice unit take to complete?
- Do SMEs regard the instructional material as accurate and well designed?

If a statement format is preferred, the first two examples might be rewritten as follows:

- To determine students' accuracy, following the instruction, in entering the data into the spreadsheet
- To identify the exercises in the recycling unit that students find most understandable and least understandable

Resources

Given the evaluation objectives (step 3), what resources are needed to address each? In the previous example, objective 1 implies the need for students to be tested, the need for computers and spreadsheets for the students to use during testing, and the need for keyboarding test(s) for measuring the degree of change from pre- to postinstruction. Objective 2 also involves gathering data from students, but this time using a survey or interview to determine the exercises they most and least prefer. The resources needed therefore differ from objective to objective. Common types of resources include these:

- Trainees/students
- SMEs
- Instructors
- Data collection and analysis instruments
- Copies of materials
- Physical facilities and equipment

Evidence

In conjunction with identifying resources, careful consideration must be given to the types of evidence that will be acceptable for addressing the evaluation objectives. For objective 1 in our example, we obviously want to obtain keyboarding scores, but will scores from, say, five students on one test suffice, or will additional students and/or multiple testings be required? For objective 2, thought must be given to the type of student reporting (in reacting to the exercises) that will be most valid and informative. We might be skeptical, for example, about the validity of impressions conveyed in an interview immediately following a difficult final exam. In deciding what will constitute acceptable evidence, the evaluator and the stakeholders may want to consider these points:

- Sample size
- Objectivity of the information sources
- Realism of the testing context
- Degree of control in the testing context
- Need for formal statistical reporting
- Reliability/validity of SME reviews

Data-Gathering Techniques

This step involves making final decisions about the instrumentation and data collection methods to be employed. Two key, and often opposing, factors need to be weighed: precise measurement versus feasible or practical measurement. For example, in planning a formative evaluation of a carpentry training program, the designer initially elects to rate actual projects that students complete on the job. But once the practical problems of identifying and validly assessing actual projects are considered, it is decided instead to employ a controlled assessment, specifically, a cabinet door of a specified design and size completed at the training site. Similarly, in order to reduce time and cost, planned interviews with 30 students may be reduced to include only 10 students. Or perhaps the designer may substitute an interview for a questionnaire when he or she considers that the former provides opportunities to probe for more in-depth explanations.

The data-gathering techniques available as options are the ones we discuss in the two previous chapters. They include performance tests, written tests, observations, ratings, questionnaires, interviews, portfolios, and exhibitions. At this stage, the designer should consider the advantages and limitations of each type for addressing the evaluation objectives as well as the resources necessary for each. In Chapters 10 and 11, we recommend the use of multiple measures to increase validity (through the triangulation of findings across measures) and the provision of as much relevant information as feasible. Current cognitive and constructivist paradigms have increased awareness of obtaining data regarding learning processes as well as products (Ross & Morrison, 1995). By knowing about processes—how instructional material is used—designers are in a better position to interpret products (outcomes) and, thereby, improve the material.

Analysis

Once the data are collected, the next step is analyzing the results. If the term *analysis* conjures up thoughts of complex statistics and formulas, reflect again on the main purpose of formative evaluation. It is to provide usable information for designers to improve instruction. Although the need for complex analyses should not be ruled out, the questions of interest are often best addressed by straightforward and fairly simple descriptive analyses. These types of analyses generally tell us how students performed or reacted on a particular lesson. Typical analysis procedures would include the following. Note that the first three are quantitative (involving numerical indices); the fourth is qualitative (involving impressions); both types of analyses are discussed later.

- Frequency distributions
- Frequency graphs or histograms
- Descriptive statistics, such as percentages, means, and medians
- Listing of actual comments made by respondents

Figure 12-2 shows a frequency distribution and descriptive statistics for a class on a unit achievement test (maximum score = 100%). Note that the "bars" on the graph represent the number (frequency) of scores obtained within 10-point intervals (20–29, 30–39, etc.) in which scores were obtained. From the distribution, it is clear that performances were quite spread out (range = 75) and also somewhat low for many students (mean = 68.1). While it is possible that these are desirable performances for this unit (i.e., it may be very difficult material), chances are that the designer will not be satisfied and will conclude that the instruction needs to be revised.

In many cases, an introductory-level knowledge of statistics will suffice for completing the data analysis. If more complex analyses are required, the designer can always seek assistance from a statistical consultant.

Although traditional views of data analyses denote graphs, tables, numbers, and probability values, today's educational evaluators may find that they depend just as much (or more) on qualitative analyses. These types of analyses involve categorizing, interpreting, and, in general, "making sense" out of subjective data such as observations of instruction or student learning, interview responses, and open-ended survey responses. Qualitative researchers who are collecting data for scientific study and intended wide-scale dissemination of results will want to invest

FIGURE 12-2

Histogram of test score

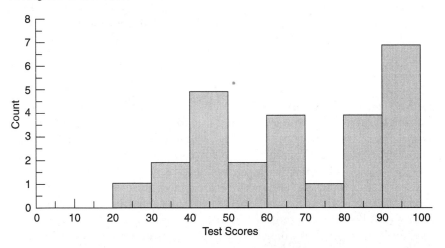

Mean:	Std. Dev:	Std. Error:
68.077	22.765	4.465

Minimum:	Maximum:	Range:
23	98	75

considerable effort ensuring high reliability in their methods, inferences, and conclusions. Consequently, the thorough and systematic procedures for qualitative data analysis recommended by such authors as Miles and Huberman (1994) should be followed. The qualitative evaluator of instruction will also want to ensure valid conclusions, but may, because of time and project needs, use a more practical, less rigorous approach. Key strategies should include the following:

- Reviewing notes and transcripts to extract major categories or themes (e.g., "The most common concerns about the training unit were inadequate length, poor readability of materials, and lack of relevance of the unit on reflective listening.")
- Providing a sense of the saliency or importance of the themes (e.g., "The inadequate length of the training was a critical weakness, as conveyed by the majority of trainees; only several, however, were concerned about the readability of materials.")
- Conducting "member checking" by having respondents review and validate, where feasible, your description and interpretation of what they said
- Providing tables that present typical responses or a complete listing so that stakeholders in the instructional design might review them
- Having more than one person participate in the data analysis so that reliability can be checked and increased by consensual agreement

Reporting

The evaluation effort will generally be of little value unless the results are disseminated to individuals involved in the instructional unit or course (e.g., instructors, administrators, or designers). The most common means is the *evaluation report*. There is no single standard reporting format; in fact, the best strategy is to adapt the report to the primary target audience with regard to content and style of writing. A "typical" report, however, is likely to include most or all of the following sections:

    I.   Executive summary (abstract)
   II.   Purposes of evaluation
       A. Evaluation objectives
       B. Description of target course/unit
  III.   Methodology
       A. Participants
       B. Instruments
  IV.   Results
       A. Analyses
       B. Findings
   V.   Conclusions and recommendations

A second common dissemination mode is oral *reporting*. Depending on the context, such reports may be formal presentations, group meetings, or one-to-one discussions.

Keep in mind that, whatever the form of reporting, the overall goal of formative evaluation is to recommend and make changes (as suggested by the results) to improve instruction. Formative evaluation results are unique to the particular project and thus will have limited generalizability to projects outside the same educational context or curriculum.

TYPES OF FORMATIVE EVALUATION

As just described, the initial planning clarifies the purpose(s) of the evaluation and the target audience for results. These decisions then dictate the evaluation approach that is most appropriate for the particular project. According to Flagg (1990), the most commonly used evaluation approaches can be classified into four categories: connoisseur-based, decision-oriented, objectives-based, and public relations–inspired studies.

Connoisseur-Based Studies

A *connoisseur-based study* employs SMEs and other appropriate consultants (e.g., media and design experts) to examine the instruction and give opinions regarding its accuracy and effectiveness. An important part of the expert's report is any recommendation for revising the instruction where improvements are needed. Expert review can be useful at all stages of the design process, from initial drafts of instructional material to the completed versions.

In using expert review, the experts are assumed to be competent and interested in the evaluation task. Important tasks for the designer are to determine the number and types of experts needed, the particular individuals who will fill these slots, and the best time(s) in the evaluation process to involve each.

Expert review can provide valuable information for refining instruction. However, an important limitation of connoisseur-based studies is that so much depends on the biases and experiences of the selected experts. Remember, experts in a subject area are not necessarily knowledgeable about instruction and learning. Therefore, it is not advisable to blindly follow a recommendation that you question, without seeking other opinions or data sources. In educational research, this type of verification process is called *triangulation,* the procedure of cross-validating a finding by using multiple information sources.

Consider this example: After reviewing a CBI lesson, a media expert suggests that children will not know which keys to press in selecting different branching options. A field test of the program reveals, however, that this problem does not occur—the children actually make very few errors. Implication: Keep the expert's concern in mind, but do not make changes in the screen design without further evidence.

It is also important that the expert is willing and able to provide accurate and objective feedback. In this regard, consider the situation described in the Expert's Edge section.

(**Expert's Edge**)

Never Let a Fox Guard the Henhouse Even If He Claims to Be a Vegetarian

The workshop had been designed by a well-known training organization and followed a systematic product realization process. The process included several "gates," each of which specified a formative evaluation requirement. Early gates required reviews by SMEs, clients, and instructional designers, whereas the penultimate gate required a formal field trial. By all accounts, the workshop passed each gate with flying colors. The problem was, however, that participants' feedback on the workshop was not as positive as the client had hoped, and the work products participants created as a result of the workshop lacked the connection to business results the client had intended.

Further investigation revealed that the formative evaluation process, while it had been followed to some extent, had been co-opted. In the interest of meeting the target dates in the project plan, "friendly" SMEs and client representatives had been selected for the reviews, and the instructional design review had been done by the project manager. Furthermore, the field trial was actually a run-through of workshop materials not before representative members of the target audience but before a small group of colleagues of the project manager. Conversations with those involved in the development of the workshop showed no malicious intent; as a matter of fact, there was no real conscious awareness that the process had been subverted.

Eventually, the workshop was redesigned following a more stringent process. But considerable damage had been done, and because of the rework required, the financial cost was significant. Reputations were sullied, client trust was weakened, work was reassigned, and jobs were lost.

Formative evaluation can take many forms, and it can follow varying degrees of formality. Despite immediate pressures to the contrary, formative evaluation need not be incompatible with speed or staying within the budget. But formative evaluation is a *sine qua non* of our profession, and ultimately we bear the responsibility to our clients and to ourselves to conduct these activities with rigor and discipline. Here are some actions you might take in this regard:

- Build the time and cost of formative evaluation into your project plans.
- Make sure your clients and management understand in their own terms the value of formative evaluation.
- Design formative evaluations so that subversion is unlikely—use outside evaluators and employ audits or evaluation panels, for example.
- Develop and strive to maintain a set of personal standards by which your work can be known.
- Create an atmosphere where the truth can be told.
- Walk away from projects where your standards cannot be upheld.

Robert Bowman is an instructional development and evaluation manager in the Lucent Technologies Learning & Performance Center. His current assignment focuses on assessing the impact of leadership development programs and converting leadership development programs to technology-based systems. His work has included a broad range of needs assessment, instructional development, and evaluation assignments.

Decision-Oriented Studies

Decision-oriented studies are designed to provide information related to particular questions about the instruction. Example concerns might include these:

- Does the lesson require too much time to complete?
- Is the amount of practice examples adequate?
- Are prerequisite math skills required?
- Should a student study guide be developed?

Given these questions, the evaluator then designs specific measures and procedures to address each.

Decision-making evaluations are naturally most valuable when program changes are still feasible and economical. Good communication between the evaluator and the program stakeholders is essential to define the relevant questions around which the decision making will be based. The limitation of decision-making studies is that their results are usually descriptive, not prescriptive. That is, they tell us how the instruction is working, but not what to do to make it better.

Objectives-Based Studies

A third category of formative evaluation approaches involves investigating how well the instructional program is achieving its objectives. The basic methodology therefore resembles that employed in summative and confirmative evaluations (discussed later in this chapter) by assessing the amount of progress students have realized from completing the instruction. Summative and confirmative evaluations, however, use such information to judge the effectiveness of the program immediately (summative) and over time (confirmative). Objectives-based studies are an appropriate choice for evaluating projects such as a distance education course to determine whether it is effective. Formative evaluation uses it as a basis for improving the instruction where outcomes fall short of goals.

Objectives-based studies frequently employ pretest–posttest designs that measure the amount of gain on measures of achievement and attitude. Their main limitation is the same one noted earlier for decision-making studies: the findings by themselves provide limited direction for making improvements. For that reason, it may make sense to combine expert opinion (connoisseur-based study) with the objectives-based results.

Public Relations–Inspired Studies

By making evaluation results known to targeted individuals, public relations–inspired studies are used to solicit financial support or backing for a project. An example comes from one of the authors' recent experiences in trying to obtain funding from a private foundation to support an elementary-school reading program. By conducting a formative evaluation of a pilot version of the program, he was able to present preliminary data that convinced the foundation representatives of the program's potential. The result was a foundation grant to expand both the program and the evaluation the next year.

These four categories should be viewed as complementary rather than exclusive. Most studies will employ combinations of two or more of these orientations, depending on the evaluation objectives. For example, in evaluating a new mathematics program for lower-achieving children, the designers might (1) employ experts to review the instructional materials (category 1), (2) administer surveys and use observation techniques to answer questions about the implementation (category 2), (3) administer achievement pretests and posttests to assess the level of reading improvement demonstrated by student participants (category 3), and (4) publicize the latter results to obtain additional funding for the program (category 4).

STAGES OF FORMATIVE EVALUATION

At this point, we have presented general approaches and a specific procedural model (see Figure 12-1) for conducting formative evaluations. A remaining question may be how formative evaluation methods might vary at different stages of the design process. Dick and Carey (1991) address this issue in their three-stage model (see Table 12-1).

The first stage, occurring toward the beginning of the process and usually repeated several times, consists of one-to-one trials or developmental testing (Thiagarjan, Semmel, & Semmel, 1974) in which the designer "tries out" the instruction with individual learners (Brenneman, 1989). The goal is to obtain descriptive information pertaining to the clarity, impact, and feasibility of initial versions of the instruction.

The second stage consists of small-group trials in which a more developed version of the instruction is used with a group of between 8 and 25 individuals. Through observational, attitudinal, and performance data, the evaluator attempts to identify strengths and weaknesses in the instruction before it is put into a "final" form.

TABLE 12-1
Stages of formative evaluation

Stage	Instruction Phase	Purpose	Learners	Main Measures
One-to-one trials	Development	Try-out impressions	Individuals	Observation, survey, interview
Small-group trials	Preliminary/ draft version	Identify strengths/ weaknesses	Small groups (8–20)	Observation, attitudes, performance
Field trials	Completed	Assess actual implementation	Regular classes	Performance, attitudes

The third stage is the field trial, which examines the use of the instruction with a full-sized learner group under realistic conditions. Based on the results from various outcome measures, the instructor would make final revisions and deliver the completed instruction to actual classes. But at this point, the need for evaluation is not over. Summative and confirmative evaluations are then required to determine whether the instructional program is achieving its goals.

SUMMATIVE EVALUATION: DETERMINING PROGRAM OUTCOMES

Too often an instructional designer or an instructor may intuitively be convinced that what is being accomplished is worthwhile and successful. It is often assumed by persons in education and training that the merits of a program are obvious to other persons in the institution or organization. Unfortunately, rarely is either of these conclusions true.

A summative evaluation permits a designer or instructor to reach unbiased, objective answers to evaluation questions concerning expected program outcomes and then to decide whether the program is achieving those outcomes. With this evidence, the designer's intuition can be supported or rejected, and he or she has the facts for correctly informing others about the program results.

The following important issues can be examined through summative evaluation procedures:

- Effectiveness of learner or trainee learning
- Efficiency of learner or trainee learning
- Cost of program development and continuing expenses in relation to effectiveness and efficiency
- Attitudes and reactions to the program by learners, faculty, and staff
- Long-term benefits of the instructional program

In this section, we examine methods for gathering data that can lead to a conclusion for each of the five issues stated earlier. Attention to these matters may be essential in proving the value of a new instructional program and then ensuring its continued support.

A summative evaluation of a course or program is more than a one-time activity. Immediately after each course or training program is concluded, the instructor should utilize some or all of the assessment methods described subsequently. By accumulating summative data, continuing positive trends in a program can be tracked over time, or deficiencies can be noted as they show up, with possible corrections being made immediately.

Evaluation versus Research

One way of measuring the value of a new program is to compare the results obtained with those of a conventionally conducted course in the same subject. Most often this comparison cannot be made fairly because the two courses were planned to achieve entirely different objectives. It is very likely that there are no stated, measurable objectives for the conventional course that can be used as a basis for the comparison. Also, the subject matter treated in the two programs may be significantly different, with the content of the conventional course often being limited to a lower cognitive domain level than that of the new program.

In some situations, evaluation is performed by using a formal research framework. This means that a carefully designed comparison study is based on control and experimental groups or classes. One or more hypotheses are stated as anticipated outcomes. Then, after instruction takes place, statistical methods are employed to gather data and report the evidence collected about learning outcomes. Conclusions are drawn that support or reject the initial hypotheses.

Such a methodology is usually more appropriate in basic or applied research studies that permit control over extraneous variables and allow for the establishment of reasonably equivalent experimental and control groups. Most instructional design projects are not planned to result in broadly applicable theories. Their purpose is to find out how well the needs that have been identified can be met. Growth in learner knowledge or skill activity, as measured by the difference between pretest and posttest results or by observing behavior before and after instruction, provides evidence of learning that can be directly attributable to the instructional program.

Sometimes the success in learning can be shown only in following up on-the-job work being done by individuals after instruction. For example, if after employees complete a safety course, accidents involving those employees are appreciably reduced (say, by more than 30 percent), then it can be inferred that the training was successful. Or, if company operating expenses decrease and revenues increase from the pretraining to the posttraining periods, then one could infer that direct benefits are due to the results of training. On the other hand, when results do not meet goals, the evaluation evidence would indicate the shortcomings. Steps can then be taken to improve the program before its next use.

Thus, for evaluating instructional design projects, it is not necessary to perform formal research involving control/experimental groups and a detailed statistical analysis. All that must be done is to gather evidence relative to accomplishments or change from preinstruction to postinstruction for as many of the five components (effectiveness, efficiency, costs, attitudes, and benefits) as are considered important for that course, then to interpret the information to reach conclusions about the success or failure of the instructional program.

A special note: For some of the procedures considered here, it is advisable (or even essential) to start collecting data from the time the program is initially planned. By doing this, you will have the necessary information to determine costs, time, and other facts pertinent to the evaluation.

PROGRAM EFFECTIVENESS

Effectiveness answers the question, "To what degree did students accomplish the learning objectives prescribed for each unit of the course?" Measurement of effectiveness can be ascertained from test scores, ratings of projects and performance, and records of observations of learners' behavior.

An analysis of scores can be prepared by hand or using a computer statistical package. The data may show the change from pretest to posttest results. Then, a summary may be presented in tabular form, as shown in Figure 12-3. The figure illustrates that the group, composed of six learners, accomplished 90 percent of the objectives. This figure is calculated by totaling the number of objectives satisfied (represented by the X marks in section c and dividing by 6, which is the number of learners). The average number of objectives accomplished per learner is 4.5, which is 90 percent of the objectives. This result can be interpreted as a measure of the effectiveness of the instructional design plan for this group of learners. The percentage may be considered an *effectiveness index* representing the percentage of learners reaching a preset level of mastery (satisfying each objective) and the average percentage of objectives satisfied by all learners.

If all learners accomplished all objectives, the effectiveness of the program would be excellent. If 90 percent of the learners accomplish 90 percent of the objectives, could you report that the program has been effective? To answer this question, the instructor, along with the administrator or training director, must have previ-

FIGURE 12-3
A sample analysis of test questions measuring cognitive objectives

a. Unit Objectives

Unit Objectives	Test Questions
A	2, 4, 11
B	1, 7
C	3, 6, 12
D	8, 10
E	5, 9

b. Learner — Correct Answers to Questions

Learner	1	2	3	4	5	6	7	8	9	10	11	12
AJ	x	x	x	x		x	x	x	x	x	x	
SF	x	x	x	x	x	x		x				
TY	x	x	x	x	x	x	x	x	x	x	x	
LM	x	x	x	x	x	x	x	x	x	x	x	
RW	x	x	x	x	x	x	x	x	x	x	x	
WB	x		x	x	x	x	x		x	x		x

c. Learner — Objectives Satisfied

Learner	A	B	C	D	E
AJ	x	x	x	x	
SF		x	x	x	x
TY	x	x	x	x	x
LM	x	x	x	x	x
RW	x	x	x	x	x
WB		x	x	x	x

ously decided the level at which the program would be accepted as effective. In a systematically planned academic course, attainment of the 80 percent level by at least 80 percent of the learners in a class could be acceptable as a highly effective program. In a vocational or skill area, 90–90 (90 percent of the trainees accomplishing 90 percent of the objectives) might be the accepted success level. Similar courses (e.g., in biology or electronics assembly) can be compared with respect to effectiveness indices and conclusions drawn for judging program effectiveness.

Realistically, it is very likely that because of individual differences among learners and a designer's inability to design ideal learning experiences, no one can hope to reach the absolute standard of mastery or competency—100 percent—in all instructional situations. (Some training programs for which life and safety are critical—medical areas or airline pilot training, for instance—may require the 100 percent level of mastery learning.)

Then another question must be asked. Assume that your own performance standard requires all learners to accomplish 85 percent of the objectives but that as a group they actually satisfy 82 percent of them. Is the effort to reach the 85 percent level worth the cost? If not, you may have to settle for a somewhat lower level of accomplishment until someone can design a revision of the program that will enable reaching the desired level of performance with reasonable effort and cost.

When evaluating the effectiveness of an instructional program, a designer must recognize that there may be intangible outcomes (often expressed as affective objectives) and long-term consequences that would become apparent only after the program is concluded and learners are at work. Both of these matters are given attention in the following sections as part of other summative evaluation components. Here, the evaluation of effectiveness is limited to those learning objectives that can be immediately measured.

Summative Evaluation Methods

The basic procedures for determining program effectiveness in summative evaluations are similar to those described earlier for formative evaluations (see Figure 12-1). Specifically, the major steps are these:

1. Specifying program objectives
2. Determining the evaluation design for each objective
   a. Pretest–posttest with one group
   b. One-group descriptive
   c. Experimental-control group
   d. Analysis of costs, resources, implementation
3. Developing data collection instruments and procedures for each objective
   a. Questionnaires
   b. Interviews
   c. Observations
   d. Achievement tests

4. Carrying out the evaluation
   a. Scheduling the data collection
   b. Collecting the data
5. Analyzing the results from each instrument
6. Interpreting the results
7. Disseminating the results and conclusions
   a. Evaluation report
   b. Group meetings
   c. Individual discussions

Data Collection Instruments. As with formative evaluations, data collection addresses one or more of the three domains of skills/behavior, cognitive, and affective. The main difference in summative evaluation is judging a completed rather than developing program.

For assessing skills, key information sources (as in formative evaluations) are as follows:

- Direct testing
- Analysis of naturally occurring events
- Direct/indirect observations
- Portfolios
- Exhibitions

For assessing cognition, measurement options include objective tests (multiple-choice, true/false, matching) and constructed-response tests (short-answer, essay, and problem solving).

Assessments of affective outcomes entail gathering reactions from both learners and the instructional staff as they look back on the program just completed. Three categories of reactions may be given attention:

- *Opinions:* Judgments about the level of acceptance of course content, instructional methods, assistance from and relations with instructor and staff, study or work time required, grading procedure, and so forth
- *Interest:* Responses to the value of topics treated, learning activities preferred, and motivation for further study or work in the subject area
- *Attitude:* Reactions to the total program in terms of degree of its being pleasurable, worthwhile, and useful

Examples of types of questions for gathering subjective reactions are shown in Figure 12-4.

PROGRAM EFFICIENCY

In evaluating efficiency, three aspects of a program require attention:

- Time required for learners to achieve unit objectives
- Number of instructors and support staff members required for instruction and the time they devote to the program
- Use of facilities assigned to the program

FIGURE 12-4
Types of questions for gathering subjective responses

Checklist

Check each word that tells how you feel about the group projects and oral presentations used in this course.

__ Interesting	__ Informative	__ Difficult
__ Dull	__ Practical	__ Important
__ Exciting	__ Worthless	__ Stimulating
__ Boring	__ Useful	__ Unpleasant

Rating Scale

Compared with a typical lecture class, how useful was the format used in this experimental class for *learning the course material*? (Check one response.)

__ Better   __ About the same   __ Not as good

Now that you have completed the course, rate your feelings about history as a subject. (Circle the number that best reflects your reaction.)

Dislike very much	Dislike somewhat	Neutral	Like somewhat	Like very much
1	2	3	4	5

Rating

Please rank these topics as treated in the management course. Consider their value to you and your job. (Start with number 1 as the topic having the *highest* value.)

__ Planning	__ Organization and management
__ Self-assessment	__ Development
__ Stress	__ Personnel management
__ Labor relations	__ Performance appraisal
__ Effective presentations	__ Internal affairs management
__ Budgeting	__ Media relations
__ State-of-the-art technology	

Open-Ended Questions

What is your general reaction to this course: the objectives treated, the way it was conducted, your participation, its overall value to you, and so on?

Learner Time Required

Educational programs are designed typically in terms of available time periods—semesters, quarters, or other fixed time intervals (week, weekend, etc.). It is only when some flexibility is permitted that efficiency can be measured. If a conventional training program can be reduced from a period of possibly six to five weeks with the same or increased effectiveness in learning, the program can be considered to be efficient.

Efficiency can be used for measuring outcomes primarily of programs that give major emphasis to individualized or self-paced learning activities. From the learner's standpoint, the time required to satisfy unit or program objectives would be a measure of efficiency. Mathematically, this measurement is the ratio of the number of objectives a learner achieves compared with the time the learner takes to achieve them. Learners can be asked to keep records of time (a time log) spent studying a unit or set of objectives. Or, in a more subjective fashion, an instructor can observe and make notations to indicate the number of learners at work in a study area during time periods.

For example, Mary satisfies seven objectives in 4.2 hours of study and work. By dividing the number of objectives Mary achieves by the amount of time it takes her to accomplish them, we find that her efficiency index is 1.7 (7/4.2). Bill achieves the seven objectives in 5.4 hours. His efficiency index is therefore 1.3. Thus, the higher the index, the more efficient the learning. Such an index can be calculated for each unit, then averaged for each learner to give an efficiency index for the course.

Keep in mind that many instructional programs will not yield such easily attainable and concrete measures of mastery over time. Also, efficiency indices may not be comparable across different units of instruction because of the nature of the material taught and the characteristics of the students. But where feasible, an efficiency index or some other quantitative measure can provide highly useful information for evaluating allocations of time and resources. A clear advantage, especially in working in business contexts, is that quantitative measures are often expected and given more credibility by stakeholders than are subjective types of evidence.

Faculty and Staff Required

The number of faculty and staff positions required for instruction, supervision, or support of an instructional program also relates to efficiency. The question is, "How many learners are being served by the staff?" If a course requires a half-time faculty position plus the equivalent of one full-time position in assistants and technicians to serve 48 learners, then the faculty-to-learner ratio would be 1:32 (1.5:48). If the institution-wide ratio of faculty-to-student load is 1:20, then the lower ratio of 1:32 indicates a more efficient use of faculty and staff personnel. Greater efficiency, however, may not necessarily mean greater effectiveness.

The ratio of 1:32 may be reported on paper, but the actual working time of faculty and staff in the program can give another indication of efficiency. Let's assume that the same instructor and support staff (1.5 positions) are spending 60 hours a week on the program (preparation, teaching, consulting with learners, evaluating performance, marking tests, providing resources, etc.). If normal time devoted to a course is 45 hours per week for a staff of similar size, then the procedures may need some revision.

Use of Facilities

Another factor of efficiency is the time that learning facilities—classrooms, learning labs, and so forth—are available during a day, a week, or other time period. If a facility is used 12 hours a day, this may be considered an efficient use of space. By obtaining these data as a program is expanded, the need to increase use or to provide for additional training space can be evaluated.

A second component of efficient space utilization is the number of learners using the facility during a time period. When 110 learners are being served in a 15-station microcomputer lab on a weekly basis, this may be seen as an efficient use of space. Keep records so that the time learners and staff spend in the program and facility can be calculated and objectively related to this factor of efficiency.

PROGRAM COSTS

Historically, a major concern in educational programs is the cost of instruction. Expense categories, such as personnel, equipment, and supplies, are established to aid the administration in controlling and reporting about programs. Standard bases that are frequently used for allocating funds in educational budgets are average daily attendance (ADA) in public schools, full-time equivalent (FTE, the number of students equated for taking a full course load) in higher education, the number of faculty assigned in terms of FTE, and student credit hours or student-to-faculty contact hours. These bases for allocating funds are mainly accounting methods. They provide little information about the real costs of a single program.

Although a school or college is not the same as a business operation, for both we can identify specific factors affecting costs that can be controlled. The education and training literature contains numerous explanations and reports on how program costs can be derived. Formulas that consider many of the variables that affect costs are presented in detail and their complexities are interpreted. Such terms as *cost effectiveness, cost efficiency,* and *cost benefits* are frequently used. Our concern here is simply to answer the question, "What does it cost to develop and operate a specific program for the number of learners served?" Once we have this essential information, we are able to relate costs to effectiveness, efficiency, and resulting benefits; thus, we are able to judge the acceptability of program costs.

Any new course or a program being revised requires attention to the two major categories of costs: developmental and operational costs.

Developmental Costs

As an instructional project is being planned and developed, some or all of the following costs, sometimes called *start-up costs,* may be incurred:

- Planning time: percentage of salary for time spent by each member of the planning team on the project, or number of hours spent by each member, multiplied by his or her hourly or monthly salary rate, and fees for consultants
- Staff time: percentage of salary for time spent by each member engaged in planning, producing, and gathering materials, or the number of hours spent by each person, multiplied by his or her hourly salary rate
- Supplies and materials for preparing print, media, and other materials
- Outside services for producing or purchasing materials
- Construction or renovation of facilities
- Equipment purchased for instructional uses
- Expenses for installing equipment

- Testing, redesign, and final reproduction of resources in sufficient quantity for operational uses (includes personnel time and costs of materials and services)
- Orientation and training of personnel who will conduct instruction
- Indirect costs: personnel benefits such as retirement and insurance, related to time and salary charged to the project (this information is typically available from the personnel department)
- Overhead: utilities, furniture, room and building costs or depreciation allowance, proportion of other institutional services charged to the project (this information is usually available from the business manager or the controller of the organization)
- Miscellaneous (office supplies, telephone, travel, etc.)

Here is an example of the developmental costs for a general education college-level course involving two instructors. It includes large-group presentations incorporating PowerPoint presentations, student self-directed learning with 10 interactive multimedia units, study guide, and small discussion sessions.

Design Time

2 instructors, 1 month summer	$15,500
Instructional designer, 1 month summer	$8,500
Graduate assistant, 100 hours	$2,500
	$26,500

Development Time

2 instructors, 0.25 time, 1 semester	$20,000
Instructional designer, 0.25 time, 1 semester	$13,250
Programming	$20,000
Graphic artist, 80 hours	$3,000
	$56,250

Materials and Supplies

Office supplies	$200

Equipment

20 computers for lab	$24,000

Renovative Facility

20 learning stations	$15,000
Electrical wiring	$8,000
	$23,000

Other Costs

Formative evaluation and revision costs	$10,000
Staff benefits	$13,556
	$23,556

Total Development Costs	$153,506

Operational Costs

When the project is fully implemented and instruction is taking place, the recurring operational costs include the following:

- Administrative salaries (based on percentage of time devoted to project)
- Faculty salaries for time spent in the program (contact hours with groups and individual learners, planning activities, evaluating program, revising activities and materials, personnel benefits)
- Learner or trainee costs (applicable in business-oriented training programs: salary, travel and lodging, income for company reduced while trainee is not on job, or replacement cost of a person substituting for a trainee job)
- Salaries for assistants, maintenance technicians, and others
- Rental charges for classroom or other facilities if offered at an off-campus location
- Replacement of consumable and damaged materials
- Repair and maintenance of equipment
- Depreciation of equipment
- Overhead (utilities, facilities, furnishings, custodial services, etc.)
- Evaluation and update of materials (time and materials)

Here is an example of the operational costs for the college-level course shown in the previous example over a one-semester term:

Salaries

2 instructors, 0.25 time	$20,000
Benefits	$4,500
2 graduate assistants	$22,000
Subtotal	$46,500
Replacements and repairs	$2,500
Total Operating Costs	**$49,000**

Instructional Cost Index

We cannot attempt to judge whether the costs of an instructional program are acceptable by looking solely at the gross amount expended. If it costs a company $1,000 to manufacture pencils, this sum must be related to the number of pencils made. Then the price per pencil has meaning and can be compared with the price per unit manufactured by other companies. In an instructional program, costs should be related to the number of learners served in the program.

With data available on developmental and operational costs, we can calculate the cost per learner for a program. This is the important bottom-line amount that allows for comparison of costs between programs leading to the acceptance of expense levels. Cost per learner or trainee may be labeled an *instructional cost index*. It is determined by the following procedure:

1. Spread the developmental costs over a series of time periods (e.g., 10 training sessions or 5 semesters). This would be the anticipated life of the program before it should require major revisions or cease to be useful. This procedure is known as *amortizing the cost*.
2. Add together the preceding prorated amount of the developmental costs (for 3 years) and the operational costs for one use period (a complete training class or an academic semester).
3. Determine the average number of learners known or anticipated to be in the program with each use. Divide the total in step 2 by this number. The result is the cost per learner, or the instructional cost index.

An example of an instructional cost index calculated from the previous example of developmental and operational costs follows:

Total operational costs	$49,000.00
Portion of developmental cost ($135,256/6)	25,584.33
Total cost per semester	$74,584.33
Number of learners in program	340
Instructional cost index ($74,584.33/340)	$219.37

(This is the total cost for each learner over one semester.)

If this program continues beyond five semesters (at which time all developmental costs will have been amortized) and the number of learners remains the same, the instructional cost index will then drop to $144.12 ($49,000/340). During this period, limited funds are included for minor updates and revision of materials. At the end of five semesters, a reexamination of the program for this course may be advisable. The course then may be continued as is, or new developmental costs—hopefully lower than the original ones—would be required. These would affect the ongoing instructional cost index.

The index number itself has little meaning. Calculations could be made in the same way for traditional program costs in a comparable training or subject area. As previously stated, it is difficult (and usually unfair) to make a comparison between a new program with carefully structured objectives and a traditional program based on generalized objectives. It would seem more appropriate to compare two skill-type training programs, two math classes, or a biology and chemistry course if each one has been systematically planned and implemented. Once an instructional cost index has been calculated, the instructor or designer should ask these questions:

- Is the program cost-effective? This is a subjective decision, but useful information can be obtained by relating the instructional cost index to the level of learning outcomes (e.g., 90% of the learners accomplish 84% of the objectives). If a satisfactory learning level is reached and the instructional cost index seems to be within reason, the program would be considered cost-effective.

- Is the program cost-efficient? Relate the instructional cost index to efficiency factors (time required by learners to complete activities, staff time required for instruction and support, level of facilities' use). If the efficiency index seems acceptable, with a reasonable instructional cost index the program would be cost-efficient.
- Are the costs justified in terms of resulting benefits (cost/benefit analysis)? Relate the instructional cost index to the benefits that a company or other organization derives from personnel who complete the training program. (See the following section for details and discussion of potential benefits resulting from training.) If the benefits are high and costs acceptable, then the question can be answered in a positive way.

If the outcomes of a program prove to be acceptable but the instructional cost index remains higher than desired, certain steps might be taken to lower the operational cost portion of the index, as follows:

1. Consider the feasibility of including more learners in the program (as in a distance-learning course using television). Perhaps more individuals can be served without reduced quality of instruction.
2. Decide whether assistants might replace instructors for certain activities without lowering the effectiveness of the program. This would reduce the higher cost of instructor time.
3. Plan to relieve instructors of some learner contact time by developing additional self-paced learning activities for learners.
4. As a last resort, reduce the training time or lower some of the required performance standards. Shorter instructional time would reduce instructor time and thus costs.

An alternative cost index measure is to calculate the index in terms of total contact hours. Thus, a weeklong course for 20 people has 800 (40 hours × 20 people) total contact hours.

CONFIRMATIVE EVALUATION: DETERMINING OUTCOMES OVER TIME

Instructional programs are most often offered for three general reasons:

- To "educate" individuals so that they may participate as informed, cultured, and productive citizens in society
- To prepare individuals for a gainful vocation
- To improve or upgrade competencies of individuals in a specific task or in certain aspects of a job

For each of these reasons, determining the success of an instructional program requires attention to important outcomes beyond the results of written and performance tests given at the end of a unit or a course. Often the accomplishment of major goals or terminal objectives stated for a program can be assessed only some time after instruction is concluded. As emphasized throughout this chapter and the preceding ones, the evaluation of instruction needs to be *continuous*. In our view, the constructs of formative, summative, and confirmative evaluations are mainly important in distinguishing between what the evaluation is likely to emphasize and when in the instructional design and implementation process it will be conducted. From an operational standpoint (e.g., planning, instrumentation, data collection, and analysis) the three evaluation types are much more similar than different.

Confirmative evaluation represents a continuation of summative evaluation. Both approaches are designed to judge the effectiveness of instruction, summative soon after instruction is completed and confirmative after some time has passed. Our practical view of both summative and confirmative evaluation is that rarely will either be used solely to pronounce an instructional program as "working" or "not working" and then conclude. In the real world, there will typically be opportunity to use the results of these evaluations to make improvements in future training. Thus, the important aspects of formative evaluation continue to be employed and the instructional program regarded as never fully "completed."

Confirmative evaluation may encounter a few hurdles that earlier evaluations do not. After a course is completed, the learners or trainees move to other courses or work at different locations. Observations of them at work or communication with them may require an extra effort. Some important outcomes are in the affective domain. These may be difficult to identify and measure. Responses for evaluation may be needed from other persons (colleagues, supervisors, and others) who may not be understanding or cooperative. Regardless of these obstacles, attempts should be made to follow up on learners after an instructional program has ended. Evidence of follow-up benefits could be the most important summative results to measure.

Educational Programs

Traditionally, the general, long-term benefits of educational programs are measured through statewide and national standardized tests given to students in public schools; college students take undergraduate and graduate admission examinations; and regional or national opinion surveys are conducted at various times. Such tests measure broad, fairly general objectives. One limitation is that gains on these tests may not show up immediately after a new instructional program is implemented. The summative evaluation, therefore, may not indicate success, but a year later, a confirmative evaluation might. A second limitation, which affects both evaluation approaches, is that the objectives measured may be too broad to provide useful information on how well a particular course accomplished its specific instructional objectives. Concerns may also arise about the circumstances under which students prepare for or complete the standardized tests (Haladyna, Nolan, & Haas, 1991).

The long-term outcomes of the objectives of specific courses are frequently not examined or examined only casually. Within the framework of the goals and terminal objectives of a program, the following categories of outcomes might be considered:

- Capabilities in basic skills (reading, writing, verbal expression, and mathematics), as required in following courses
- Knowledge and competencies in a subject as bases for study in subsequent courses
- Proficiencies to carry out job tasks and responsibilities in occupational employment
- Fulfillment of roles as good citizens (law abiding, participating in democratic process, etc.)

As indicated at the beginning of this section, data concerning these outcomes are not easy to obtain. The following methods are commonly used in continuing (i.e., confirmative) evaluations to gather information:

- *Completing questionnaires:* Ask former students, present instructors, or employers to respond to a questionnaire designed to indicate learners' present proficiencies as related to competencies derived from the course or program being evaluated (see Figure 11-2).
- *Conducting interviews:* Meet with former learners, present instructors, or employers to inquire about the present proficiencies of learners as related to competencies from the courses or programs being evaluated.
- *Making observations:* Observe learners in new learning or performance situations and judge their capabilities as a follow-up of competencies acquired in the course being evaluated.
- *Examining records:* Check grades and anecdotal records of former students in school files to ascertain how they are now performing in their classes as based on competencies gained in the course being evaluated. (Note: Because of privacy laws, this procedure may require permission from the former students before records can be made available.)

Training Programs

A training program within a business concern, an industrial company, a health agency, or other organization usually has clearly defined outcomes to be accomplished. These planned results may have initially been identified when a needs assessment (see Chapter 2) was first made. The consequent benefits are expected to result in improved job performance and often can be translated into dollar savings or increased income for the company.

Three areas may need attention in posttraining evaluation, which is discussed next.

Appropriateness of the Training.   Although the program was developed according to identified needs, changes in on-the-job operating procedures and the equipment used could necessitate different job performance from what was taught. Use confirmative evaluation to determine whether modifications are required before training is conducted the next time.

Competencies of Employees.   It is one thing to pass written tests and perform satisfactorily in the controlled environment of a classroom or laboratory but potentially another to be successful in transferring the learning to a job situation. Determine how well the former trainees now perform the job or tasks they were trained to do.

Benefits to the Organization.   The advantages need to be measured in terms of the payoff to the organization as well as to the individual. Some of the criteria that indicate that a training program has been beneficial to the organization are these:

- Increased safety through reduced number of accidents
- Increased service abilities, including both work quality and performance speed
- Improved quality of products being produced
- Increased rate of work or production
- Reduced problems with equipment due to malfunctions and breakdowns
- Increased sales of products and greater services, or more income being generated (referred to as "return on training investment")

With respect to affective-type outcomes, the following may be some of the expected results:

- Less employee tardiness and absenteeism
- Less employee turnover on jobs
- Greater job satisfaction
- Higher level of motivation and willingness to assume responsibilities
- Increased respect for the organization

The same methods for gathering information for educational programs would apply to measuring the follow-up benefits of a training program: questionnaires, interviews, observations, and examining records. In terms of actual performance levels, if careful records are kept, comparisons can be made between pretraining and posttraining competencies. A key method of follow-up evaluation can be related to reduction in expenses or greater revenue generated for the company. This approach requires a comparison of pretraining cost factors with the costs and income data determined at a reasonable time after training is completed. This evidence can be one of the best measures to relate training benefits to the bottom line with which a company is most concerned. Keep in mind, though, that not all training courses will have a direct, measurable impact on the bottom line (e.g., courses in interpersonal relations, public speaking).

In summary, confirmative evaluations take up where summative evaluations leave off—once the instruction is completed and the application of learning begins and continues over time. Confirmative evaluations will tend to include the following characteristics:

- Continuous (repeated over time, where feasible)
- Occurs in realistic contexts (on the job, in practice)
- Emphasizes performance rather than simply knowledge
- Includes learner reactions as direction for improvement
- May address new evaluation questions, as performance requirements or contexts change over time
- May use smaller samples (more case studies) due to attrition of original learner cohort
- May use indirect measures (colleague, supervisor, and self-ratings; data from naturally occurring events) because of the difficulty of collecting follow-up data in the field

REPORTING RESULTS OF SUMMATIVE AND CONFIRMATIVE EVALUATIONS

The final step that needs to be taken in evaluations of instruction is to prepare a report of the results for others to read and examine. Careful attention should be given to this activity. Future support for the program, as well as the assistance required for additional instructional design projects, can be influenced by the manner in which a summative or confirmative evaluation is reported.

First, the evaluator must decide for whom the report is to be prepared—administrators/training managers, instructors, or another supporting agency. By considering those persons who are to receive the report, emphasis or special attention may have to be given to certain phases of the evaluation. Explaining how and where funds have been spent may be of primary interest, or evidence of follow-up benefits may be of more value than are the efficiencies or effectiveness of instruction.

Second, the evaluator must decide on the format of the report. Should it be on paper for individual reading, or will it be presented to a group with the support of slides or overhead transparencies? In either case, plan to report results attractively. Not everyone will be as highly interested or as well informed about the project as the designer has been. Here are some suggestions:

- Give the report an interesting title.
- Summarize highlights so the key outcomes can be grasped quickly. Do this by setting them off on a page with white space or boxing each statement.
- Describe supporting data in visual ways with graphs rather than as detailed tables; use artwork as appropriate.

- If slides or transparencies will be prepared, limit the information displayed to only the key points. Prepare printed materials that correlate with the visuals and contain the details of information for the audience to retain.
- End by making appropriate recommendations for continuing, extending, modifying, or terminating the program.
- Where feasible, adapt the style and content of the report to the main target audiences. Different stakeholder groups will have different backgrounds, interests, and expectancies for what the report will convey.
- The reporting format outlined in the "Reporting" section for formative evaluations is generally appropriate as well for summative and confirmative evaluations.

SUMMARY

1. Formative, summative, and confirmative evaluations serve the complementary purposes of assessing developing and completed instructional programs.
2. A basic model for planning formative evaluations addresses eight areas: purposes, audience, issues, resources, evidence, data-gathering techniques, analyses, and reporting.
3. Common formative evaluation approaches can be classified as (1) connoisseur based, in which expert opinions are sought; (2) decision oriented, in which information related to particular questions is gathered; (3) objectives based, in which assessments are made of the degree to which particular objectives are obtained; and (4) public relations inspired, in which financial support or backing for a project is solicited based on the evaluation findings.
4. Three major stages of formative evaluation consist of one-to-one trials, small-group trials, and field trials. Each successive stage focuses on a more developed version of the instructional program, using larger samples of students.
5. Summative evaluations, unlike experimental research, are designed to provide information about specific instructional programs. They are not used to test general theories and thus do not require rigorous research methods or control groups.
6. Program effectiveness is determined by analyzing test scores, rating projects and performance, and observing learner behavior.
7. Summative evaluations involve similar planning procedures and methodologies as formative evaluations. The emphasis in summative studies, however, is on the full, completed program rather than on preliminary versions of the program.
8. A useful outcome measure for summative evaluations is program efficiency, computed as a ratio of number of objectives achieved to time taken to achieve them.
9. Program costs are evaluated by determining both developmental costs (the expense of designing the program) and operational costs (the expense of offering the program). The instructional cost index is the total cost per learner or trainee.

10. Confirmative (follow-up) evaluations should be conducted after the student leaves the program. In the case of educational programs, the important outcomes are basic skills, knowledge, competencies, and performance in occupational settings. For training programs, important outcomes include appropriateness of the training, competencies of employees, and benefits to the organization.
11. The evaluation report should be carefully prepared and attractive in its appearance. Adaptation of content to stakeholder backgrounds and interests is highly important.

THE ID PROCESS

Inexperienced designers sometimes view formative and summative evaluations as discrete strategies that respectively come at the "beginning" and at the "completion" of the design process. Our approach is to see them, along with confirmative evaluations, as overlapping processes having more similarities than differences. Although every design project is different in content, context, and goals, we offer the following as general guidelines based on our experiences.

Make continuous evaluation a primary component of the initial design plan. Once a project is launched, it seems to be human nature to want to devote more time and money to designing and implementing the instructional program. It is generally difficult to add "more" evaluation if it is not built in at the front end.

In most contexts, being sensitive to the political aspects of a design project is critical to the project's success. Of the many stakeholders concerned (e.g., sponsors, learners, administrators, and instructors), there are likely to be both supporters and detractors. Evaluation, therefore, not only becomes a tool for refinement and judgment, it becomes a valuable means of communicating (with data) what is being accomplished. We have discovered many times that "data talk" convincingly, particularly when there is disharmony among stakeholders on such matters as the need for the course, its content, how and when it is offered, the costs involved, or the delivery methods used.

While the distinction between the three types of evaluation is useful as a heuristic for evaluation timing, emphasis, and orientation, it seems most important to employ each as the evaluation objectives and conditions dictate at each point in time. There will be times when a formative evaluation that is conducted very early in the design process must produce preliminary data to satisfy the new training manager who wants some indication of the project's impact in order to support it. Such situations are not a matter of how the "book" says a pure formative evaluation must be done. Simply put, unless that particular manager receives some outcome data, there will be no project on which to conduct a pure formative evaluation! And there will be situations (probably many) when it makes perfect sense in a summative or confirmative evaluation to gather information for improving the design. Judging from our experiences, the art and science of instructional evaluation in the real world often necessitates developing well-constructed hybrid designs adapted to situational needs.

A final consideration in all phases of evaluation is to what degree outside experts should be employed. Different types of experts can be particularly valuable. The SME (e.g., a database administrator consulting on a course on database management) should be helpful in validating the content of the instruction. A media expert may be needed to help with instructional delivery using specialized technology (e.g., distance learning) with which the designer is less familiar. An external, professional evaluator may be needed to design the study, develop instruments, and analyze and interpret the data. When funding permits, we strongly recommend using experts. Not only is their knowledge important, what they say adds objectivity and credibility to the project. Expert data usually talk very convincingly.

APPLICATIONS

You are designing an instructional program to be used at kiosks in an art museum to acquaint visitors with the museum layout and exhibits. It is important to the philanthropic foundation that supported the stations that visitors (1) actually use the program and (2) find the information useful and interesting. Using examples, describe how each of the following types of formative evaluation might be used: connoisseur based, decision oriented, objectives based, and public relations inspired. Which of these orientations might you also apply in summative and confirmative evaluations?

ANSWERS

Assuming that you are not highly knowledgeable about the particular art museum or art exhibits in general, connoisseur-based evaluation would be useful to confirm the accuracy of the content of the program, its organization, and its presentation. Decision-making evaluation might focus on questions such as, "Is the program economical to update as new exhibits are featured?" Answers to these questions will provide useful suggestions for refining the design. Objectives-based formative evaluation might focus on the criterion questions posed by the sponsoring foundation (as well as other relevant outcomes): "What percentage of visitors use the program and for how long?" and "Do users find the program to be helpful and interesting?"

Given that this evaluation is formative, the results will be used less to judge its effectiveness than to provide directions for its improvement. For example, infrequent use of the program may lead to the decision to place the information stations in more visible locations in the museum lobby. Public relations–inspired evaluation may involve providing the foundation with preliminary information showing that good progress is being made in the program design and implementation.

For summative and confirmative evaluations, the two most important orientations will most likely be objectives based, to determine how effectively the completed program is achieving the desired outcomes, and public relations inspired, to keep the foundation satisfied and perhaps (assuming the program is successful) attract additional funding for related projects. With a completed program, connoisseur-based evaluation would probably not be needed. Assuming that the "completed" program can still be improved, decision-based evaluation, however, might prove to be a helpful supplement by providing data on how effectively different program components are working.

SAMPLE DESIGN PLAN

FORMATIVE EVALUATION

SME Review

I have been looking at this instruction for too long and too intently. I can't possibly be an objective evaluator. I'm fortunate though in that the Student Services director as well as two of the learning consultants are eager to review this design document. This is really valuable because not only are they SMEs, but they also have first-hand experience with the target audience! I plan to attach a brief explanation about the purpose and pieces of an instructional design document and send that along with copies of the document itself. Each SME will review the document independently of the other, making comments on the objectives, sequencing, and strategies. We will then meet as a group, and I will gather their comments, work toward consensus where necessary, and then make the recommended changes. The training materials will then be created.

Target Audience Review

I plan to introduce a beta version of this unit during the new-student orientation events in August. I have made arrangements with a vendor to provide plug-ins for the PDAs of the first 300 people who agree to test the instruction and complete a brief online evaluation form. I'm looking for feedback on usability, motivational elements (i.e., are the examples relevant? does the section on using the PDA engage you more deeply with that technology?), and ease of accessibility. Based on their comments, I'll make any needed changes, run the instructional package past my SMEs, and then go into production.

REFERENCES

Brenneman, J. (1989). When you can't use a crowd: Single subject testing. *Performance and Instruction, 28*, 22–25.

Dick, W., & Carey, L. (1991). *The systematic design of instruction* (2nd ed.). New York: Harper-Collins.

Flagg, B. N. (Ed.). (1990). *Formative evaluation for educational technologies.* Hillsdale, NJ: Erlbaum.

Gooler, D. D. (1980). Formative evaluation strategies for major instructional development projects. *Journal of Instructional Development, 3*, 7–11.

Haladyna, T. M., Nolan, S. B., & Haas, N. S. (1991). Raising standardized achievement test scores and the analysis of test score pollution. *Educational Researcher, 20*, 2–7.

Miles, M. B., & Huberman, A. M. (1994). *Qualitative data analysis: An expanded sourcebook* (2nd ed.). Thousand Oaks, CA: Sage.

Ross, S. M., & Morrison, G. R. (1995). Evaluation as a tool for research and development. In R. D. Tennyson & A. Barron (Eds.), *Automating instructional design: Computer-based development and delivery tools* (pp. 491–522). Berlin: Springer-Verlag.

Thiagarjan, S., Semmel, D., & Semmel, M. (1974). *Instructional development for training teachers of exceptional children: A sourcebook.* Bloomington, IN: Center for Innovation in Teaching the Handicapped.

CHAPTER 13

The Role of the Instructional Designer

GETTING STARTED

Your work with a leading copy machines manufacturer has led you to identify a major problem with the way field service technicians repair "broken" copiers. It seems that their approach is more one of replacing each part until the copier works rather than using the built-in diagnostics to identify the actual problem. You have sold management on your idea of creating a new troubleshooting course that will focus on identifying the faulty part. To help you with the project, the warranty and service manager has assigned one of his top design engineers as your subject-matter expert (SME). Although this individual is a few years younger than you, she has the respect of many in the company as one of the most knowledgeable and capable people in her area.

During your second meeting, you, your SME, and a service technician are visiting a customer's location that has three broken copiers. You are amazed with how your SME is able to lead the service technician through the troubleshooting process. In an instant you know that this project will be easy because of your SME's knowledge. On the way back to the office, you ask the SME some additional questions to complete the first draft of your task analysis. She asks what you are doing and why you're taking notes. After you explain, she says that she sees no reason for you to do this project as she and the other engineers in her department are more than capable of developing this training without your help, and they can do a better job than you. It is obvious that she has no desire to work with you on this project. Since you and management are highly committed to this project, what do you do?

"How do I distinguish between the SME and client?"

"What responsibilities does the instructor or client share in the design process?"

"How does an instructional designer work with media personnel and other support staff?"

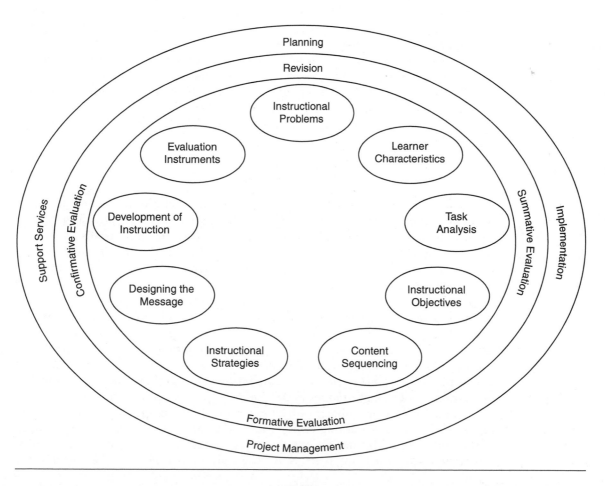

The instructional designer is often the individual solely responsible for implementing and following a systematic design process. This chapter focuses on the role of the instructional designer as a designer; that is, the individual who has the primary responsibility for designing and developing the instruction. The designer's role as a project manager is addressed in the next chapter. At times, the roles may appear to conflict with one another, but mostly they will complement each other.

THE ROLE OF THE DESIGNER

The instructional designer has the primary responsibility of ensuring that the instruction is designed, developed, and produced in a systematic manner that will consistently produce efficient and effective learning. This task is accomplished by carefully following an instructional design model. A distinction is needed between rigidly following a model and applying a model to solve an instructional problem. No model is so carefully planned and flexible that it can account for all conditions in all projects. Following a model in a rigid fashion will result in a misallocation of resources and lost time fulfilling the "needs" of the model rather than solving the instructional problem. The design model should serve as a guide for designing the instruction. Those steps that are not relevant to the particular problem are skipped, so that the effort can be concentrated on the parts of the model that are most applicable.

With each project the designer must decide how much design is required. This decision is influenced by the time frame for addressing the problem, the nature of the delivery, and the resources available. The following sections describe each of these decision factors.

Time Frame

First, consider the issue of the time frame. Some problems require immediate attention either because of the number of individuals affected or the critical nature of the problem. For example, suppose a company or organization installs a new telephone system and all phones are switched at midnight Monday. Thus, everyone reporting to work on Tuesday has an immediate need to know how to use the telephone system. After Tuesday, the need is gone except for the occasional new employees. Thus, the training is short term; the problem exists only for a day. A designer needs to determine whether this need is best addressed by a major instructional design project that could take a month or more to complete or whether the designer should spend a few hours with an SME preparing a group presentation or a job aid. Another example is the installation of new software or a major update that affects purchase orders or other essential business tasks. There is a need for immediate training of a large number of people that typically drops rather dramatically.

An instructional problem with a longer time frame might be a technical training issue, such as determining whether an acid treatment will improve the production of an oil well. This need is one that will probably apply to all new engineers in a particular area for many years. Since the training is repetitive (i.e., offered for each new employee), the need would justify a carefully designed unit of instruction if there is a sufficient audience. Similarly, you might decide to create a unit of instruction for students who serve as office assistants to teach them how to correctly answer the phone and take messages. Again, this is a need that will apply to new student workers each year until either the school's name changes or the phone system is changed.

The designer's role is likely to vary between two extremes. First, the designer can serve as a consultant to an SME for a short time period to help the SME organize and sequence the content. The actual design and delivery is left to the expertise of the instructor/SME. Second, the designer can assume a more active leadership role and carefully design a project following an instructional design model. Compared with the role as a consultant, the designer is more likely to assume a leadership role and direct the full development of a self-paced or mediated unit of instruction. The designer's role then becomes central to the project as he or she is responsible for the content analysis, objectives, instructional strategies, test items, formative evaluation, and, possibly, the actual writing of the materials.

Nature of Delivery

In Chapter 9, we describe several strategies for delivering instruction to large groups, small groups, and individuals. The type of delivery method selected often influences the role of the designer. Let's consider two examples.

An instructor approaches a designer for help in structuring a new course that involves lectures. The designer's role could take one of three possibilities. First, the designer could assume a proactive design and leadership role. In a proactive role the designer serves as a leader and uses a model to guide the design of the project. Second, the designer and SME could agree on a cooperative relationship in which they share the responsibility for design. In this role, the SME/instructor often assumes responsibility for defining the problem and for doing the task analysis. The designer then works with the SME or instructor to design the strategies for each individual lecture. Third, the designer's role is one of a consultant who is a sounding board and a resource for the SME's ideas. When designing a lecture-based course, the SME is likely to maintain a more dominant role in the design of the instruction, since he or she will ultimately deliver the information.

A second example involves the development of a multimedia unit that is delivered as individualized instruction. When the delivery method is individualized, the designer is more likely to assume a proactive role in design and leadership. The SME, then, tends to be the consultant to the project. This shift in roles may be due to the shift from the classroom, where the SME typically has control, to an individualized environment that may utilize a form of technology to deliver the instruction.

A third example is a teacher who serves as an instructional designer with a team of other grade-level teachers on a development project. The designer/teacher has two options. One is to assume the role of an instructional designer and lead the group through the design process. Such a role normally requires an agreement among the other teachers to follow the process. Second, the designer/teacher can serve as both an SME and a design consultant.

Resources Available

The final factor that can influence the role of the designer is the resources available for the project. The primary resources—personnel, time, and money—can influence the designer's role on a continuum from consultant to proactive designer and leader. A lack of design staff personnel, short time lines, or a lack of funds may require the designer to accept a role as a consultant as opposed to a proactive designer. Working under such constraints, the designer may need to question the acceptance of the consulting role on the basis of the amount of impact the designer can or will have on the project. The decision, however, must also be based on organizational and political factors.

Expert's Edge

The ibstpi Code of Ethical Standards for Instructional Designers

The International Board of Standards for Training, Performance and Instruction (ibstpi) was founded as a not-for-profit corporation in 1984. Its mission is to improve individual and organizational performance by articulating and promoting the integrity of professional practice through research, development, definition of competencies, and education.[1] The following is the code of ethical standards for instructional designers published by ibstpi.[2]

    I.   Guiding Standards: Responsibilities to Others

        A. Provide efficient, effective, workable, and cost-effective solutions to client problems

        B. Systematically improve human performance to accomplish valid and appropriate individual and organizational goals

        C. Facilitate individual accomplishment

        D. Help clients make informed decisions

        E. Inform others of potential ethical violations and conflicts of interest

        F. Educate clients in matters of instructional design and performance improvement

    II. Guiding Standards: Social Mandates

        A. Support humane, socially responsible goals and activities for individuals and organizations

        B. Make professional decisions based upon moral and ethical positions regarding societal issues

        C. Consider the impact of planned interventions upon individuals, organizations, and the society as a whole

III.   Guiding Standards: Respecting the Rights of Others
  A. Protect the privacy, candor, and confidentiality of client and colleague information and communication
  B. Show respect for copyright and intellectual property
  C. Do not misuse client or colleague information for personal gain
  D. Do not represent the ideas or work of others as one's own
  E. Do not make false claims about others
  F. Do not discriminate unfairly in actions related to hiring, retention, and advancement
IV.   Guiding Standards: Professional Practice
  A. Be honest and fair in all facets of one's work
  B. Share skills and knowledge with other professionals
  C. Acknowledge the contributions of others
  D. Aid and be supportive of colleagues
  E. Commit time and effort to the development of the profession
  F. Withdraw from clients who do not act ethically or when there is a conflict of interest

[1]www.ibstpi.org.

[2]Richey, R. C., Fields, D. F., & Foxon, M. (2001). *Instructional design competencies: The standards* (3rd ed.). Syracuse, NY: ERIC Clearinghouse on Information and Technology.

THE CLIENT AND THE SUBJECT-MATTER EXPERT

Each design project has a client and an SME; however, these individuals are not always easily identifiable. The following section describes the participants of a design project in a business organization, higher education, and a company that develops materials for other companies.

Business Training Environment

In this business environment, all the participants are usually employed by the same company; however, they may be separated geographically in different offices, buildings, states, or countries (Morrison, 1988). The client is typically the individual who "owns" the problem. The client/owner is usually a manager or supervisor of the target audience (the individuals with the problem). Transfer of real or paper money does not always identify the client. Another manager, a vice president, or even the training manager might "pay" for the instructional product. A client's primary responsibility in this environment is to provide access to the target population and to identify qualified SMEs.

The role of the SME is that of a consultant who often is not an employee of the training or instructional design group. The SME usually has some association with the target population (e.g., he or she worked at that level and was promoted), but is seldom the client. The primary responsibility of the SME is to provide accurate information during the task analysis and verify the accuracy of the products. This separation of roles between the SME and client allows the designer to contract with the client for the work and to assume the role of a proactive designer and leader.

Higher Education Environment

The client in the higher education environment is usually the professor who approaches the instructional designer for assistance (Tessmer, 1988). Since the professor both owns the problem and is the SME, the professor typically maintains the leadership role. The structure of the higher education environment and the organizational environment is often responsible for placing the instructional designer into a consulting role rather than a proactive designer role.

The SME is responsible for the accuracy of the content. If the designer assumes the role of a consultant, the client/SME may see the designer in a service role and limit requests to assistance with media production. On projects requiring the development and use of multimedia technologies, the client/SME may request that the designer take a more proactive role.

The role of the instructional designer and SME often changes when the focus of the project is on the design of distance education instruction. The client is often the university administration that contracts with a designer and professor who assumes the role of the subject-matter expert. The designer is often the project leader in this environment, with the designer and SME having almost equivalent responsibilities or even shared responsibilities. In some cases, the professor may not be the instructor of record for the course when it is delivered.

The role of the designer is often influenced by the function of the instructional group. If the department or group is perceived as providing a service to faculty members (e.g., preparing overhead transparencies), the designer's role may be seen as simply offering a service of suggesting and producing media. If the group's role is one of providing instructional design guidance or assistance to the faculty, then the designer's role may be perceived as a team member or even team leader.

Developing Training for Third Parties

The final illustration is a business that develops instructional materials for other companies under a contract. There may actually be several clients (Foshay, 1988). First, the individual who signed the contract is one client, but he or she may not have any additional further involvement in the project until the final product is delivered. A second client includes the individuals in the contracting company who will judge the technical accuracy of the instructional materials. Finally, the third client is the instructional designer's manager who may manage the contract. The designer has the responsibility of addressing the needs of each client and resolving conflicts between their needs. Correctly identifying all of the clients is essential for a project of this nature.

When doing contract work, the SME can be an employee of the contracting organization, an employee of the designer's organization, or an independent consultant hired for the duration of the project. If the SME is an employee of either organization, the designer may face problems negotiating for the SME's time. If the SME, however, is hired specifically for the project, then access to the SME is seldom a problem.

Typically, in contract work the designer has the responsibility of assuming a proactive role for instructional design. This role is usually facilitated by the nature of the relationship between the clients and SME. Sometimes, the designer must also fulfill the role of the project manager. While the project manager role can enhance the role of a proactive designer, the burden of administrative responsibilities can reduce the time a designer can spend on the design role. A designer fulfilling both roles will need to maintain a balance between the two roles.

PREPARING FOR THE JOB

There are three additional skills designers need that are not often explicitly taught in graduate programs. Designers need to develop time management, computer, and group process skills.

Time Management

When working as an instructional designer, planning your time and setting priorities is an extremely important skill because you will typically have more than one project in progress at a time. A designer must know how to establish priorities and budget time. A new instructional designer may find that a course or book in time management is helpful. There are several planners (e.g., Day-Timer, Franklin Planner) and personal information managers (PIMs) that work on a personal digital assistant (PDA) and/or computer that provide useful tools for planning your time and setting priorities. In addition, a planner, PDA, or calendar is useful for tracking the amount of time associated with a particular task. This information is then summarized at the end of a project and used for billing and/or planning and pricing future projects.

Computer Skills

Computer skills beyond basic literacy are a requirement for an instructional designer in most any environment today. Proficiency with a word processor can increase your productivity and reduce your reliance on a typing pool. With practice and experience, you should develop your proficiency to the level of being able to compose your documents at the keyboard. Development and turnaround time for materials can be considerably reduced, which results in increased productivity. The next step is to develop desktop publishing skills that you can use to produce print materials for your projects.

Developing a working knowledge of database, spreadsheet, presentation, and project-planning applications can assist you with the project management responsibilities. Databases are useful for tracking the personnel associated with the project, the status of individual components (e.g., under development, in review), and planning and budgeting the total project. Spreadsheets are useful for calculating and managing budgets; presentation software is useful for preparing reports for management and clients as well as presenting prototypes to the client; and project management software is useful for planning and managing the time lines for a project.

Group Process Skills

As a designer, you will lead several groups during the life of a project. For example, at the beginning you will need to lead a planning meeting to discuss the goals and direction of the project. Having the necessary skills to organize and lead a meeting is essential for the success of the project. A designer should know how to plan a meeting, prepare an agenda, keep the group on track, lead discussions, and resolve conflicts.

WORKING WITH SUPPORT PERSONNEL

As a design project grows in complexity, the number of support personnel involved also grows. This section describes some of the personnel who work on instructional design projects and their role in the process.

Working with Media Production Specialists

Instructional design projects produce instructional materials that may include a range of activities and the use of numerous media for delivery. The services of various support personnel are often required for preparing materials, locating commercial items, making materials available to learners, selecting and installing equipment, adapting facilities, or filling other needs. The instructional designer is responsible for involving the necessary support personnel and coordinating the preparatory work.

Graphic Artists.   Projects ranging from print to video production to multimedia units to projected materials for lectures often utilize the help of graphic artists. These individuals can help with the creative layout of pages, computer screens, slides, overhead transparencies, computer-generated animations, and templates for PowerPoint presentations. For print production, their early involvement can help you create a template for your word processor documents that can streamline the print production process. Providing the graphic artist with information early in the project allows him or her to help create a consistency and identity for the materials.

Requests for technical drawings to cartoons for the final production must include clear and detailed instructions to make efficient use of a graphic designer's time.

Scriptwriters. Some design teams employ professional scriptwriters for video and audio productions as well as any dialog that might be incorporated into other media such as role plays. The scriptwriter should join the project once you have completed the design plan and have a detailed description of the purpose and content of the script.

Video Production Staff. The video production crew is often assembled and managed (i.e., directed) by either a producer or videographer. The staff can include one or more camera operators, sound-recording specialist, lighting specialist, on- and off-camera talent, editors, video or picture researchers, and a director. For large or high-quality productions, the producer may join the team during the design phase and coordinate the development of the script with the scriptwriter. Other video production personnel are typically hired on an as-needed basis.

Still Photographers. Photographers are used to provide photos for printed materials. Since these individuals are often hired on a contract or hourly basis, you will need to scout for the appropriate shooting location and assemble the needed models and equipment. You can save additional costs by discussing your needs with the photographer (i.e., color versus black and white, pictures of equipment versus people, and indoor versus outdoor shots) so that he or she is properly prepared for the task.

Programmers and Multimedia Designers. We might think of this individual as developing the code for a computer-based or multimedia unit. This programmer takes our script or storyboard (see Gibbons & Fairweather, 1998; Morrison & Ross, 1988) and creates the appropriate materials. Others such as web designers might be hired to create appropriate web-based tools or websites for a project. Last, a design team might need to hire a database programmer to create a database to manage and track enrollment in a course(s). The requirement for each programmer is to carefully define what the programmer is to create.

Network Administrators. Network administrators/specialists are often needed during the development and delivery of a project. They can help identify and plan for servers, computers, and telecommunications. If you are developing a course that will be offered at various sites and that requires computers and/or access to the Internet or company computing resources, the network administrator will need adequate time to plan and install the resources.

Working with an Evaluator

The size and scope of the evaluation and testing activities (see Chapters 10, 11, and 12) determine the need for an evaluator. Projects requiring extensive evaluation

Expert's Edge

Sharing Goes beyond Sharing One's Toys

The ways in which instructional design teams interact in the creation of online learning environments are critical to both the success of the project and the effective delivery of the instruction. Based on our experiences with development teams in higher education, we emphasize the importance of establishing communication, developing relationships, and enabling shared understandings of the strategies and purpose within the project team. In this brief report, we identify the significant factors that impact creating a successful team dynamic, specifically with respect to engaging the subject-matter expert (SME) with the expectations of the instructional development process.

Team Roles

Our work units focus on three discrete subteams within the instructional development cycle—the *development support* team, the *faculty* team, and the *user* team. Each of these has a critical role that can be performed effectively only when the complete team has a shared understanding of its purpose and goals.

Within the development team we identify a major player as the *educational designer* who is responsible for educational advice, curriculum design, and strategic decisions for the instructional design. In addition, this role often encompasses project management and team leadership, even if a tacit implementation. This individual typically coordinates other members of the team, specifically focusing on courseware development and maintaining interaction and rapport with the SME. Other development team members include the *interactive architect*, responsible for ensuring the online interactions and communications are consistent with the design; the *information analyst*, responsible for ensuring all required learning resources and objects are available; and *online developers*, *network specialists*, and *technical specialists* who have responsibility to both advise and be advised on required and/or appropriate learning environments.

The second team is the *faculty* or subject-matter expert, consisting of the academic staff responsible for the content and for defining all learning outcomes, learning activities, and assessment tasks. We contend that it is the relationship with and shared understanding between the development and faculty teams that are critical to the ultimate achievement of project goals—on-target completion of project deliverables and learning outcomes being realized.

The third team essential for our projects is the *user* team, or "try-out" learners, who have a major role in assessing the quality of the design process and communicating their evaluation data back to the development team. When possible, this group should try an initial prototype of a learning episode and provide feedback that can then be incorporated into the design.

It is by developing and building effective communication paths between each of these three groups that a shared understanding of the project goals and learning outcomes can be established. Without this rapport being established, we have found that educational quality and the effectiveness of online teaching and learning environments are compromised.

Building Shared Understanding

In our work environments we have found that identifying clients, providing leadership, and building rapport are essential for developing good working relationships between the SME and the project groups. It is critical to establish who communicates with the SME to elicit the appropriate content within the time frame prescribed by the project plan. While we can establish formal mechanisms, we have found that it is the informal conversation with the SME that elicits clues by which the educational designers and producers can interpret the SME's intentions for the instruction. The trick behind developing this rapport is for the SME to have the confidence that the educational developer and interactive architect are able to translate his or her concept into an effective online environment. This informal but important connection between team members is often fostered through the use of synchronous online technologies such as ICQ, enabling dialog around certain current aspects of courseware development

Maintaining Communication

The process we are implementing to align the development process with the modus operandi of the academic staff is to stagger the creation of online materials over a number of delivery cycles and to work with the faculty and learners (users) during actual course delivery. This process has three discrete phases: first, environments are established to provide fully functional online teaching and learning components; second, feedback from the teacher and learners is used to make modifications to the environment; and third, these environments are monitored and maintained for quality. To maintain the communication it is essential that the teams, as far as possible, remain cohesive for the long term by maintaining the shared understanding and rapport between themselves.

The success of this shared understanding requires all members of the development team to reconceptualize their roles in the design and delivery of online educational resources. For teachers, there is the option to collaborate with an online development expert while delivering the course to implement modifications based on student feedback; for learners, there is the opportunity to contribute to both the content base and the educational strategies. For educational designers and media producers, there is the opportunity to learn more about each other's work.

Deborah Jones is an educational developer within the Teaching and Learning Unit of RMIT Business Online at RMIT University, Australia. In this role, she is responsible for the design, development, and implementation of online, off-campus courses and the communication between academic staff and the educational developers. Her insights into team-based process and collaboration are a result of current work practices within the Teaching and Learning Unit.

Roderick C. Sims, Ph.D., is associate professor and director of the Teaching and Learning Support Unit at Deakin University, Australia. He is responsible for the educational design and quality assurance of online teaching and learning environments as well as the provision of academic professional development for the university faculties. Dr. Sims has over 20 years of experience with instructional design and educational computing, specializing in the learner-computer interface and visual communication.

often require an independent evaluator. Similarly, a designer may wish to include an evaluator in the project if extensive test items, specialized test items, or certification tests are required.

If the services of an evaluator are required, typically it is the designer's responsibility to bring this person into planning meetings at suitable times. The evaluator is responsible for planning the evaluation and developing tests and other measurement instruments. Sometimes an "outside" evaluator (someone who is not part of the program) is employed to conduct summative and confirmative evaluations. To be as objective as possible, such a person should have had no previous contact with the project and may need a limited orientation to the program.

For projects requiring extensive formative evaluation, the evaluator needs access to other SMEs to review the materials for accuracy and members of the target population for field testing. Projects of this size typically include the evaluator during the early stages of the design process so that review and evaluation can begin with the completion of the instructional objectives.

Working with the Performance Consultant

We describe the larger field of performance consulting in Chapter 1. When you identify a problem for which an instructional intervention is not the appropriate solution (see "Performance Assessment" in Chapter 2), you may need to work with a performance consultant or other specialist to develop an appropriate solution. For example, if the problem requires the restructuring of the workstation, you may need to involve a human ergonomics specialist. For problems that require the implementation of incentives or restructuring of the job, you may need to involve a human resources specialist. Solutions for performance problems can involve a number of specialists, ranging from a manager who can coach a peer to an organizational development specialist who can help with conflict management problems.

WORKING WITH THE SUBJECT-MATTER EXPERT

The instructional designer and the SME play the two most critical roles in an instructional design project. The relationship between the two roles varies from complementary and collaborative to adversarial. Disagreements are often centered on content issues, with the SME desiring to include content that the designer perceives as "fluff" or unrelated to the achievement of the objectives. The following section provides eight guidelines for working with SMEs (Morrison, 1987).

1. *Recognize that the SME's main priority is to produce income for the organization, not to develop instructional materials.* A professor's major role in a university is to teach assigned classes, provide service, and conduct research. An SME's role in business is to perform the assigned tasks that contribute to the profits of the company. Thus, the SME may see instructional design as intrusion into his or her work time and productivity. Keeping this perception in mind, you as the designer need to prepare adequately for each meeting with the SME. You should determine the goals for the meeting, prepare for the meeting by checking your understanding of the instructional problem, and gather the necessary materials.

2. *Build rapport and gain the SME's confidence.* For many SMEs, this project may be their first encounter with the instructional design process. Because of the nature of the design process (e.g., task analysis and formative evaluation), the SME will be placed in an unfamiliar role in which his or her knowledge and expertise are revealed and often questioned. You as the designer must develop rapport with the SME and gain the SME's confidence for a successful project. Your background and that of the SME are usually quite diverse, so a common ground of interest (e.g., sailing, woodworking, sports, family) is often needed to establish rapport. Confidence is often built by involving the SME in the design process and recognizing the SME's contributions.

3. *Avoid confusing the SME with instructional design jargon.* Find some common words to use when you need to explain the design process or specific steps. For example, when explaining formative evaluation, simply describe it as a process to test the materials to see whether they work as expected rather than as "a systematic assessment process to ascertain the functionality of separate instructional components."

4. *Do not coerce the SME to follow an ID methodology directly.* An SME is not likely to understand the instructional design process; he or she may even resist following the steps. As a designer, you should attempt to be as flexible as possible to accommodate the SME. For example, if the SME does not want to write objectives, ask him or her to write a single test item that would measure the learning. You can then translate the test item into an objective.

5. *Avoid us–them conflicts with the SME.* As a designer, you may find a situation in which a client or another stakeholder (i.e., someone with an interest in the project) wants to influence an aspect of the project, such as including specific content, and the SME disagrees. Consider having the client or stakeholder attend a meeting with the project team to explain his or her position. Using this approach can keep you from having to explain and defend the stakeholder's interest, thus reducing the chances of placing you

in the middle of an us–them conflict if the members of the project team disagree.

6. *Develop a sense of material ownership in the SME.* An instructional design project is successful only if it is adopted and used by the target audience. A project can be successfully "sold" if the SME feels a sense of ownership in the program and promotes it to his or her superiors, peers, and subordinates. A sense of ownership can be developed in not only the primary SME but in those individuals involved in the initial planning and review processes by encouraging their input and then incorporating the input. For example, you might ask an important individual to provide an example page from a report for use as an illustration.

7. *Recognize that motherhood, apple pie, the flag, and the SME's favorite ideas are sacred cows.* All of us have ideas of what content is needed in a course. These ideas, however, often conflict with the instructional design process that tries to limit the content to *only* the information needed to achieve the objectives. It is highly probable that you will encounter a situation in which the SME insists that certain content be included in a particular project. Attempting to slay this sacred cow is a risky proposition. For example, you might approach the client or a manager for help, only to result in a higher form of blessing on the idea. Allow the SME to slay a sacred cow to maintain rapport and avoid a conflict with the SME, even though this process takes time and some manipulation. Often, the SME will recognize that the content does not fit with the unit and will suggest that it be deleted. Another tactic is to mention that you are approaching the maximum page count (or time limit for film or video) and something must be deleted. *Hopefully,* the SME will delete the unnecessary section.

8. *Approach evaluations and reviews diplomatically.* Evaluating and determining the action needed to deal with reviewers' comments are often difficult tasks, especially for the SME. Most SMEs are not accustomed to having their work reviewed and critiqued by their peers in the manner required by formative evaluation. You need to protect the SME's ego and filter the comments. For example, some reviewers may make comments that directly question the SME's competence. Your responsibility is to determine why the comment was made and then translate it for the SME. Providing the SME with a series of critical rather than constructive comments could damage the working relationship and endanger the success of the project.

SUMMARY

1. The role of the instructional designer varies between consultant and proactive designer and leader. This role is affected by the time frame of the problem, the form of instructional delivery, and the resources available. Economic and time constraints also influence the amount of instructional design a designer can contribute to a project.

2. Each project involves a client who owns the problem, an SME who provides accurate content, and an instructional designer who is responsible for the design of the instruction. At the beginning of each project, a designer must identify the various roles, the number of clients, and other stakeholders so that each of their needs is addressed. Failure to identify these individuals and their needs can result in problems both with project development and implementation.

3. Finally, the designer must establish a good working relationship with SMEs. Three aspects of instructional design—identifying the clients, providing leadership, and building rapport—are essential for the success of the project. A successful designer is a good listener and flexible in his or her approach to instructional design.

THE ID PROCESS

Instructional designers are often the jack-of-all-trades. On a small project, the designer might serve not only as the designer but as the graphic artist, evaluator, programmer, photographer, copy machine operator, and project manager. A designer who has some basic graphic, desktop publishing, and photography skills can easily prepare a printed unit in a timely and cost-effective manner. On the other hand, the different tasks including project management can distract the designer from the more important instructional design tasks. As a designer, you must maintain a balance between your different roles. At times, you will need to make a decision between doing a task yourself (e.g., taking pictures) or hiring a professional to do the task. A more difficult decision is making trade-offs between instructional designer tasks or project management tasks, especially if you are the only instructional designer on the project.

APPLICATIONS

If you have had your car serviced recently or used a service company, you may have received a survey asking for your opinion of the service. Create a similar survey that you could (hypothetically) mail to an SME, evaluator, or other stakeholder to evaluate your instructional design services. The survey should include five to eight items.

At the end of Chapter 1, you created a job description for an instructional designer. Reconsider your job description. How would you revise it now that you have studied most of the elements of the instructional design process and read about the various individuals associated with a project?

ANSWERS

Instructional Design Survey.   Thank you for working with our instructional design staff on a recent project. Would you please take a few minutes to complete the following survey to help us improve our services?

1. The instructional designer was very flexible in his/her approach to the task.
   Strongly Agree   Agree   Neutral   Disagree   Strongly Disagree

2. The instructional designer was open to new ideas and approaches to teaching the content.
   Strongly Agree   Agree   Neutral   Disagree   Strongly Disagree

3. The instructional designer used the feedback from the trials to improve the instructional materials.
   Strongly Agree   Agree   Neutral   Disagree   Strongly Disagree

4. The instructional designer was an effective group leader.
   Strongly Agree   Agree   Neutral   Disagree   Strongly Disagree

5. The instructional designer developed an appropriate time line for the project.
   Strongly Agree   Agree   Neutral   Disagree   Strongly Disagree

6. The instructional designer sought input from all the team members on each aspect of the project.
   Strongly Agree   Agree   Neutral   Disagree   Strongly Disagree

Job Description.   How would you describe the changes to your job description? How has your view of instructional design changed? Is it broader or narrower than your view in Chapter 1? What is the most significant change you made in your job description? Does this change reflect an interest or a different perspective of the instructional design process?

REFERENCES

Foshay, R. (1988). I don't know is on third. *Performance and Instruction, 27,* 8–9.

Gibbons, A. S., & Fairweather, P. G. (1998). *Computer-based instruction: Design and development.* Englewood Cliffs, NJ: Educational Technology Publications.

Morrison, G. R. (1987). Nonviolent instructional development. *Performance and Instruction, 24,* 25–27.

Morrison, G. R. (1988). Who's on first. *Performance and Instruction, 27,* 5–6.

Morrison, G. R., & Ross, S. M. (1988). A four-stage model for planning computer-based instruction. *Journal of Instructional Development, 11*(1), 6–14.

Tessmer, M. (1988). What's on second. *Performance and Instruction, 27,* 6–8.

Planning and Project Management

GETTING STARTED

Your newly created instructional design consulting company has just received a request for a proposal (RFP) from a major manufacturing company to develop training for its designers using a new software product. You have 10 days to prepare a proposal and submit it. What would you include in a proposal that would produce over $1.5 million in revenue for your company and take approximately one year to complete?

QUESTIONS TO CONSIDER

"Where is the instructional design department located within the structure of an organization and how is it financed?"

"Are special facilities required to support the instructional design efforts?"

"What are the legal responsibilities of the instructional designer?"

"How can I evaluate the benefits of the instructional design departments to the organization?"

"How do I prepare a proposal and manage an instructional design project?"

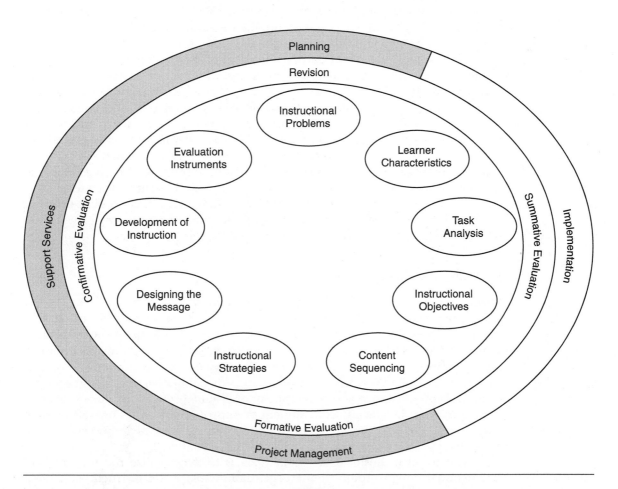

ID IN AN ORGANIZATION

If instructional design activities in an organization are to require more than only casual or single-project attention, then a plan for supporting and managing the group is needed. The structure of an instructional design group or service requires a statement of (1) purpose, (2) the service provided, (3) placement of the program within the organization, (4) staffing and facility requirements, (5) budget required to accomplish the objectives, and (6) operational policies. The manager is also responsible for the continual evaluation to determine the benefits of the effort.

Purposes and Services

The application of instructional design is based on the assumption that productivity and learning are improved through the application of a systematic planning process. It follows that a person who is skilled in applying an instructional design procedure can work with subject-matter experts (SMEs) to design effective instruction. To continue to function as a group, the decision makers in the organization must realize the benefits of the instructional design process.

The group's purpose is partially determined by the function it serves. For example, most instructional design or training groups have a primary mission in the organization. In education, most groups provide a service to faculty members and departments. In business, a design group also offers a service, but the nature of the service can vary. In some organizations, the group provides a service to others based on needs or requests. Such groups are classified as *cost centers*. Other organizations see the group as a *profit center* as the services or courses are sold both inside and outside the company to generate income. Although the purpose of both groups is to improve productivity by improving both instruction and learning, the mission can influence which projects are selected. The group that is viewed as a profit center will most likely take a more entrepreneurial attitude when selecting projects. A group seen as a cost center can use a variety of criteria for selecting projects.

Placement within the Organization

Within a university or college program, instructional design groups benefit from administrative placement as close as possible to the chief academic officer (e.g., academic vice president). Services are readily available to any academic area through simple requests. One popular location for instructional design groups is either in a faculty improvement or development center or in a distance education center. The type of services often vary, with the the distance education designers focusing almost exclusively on the design and development of distance education courses. Instructional designers in a faculty development or improvement center may also design and develop courses, but will be involved in other activities, including evaluation, coaching, workshop planning and delivery, and facilitation.

The trend in business in recent years is to decentralize the training and instructional design groups. Some organizations place the instructional design group or staff in the personnel or human relations department. The mission of this group is often to provide management, secretarial, and new employee training. Instructional design groups providing support for technical or sales training are often placed in the department they are supporting. For example, in an airline company there may be one instructional design group associated with the ground operations and another associated with flight training. In a manufacturing company, the design group may reside in the customer service department or field services department, depending on the clientele served. Similarly, a separate design group might work on only technical training for the sales staff.

In all situations there is a direct working relationship among instructional design, reproduction, and media departments. If a separate testing or evaluation office exists, it should have close ties with instructional design. All these groups should report to the same manager or administrator so that project activities can easily involve each department in a cooperative fashion.

Staffing

The staffing of the department should match the needs of the organization. In some organizations, the manager and secretary may manage the group and perform the required instructional design services. In larger organizations, a distinction is often made between organizational management and project management. Organizational management might include a broader scope of all training functions (e.g., design and delivery) requiring one or more managers, an administrative assistant, one or more secretaries, and a registrar to register and track employees enrolling in courses. The instructional design staff might include a manager and instructional designers. If the mission includes both the design and delivery of instruction, the group might also include instructors and/or SMEs (Figure 14-1).

SMEs are usually not permanently assigned to an instructional design group. Since each project requires its own SME, such individuals are drawn from

FIGURE 14-1
Training department organization

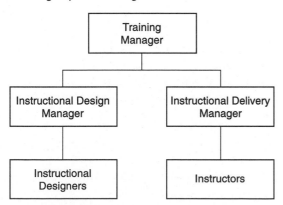

appropriate teaching or operational departments in an organization or institution. The assignment, then, is usually temporary, which can range from full-time to only a small percentage of the SME's time during the life of the project.

The roles of the project manager (often the designer) and the organizational department manager vary from organization to organization. The responsibilities of the project manager often include the following:

- Communicating the purposes of the project to all personnel involved
- Assigning tasks and responsibilities
- Setting schedules and ensuring that deadlines are met for completion of all components
- Arranging for resources as needed (e.g., media, production, evaluation)
- Approving and checking budgetary expenses
- Making certain that ongoing evaluations take place at specified approval points, including completion of instructional design components, resource design, resource completion, formative evaluation, and project completion
- Reporting status of project periodically
- Reporting when program is ready for use
- Reporting program results after implementation
- Serving as primary contact with client, especially if client is in another company

The organizational management functions performed by the group's manager include the following items:

- Normal administrative functions, such as assigning personnel to projects and managing organizational budgets
- Informing superiors of progress of projects and related activities
- Preparing reports
- Anticipating problems and resolving conflicts
- Participating in long-term planning and allocation of resources
- Participating in identifying areas of need

Facilities

Facilities should include offices for the staff and one or more conference-type planning rooms. A conference room should project an informal, congenial atmosphere, with a table for seating at least six people. One wall should contain a large whiteboard for the planning sessions. Provisions are also needed for a projection screen to review materials. Access to flip charts, a video projector, and a laptop computer is valuable for some tasks and meetings.

BUDGETARY SUPPORT

The method of funding and selecting instructional design projects differs between businesses and educational institutions.

Business

An instructional design group's budget in business is usually influenced by its mission (e.g., cost center or profit center). There are four general types of funding. First, the department is given a *fixed budget* either to complete a specific number of projects or to remain operational during the year. Projects are selected based on need, number of individuals impacted, cost, or other benefits.

Second, the group can work on a *direct charge-back system,* in which other departments contract for the work and pay for the instructional design effort out of their budgets. A market economy is used to select the projects, although management may provide additional funding for critical needs.

Third, there is an *indirect charge-back system*, in which the costs of the instructional design department are included in the general overhead costs. Projects are often selected on a similar basis as a department working on a fixed budget.

Fourth, a department with a mission to produce a profit may approach management as any other department and request funds in the terms of a *loan to develop a project*. Management views the instructional project as another product that the company can produce for profit, even though the customers are often members of the same company. With this type of funding approach, projects with the greatest potential to return a profit are most likely to receive funding.

Funding is used in part to pay for the personnel and resources for a project. This funding may include time spent by the instructional designer, the SME, the evaluator, and the support staff. Also, costs are covered for such expenses as those incurred for developing or purchasing materials and equipment, adapting facilities, or meeting overhead charges and other requirements.

Education

There are four ways to provide financial support for instructional design activities in an educational environment. First, money is budgeted for the projects from the institution or organization. Allocations are made to fund personnel time and designate costs for projects that are commissioned, selected through a competition, or requested. Second, an academic department or a division uses its funds to contract for a specific project. Third, an administrator can provide funding to faculty as an incentive to create distance education courses or to develop innovative uses of technology. Fourth, funding from outside the institution is obtained as a grant or contract specifically to support a project. The last two methods usually require the submission of a written proposal that is evaluated according to certain criteria, often in competition with other proposals.

PROPOSAL PREPARATION

For some projects, a client or funding agency may request a proposal or bid. Such a request is often referred to as a *request for proposals,* or RFP. Some agencies (e.g., the National Science Foundation) provide a number of forms and specific instructions on how to prepare and submit the proposal. Internal proposals or proposals prepared for corporate clients may not require a structure. Regardless of the client, a proposal should include the details of the project. A proposal should include six parts.

1. *Statement of purpose.* This section should describe the need or problem the project will address and a statement of goals. It should focus your reader's, the proposal evaluator's, or client's attention on the primary purpose of the proposal. Using signal words such as, "The purpose of this proposal is" or headings such as "Project Purpose" or "Project Goals" helps direct the reader's attention.

2. *Plan of work.* This section might include a brief description of the instructional design process that you will use. The reader is probably unfamiliar with the instructional design process and the terminology, so the section should be written in terms a layperson can understand. Your reader should gain an understanding of what you will do if the project is funded.

3. *Milestones and deliverables.* Milestones are major accomplishments of the project (see "Project Management"). Typical milestones might include the completion of the needs assessment, completion of the design and proto-types, final version of print units, rough edits of videotapes, and comple-tion of the field test. Deliverables are those objects such as unit, videotape, or report that you will give to the client. Again, the design model can help identify the milestones and deliverables.

4. *Budget.* The fourth part of the proposal is the budget, which details all the costs associated with the project. One approach to doing a budget is for the designer to complete a task analysis for each of the milestones to identify the tasks associated with each. Then, the designer must determine the per-sonnel, travel, and other costs associated with each task.

5. *Schedule.* This section includes a time line or schedule describing the work on each milestone. The amount of detail in your schedule will vary depending on the requirements of the client or funding agency. Some pro-posals may only require a schedule for milestones and deliverables while others may only request a date for completion of the total project.

6. *Staffing.* The final section describes the project personnel, perhaps a brief biographical sketch of individuals or a vita or résumé. Often, clients and funding agencies want to know who will work on the project. This section needs to present each staff member in an honest and appropriate manner.

When writing a proposal, the designer should always keep the readers' per-spective in focus and write the proposal for the reader, not for other instructional designers. Many agencies place a page limit on the proposal (e.g., 25 pages of nar-rative). A good proposal is concise and addresses the purpose. An unnecessarily long proposal may bring negative results. The following checklist will help you assess your own proposal:

1. Does the project title describe the purpose and nature of the project?
2. Are the goals or major objectives of the project clearly defined?

Expert's Edge

Damn the Torpedoes . . . the Schedule, Full Speed Ahead

"Once you have the material reformatted and reorganized in a logical sequence, then I will read and approve the course." This was our first meeting with Ted. He was the new project lead manager for our client and had very definite ideas of how training should take place. He did not want the learning strategy or leader's guide format that his predecessor had *approved*.

Changing Project Leads

The productivity workshop that we were designing for Kaptain Kidd Enterprises was the second in a series. The first workshop on time management was well received by the employees, and management saw the positive effect that the workshop had on production. They requested a second workshop and stipulated that it should follow the same format and learning strategy as the first.

We were a week away from our third meeting when one of the team members from Kaptain Kidd mentioned that the project manager for this workshop was being transferred to another location and a new project manager was being assigned.

It was at the third meeting that we met Ted. According to our time line, the third meeting is a paper walkthrough during which the revised course, workbook, and video scripts and/or audio scripts are reviewed to ensure continuity and accuracy in the course. The next phase is producing any video or audio and sending the drafts of the course and workbook to typesetting. Instead, Ted told us that we would receive samples of the new format in the morning. We should revise the course and reformat it accordingly. He did, however, expect that we would meet the deadline for delivery.

Havoc on the Time Line

The difference between the old format and the new format required more than 40 additional hours of work. These changes affected not only the writer, but the video production team, the desktop department, printing, and fulfillment. Video could not begin to shoot until the script was approved. The desktop design department could not produce the galleys for printing. And fulfillment had nothing to ship until all the material was printed. Everything from this point in the time line was delayed, except for the deadline. In addition, there was a four-day holiday in this time frame.

Meeting the Challenge

Everyone on the team worked longer hours and the weekend to shorten the delay time. The video costs were increased because the shoot was postponed. The printing and shipping costs were also higher because of the delay. Despite the time constraints and the cost overruns, the deadline was met.

Future Considerations

The event that led to this time crunch was not completely within our control. Project leads can change in the middle of an assignment and the new project lead may have his or her own standards. What we will do differently in the future is act immediately when we hear of a personnel change. If we had approached the new project lead before the third meeting to learn his expectations on the course, we might have learned about his views on the delivery of training material and his bias toward a certain layout of the material. We had the time *before* the third review, when we were incorporating the changes from the second review. Reworking the material at that time would have saved us the cost and frustration of trying to complete the project on time.

Linda M. Watson is a freelance instructional designer with over 10 years of experience. She has developed a variety of training products for the automotive and retail industries that were delivered as workshops, videotapes, interactive videodiscs, computer-based instruction, web-based instruction, and interactive distance learning.

3. Is the procedure to develop the materials clearly defined?
4. Are the personnel, resources, facilities, and departments required for the project identified?
5. Does the budget clearly describe the costs of personnel, materials, travel, resources design and production, reproduction of print and nonprint materials, evaluation departments, and other departments? These estimates should be based on the work effort required to complete the project.
6. Are the time frame, including completion, evaluation, and reporting points, and other requirements for carrying out the project included?
7. Are the approval and sign-off points by the client identified?
8. Are the actual products, including instructional and learning resources, stated?
9. Is any subcontract work identified and explained?
10. Is the payment schedule described? (Payments are often requested at the completion of planning steps, design of materials, final preparation of materials, formative testing, or final completion.)
11. Are the qualifications of primary project personnel described?
12. Are other important matters (how to proceed with the project; other personnel, resources, or departments you might call on for use, etc.) included in the proposal?

OPERATING POLICIES

Another aspect of managing an instructional design function is the need for general policies.

Sometimes provision for incentives or rewards is advisable or even necessary for the instructors or SMEs who participate in an instructional design project. In a business organization, such inducements may not be of serious concern because employees are rarely free to reject a directive for participating in a project. With success of the project, they may receive a promotion, a raise in salary, or an extra pay incentive ranging from enough money for a nice dinner for two to several thousand dollars. A manager may present a simple plaque or commemorative to recognize cooperative individuals and foster future projects.

In an academic institution, participation is much more voluntary. Therefore, it is advisable to recognize, encourage, and reward participation in acceptable ways. These may include the following:

- Release time to participate in the project as opposed to required overtime for the work
- Extra monetary payment for time devoted to the project (during vacation or summer, or as extra compensation)
- Travel funds
- Funding to purchase equipment such as a laptop computer
- Recognition of success in project work through acclaim by colleagues
- Opportunities to report on project procedures and results through presentations at meetings and acceptance of articles written for professional journals
- Opportunities to follow up with additional projects or other desirable activities
- Recognition of work as support for tenure and/or promotion in professional rank

Royalty Payments for Programs or Materials

Another area for management decision making relates to the ownership of materials and programs developed during a project. In a business, program resources usually remain the company's property. They may even be marketed to other organizations for use in their training programs. Each corporation and institution has a policy on including the names of individuals who developed the materials. Many corporations do not allow the authors and/or instructional designers to include their names in the finished product, whereas others encourage the inclusion.

An academic institution may establish a policy that allows the institution to hold title to all program components of a project it funds. On the other hand, a different policy may allow an agreement to be made between the institution and faculty members to share royalties on the sale of materials. Also, a faculty member can utilize experience gained in developing instructional materials for a project and redesign them completely outside of the institution. The instructor can then contract with a publisher, or other distributor, to handle sales.

If an organization receives money for the sale of materials resulting from instructional design projects, such funds could justifiably be returned to the instructional design office to support further projects. This income could prove to be a sizable amount of money.

LEGAL LIABILITIES IN TRAINING

Consider the following situations:

> "I was not told these chemicals could hurt me."
> "I did not know that operation of this equipment was dangerous."
> "I was not shown how to protect myself while carrying out this procedure."
> "I did not understand what was explained about safe practices during training."
> "It became stressful when I was not able to do the job properly."

Each of the preceding situations could lead to a legal claim that training was inadequate. The individuals designing the training or the instructor might be held liable for not developing or delivering competent training. Therefore, anyone involved in instructional design work should be aware of regulations and statutes that can affect instructional requirements.

State and Federal Mandates

It is important to become familiar with legislative enactments, judicial precedents, and local administrative regulations that can impact education or training. For example, some major federal statutes to examine include the following:

- Occupational Safety and Health Act (OSHA)
- Equal Employment Opportunity Commission (EEOC)
- Americans with Disabilities Act (ADA)
- Environmental Resources Act (ERA)
- Toxic Substance Control Act (TSCA)

In addition, other governmental agencies regulate work in different environments.
While some statutory provisions may specify topics or actions that require attention in training, planning, and implementation methods, others are left to local decision makers. You can ensure compliance by consulting with appropriate SMEs and the legal department and by keeping records of all evaluations that require students to demonstrate achievement of the objectives.

Contracts

Occasionally, a need arises when some or all of the instructional design effort is contracted with outside consultants or vendors. Several situations could prompt such a need:

- Resources (e.g., time, money, or personnel) are not available to complete the project.
- Current staff lack the necessary skills required for the project (e.g., producing a multimedia application, duplicating a videotape for foreign distribution, or translating materials to a foreign language).

- A consultant is needed to fill a particular instructional design role—assessing needs, advising on instructional procedures, SME, or evaluating a completed project.

A project director is required to draw up a proper legal contract when hiring a subcontractor to perform a task. You should check with the organization's legal department and personnel department for specific guidelines and policies before you make the initial contact with any contractor. Any contract or letter of agreement should be either initiated or approved by the legal department.

Common Legal Problems in Training

Eyres (1998) has identified 10 different legal problems that affect those in the training field. The following paragraphs provide a brief description of these problems.

Failure to Perform Training.   Some industries are mandated by the federal government to train employees in specific areas. For example, the oil industry must provide training on hydrogen sulfide and carbon dioxide for employees who work in areas where those hazards are present. Companies that accept packages for shipping via air must train employees in the acceptance and rejection of hazardous goods. An employee can sue a company that fails to provide this training. A broader issue is that of providing a discrimination-free work environment. According to Eyres (1998), employers have an obligation to train employees on what constitutes unacceptable behaviors.

Emotional Trauma or Physical Injury from Training.   Nontraditional training programs (e.g., new age) that challenge an individual's comfort zone have provided the basis for legal action against the facilitators and company. Programs that include physical or wilderness activities have resulted in lawsuits from physical injury as well as charges of discrimination against disabled employees.

Intellectual Property Infringement.   It seems that at least once per week, we find one or two cartoons that would be great icebreakers for meetings, lectures, or even as additions to this book. Cartoons, quotes, exercises, and ideas conceived and developed by others have intellectual property right values that are protected by law. Scanning a cartoon from the morning paper to include in your PowerPoint presentation may be a violation of the artist's intellectual property rights and probably of the copyright laws. Similarly, using an exercise that you have observed another person present at a workshop could also leave you liable. If you want to use ideas or materials developed by another individual, you need to obtain that person's permission or even pay a fee.

Content Is Discriminatory.   Most professionals would agree that one could be liable for including discriminatory (e.g., racial, ethnic, or sex-biased) materials in a training program. Eyres (1998) indicates that an activity designed to improve diversity could be used as evidence of discriminatory practices. For example, having supervisors list examples of statements that are discriminatory could be used as evidence against the company at a later time.

Injury Due to Human Error.   A mandate to provide training can lead to legal action if the *appropriate* and *safe* training is not provided. Individuals conducting the training must have adequate training and preparation. When the training involves the use of actual equipment, appropriate precautions must be taken to provide a safe environment for the trainee and trainer.

Access to Training.   Employees must have equal access to training within a company. Screening methods must be applied equally to all groups and be nondiscriminatory.

Testing and Evaluation.   Conducting criterion- or performance-based tests at the end of the training must not discriminate against any group of individuals. Any testing must be related to essential job tasks (see the Expert's Edge in Chapter 11).

Failure to Perform.   Individual consultants and companies that provide instructional design and training services to other companies typically do so under a contract for the service. Failure to perform as defined in the contract can lead to legal action. For example, a client may take legal action if you have delayed the delivery of a training product. Such actions are often avoided by keeping the client informed of your progress and any problems encountered. Another basis for legal action occurs when qualifications are overstated for a member of the project. For example, the qualifications of a consultant you plan to hire as the SME might be misleading (e.g., suggesting the individual has a doctorate in the field when she has only a master's degree) and could result in legal action.

Inadequate Documentation.   Many federal agencies require companies to maintain records of when employees are trained. Failure to maintain these records could result in fines or legal action in the case of an accident.

Unlawful Conduct.   If you are confronted with a situation that requires you to make an ethical judgment, you are expected to make an appropriate decision that considers both legal and ethical issues. These issues might include protecting intellectual property, client confidence, as well as your own professional integrity. In some cases, you may decide to you need to report illegal actions to the appropriate authorities. Eyres (1998) states that it is good judgment to avoid participating in illegal activities.

REPORTING ON SERVICES

Any new endeavor like an instructional design group must be accountable for proving its value within an institution or organization. Therefore, careful and detailed records should be kept on planning, progress, personnel time required, and costs incurred. Reports should indicate not only the number of courses developed, number of students served, and related statistical data but also benefits of the department to the organization. Recall the statement near the beginning of this chapter about the importance of the decision makers' understanding of the value of the department. The reporting process can aid the understanding and justification of the group.

Reported benefits should specify the contributions that successful projects make to increasing the organizational effectiveness, efficiency, and productivity, as well as the resulting cost benefits. (See Chapter 12 for how these outcomes are determined.)

Keeping people in the institution or organization informed about instructional design activities, progress, and successes is often essential for continued support and requested increases in personnel and funding for projects. You may find that weekly, biweekly, monthly, or quarterly status reports are helpful for keeping others informed. Projects funded by agencies such as the NSF often prepare newsletters or web pages to inform others of their progress.

In addition to separate reports on individual projects and annual reports of all yearly activities, consider a cumulative report for a longer period, perhaps five years. This report can illustrate the ongoing, overall benefits to an organization that supports strong instructional design departments.

Progress reports on an instructional design project can take two approaches. One approach is to detail the completion of each step in the instructional design process. A second, more desirable approach is to follow a product-based reporting process. Rather than reporting the completion of each step, develop a report for each milestone in the instructional design process. For example, a project might submit the first report (product) when the problem is identified or the goals are established. The report would describe the problems and/or goals. The second product might be a listing of the objectives developed after the task analysis. A third product is the design plan, which describes the instructional strategies and delivery plans. A fourth product is the results of the formative evaluation and field test. The last report would include the final product. It might summarize the accomplishments of the milestones and critique the instructional design and project management processes, with recommendations for future projects. A product-reporting approach gives managers or administrators solid evidence of the project's progress. The next section on project management describes how you can integrate your reporting with the project management process.

PROJECT MANAGEMENT

In the previous sections of this chapter, we address some of the issues with managing an instructional design group or department. In this section, our focus is on how to manage a specific instructional design project. Instructional design projects vary in complexity from creating a simple job aid for making internal, local, and long-distance calls to the development of a major course such as a semester-long college chemistry course delivered as a distance education course or 100 web-based units on computer product design for your company's designers. Similarly, you might work on the development of a course for network technicians that includes modules on cabling, network design, controllers, modems, and so forth. A project or course that involves the design, development, and production of 15 or 100 different modules presents a unique problem—how does an instructional designer manage the process? We have divided the project management process into two major parts. First is the planning aspect, and second is management of the product.

Project Planning

The planning of an instructional design project requires a scope of work, scheduling, and budgeting. These three tasks are often done for proposals as well as for projects.

Scope of Work.   The scope of work provides a definition of the boundaries of the project. This definition is used to gain a consensus among all the stakeholders as to the purpose of the project, why it is done, and the expected outcomes or products (Duncan, 1996). The project's scope may need to be modified during the life of the project to reflect changes.

Scheduling.   Developing a schedule for the design of a single unit is rather straightforward; however, developing a schedule for several units for a specific project becomes a complex task in logistics. The project manager must determine who is available when, what must be done first, and how to make efficient use of employees' time.

Scheduling is dependent on identifying the tasks needed to complete the project. Identifying these tasks is accomplished by applying your task analysis skills to the instructional design process. There are two types of tasks. *Fixed-duration tasks* take a set amount of time. For example, viewing a 30-minute videotape will take 30 minutes. The time required to complete the task is a function of the nature of the task. Other tasks that have a variable duration are referred to as *resource-driven tasks* (Stevenson & Marmel, 1997). You can change the amount of time it takes to complete a resource-driven task by adding more resources. For example, it might take a graphic artist four days to complete 16 drawings, but we can complete the 16 drawings in one day by using four graphic artists. It still takes a total of four days of effort; it just happens that all four days of effort happen on the same day, and that shortens the time line.

A key term in scheduling is the *critical path*. The critical path is the series of tasks you must complete to keep a project on time. For example, if you are wallpapering your kitchen, you must first remove the old wallpaper *before* you can apply the new wallpaper. The critical path would include removing the old wallpaper and installing the new wallpaper. Returning the wallpaper-removal equipment is not critical to finishing the project on time.

Some tasks can be completed at various times before they cause a delay in the project. Selecting and purchasing the wallpaper can be done almost any time prior to the removal of the last strip of old paper. Selecting and purchasing the new

Expert's Edge

The Recipe for Success Requires the Right Mix

Managing an instructional design project in the context of higher education has become a new challenge, with new technologies and new paradigms converging and conflicting with established practice and interactive learning literacy. Within our unit at Deakin University, specifically where projects integrate online learning environments, we are developing a different approach to the management of instructional design projects by focusing on the long-term delivery of those environments and the dynamic nature of the educational content. This management approach integrates the essential features of instructional design while catering to the unique elements of online access (interactivity, collaboration, communication) and off-campus delivery (access, convenience, service) as well as the associated professional development and support (scaffolding) in online teaching and learning strategies for the academic staff. This brief synopsis highlights what we consider to be the six essential success factors for the management of our instructional design projects.

The first and most critical aspect of managing our instructional design projects is to ensure that we have established effective *liaison* with the "client," usually the course or program chair, who has overall responsibility for the effective delivery of the course of study. Until recently, it was assumed that our clients' familiarity with both educational design and online learning was sufficient to enable translation (instructional design) of the content material to the interactive medium without requiring additional professional development. What we have discovered, however, is that familiarity with these concepts is varied and that often extensive professional development is required to maximize the effectiveness of any instructional design and development projects. This situation is also consistent with evidence from other training and learning contexts that have manifested limited levels of competency in utilizing the online milieu effectively. In our situation, when professional development needs were identified, it was often during the development process, with the consequence that the output of content into the online environment became little more than a digitization process. Our revised approach, working closely with senior faculty, is to establish the necessary communication and understanding between client and designer and to delay formal instructional design work on the project until any necessary professional development and training have been completed.

The second factor relevant to the effective management of instructional design is to work with the client to confirm the project *scope* and the subsequent project specifications. In our context, the scope refers to the overall requirements for the project that focus on the educational rationale (what is going to be achieved by undertaking the work), the project deliverables (what we as a development team will produce for the client), the project responsibilities (the people who have been nominated to undertake specific tasks), the project plan (estimating when essential tasks will be completed), and the project resources (the people, equipment, and funds necessary to create the deliverables by a target date). While this model is consistent with accepted commercial practice, our experience has been that projects too often follow their own paths, becoming unwieldy, rather than conforming to an articulated plan. Once both the client and our development group have accepted and agreed to the project scope, more detailed specifications are generated. It is also important to note that this process assumes that the client is responsible for the provision of content and the statement of learning objectives, with strategies for teaching and learning being developed in consultation with educational designers from our development group.

Before embarking on the project, the third critical element for the manager is to ensure that the development team has the appropriate *skill mix*. Prior to the growth of online environments for off-campus delivery, our main mode of media production was print-based study guides and readers that were developed using a specific sequential process and clearly articulated roles. This linear process, however, is not suitable for online environments, and we are now emphasizing what skills are required to complete the instructional design project and the roles different people play in that process. The critical roles for the successful design and implementation of online resources include the educational designer, the teaching and learning innovator, and the visual/interactive designer. Rather than operating with a mind-set that we are creating text online, we must focus on providing engaging communication between learner and material presented. This requires project roles in which individuals can take on a wide range of skills relevant to the project—creating online material, integrating appropriate graphical or interactive objects, applying educational design to the course structure, and undertaking operational effectiveness (quality assurance) checks.

This last role highlights the fourth success factor that must be included in our instructional design projects—*quality assurance*, which takes a number of different forms. In the first instance, quality checks are established to ensure the overall design is consistent with the original plan and, where necessary, to correct different design components such as screen layout or graphics. This process also provides feedback to team members who have expressed a need to better understand the impact of their work on the overall design effort. Subsequent quality checks are undertaken by independent experts to provide feedback to the team and the client on the overall impact of the product and any potential delivery issues. Through an iterative sequence of successive approximations, the instructional design effort is monitored for quality and educational effectiveness.

The fifth factor is to ensure that the *time lines* and *milestones* that are prescribed for the project are closely monitored and corrected to meet the objectives of the project. While this is clearly a standard component of any instructional development project, a major issue that we face is that traditional development has focused on completing the instructional design activities prior to delivery. Typically, this has been undertaken on a semester basis, with development in semester 1 for delivery in semester 2. However, this does not provide adequate time to ensure the ongoing effectiveness of teaching and learning resources in the context of higher education, and we are now conceptualizing the project as extending over a sequence four or five delivery cycles, with each cycle implementing changes based on information from evaluation of the prior delivery cycle. The significant difference with this approach is that projects are conceptually always "under construction." This links to and highlights the sixth and final success factor, the ongoing *maintenance* of resources. Until recently, we had undertaken projects on a year-by-year basis and are now establishing a process by which a single project is scoped for development work over a number of years. Our projects are therefore conceptualized as the development of a series of resources that will be subject to ongoing change as a result of course evaluation and disciplinary developments. Moving from a mind-set that focuses on completion of these resources (and therefore the end of the project) to one in which resources will (theoretically) never be "complete" requires a new approach to the management of instructional design projects.

These success factors are critical in our current environment because we are moving rapidly to new ways of designing and delivering teaching and learning environments. Unless we change the way our clients think and our developers undertake projects, we will not be aligned to the appropriate methods for effective instructional design in the context of online teaching and learning in higher education.

Roderick C. Sims., Ph.D., is associate professor and director of the Teaching and Learning Support Unit at Deakin University, Australia. He is responsible for the educational design and quality assurance of online teaching and learning environments as well as the provision of academic professional development for the university faculties. Dr. Sims has over 20 years of experience with instructional design and educational computing, specializing in the learner-computer interface and visual communication.

wallpaper has *slack* time. That is, there is a time period for completing the task *before* it becomes part of the critical path. Thus, if we wait until after we have removed the old wallpaper to buy the new, then the selection and purchasing task becomes part of the critical path. Some tasks are also *dependent* on other tasks. Applying the new wallpaper is dependent on removing the old wallpaper and purchasing the new wallpaper. But removing the old paper and buying the new paper are not dependent on each other.

Milestones are the completion of major accomplishments in a project. A milestone is actually a point in time. For example, one of our milestones is the purchase of the new wallpaper, a second is when the old wallpaper is removed, and a third is when the new wallpaper is applied. Each of these milestones indicates the completion of a phase or major task, not the time needed to complete the phase or task. In a design project, milestones might be the completion of the task analysis, learner analysis, statement of objectives, strategy design, approval of the design document, and first draft of the instruction.

Often, there is a product associated with a milestone. These products are *deliverables*. A deliverable is a tangible item that you can give to a manager or client. The item might be a prototype of a screen design for a web page or a report, such as the results and recommendations of the formative evaluation.

The scheduling process involves translating planned activities into the various tasks; determining the dependent tasks, milestones, deliverables; and then identifying the most efficient path for completing the project.

Budgeting.   Some projects require a budget, some projects only require that you track costs so they can be charged back, and others do not budget or track the costs. Once you have identified the tasks and their durations, you can determine how much effort is needed by the different team members and what resources are needed to complete the task. Resources can include offices, labs, video studios, videotape cassettes, computers, clerical support, SME consultants, and financial support. Assigning a dollar value to the effort and resources produces a budget. Businesses often have a daily consulting rate for employees that includes overhead costs (e.g., insurance, vacation, retirement), or the calculations are based on the annual salary and the organization's indirect cost rate that covers telephone, office space, and employee benefits.

Management Activities

The initial scheduling and budgeting are completed prior to the beginning of the project. Once the project is under way, the project manager is responsible for managing, tracking, and reporting the progress. Management involves coordinating the work of others, hiring consultants, facilitating the work, and managing the resources.

Managing Resources.   The project manager is responsible for ensuring that adequate resources (human, material, and financial) are available to complete the tasks. A project manager must determine when the video production crew is needed and have it arrive at the appropriate time rather than a week early or a week late. When a project falls behind, the project manager may need to add additional resources to resource-driven tasks. For example, additional graphic artists could be hired to finish the graphic work, or additional programmers could be added to complete a multimedia project. Similarly, the project manager may ask the team to work six days a week or longer hours to complete the project on time.

Tracking.   During the life of a project, tracking the completion of tasks and the budget are essential for completing the project on time and within budget. A project manager will need to establish processes and procedures (e.g., weekly status reports) for collecting information from the various team members to track the project. Similarly, weekly or scheduled team meetings are used to identify problems and successes so that personnel can be shifted to keep the project on schedule.

Project Reporting.   A project manager has the responsibility to keep management and the client informed of the project's progress. The type of reporting is dependent on not only the length and complexity of the project, but on what information management and the client want. Some organizations may want a weekly or monthly report, whereas the client may only want a final report. A project manager needs to determine the type of reporting at the beginning of the project and be willing to make changes as the project progresses. If management and the client do not want reports, we have always found it wise to maintain our own file of reports in case someone asks a question about the project. Similarly, it is always useful to keep phone logs with the client and to document changes to the project.

Starting the Project

Successful projects typically start with a project launch meeting that includes all the stakeholders and key team members. The project manager and team members can explain the project, the milestones, and deliverables to clarify any misconceptions. This meeting provides a means for the team to develop rapport with the stakeholders and to explain the instructional design process. It also provides the client with a forum to ask for explanations and to clarify their expectations.

Managing the Project

Planning and managing a project may seem like an overwhelming task. The project management responsibilities often conflict with the instructional design responsibilities, leaving instructional designers in the position of determining which task to neglect to cause least negative impact on the project. Project management software is a valuable tool that can help the instructional designer manage a project. These software tools can streamline the scheduling, budgeting, tracking, and reporting processes.

SUMMARY

1. The first step in establishing an instructional development service within an organization is to recognize that systematic planning can make an important contribution to education or training.
2. The service should be directly responsible to either the chief academic officer or the director of training.
3. There are practical reasons why design services outside the organization might be utilized.
4. Staffing considerations should cover both administration and management of the services and management of projects with facilities and budgetary support provided.
5. Establish a format and procedure for preparing proposals to be considered for outside support.

6. Decide on operating policies for managing projects and recognizing professional work with royalty payments.
7. Be alert to legal liabilities and responsibilities relating to instructional program design and implementation.
8. Develop a project management plan for a project and determine who is responsible for managing the project.
9. Keep persons within the organization informed by reporting progress and results in writing.

THE ID PROCESS

The placement in an organization and the department funding process impacts the success and life of an instructional design group or function. A design group placed in the human relations department may have a different function, role, and impact on the organization than a group placed in a profit center, such as customer or warranty service. Similarly, a group whose charges and expenses are considered part of company or organizational overhead may select projects differently than a group that is considered a profit center and that must obtain funding for all projects. When you interview for a position, determine where the group is placed in the organization and how it is funded.

The way a group is funded and operates can also impact your approach to instructional design. A group that works on large projects or with funding from outside sources may require a greater emphasis on project management. Often, the project management responsibilities may conflict with the instructional design requirements, especially if you are the single instructional designer on a project and the project manager. Similarly, a consulting group or a group that must obtain funding for all projects will help you sharpen your proposal development skills.

APPLICATIONS

Your organization has just received a request for a proposal (you are the sole source/bidder) to develop a basic store manager course for a new drugstore chain. The course can include no more than 40 hours of classroom instruction. The drugstore company will provide the instructors who will use the materials you have developed. The proposal has suggested that the instructional design company hire a number of SMEs with expertise in store management, pharmacy management, human resource development, and security. The company will provide you with access to six of its successful store managers during the proposal development. You will receive compensation (up to $10,000) only for the proposal and work associated with it if you are funded.

What personnel will you involve from your organization and how will you proceed?

ANSWERS

First, we would interview the six store managers to determine the scope of their work and responsibilities. This information would be used to define the scope of work. Second, we would identify a potential SME to define the initial goals for the course. Third, we would develop the project management plan to use as a resource to create the budget and schedule.

Individuals involved from our staff would be one or more instructional designers, an evaluator, support for developing the budget, and clerical support. Since we are hiring an outside consultant, we will need to use an existing contract or ask a company lawyer to prepare a contract.

REFERENCES

Duncan, W. R. (1996). *A guide to the project management body of knowledge.* Newtown Square, PA: Project Management Institute.

Eyres, P. S. (1998). *The legal handbook of trainers, speakers, consultants: The essential guide to keeping your company and clients out of court.* New York: McGraw-Hill.

Stevenson, N., & Marmel, E. (1997). *Microsoft Project 98 bible.* Foster City, CA: IDG Books Worldwide.

CHAPTER 15

Planning for Instructional Implementation

GETTING STARTED

Your needs assessment of the network-engineering group found that it often selected a backup generator for clients that was much too large and costly. As a result, your company was losing a fair number of contracts because of the price. The analysis indicated that the network engineers had very little knowledge of how to develop the specifications for a backup generator and tended to rely on the generator sales representative for the design and specifications. As a result, you worked with two senior engineers who are highly respected in the company to design a course on how to prepare the specifications for backup electrical generators. Your pilot test results suggest the course is very effective—engineers completing the course were capable of developing specifications for a backup generator that were appropriate for the installation. The problem, however, is that some of the 14 division managers do not believe their engineers need this type of training. "Any good network engineer should know how to develop the specifications for a generator, and all my engineers are good" is a common response from the managers. Of course, the data from your needs assessment suggest a different conclusion. How will you convince these managers to send their employees to this course?

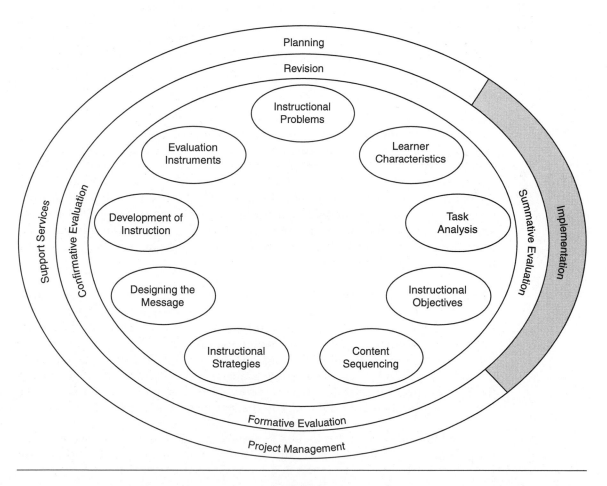

PLANNED CHANGE

It would seem that if we have created the instruction necessary to solve a problem that would increase productivity, we could simply enroll students in the course or observe people accessing our web-based instruction. The managers, instructors, and learners would see the advantage of learning the information and readily embrace the instruction. Sometimes, training programs, multimedia, web-based instruction, and print units are readily adopted by our target audience. There are other times when we have to sell the clients on our product. That is, we try to change their ideas so they will use the product. When working within a company, university, or school to implement an instructional product, the designer's effort is often focused on working with the individual in a collaborative manner. Bhola (1982) labels this process as *planned change*.

Selling is an aspect of the processes referred to as *diffusion* and *adoption*. Diffusion is the process of communicating information to a client and target audience about an innovation (i.e., an instructional intervention) (Rogers, 1995). Adoption is the decision to use the innovation. According to Rogers, there are four components of the diffusion process—the innovation, communication, time, and the social system. The following paragraphs describe each of these components.

Innovation

An *innovation* is something new to an organization, manager, worker, teacher, or student who is considering using it. For example, a recent radio advertisement made an offer to the "last person on earth" who does not have caller ID. To those of us who have had caller ID for several years, it is an old idea; however, to the household that does not have caller ID, it is still an innovation. When we produce an instructional intervention, it is an innovation for our users. If you were to develop a course on conflict management, upgrading the computer in a copy machine, or how to use a spreadsheet for sales forecasting, then the course would be an innovation. If and when the client or users decide to use the product is dependent on five characteristics of the intervention (Rogers, 1995).

The Advantage of the Innovation.   Each training product is judged on its relative merit. If the users perceive it as providing useful knowledge, then they are more likely to adopt it. Although the training program might have many advantages and make an employee more productive, leading to monetary or efficiency rewards, the user has to perceive it as being advantageous. For example, providing sales personnel with laptops and access to company databases while on the road has the potential for making the sales force more productive. Computer-naïve salespeople, however, might not see the advantage to the laptops and may resist using them.

Compatibility with Values, Needs, and Experiences.   Our users will evaluate a training program or instructional innovation to determine whether it is compatible with their values, matches their needs, and is compatible with what they have learned in the past. For example, in recent years there has been a push for professors and teachers to adopt a more student-centered approach to their teaching. This approach requires the professor or teacher to change roles from that of a lecturer to one of a facilitator. Some may perceive this role shift as incompatible with their values—teachers need to lecture to teach the student.

Innovation Complexity.   If the users perceive the innovation as complex or difficult to use, they are more likely to resist using it. This perception of complexity can become a major obstacle to adoption of the innovation. Consider the difficulty you might face implementing web-based instruction for instructors who have limited experience with the Internet. If the software required them to create pages using Hypertext Markup Language (HTML), participate in online chats, and create PowerPoint presentations with streaming audio, they would probably view this innovation as too complex to adopt. Similarly, consider the problems you might have implementing a maintenance and work order computer application in an organization in which most users have minimal, if any, computer skills. The complexity of such a system could cause resistance to adoption by the users.

Ability to Try the Innovation.   Users often like to try an innovation on a small scale first. For example, a company introduces a new course for accountants on how to use an innovative software package for auditing clients' books. Some divisions in the organization might resist sending all of their accountants to the training during the first offerings. Allowing a division to send one or two employees to the training allows them to sample or try it on a small scale and then determine whether they want to adopt it for everyone. Similarly, a school district might identify a need to use a wireless network in the schools where the students all have laptop computers. Rather than purchasing equipment for all the schools, the network administrator might install it in one or two classrooms to determine whether it will meet their needs. If it works, then they may make the decision to install it in all the schools.

Observability of Results.   A training program is more likely to be adopted when the users can easily see the benefits. For example, if the managers and other accountants can see a benefit of the training for the new auditing software, they are more likely to send others to the training. However, if an accountant returns from the training and either refuses to use or seldom uses the new software, others will not see the benefits and may not attend the training. Also, if a critical mass of users is not trained, the training may become a wasted resource because those using the software will not have the support of management or other employees.

　　As we plan an implementation strategy for a new instructional product, we must consider how to communicate the advantage of the product, its compatibility with existing ways, how the user can try it out with minimal risk, and how to make the results observable. We also must show that it is not a complex process.

Communication

Communication is central to the diffusion process. We have to communicate information about the innovation to our potential users so they can make a decision to use it. Although the instructional designer can prepare materials such as informative memos and presentations, the designer might not be the best individual to communicate the information or "advertise" the course. The most effective communication occurs between individuals who are similar, such as those belonging to the same peer group or having similar interests (Rogers, 1995). A designer needs to consider who could best communicate information on a new course for plant electricians. Is it the instructional designer, or is it the master electrician who served as the SME for the project? The master electrician is a member of the group of electricians and probably has more in common with group members than the instructional designer. Selecting the master electrician to sell the course may be more productive than having the instructional designer sell it, since the electrician has more in common with the target group.

Time

Users make decisions to adopt an innovation at different times in the life of the innovation. You are probably familiar with an individual who is the first to have the latest computer, television, or electronic gadget, and, on the other hand, the individual who still has a 13-inch black-and-white television. Rogers (1995) classifies these adopters into five categories. The "first adopters" are the innovators who rush out to adopt innovations as soon as possible. Sometimes these early adopters are willing to accept prototypes or test versions of a product. The "early adopters" are the second group to adopt the innovation, often as soon as it is available in "commercial" form. The "early majority adopters" are the third group and comprise the first 50 percent to adopt the innovation. Fourth are the "late majority adopters" who adopt after it appears safe. The final group is the "laggards" who are the last to adopt an innovation or perhaps never adopt it.

The actual time frame for adoption varies depending on the nature of the instructional product. It is conceivable that the adoption cycle could be a week or less for a small project and upward of a year or more for a complex project.

Social System

The social system describes the networks and relationships between the members of our target audience. Decisions to adopt a training program or instruction are typically influenced by the opinion leaders' views about the consequences of adopting the program. Identifying the opinion leaders and other stakeholders early in the implementation-planning process will identify one group to target with communications. At the same time, we must identify the various networks in the social system that can help us communicate information about the instructional intervention. These networks of people, however, may also resist the adoption process.

Understanding the role of the innovation, communication, time, and the social system can help us develop a plan for implementing our product. In the next section, we examine how to use this information to develop an implementation plan.

THE CLER MODEL

The implementation strategy is a means of specifying to whom and how to communicate information about an instructional product. One strategy for preparing an implementation plan is Bhola's (1982, 1988–1989) CLER model. *CLER* is an acronym for configuration, linkages, environment, and resources, components that are used to facilitate the diffusion and adoption processes to implement an innovation.

So, the CLER model, or the configurational theory of innovation diffusion, defines diffusion of an innovation D_i, or implementation, as a function of social (C) configurations, (L) linkages between the designer system and client system, (E) the surrounding environment, and (R) resources available to the designer and the client:

$$D_i = f(C, L, E, R)$$

The following paragraphs further explain each component of the CLER model.

Configuration

Configuration represents the network of relationships of various social units in the organization and the individuals who play a variety of formal and informal roles in the "in" group. These relationships include the designer system and the client system. The designer system includes the instructional designer, the evaluator, and the manager of the instructional design department. The client system includes the target audience as well as the managers and other stakeholders. Identifying these configurational relationships and the roles of the various individuals helps us to develop a communication plan for implementation strategy.

There are four types of configurational relationships—individuals, groups, institutions, and cultures. *Groups* are formal workgroups within an organization such as the accounting department or the electricians. *Institutions* are the formal organizations such as businesses or schools. *Culture* describes subcultures or communities. For example, there may be several accounting, marketing, finance, and engineering groups in a business (i.e., institution). One group might include individuals from engineering, finance, and marketing. Engineers from all these various groups also belong to an engineering subculture that is open only to engineers.

When preparing an implementation plan, the configuration describes both the instructional designer (e.g., innovator) and the client or adopters. Using the four types of configurations, Bhola (1982) identified 16 possible relationships (Table 15-1).

Table 15-1 lists the various configurational relationships for interactions between the instructional designer and the client. For example, the instructional designer could act as an individual on the various client relationships. Similarly, the instructional design group or department could act on the various client configurations. While Bhola (1982) identifies 16 possible configurations, the most effective are those that are one on one. Although you might identify several different relationships such as managers "in" with the accounting managers (a group), the most effective way to communicate information about your instructional product would be by having your manager talk individually to each of the accounting managers.

TABLE 15-1
Configurational relationships

Instructional Designer	Client			
	Individuals (I)	Groups (G)	Institutions (IS)	Cultures (CL)
Individuals (I)	I–I	I–G	I–IS	I–CL
Groups (G)	G–I	G–G	G–IS	G–CL
Institutions (IS)	IS–I	IS–G	IS–IS	IS–CL
Cultures (CL)	CL–I	CL–G	CL–IS	CL–CL

Linkages

Linkages represent networks or relationships between and within the instructional designer and client organizations. Formal linkages exist within the context of the group and institutional configurations as defined by the management structure. Informal linkages result from partnerships, friendships, and working relationships. These informal relationships often bypass traditional organizational structure. For example, consider a friendship between a vice president and a salesperson who happen to have children who take gymnastic lessons from the same coach. Although they both work for the same organization, the friendship is informal rather than formal. Identifying these different linkages can provide a rich source of communication links for the implementation plan.

Environment

The *environment* represents the physical, social, and intellectual forces operating within a configuration. Environmental forces can provide a supportive, neutral, or inhibiting atmosphere for adopting an innovation. Consider, for example, a school that wants to provide students with their own laptop computers they can use in each classroom. A new school could create a supportive environment by providing training and readily available technical support for the teachers. An older school might have a more difficult time due to the physical environment. For example, the lack of electrical outlets placed around the room could make it difficult to charge the batteries during class. Similarly, the desks or tables may not be ergnomically correct or of the right size to hold the laptops. These environmental variables could hinder the adoption.

Resources

Resources are used to support the implementation process. There are six types of resources an instructional designer can use to support the implementation of a project (Bhola, 1982).

Conceptual Resources.   Technical skills and support are one type of *conceptual resource* that is often needed for implementing projects involving the use of technology. Consider the technical support needed to offer a database administrator course at a hotel. The course needs computers, software, and access to the company's intranet. Successful implementation of this course requires the needed networking and technical expertise from a variety of individuals. Other conceptual resources include management abilities and planning assistance.

Influence Resources.   Goodwill, brand names, incentives, shaming, and threatening are examples of *influence resources* one can use in the diffusion of an innovation. An instructional designer who has developed goodwill during the development phase will have a resource to act on with the client. Other types of influence resources include incentives such as bonuses or monetary incentives, faculty release time from teaching a course, and travel benefits. Negative influence resources could include the withholding of monetary or promotional incentives.

Material Resources.   Financial backing is one type of resource that is often needed to implement a product. Other material resources could include computers, software, books, televisions and VCRs, video projectors, and physical facilities that can facilitate the implementation.

Personnel Resources.   Depending on the size of the project, worker resources can be a critical issue during the implementation phase. Having a number of individuals who can be available at the right time to provide essential training or facilitation is essential if the product implementation is needed in a short time frame.

Institutional Resources.   The infrastructure provided by the institution including both the technology/communication and personnel infrastructure is considered an *institutional resource*. Other resources can include institutional capabilities, such as printing and shipping instructional materials. For web-based instruction, a server either on the Internet or intranet is considered an institutional resource necessary for implementation. Consider again the introduction of laptop computers. A new school could provide tables for using the laptops that have built-in electrical outlets

$\left(\text{Expert's Edge}\right)$

Never Put the Cart after the Horse

Traditional instructional design models tend to treat implementation as a phase, like design or development. As a phase, it's something you start when the preceding phase is done. I'm overstating the case, but that's the essential logic of phased approaches: first, we analyze; next, we design; and then we develop. And when the product is ready to go, we implement.

One important consequence of this approach is that there are lots of implementation horror stories. A session at an AECT (Association for Educational Communications and Technology) conference a couple of years ago described several implementation case studies and most had one or another serious problems (Wilson, 1997). I have contributed my own to these field stories with a chapter in the *ID Casebook* (Spannaus, 1999).

Implementation seems to go much better when it is part of the project from the beginning. If we treat the whole project as a change management process, involving key decision makers and stakeholders from the beginning, implementation will be successful.

Let's consider a specific implementation problem. A company is considering moving to a new CAD/CAM (computer-aided design/computer-aided manufacturing) system. It goes without saying that training would be an important part of the plan. If the information technology (IT) people go to engineering and announce the change, they will encounter resistance. If, on the other hand, the IT people go to engineering and ask for a study, then the decision will be one supported by engineering and IT. There is, of course, a risk that engineering won't want to make the change. Given that they are major users of the CAD/CAM system, they should have a key role in the decision.

From the beginning, the change team should include, besides engineering and IT, other stakeholders, such as manufacturing (a downstream customer of the CAD products), human resources, training, internal corporate communications, and finance. With this broadly representative team, implementation is a natural result of the team effort. There is no need to sell the change because the people being sold made the decision up front.

Implementation has switched from a top-down, expertise-driven approach to a bottom-up, consensus-driven approach. Such a change model is messy and unpredictable. It requires cooperation among several disciplines, meaning that many leaders will find themselves in a supporting role. But the result is change that works and remarkably reduced resistance to change. (Spannaus, Binkert, & Lippit, in press)

Spannaus, T. W. (1999). Jim Huggins. In P. Ertmer & J. Quinn (Eds.), *ID casebook: Case studies in instructional design*. Upper Saddle River, NJ: Merrill.

Spannaus, T. W., Binkert, J., and Lippit, L. L. (in press). Performance improvement team: An interdisciplinary approach. *Journal of Courseware Engineering.*
Wilson, B. (1997). "If You Build It, Will They Come?" Panel discussion at AECT, Albuquerque, February 23.

Timothy W. Spannaus is CEO of the Emdicium Group, Inc. He has worked as an instructional designer for over 30 years, mostly in technical areas, with technology-based training delivery. He is president of ibstpi, the International Board of Standards for Training, Performance and Instruction, and was previously president of ADCIS, the Association for Development of Computer-Based Instructional Systems.

and network connections. An older school's building could inhibit the use of laptops because the individual desks are too small to hold the laptops, only one or two electrical outlets are in the room, and a single network connection is on the front wall.

Time Resource.   Implementation and adoption of a product can take time for all the users to make the adoption. The time needed for the implementation must consider all the adopters, from the innovators to the laggards. Trying to implement the program in an unreasonably short time frame can result in poor results.

PLANNING THE IMPLEMENTATION WITH THE CLER MODEL

An implementation plan identifies the various configurational relationships and then identifies ways to manipulate and capitalize on the configurations to facilitate the process. This section describes how to use the CLER model to plan an implementation. We use our earlier example of the implementation of a course for network engineers on how to develop specifications for a backup generator. The two SMEs, you will remember, were respected network engineers in the company.

Configuration

The key configurational relationships are the instructional designer (individual), the instructional design department (group), and the company (institution). There are several key relationships on the client side. First are the individuals, who include the chief network engineer, the vice president of the group of network engineers, the individual regional managers, and the 143 individual network engineers. The client group includes the 14 regional network-engineering departments. The institution is the same for the instructional designer and client. There is also a culture configuration. The individual engineers, their managers, and the chief engineer all belong to a subculture of those who share the same interest and expertise in network engineering.

Linkages

Both the instructional design and client groups have the same formal management linkages. There are a number of valuable informal linkages. First is a strong rapport between the instructional designer and the two SMEs. The two SMEs have ownership of the course and respect the designer's efforts. Second is the informal linkage the SMEs have with the regional managers and engineers. Third is the linkage between the instructional design manager and the vice president and chief engineer. Fourth are the various informal relationships among the engineers, resulting from transfers, promotions, and collaborative efforts, that go across boundaries.

Environment

The environment created by management is considered supportive of the project. The "word" has come down that the engineers will improve their design of the generators by relying less on the outside vendors.

Resources

Management has indicated that they will provide the needed resources to complete the project. There is a lack of technical resources to answer questions an engineer might have concerning the design of a generator package. Similarly, the vice president has indicated that he wants the training to be implemented as quickly as possible to avoid the loss of any additional bids. On the positive side is the goodwill toward the project generated by the association of the SMEs and the involvement of a number of engineers in the review of the instructional materials. There is also adequate support provided for delivery of the course.

Analysis of the Situation

There is resistance by several of the regional managers to the need for the course. They believe that their engineers know how to develop the specifications successfully (even though there is adequate evidence to the contrary). These managers are hesitant to enroll their staff in a three-day course.

Implementation Plan

The following is the plan for the manipulation of each component of the CLER model.

Configuration and Linkages.   We can create a one-on-one relationship by using the SMEs to communicate to each of the 14 regional managers. Our initial effort is to focus on this configurational relationship and linkage as it can provide a positive, supportive environment for the implementation. All the engineers are in the same subculture and speak a similar technical language. This homogeneous grouping should produce a more effective communication than between the instructional designer and the regional managers (Rogers, 1995). As a last resort, we can use the linkage between the instructional design manager and the vice president to offer incentives or some other inducement to implement the training.

Environment.   During the implementation by the adopters, the company has agreed to provide technical support that should result in fast resolution of any problems. The backing of upper management should help create a supportive environment for the adoption of the materials.

Resources.   The most important resource may be the goodwill the instructional designer has developed with the engineers and the ownership the two SMEs have of the project. This support should provide a perception of low complexity for the project. The training materials are readily available as is a support staff to make arrangements for the course offerings. Financial support for the project would allow the instructional design department to pay for one to two engineers from the slow-adopting divisions to attend training. This opportunity can provide a regional manager with an opportunity to test the training on a trial basis before fully investing in the product.

First Course Offering.   We will work with the SMEs to identify one regional manager who is a respected innovator. The first course offering will be in this district. By implementing the course in a region that supports the innovation, we would expect to see increased productivity. The observable benefits of the innovation would then reduce the risk and complexity perceptions of managers in other regions and increase the probability of adoption.

IMPLEMENTATION DECISIONS

A training program in industry requires an infrastructure to implement and deliver instruction. The following sections describe the implementation decisions related to instructional delivery, instructional materials, scheduling, and instructors.

Instructional Delivery

Some training departments have a support person or group that manages the delivery of the instruction. The complexity of this task grows with the number of different sites and the number of courses offered.

Classroom Facilities.   Training rooms at a company, university, or school are often booked months in advance. Once you have a schedule for a course offering, reservations are needed for an appropriate room. Options for the room include the organization's conference and training rooms or a room at a hotel or conference center. Some rooms are flexible and can be arranged in various formats while a conference room with one large table offers very little flexibility. Careful consideration must be given to the type of room arrangement needed for the course. Some courses require one large lecture-style classroom with several breakout or small-group meeting rooms. A course such as the network-engineering course might require each student to review blueprints or other large documents. To accommodate these materials, you may need a room with a large table for every two students. Courses that use computers will require a different type of table and layout.

Media Equipment.   Arrangements for media equipment also must be made early in the planning process. With adequate notice, overhead projectors, video projectors, and VCRs with monitors are often readily available at various facilities. Providing compressed video facilities may require additional planning and scheduling at both the course location and the speaker's location. Visit the classroom before the first course offering and make note of existing projection screens, the need for additional screens, and other factors that may affect instruction and learning. This visit is also a good time to consider the layout of the room and position of the equipment.

Providing computer labs presents a variety of problems especially if the learners need access to the Internet, intranet, or the organization's computing resources. Once this need is identified, the information technology and/or network support staff should become part of the planning team. They can help arrange for the installation of software and the necessary networking.

Other Equipment.   Technical training courses often require access to other equipment and labs for hands-on training. These needs can vary from cutaway engines to actual copy machines that repair technicians can practice repairing. Similarly, arrangements may be needed for tools and test equipment during the course.

Transportation.   There are two levels of transportation planning. First is transportation from the learner's home to the training site, which might require air transportation and either a shuttle service or rental car. This level also includes transportation for instructors and guest speakers. Second is group transportation for field trips during the course. Buses or vans from either the company car pool or from a private company can be used for field trip transportation.

Housing.   Some companies have training facilities resembling a small college campus that include not only classrooms but also dormitories and cafeterias. Other options include using a hotel that could also provide the classrooms. Again, these facilities must be scheduled in advance to obtain an adequate number of rooms at one location.

Food.   Hotels and many corporate training facilities provide a wide range of food services. Other options include catering the lunch or allowing the learners to leave the "campus" for the noon meal. In addition to the regular meals, arrangements must be made for snacks and drinks during the day. The facility's food services manager or a dietician can help you select appropriate meals, snacks, and drinks.

Materials

Coordinating the instructional materials for a course can require a substantial amount of time. The instructional designer is often responsible for the packaging, duplication, warehousing, and shipping of the materials. An organization may provide support staff to help with these tasks; however, the designer is usually responsible for initiating and monitoring the process. Be sure to allow enough time to follow the normal procedures of the support staff.

Packaging.   Any type of print materials needs some form of binding, ranging from a single staple, to three-ring binders, to textbook-style binding. Three-ring notebooks, spiral binders, and comb binders are popular for when the number of copies is limited or the materials must lay flat while in use. Another feature with three-ring notebooks and some spiral and comb bindings is the option to add tabs to divide the different sections. The print materials also need a cover, a cover design, and copyright information. A graphic artist or an individual in public relations or communications can provide information on printing standards and use of logos.

Packaging nonprint materials such as CD-ROMs, videotapes, and computer disks requires some type of labeling and packaging. CD-ROM production houses will often print your design on the CD and provide jewel cases with printed inserts or simple cardboard mailers. For short runs of computer disks and CDs, you can purchase labels at an office supply store or contract with a printer for a larger quantity.

Duplication.   The duplication of print materials can take just a few minutes at a copy machine to a week or more at an offset printer. Discussions with a representative of the group doing the duplication should start early. Initial meetings can include helpful information on page and margin sizes for your layouts as well as for scheduling the duplication. You will need to coordinate the duplication of the materials so that they are ready for the initial (and subsequent) course offerings. It is prudent to check the final materials for accuracy of duplication, collation, and assembly *prior* to the beginning of a course. The same considerations must also be given for nonprint materials such as videotapes and CD-ROMs.

Warehousing.   It is easy to imagine an instructional designer ordering 1,000 copies of a training manual in a three-inch ring binder and then trying to find storage space for them when the printer's truck arrives! A training department located at the organization's headquarters is often faced with the problem of finding adequate office space. Finding a room to store the materials is an almost impossible task. Consideration must be given to warehousing all training materials *before* they are ordered.

Shipping.   Some companies offer their courses all over the country and world. Special arrangements have to be made to box and ship the student materials prior to the course. If the materials are going to another country, special forms must be completed for customs and time must be allowed for the packages to pass through customs when leaving the country and upon entering the destination country. Another option that also solves the warehousing issue is to upload or e-mail electronic documents, such as word-processing files, to a commercial copy center near the training site. The copy center can duplicate, bind, and deliver the materials to the training center a day or two before the training begins.

INSTRUCTORS

The last implementation decision concerns the instructors. The two primary issues of concern are the scheduling and training.

Scheduling

Some companies have a group of professional instructors or they may rotate individuals through the training department to serve as instructors. Another option is to use experts, such as in the example of the network-engineering course presented in this chapter. Regardless of the source of the instructors, careful planning is required to schedule their time. Using company experts as instructors assumes that their manager will allow them to leave their job several times a year to teach a course. Scheduling a course requires consideration of their workload to minimize the impact on their productivity.

Instructor Training

There are two reasons to provide instructor training. First is to improve the instructors' teaching and presentation skills. In business, many of the individuals who serve as instructors have not had any formal training in teaching. One or more basic courses in presentation, facilitation, and teaching strategies can help them improve their skills. Second is to train instructors on how to teach a specific course. For example, the implementation plan for the network-engineering course example planned to use the two SMEs as the instructors for the first six months. New instructors with the necessary technical knowledge and skills will be needed to conduct future courses. These new instructors may need to attend the course one or more times and receive tutoring or coaching to develop their technical expertise to teach the course.

S U M M A R Y

1. The successful adoption of an instructional product is dependent on how the merits, compatibility, complexity, and visibility of results are perceived and on the ability to try it.

2. An implementation plan includes the analysis of the configuration, linkages, environment, and resources and how these elements can be optimized to provide for effective communication between the instructional designer and the client. The CLER model provides a framework for developing the implementation plan.

3. When planning the implementation of a course, careful consideration is needed to schedule the facilities, equipment, transportation, housing, and food services.

4. The instructional designer is often responsible for the packaging, warehousing, and shipping of the various instructional materials. This planning often requires involving individuals such as a graphic designer early in the design process to develop a cost-effective layout for the duplication process.

5. Instructor scheduling and training is an important aspect of the course implementation process.

THE ID PROCESS

Implementing a project begins during the problem identification process. A designer can use a needs assessment or goal analysis to generate interest and goodwill toward the project. During the design and development phases, individual buy-in may be developed by soliciting reviews and examples from various stakeholders. For example, we needed a sample diary page for an example in a training manual. We asked one of the regional engineers who was an opinion leader if he could provide us with a sample page from his diary. By using his example, we were able to give him both recognition and involvement in the project.

Implementing a training product may require extensive traveling, meetings, and special training to gain adopters. For some courses that solve a real problem, the plan is as simple as informing managers and employees that the course or materials are available. Courses that conflict with existing values or methods typically require a more elaborate approach for convincing your clients of the value of the training.

APPLICATIONS

You have just completed the development of a major management training program for a national retail chain. Using existing classroom materials, your team has created a hybrid course that incorporates both web-based instruction and traditional classroom instruction while significantly reducing the classroom time. This is your client's first experience with web-based instruction.

At the first implementation and instructor training meeting, you found resistance to the web-based components by the instructors in the New England region. The regional training manager fully supports the concept, but the instructors refuse to use the materials. The course was well received by managers and instructors in the other two regions that have completed the instructor training and implementation.

You have four remaining regions that need the implementation and instructor training. You now see a need to develop an implementation plan for the remaining regions plus the New England region. How would you develop the plan?

ANSWERS

We would start first by identifying the different components of the CLER model. First are the configurations. The primary players include the design team, the regional managers, and the instructors. Most of these configurations will probably be the design team and managers and the design team and instructors. We would also want to identify individual-to-individual configurations where possible.

Second, we start searching for linkages that help us implement the project. The formal linkages, such as regional manager to instructors, are easy to identify with an organizational chart. But more important are the informal linkages that we might use. For example, we might identify an instructor who buys in to the course and who has worked with an instructor who is resistant to adopting the course design.

Third, we would want to identify the environment in each region and within the company. For example, the New England region might not have the ready and easy access to the intranet that the other regions have. Correcting this environmental constraint might increase the adoption of the course. We would also want to identify the climate created by the regional managers to identify other constraints to the implementation.

Fourth, we would want to identify the resources available to help the implementation. One example might be the use of an instructor from one region offering a course in another region and serving as a model for the instructors. Finding informal linkages between instructors could help us identify instructors that would have the most potential for helping us implement the project.

Using this information, we could develop an overall implementation plan as well as plans adapted to specific regions.

REFERENCES

Bhola, H. S. (1982). Planning change in education and development: The CLER model in the context of a mega model. *Viewpoints in Teaching and Learning, 58,* 1–35.

Bhola, H. S. (1988–1989). The CLER model of innovation diffusion, planned change, and development: A conceptual update and applications. *Knowledge in Society: The International Journal of Knowledge Transfer, 1,* 56–66.

Davies, I. K. (1982). The CLER model in instructional development. *Viewpoints in Teaching and Learning, 58,* 62–69.

Rogers, E. M. (1995). *Diffusion of innovations* (4th ed.). New York: Free Press.

Sample Instructional Design Documentation

PROPER BAGGING PRACTICE IN A SUPERSTORE ENVIRONMENT

PROBLEM IDENTIFICATION

Bagging customers' groceries and other purchases properly promotes customer satisfaction through personalized service and care for their purchases. It is important that the bag be presented to the customer based on solid principles of packing and handling. A poorly packed bag can lead directly to the ruin of the contents before customers can reach their destination. At busy times, many store team members are called upon to assist register personnel so that the bagging process does not delay and inconvenience the customer being served or those waiting in line. High employee turnover and the involvement of personnel not normally involved in bagging, along with the importance of proper bagging, indicate the need for efficient training. The bagger has the last and most sustained customer contact. Based on the goals, the opportunities of training include the following:

- Better personal and efficient customer service, promoting repeat business
- Better utilization of bagging supplies and job performance
- Better protection of the customer's purchases

Based on a project by Donald L. Boase

GOAL ANALYSIS

Aim

Promote customer satisfaction and repeat business through improved bagging and service at time of checkout.

Set Goals

- Use the proper bag for the job.
- Be sure bags are properly stocked before beginning shift.
- Bag together items that belong together.
- Promote the protection of the customer's purchases.
- Promote customer satisfaction through courtesy.
- Work efficiently.
- Support the team effort of customer service.
- Help the register personnel ensure that all items are checked.
- Exhibit good hygiene.
- Run errands when necessary.
- Help customers even when away from the checkout lane.
- Use the principle of looking ahead.
- Know what is not bagged.
- Know which bag to use.
- Use principles of how items are grouped.
- Select items for "walls."
- Select items for "foundations."
- Select items for "fill."
- Use the principles of proper bag building.
- Place bags and items into the cart properly.
- Check supplies and stock bags.
- Place bags properly at the checkout lane.
- Put the proper number of each bag at the checkout lane.
- Get bags from the stock room area.
- Hang the bags at the checkout lane.
- Stock additional bags.
- Use the principles of customer service opportunities.
- Use the area service rule—within 10 feet make positive contact.

Refine Goals

- Use the area service rule—within 10 feet make positive contact.
- Help customers even when away from the checkout lane.
- Use the proper bag for the job.
- Bag together items that belong together.
- Work efficiently by looking ahead.

- Know what is not bagged.
- Select proper items for "walls."
- Select proper items for "foundations."
- Select proper items for "fill."
- Place bags and items into the cart properly.
- Be sure bags are properly stocked before beginning shift.
- Put the proper number of each bag at the checkout lane.
- Get bags from the stock room area.
- Stock additional bags.
- Help the register personnel be sure all items are checked.
- Run errands when necessary.

Rank Goals

1. Be sure bags are properly stocked before beginning shift.
2. Put in the proper number of each bag at the checkout lane.
3. Get bags from the stock room area.
4. Stock additional bags.
5. Help the register personnel be sure all items are checked.
6. Bag together items that belong together.
7. Work efficiently by looking ahead.
8. Know what is not bagged.
9. Select proper items for "walls."
10. Select proper items for "foundations."
11. Select proper items for "fill."
12. Place bags and items into the cart properly.
13. Use the proper bag for the job.
14. Run errands when necessary.
15. Use the area service rule—within 10 feet make positive contact.
16. Help customers even when away from the checkout lane.

Second Refinement

1. Demonstrate the job responsibilities, including maintenance and use of supplies, efficient work practices, and team member support.
2. Identify examples of walls, foundations, and fill for bagging.
3. Demonstrate how to use walls, foundations, and fill to complete a full bag.
4. State the customer service philosophy and practice including the "10-foot rule."

Final Ranking

1. State the customer service philosophy and practice, including the "10-foot rule."

2. Demonstrate the job responsibilities, including maintenance and use of supplies, efficient work practices, and team member support.
3. Identify examples of walls, foundations, and fill for bagging.
4. Demonstrate how to use walls, foundations, and fill to complete a full bag.

LEARNER ANALYSIS

Audience Definition

General Characteristics.   The primary audience is composed of both male and female team members in their mid teens. Often this is their first job. This is a high-visibility position and requires a responsible individual with good grooming habits and a pleasant attitude. Although there is a high turnover in this position, many individuals who go on to a career in retail management start here.

Retired people make up the next group. Often, these individuals have reentered the work place as a means to stay active.

Other audiences include other store personnel, including the register operator in off-peak times. While already understanding many of the store philosophies and people issues, this group still needs to know the best way to pack a bag.

Specific Characteristics.

Four Distinct Audiences.
1. Both genders, 14- to 17-year-olds, may be first job (primary audience)
2. Retired or older people
3. Register personnel (handle checkout and bagging at off-peak times)
4. Other store personnel who may be called on at peak times

Physical Requirements.
- Should be able to lift and manage a 20-pound bag
- Good hygiene and grooming characteristics

Specific Educational or Training Requirements.
- Basic literacy consistent with a 14-year-old-student level
- Company orientation training

Contextual Analysis

Orienting Context.   There are two factors we want to focus on with the orienting context. First, we want to make sure the instruction is directly relevant to the learners' jobs so they perceive a high utility for the information. Second, the store supervisor or manager must stress the learners' accountability for bagging groceries properly and how this training will help them better perform their job tasks.

Instructional Context.   Each store has a training room that has two or more carrels where students can access a CD-ROM to use the training materials or complete online instruction. There are also two more carrels for working on paper-based instructional materials. This room is available approximately 14 hours a day. It is supposed to be reserved strictly for training. Learners can obtain their training materials from the manager's office. However, company policy dictates that the materials must stay in the store. The training should be designed so that individual units can be completed in less than one hour. Each manager arranges times for the training of new employees that fit the schedules of the room and the new employee.

Transfer Context.   The training should be scheduled as close to the employee's start day as a bagger as possible to enhance the transfer of the training. In addition to scheduling the training, the employee's first day on the job is coordinated with the head cashier to ensure that a coach is provided for the first hour or so on the job.

TASK ANALYSIS

A. Check to see that supplies are sufficient and, if necessary, restock bags.
  1. A fully stocked lane will have 400 medium bags, 100 small bags, and 200 large bags.
  2. Bags are to be brought up from the storeroom.
B. Stand at the end of the checkout lane holding area so you can see the conveyor belt and have a view of the whole basket.
  1. The bag rack should be positioned directly in front of you.
C. The area of service is defined as a 10-foot radius around you wherever you are on store property.
  1. Whenever customers are in your area of service you should:
    a. Make eye contact.
    b. Greet them by smiling and saying hello.
    c. Offer to be of service.
  2. Always greet the customer when eye contact is made.
  3. Present an attitude of helpfulness.
D. As purchases are placed on the belt, begin looking at the nature of the items and think in terms of grouping and building the bag.
  1. Items similar in nature should be grouped together.
    a. Never mix food items with cleaning or toxic materials.
  2. The following six categories should be followed for grouping:
    a. Fresh produce, such as tomatoes and carrots.
    b. Packaged food—boxed and prepared items.
    c. Frozen food (wet items—condensation).
    d. Cleaning or toxic items.
    e. Other store items.
E. As the last items are placed on the belt, help the register personnel be sure all items have been accounted for.
  1. Double check that nothing is missed underneath the basket.
    a. Think "IOU"—inside, outside, underneath.

        b. The places an item may be missed during checkout are inside another item, outside the basket, or underneath.

        c. The register personnel are very busy with the transaction and may miss something that is outside the basket.

        d. As a checkout team member, you are providing backup for the register personnel.

        e. Be sure all items are accounted for through the checkout.

           (1) Items may be inside larger products.

           (2) Although it is the primary responsibility of the register personnel to check, you are a team member and you should follow up if an item was not checked.

   2. The customer may be absentmindedly holding an item, or the item may be underneath the basket in the bottom of the cart.

   3. Some items are too big or awkward to be placed on the belt. Assist the register personnel with the scanning if necessary.

F. As items are fed through the scanner and gather in the holding area, begin bag building.

   1. Choose the right bag and build the bags following the principles for solid construction.

        a. Plastic and paper bags are available for bagging.

        b. Plastic is the best based on cost, ecology issues, and ease of use.

        c. Paper is best if the customer asks for it.

        d. Paper bags are stored beneath the holding area, where they can be easily retrieved for use without promoting their use through high visibility.

   2. Choose from three sizes of bags or not at all.

        a. Match the size of the bag to the purchased item.

        b. The standard or medium-sized bag most commonly used for groceries is stocked in bales under the holding area.

           (1) A supply is hung on the bagging racks at the end of the lane, ready to use.

           (2) These are prepared for use by placing the loops on each side of the bags over the left and right arms of the rack, stretching the bags across the back of the rack.

        c. What not to bag:

           (1) Oversized items, such as bagged dogfood

           (2) Items with built-in handles, such as milk or bleach

           (3) Some things, such as goldfish, just should not be bagged and need special handling. Find out from the customer how the item should be handled.

G. Construction principles:

   1. Build the walls:

        a. Walls are built with items that can give structure and support to the bag.

      b. Usually, packaged items that have some rigidity, such as a box of cereal or even a package of napkins, will work.

      c. Wall items are placed at both ends of the bag (left and right sides as you face the hanging bag), with the center open for other items.

      d. Examples:

          (1) Boxes of cereal, crackers, or cake mix

          (2) Rigid items, such as carrots, celery, or even bananas

          (3) Packaged items, such as napkins, cookies, or plates

2. Lay the floor:

      a. After the walls are established, lay the floor.

          (1) Use heavy items first, such as canned goods.

          (2) Place heavy items between the walls to provide a solid base to support continued filling.

      b. Examples:

          (1) Canned goods, such as green beans or soda pop

          (2) Heavy packaged items, such as sugar or flour

          (3) Glass jars, as used with jelly or mayonnaise

3. Fill the space:

      a. Now fill the rest of the bag with lighter or more fragile items, such as bread or chips.

          (1) They will be protected within the walls and will not crush the items beneath. The bag is not built until it is full.

      b. Examples:

          (1) Thinly packaged items, such as bread and chips

          (2) Small items, such as pudding boxes, drink mixes, and cosmetics

          (3) Fragile items, such as eggs and tomatoes

H. As bags are built, place them back into the cart, keeping in mind the same principles apply to the cart as they did to the bag.

I. If customers appear to need assistance getting to their vehicles, offer to help.

    1. Be aggressive in helping.

OBJECTIVES AND PRESENTATION STRATEGIES

Objective 1

After completing this unit, the learner will correctly answer short-answer questions about individual responsibility, scope (10-foot rule), customer position, and importance of bagging to demonstrate a personal understanding of customer service.

Fact–Recall

Initial Presentation.   An example will be used to show a bagger demonstrating the company's philosophy, the principles of customer satisfaction, and the responsibility of the bagger to fulfill it.

Generative Strategy.   The student will provide an example of how he or she would demonstrate the philosophy, achieve customer satisfaction, accomplish the bagger's responsibilities.

Test Items.
> We provide bagging to build customer _____.
> Your responsibility is to ensure our customers are _____.
> Your *area of service* is _____ ft. around you.
> The customer comes _____.

Objective 2

After completing this unit, the learner will demonstrate how to restock bagging supplies with 100 percent accuracy.

> *Procedure–Application*

Initial Presentation.   Eg–Rule: The principles for bagging preparation and practice are presented and then are followed by examples of application.

Generative Strategy.

> After the presentation, describe the process for restocking the bagging supplies. Using the demonstration area, practice stocking the bagging supplies.

Checklist.

Appropriate number of size of bags are stocked.	Yes	No
Bags are properly stacked or attached for use.	Yes	No

Objective 3

Given a display of 20 items, the learner will correctly select the appropriate bag to use for each item with 90 percent accuracy.

> *Principle–Application*

Initial Presentation.   Eg–Rule approach is used to illustrate the type of bag for various items and to illustrate the size of bag.

Generative Strategy.   The learner is shown four groupings of grocery items and is asked to explain the size and type of bag needed for each.

Test Item.   The learner is shown individual items and groups of items and selects the appropriate bag for each item or group.

Objective 4

Given a grocery cart, the student will demonstrate the procedure for ensuring all items have been scanned.

Procedure–Application

Initial Presentation.   The student will read a section with an illustration indicating the procedure to look inside, outside, and underneath the cart.

Generative Strategy.
   A mnemonic device, IOU, will be given to the learner with instructions to rehearse it.
   Using the demonstration area, the learner will practice indicating how to check that all items have been scanned.

Test Item.   Using the drawing, indicate with arrows where you need to look for items that have not been scanned.

Objective 5

Given a list of 40 products, the learner will correctly assign 90 percent to the correct category.

Concept–Application

Initial Presentation.   For each of the six categories, learners are given a description and a best example of the concept.

Generative Strategy.   Provide the learner with a list of items for each category and have the student match the item with the correct category.

Test Item.   Provide the learner with 40 products on a table with a number on each product. The student writes the category beside the number of each item on the answer sheet.

Objective 6

Given a picture of a group of grocery items on a table, the learner will correctly select two examples of walls, foundations, and fill.

Concept–Application

Initial Presentation.   For each of the three concepts, learners are given a description and a best example of the concept.

Generative Strategy.   Provide the learner with a list of items for each concept and have the student match the item with the correct category.

Test Item.   Provide the learner with 20 products on a table with a number on each product. The student classifies each item as use for a foundation, wall, or fill.

Objective 7

Given a group of 30 grocery items in a single line, the learner correctly bags the group following acceptable practice.

Procedure–Application

Initial Presentation.   State each rule for bagging concerning grouping, walls, foundations, and fill, and then illustrate the rule.

Generative Strategy.
    The student will paraphrase the process for building a bag.
    Using the demonstration area, the learner will practice bagging three carts of
        groceries.

Performance Checklist.

1. Most bags have walls, foundation, fill.	Yes	No
2. Each bag has appropriate items.	Yes	No
3. Heavy items are on the bottom.	Yes	No
4. Fragile items are not broken.	Yes	No

PREINSTRUCTIONAL STRATEGY–ADVANCE ORGANIZER

The instruction will be built around the metaphor of building as in constructing a home. The learner will be introduced to the content in the opening copy and illustration through a building concept. The metaphor will be used to support the sequencing strategy. It will improve retention by providing a conceptual grid to hang the information on and by emphasizing the deliberateness and care that should be given the job of customer service through proper bagging and teamwork with imagery that an audience young or old would readily understand.

Pretest as a strategy was not chosen because of the predominately entry-level job position. However, an argument could be made to use the pretest as a way of exposing preconceived attitudes, but then it would not lend itself well to support the balance of the cognitive objectives.

Behavioral objectives as a strategy was not chosen because of the predominately youthful audience. The "why" of the training needs to be established as well to provide meaning and context for the objectives. Although a clear statement of training purpose would leave no room for confusion for this first-time employee, the raw objectives could come across too sterile and result in a negative response.

Overview as a strategy was not chosen because of the lack of experience of a key target audience to build on. More is needed to establish the foundation and context of the workplace before presenting an overview.

SEQUENCING CONTENT—TEMPORAL RELATION

Following through with the building metaphor, the content will be sequenced based on the chronological progression of the job—organizing the work site, planning, and working together to perform the tasks. The content will be presented, as the need to know is progressively established through the job/tasks sequence.

FORMATIVE EVALUATION

SME Review

Based on research, interviews, and assumptions, a design document will be prepared for validation by project stakeholders. This review will be performed in a group meeting covering the objectives, content, and creative treatment through a guided reading of the design document. Comments, concerns, or new direction will be captured, noted on the designated master document, and agreed to by the group for implementation. A final design document will then be generated to facilitate development and report changes.

Target Audience Review

Once the initial training materials are prepared in prototype form, usability testing on a representative small sampling of the target audiences will be performed with an opinion survey to capture additional information outside the inherent course testing and to document the results. For this evaluation, the participants will go through the course as designed. This will be a last check before publication. (See attached survey.) Based on the results, modifications would be made and submitted for final SME approval.

FORMATIVE EVALUATION

Date: _____

Course Title: _____

What is your current job title? _____

How long have you been at this job?
- ☐ 1 year or less
- ☐ 1–3 years
- ☐ 3–5 years
- ☐ 6–10 years
- ☐ 11 years or longer

Will the course help you do your job better?
- ☐ Significantly better
- ☐ Somewhat better
- ☐ About the same
- ☐ Worse
- ☐ Significantly worse

How did you find the course?
- ☐ Very interesting
- ☐ Somewhat interesting
- ☐ Fairly interesting
- ☐ Not very interesting
- ☐ Boring

Was the course easy to follow?
- ☐ Extremely easy
- ☐ Very easy
- ☐ Fairly easy
- ☐ Not too hard
- ☐ Very hard

Was the course challenging?
- ☐ Extremely easy
- ☐ Very easy
- ☐ Fairly easy
- ☐ Not too hard
- ☐ Very hard

Did you always know what to do?
- ☐ Very clear
- ☐ Somewhat clear
- ☐ Fairly clear
- ☐ Not very clear
- ☐ Confusing

Would you recommend the course to someone else?
- ☐ Yes
- ☐ No

What would you change?

What did you like?

A Sample Instructional Unit

Building Bags

BUILDING CUSTOMER SATISFACTION

We are continually building our business, and we do it by filling one bag at a time. Customer service is the cornerstone. A cornerstone is the foundational stone in a building on which all the rest stands. It supports the weight and ensures the integrity of the structure. We are building on customer service every day through every opportunity we have. We are providing a special personal service to our customers through bagging.

As a bagger it is your responsibility to ensure our customers are served in a professional manner providing the best in attitude and practice. We build our bags better to build customer satisfaction.

Like building a house, you prepare, plan, and build with a purpose. And like a house, a properly built bag has walls and a floor protecting its contents. It sets upright on a solid foundation.

BUILDING CUSTOMERS

The Customer Comes First

Whether at the checkout lane or anywhere on store grounds, when you gain eye contact with customers greet them and present an attitude of helpfulness.

Based on a project by Donald L. Boase

Also, whenever customers are in your area of service you should make eye contact and greet them. Your area of service is defined as a 10-foot radius (Figure B-1) around you wherever you are on store property.

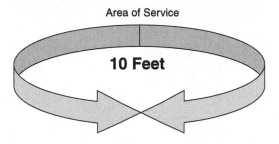

Area of Service

10 Feet

FIGURE B-1

See the Opportunities

As you watch the videotape of a morning at the store, can you identify examples of baggers helping customers?

The following situations describe opportunities to build customer satisfaction.

- You are passing a customer who cannot reach an item on the top shelf, and you retrieve it for him.
- You are sent out to retrieve carts and while in the parking lot you pass a customer holding her bags while trying to get her keys from her purse. You offer to hold her bags.
- You pass a customer with his hands full and offer to get him a cart.
- A customer stops to ask you where the service desk is, and you show her where it is.
- You see a customer obviously looking for something and inquire whether you can help.

NOW YOU CAN MAKE THE OPPORTUNITIES

Write in two situations you can think of where you could help.

1. _____

_____

_____

2. _____

_____

_____

PREPARING TO BUILD

First check your supplies. When you come on shift, first check to see whether supplies are sufficient, and if necessary, restock the bags at your lane. A fully stocked lane will have 400 medium bags, 100 small bags, and 200 large bags (Figure B-2).

The bags are packaged in bales of 200. Usually you will need to bring a fresh bale or two from the storeroom to the checkout lane at the beginning of your shift. Your supervisor will show you the storeroom and show you how to hang the bags at the checkout.

The bags are prepared for use by placing the bag handles over the left and right arms of the rack, stretching the bags across the back of the rack. The rest are stored under the holding area at the end of the lane.

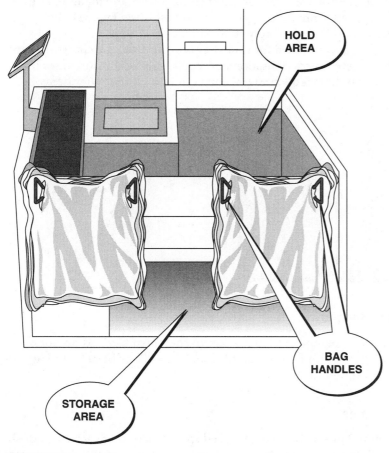

FIGURE B-2

It Is up to You

Describe what you should do at the beginning of your shift.

_____

_____

_____

Using the demonstration area, practice stocking the bagging supplies.

Bags Come in Three Sizes

So, which bag to use? Just match the bag to the size of purchase. The most commonly used bag is the one you are probably most familiar with, the medium or standard-sized plastic bag used primarily for grocery purchases (see Figure B-3).

The large bag is used for other store items such as clothing.

The small bag is obviously used for small items or for food purchases that are very cold. Cold items develop condensation and could ruin other purchases if the water that condenses on them is allowed to be in contact with the other items.

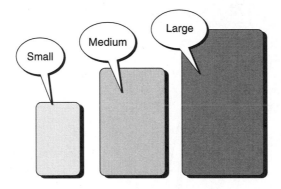

FIGURE B-3

Not Everything Is Bagged

Oversized items such as dogfood or charcoal are in their own bag and do not need additional bagging. Items with built-in handles such as milk or bleach are bagged only if the customer requests it.

Talk to Your Customer

Some things just should not be bagged and need special handling such as goldfish or a large plant. Talk to your customer and ask how he or she would like the item handled. The register personnel will ask the customer about single-item purchases. Quite often, single-item purchases are also not bagged with the customer's consent.

Paper or Plastic?

Plastic or paper bags are available for bagging. Plastic is the preferred based on cost, ecology issues, and ease of use. Paper is best if the customer asks for it.

Paper bags are stored beneath the holding area where they can be easily retrieved for use without promoting their use through high visibility.

The Right Tool for the Job

Select the appropriate bag for the items in Figure B-4.

Now that your supplies are checked and ready, stand at the end of the check-out lane holding area so you can see the conveyor belt and have a view of the whole basket. The bag rack should be positioned directly in front of you. You begin by greeting the customer with a smile and saying hello. Be ready to help.

As purchases are placed on the belt, begin looking at the nature of the items and think in terms of grouping the items and building the bags. Briefly use the holding area to help arrange the purchased items into groups. However, do not let too much accumulate before bagging.

Group together items similar in nature and never mix food items with cleaning or toxic materials. Later we will look at how within the groups there are best

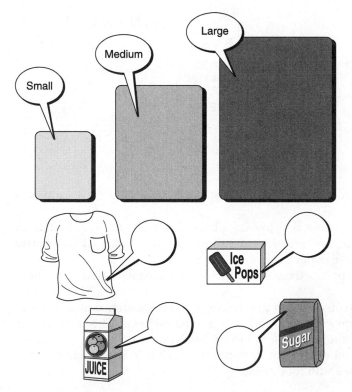

FIGURE B-4

ways to build the bag based on weight, shape, and toughness. These are principles that can be applied to anything we sell.

Types of Grocery Items

Grocery items are usually put away at home in the same way you should group them. Not only does this help you in bagging, but it also helps the customer in putting the items away. When our customers return home, they will appreciate the extra thought and consideration.

Take a look at the following five categories that should be followed for grouping your bag-building items and its representative product in Figure B-5:

1. Fresh produce

2. Packaged food

3. Frozen foods

4. Cleaning or toxic items

5. Other store items

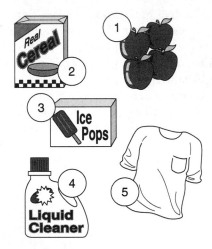

FIGURE B-5

Group Descriptions

Fresh produce includes food items that are not prepackaged, such as fruits and vegetables.

Packaged foods are those that are in a box or sealed package. Examples include cereals, boxed mixes, meats, and canned goods. Packaged foods also include some dry goods like paper plates and tissues.

Frozen foods are kept in a freezer and include ice cream, frozen vegetables, and frozen pizzas.

Cleaning or toxic items are used to clean or to kill pests such as ants or mice. They should always be kept separate from other purchased items. This includes bar soaps, automotive fluids, ant killers, and window cleaners.

Clothing as well as other types of store purchases should have their own bag and should not be grouped with food items.

Preparing to Build

Match the item on the left with an example from the group on the right in Figure B-6.

1. Fresh produce

2. Packaged food

3. Frozen foods

4. Cleaning or toxic items

5. Other store items

FIGURE B-6

BAG BUILDING

Construction Principles

Build the Walls First.   Bags do not have built-in support. Walls need to be built with items that can give structure and define the shape of the bag (see Figure B-7). Items that look like walls, such as a box of cereal or cookies, make good walls. Then, also look for items that are packaged like a wall such as napkins or even rolls of toilet paper. Finally, look for items that can give stiffness to the sides of the bag even if they are not square, such as celery, carrots, or paper plates.

Wall items are placed at both ends of the bag to square off the bag (left and right sides as you face the hanging bag) with the center open for other items. Walls are always built first and then you should not have to move them. Also, never place an item between a wall and the bag. The bag could be torn by it.

Lay The Floor.   After the walls are established, the floor is laid (Figure B-8). Heavy items placed between the walls provide a solid base to support continued filling.

Put items like canned goods, flour, sugar, and glass jars between the walls. And always plan ahead. Put aside any other good wall builders you may come across for the next bag or until that is all you have left.

When you square off the sides and fill in the bottom, the bag stands up and holds the contents in during the ride home. A loosely packed or top-heavy bag tips over and spills.

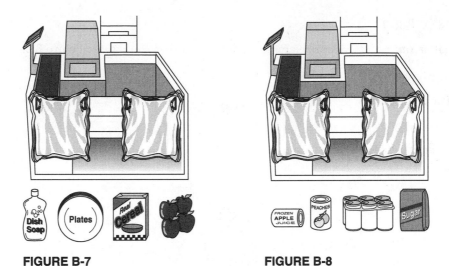

FIGURE B-7   **FIGURE B-8**

Fill the Space.   Once you've got a solid, tight floor across the bottom, fill up the bag with items such as boxes of pudding, drink mixes, cosmetics, and other small, lightweight items (Figure B-9). Never build more than one layer of heavy items. More than one layer of heavy items makes the bag too hard to carry and top heavy.

Fill the rest of the bag with lighter or more fragile items. They will be protected within the walls and will not crush the items beneath. But remember the bag is not built until it is full. Top off the bag with a small loaf of bread, a bag of cookies, or a bag of chips. But put only one or two crushable items on top. If you have more,

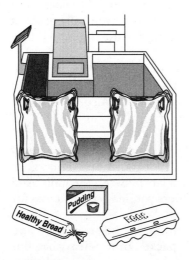

FIGURE B-9

put them all together in one bag. Keep in mind that the more bags that are used means more handling for our customers as well as wasted supplies.

The Building Parts

Label each of the following items as a wall, foundation, or fill (Figure B-10).

FIGURE B-10

The Building

Describe the process for building a bag.

_____

_____

_____

_____

_____

Using the demonstration area, practice bagging groceries from three carts.

BUILDING TEAMWORK

Inside, Outside, Underneath

As the last items are placed on the belt, help the register personnel be sure all items have been accounted for. Double check that nothing is missed underneath the basket. The places an item may be missed during checkout are inside another item, outside the basket, or underneath (Figure B-11). The register personnel are very busy with the transaction and may miss something that is outside of the basket. As a checkout team member, you are providing backup for the register personnel. Be sure all items are accounted for through the checkout.

Items may be inside larger products. Although it is the primary responsibility of the register personnel to check, you are a team member and should follow up if an item was not checked. The customer may be absentmindedly holding an item or the item may be underneath the basket in the bottom of the cart. Just tell the register person you owe them one. This lets the team member know what to look for without embarrassment to the customer.

Remember *IOU* to help your recall *inside, outside,* and *underneath* the cart. Practice saying this until you have memorized it. Now, use the demonstration area and practice checking two carts.

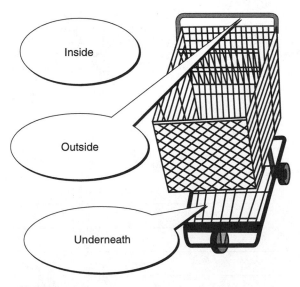

FIGURE B-11

Glossary

Affective domain   That area of learning devoted to developing attitudes, values, or appreciations

Application   Performance requiring the learner to use or apply the information

Assessment   The systematic collection of data pertaining to programs or people

Behaviorism   Learning theory in which subject content is divided into a series of small steps; the learner participates actively, receives feedback on effort, and is guided to success

CD-ROM   A compact disk containing a quantity of verbal and pictorial information

Client   Person for whom instruction is being planned and who may serve as subject specialist when working with the instructional designer. May also be the individual who contracts for the training

Cognitive domain   That area of learning devoted to acquiring information, knowledge, and intellectual abilities relative to a subject or topic

Cognitive learning style   Unique way an individual receives and processes information as classified on a number of scales

Cognitive objective   An objective used to describe learning intellectual skills that are not easily defined by a behavioral objective

Cognitive strategies   Highest level of cognitive learning, typified by problem solving

Compact disc   High-quality music and other sound recording on a 4.75-inch disk that is read by a laser beam

Competency-based instruction   Providing and evaluating instruction against a specific standard as indicated by the learning objectives for the topic or task

Computer-based instruction (CBI)   Software program that displays information and instructions on a video screen, requiring learner participation and choices

Concept   Name or expression given to a class of facts, objects, or events, all of which have common features

Confirmative evaluation   A continuous form of evaluation that comes after summative evaluation used to determine whether a course is still effective

Constructed-response test   Consisting of questions requiring the learner to supply a short answer, write an essay, or solve a problem; allows for evaluation of higher-level cognitive objectives but is difficult to solve reliably

Constructivism   An approach to instructional design based on the assumption that learners generate knowledge structures in their own minds

Cost center   Service provided within an organization for instructional development service with costs carried by the department

Criterion-referenced instruction   *See* Competency-based instruction.

Culturally diverse learners   Students from various ethnic cultures

Curriculum   List of courses and content framework for a subject

Developmental costs   All personnel, resource, and service costs required to plan and develop an instructional program

Diffusion   The process of communicating information to a client and target audience about an innovation

Distance education   Instruction in which the instructor and student are separated in both physical location and time, requiring the instruction to be fully designed and developed prior to implementing the instruction

Domains of learning   Cognitive, psychomotor, and affective categories

Effectiveness   Measuring the degree to which learners accomplish objectives for each unit or a total course

Efficiency   Measuring the amount of learner time, personnel services, and facilities use required to carry out an instructional program, and then deciding whether these amounts are acceptable or excessive

E-Learning   Learning from instruction offered via the Internet or intranet

Evaluation   Using assessment or measurement to judge the worth or success of something

Evaluator   Person responsible for assisting the instructor in designing tests to measure student learning, conduct formative and summative evaluations, and analyze results

Fact   A statement associating one item to another

Feedback   Providing the learner with answers to exercises and other information relative to progress in learning

Flow chart   Visual description of the sequence necessary for performing a task, including decision points and alternate paths

Formative evaluation   Testing a new instructional program with a sampling of learners during the development phase, and using the results to improve the program front-end analysis

Goal statement   Broad statement describing what should take place in an instructional course or training program

Human performance improvement   A strategy for improving productivity by considering various interventions in addition to training

Individualized learning   Allowing learners to learn by providing each one with objectives and activities appropriate to his or her own characteristics, preparation, needs, and interests

Instructional cost index   Mathematical calculation of the cost per learner or trainee to accomplish objectives for a topic or course, taking into account a portion of the developmental cost and implementation costs

Instructional design   Systematic planning of instruction in which attention is given to nine related elements

Instructional designer   Person responsible for carrying out and coordinating the systematic design procedure

Instructional development   Managing the planning, development, and implementation procedure for instruction or training

Instructional objective   Statement describing what the learner is specifically required to learn or accomplish relative to a topic or task

Instructional systems   Another expression for the instructional design concept

Instructional technology   Resources (machines and materials) used for instruction; process of systematic instructional planning

Intellectual skills   Organizing and structuring facts for learning to form concepts, principles, rules, attitudes, and interactions

Interactive technologies   Media forms that require frequent active participation by the student as learning takes place

Interpersonal skills   Spoken and nonverbal (e.g., body language) interaction between two or more individuals

Learner characteristics   Factors relating to personal and social traits of individuals and learner groups that need consideration during planning or learning

Learning   A relatively permanent change in behavior that may or may not be the result of instruction

Learning styles   Various methods of learning that are preferred by individuals or that may be more effective with different individuals

Learning systems design   Another expression for the instructional design concept

Mastery-based instruction   *See* Competency-based instruction

Mastery learning   Indicating whether a learner successfully accomplishes the necessary level of learning for required objectives

Module   A self-instructional package treating a single topic or unit of a course

Multimedia   Computer program controlling display of verbal information along with still photographs, video, and audio sequences in various formats

Needs assessment or analysis   Procedure of gathering information before deciding whether there is a substantive need for instruction or training

Norm-referenced testing   Evaluating the results of instruction in a relative fashion by comparing test scores of each learner with those of other learners in the class

Objective test   Consisting of questions for which a learner must select an answer from two or more alternatives and persons scoring the test can easily agree on the correct answer

Operational costs   All costs of personnel resources and services incurred as an instructional program is being implemented

Organization management   Management of an instructional development service that broadly includes all design and delivery functions

Performance-based instruction   *See* Competency-based instruction

Posttest   Final examination given at the end of a course or training program (differs from pretest)

Prerequisite test   Portion of a pretest that measures content or skill preparation a learner has for starting the course or unit

Presentation teaching method   Technique used to disseminate information

Pretest   Test administered prior to the start of instruction to determine the level of the learner's knowledge and the necessary preparation relative to a topic or task

Principle   Expression of a relationship between concepts

Procedural analysis   Used to identify the steps required to complete a task or series of steps

Procedure   Sequence of steps one follows to achieve a goal

Profit center   Service provided within and outside an organization for instructional design services with costs charged to the client or sponsor

Project management   Responsibilities for all functions that relate to the conduct of an instructional design project

Psychomotor domain   That area of learning devoted to becoming proficient in performing a physical action involving muscles of the body

Reinforcement learning   Receiving feedback on success in learning, thus being encouraged to continue learning

Reliability   Ability of a test to produce consistent results when used with comparable learners

Request for proposal (RFP)   Paper form with instructions to be completed when submitting a bid or proposal for a project to be funded

Self-paced learning environment   Learning environment that allows the learner to satisfy required learning activities by accomplishing the objectives at his or her own speed or convenience

Subject-matter expert (SME)   Person qualified to provide content, resources, and information relating to topics and tasks for which instruction is being designed

Summative evaluation   Measuring how well the major outcomes of a course or program are attained at the conclusion of instruction (posttest) or thereafter on the job

Support services   Matters such as budget, facilities, equipment, and materials that require attention for the successful preparation and implementation of a new instructional program

Systems approach   An overall plan to problem solving that gives attention to all essential elements

Task analysis   A collection of procedures for analyzing the information needed to achieve the objectives. *See also* Topic analysis and Procedural analysis.

Topic analysis   A procedure for identifying and describing the topics related to a goal or need

Validity   Direct relationship between test questions and the learning objectives

Index